What Is Curriculum Theory?

STUDIES IN CURRICULUM THEORY
William F. Pinar, Series Editor

Pinar • What Is Curriculum Theory?

McKnight • Schooling, The Puritan Imperative, and the Molding of an American National Identity: Education's "Errand Into the Wilderness"

Pinar (Ed.) • International Handbook of Curriculum Research

Morris • Curriculum and the Holocaust: Competing Sites of Memory and Representation

Doll • Like Letters in Running Water: A Mythopoetics of Curriculum

Joseph/Bravmann/Windschitl/Mikel/Green • Cultures of Curriculum

Westbury/Hopmann/Riquarts (Eds.) • Teaching as a Reflective Practice: The German Didaktik Tradition

Reid • Curriculum as Institution and Practice: Essays in the Deliberative Tradition

Pinar (Ed.) • Queer Theory in Education

Huebner • The Lure of the Transcendent: Collected Essays by Dwayne E. Huebner. Edited by Vikki Hillis. Collected and Introduced by William F. Pinar

jagodzinski • Postmodern Dilemmas: Outrageous Essays in Art & Art Education

jagodzinski • Pun(k) Deconstruction: Experifigural Writings in Art & Art Education

What Is Curriculum Theory?

William F. Pinar
Louisiana State University

LEA

LAWRENCE ERLBAUM ASSOCIATES, PUBLISHERS
2004   Mahwah, New Jersey   London

Lawrence Erlbaum Associates, Inc., Publishers
10 Industrial Avenue
Mahwah, New Jersey 07430

Cover design by Sean Sciarrone

Library of Congress Cataloging-in-Publication Data

Pinar, William.
    What is curriculum theory? / William F. Pinar.
        p.   cm. — (Studies in curriculum theory)
    Includes bibliographical references and index.
    ISBN 0-8058-4827-4 (cloth : alk. paper) — ISBN 0-8058-4828-2 (pbk. : alk. paper)
    1. Education—Curricula—United States.   2. Education—Political aspects—United States.
I. Title.   II. Series.

LB1570.P552   2004
375'.0001—dc22

2003060375
CIP

Printed in the United States of America
10 9 8 7 6 5 4 3 2 1

For
Mary
and
Marla

Contents

PART III: THE PROGRESSIVE MOMENT: THE FUTURE IN THE PRESENT

PART IV: THE ANALYTIC MOMENT: ANTI-INTELLECTUALISM AND COMPLICATED CONVERSATION

Preface

Especially during this time when the academic field of education is under savage attack by politicians, it is incumbent upon us to maintain our professional dignity by reasserting our commitment to the intellectual life of our field. Such a reassertion of our intellectual commitment includes, perhaps most of all, the study and teaching of curriculum theory and history. Such study enables us to understand this terrible time and our positions in it.

Our situation is not very different from that of our colleagues in the public schools. Having lost control of the curriculum, public-school teachers have been reduced to domestic workers, instructed by politicians to clean up the "mess" left by politics, culture, and history. That is an impossible job, of course, and politicians have seized upon its impossibility to deflect their constituents' attention away from the mess they've been making of the American nation.

We education professors who work with public-school teachers are being scapegoated as well (see chap. 9). The courses we teach are "hurdles," according to the U.S. Secretary of Education Rod Paige, tripping up hoards of talented college graduates who would otherwise enter the teaching profession. Moreover, there is, we are told, "empirical" research that demonstrates that teachers who have been spared education coursework are more successful (than teachers who have not) in raising their students' test scores. This "business" model of education—the "bottom line" (standardized test scores) is all that matters—is now enforced by federal legislation and by presumably professional organizations like the National Council for Accreditation of Teacher Education (NCATE; see chap. 9, Sections II and III). We education professors are losing—have lost?—control of the curriculum we teach.

In this primer for teachers (prospective and practicing), I offer an interpretation of the nightmare that is the present. Our nightmare began in the 1950s, when gendered anxieties over the Cold War and racialized anxieties over school desegregation coded public education (not for the first time) as "feminized" and "black." The vicious character of politicians' and many parents' criticisms of public education is intelligible only as a recoding of these gendered and racialized anxieties, "deferred and displaced" from the originary events onto "school reform" (see chap. 2).

While the origins of our present political difficulties began with the exploitation of public education as a Presidential campaign issue in 1960 by a liberal Democratic candidate, subsequent exploitations have been made by candidates mostly on the right (see chap. 3). What is at stake in right-wing reform—which has converted the school into a business, focused on the "bottom line" (test scores) —is control of the curriculum, what teachers are permitted to teach, what children are permitted to study. At least from the 1960s, the right-wing in the United States has appreciated that its political ascendancy depends on controlling how and what Americans think.

And "conservatives"—especially in the mid-West and far West—have appreciated that the white South is key to Republican electoral success (see chap. 4). That fact first became clear in the 1964 Presidential campaign. The Democratic candidate who defeated Republican nominee Barry Goldwater—President Lyndon B. Johnson—understood that he was handing over the white South to an increasingly right-wing Republican Party when he signed the Civil Rights Act of 1964 (see chap. 10). We teachers—in the university, in the public schools—cannot understand our present circumstances apart from appreciating how the American nation has "gone South."

Understanding the American South is a prerequisite to any effort to reconstruct public education in the United States. Understanding the white South (and its reactionary racial and gender politics, of which school reform is a "deferred and displaced" expression) requires understanding its history. In chapter 4 we glimpse a telling and still reverberating event in that racialized and gendered history: lynching. One hundred years ago, lynching was "America's National Crime." The centrality of castration to the lynching event underscores that racial politics and violence in this country have been— still are—simultaneously a sexual politics. (The widespread white rape of black female slaves established the fact that racial domination is sexualized.) It is no accident that striking sanitation workers in spring 1968—the same strike that took Martin Luther King, Jr., to Memphis—carried signs saying simply: I AM A MAN. Of course, that sentence means "I am a human being," and it means "I am a citizen." But striking sanitation workers did not choose those categories; instead, these black men chose a gendered term. The politics of school reform is intelligible only in gendered and racialized terms (see chap. 3).

Not only history presses down upon us, so does the future, fantasized as technological and "information-based" (see chaps. 5 and 6). If only we place computers in every classroom, if only school children stare at screens (rather than at teachers, evidently) they can "learn," become "competitive" in the "new millennium." Information is not knowledge, of course, and without ethical and intellectual judgment—which cannot be programmed into a machine—the Age of Information is an Age of Ignorance.

We—schoolteachers and education professors—have not survived the last 40 years of school (de)form without scars, perhaps the most prominent of which is an internalized anti-intellectualism (see chap. 7). I cannot ascribe the anti-intellectualism of the field solely to post-1960s events; there is a history of anti-intellectual vocationalism within the scholarly field of education. There are (hardly unrelated) general anti-intellectual tendencies in the American national character which have functioned historically to restrict academic—intellectual—freedom in the schools. Education professors' struggles have hardly been helped by the prejudice we too often face from Arts and Sciences colleagues. Moreover, education professors' troubled "marriage" to public-school teachers contributes to the closure of "complicated conversation," as the gendered and racialized domestication of education has rendered the classroom not a public space for complicated, sometimes contentious, conversation in which the public and private spheres are connected and reconstructed through academic knowledge. Rather, right-wing reform has rendered the classroom a privatized or domestic sphere in which children and their teachers are, simply, to do what they are told. It is a feminized and racialized domestic sphere politicians—mostly (white) men—are determined to control, disguised by apparently commonsensical claims of "accountability."

"Complicated conversation" is the central concept in contemporary curriculum studies in the United States. It is, I argue (in chap. 8), the idea that keeps hope alive, enabling us to have faith in a future in which we—both education professors and public-school teachers—determine the curriculum, both in the university and in the public schools. Teachers' intellectual determination of the curriculum—which necessarily includes choosing the means by which we assess students' study—is one key meaning of the phrase "academic freedom." Academic—intellectual—freedom is the prerequisite to the very possibility of education. Education is too important to be left to politicians and those parents who believe them.

What can we do? First, we must understand our situations, both as individuals and as a group. For the sake of such understanding, I employ the concept of *currere*—the Latin infinitive of curriculum—to denote the running (or lived experience) of the course, in this instance, the present historical situation. This autobiographical method provides a strategy for self-study, one phase of which seeks synthetical moments of "mobilization" when, as individuals and as teachers, we enter "the arena" to educate the American public.

That arena (the public sphere)—now a "shopping mall" in which citizens (and students) have been reduced to consumers—can be reconstructed in our classrooms by connecting academic knowledge to our students' (and our own) subjectivities, to society, and to the historical moment. In so doing, we can regain (relative) control of the curriculum, at least as it is enacted as a "complicated conversation," rather than reified as conceptual products on display in a store window, or in the small-group facilitation of "learning" in the school-as-corporate office (chap. 1).

The struggle to educate the American public—that is, of course, the project of "public education"—requires us to teach not only our students, but their parents, our neighbors, anyone who will listen. Teacher unions could become useful by funding a national television campaign—featuring, perhaps, movie and athletic icons to attract viewers' attention—explaining (for starters) that education is not a business. By whatever means, we must continue teaching after the bell rings and students depart our classrooms. We must renew our commitment to our own intellectual lives and to the educational reconstruction of the public sphere in America (chap. 10).

ACKNOWLEDGMENTS

I wish to express my gratitude to my friend and colleague Bill Doll, who in the late 1980s, brought to my attention Richard Rorty's theorization of "conversation." I wish to thank Donna Trueit, who introduced me to Michael Oakeshott's book on conversation, Brian Casemore for drawing my attention to Kaja Silverman's *World Spectators,* Margaret Zaccone, who sent me Daniel Noah Moses' "Distinguishing a University from a Shopping Mall," and Renee Fountain, who recommended Ewa Plonowska Ziarek's *An Ethics of Dissensus.* My thanks as well to Nicholas Ng-A-Fook, without whose research and editorial assistance the publication of the book would have been delayed by months. My thanks to Chris Myers for permitting me to draw upon *The Gender of Racial Politics and Violence in America* for sections of chapters 1, 4, 9, and 10. Thanks, too, to Elizabeth Ellsworth for reviewing the section on her work. Thanks to the anonymous reviewers, whose comments and criticisms resulted in a revised manuscript. My thanks especially to Naomi Silverman, my friend as well as editor, without whose critique and encouragement the book may not have appeared at all.

—*William F. Pinar*

Introduction

Fellow educators—are we not lost?
Do we know where we are,
remember where we have been,
or foresee where we are going?
—Dwayne E. Huebner (1999, 231)

[T]he fundamental issue goes unnoticed:
the abandonment of the historic mission of American education,
the democratization of liberal culture.
—Christopher Lasch (1995, 177)

We are not in the world merely by virtue of being born into it;
indeed, most of us are not really in the world at all.
—Kaja Silverman (2000, 29)

This book is no comprehensive introduction to curriculum studies, as *Understanding Curriculum* (Pinar, Reynolds, Slattery and Taubman 1995) attempted to be. Although the book contains no systematic review of the scholarship in the field, serious students of the field will hear echoes of others' work on nearly every page. Indeed, I quote much more than the customs of scholarship deem prudent, precisely in order to make audible the voices of others, to underscore the fact that the field is no solo performance. Curriculum theory is a complex, sometimes cacophonous, chorus, "the sound of silence breaking" (Miller in press).

Because my academic discipline is education, my work as a scholar and theoretician is structured pedagogically. In my performance of a classroom

1

teacher, I present what has been written on the subject, invite comments and questions, and in the process try to contribute commentary (hopefully clarifying and provocative) to the conversation myself. As a teacher, my commitment is the complication of students' understanding of the subject they are studying—in this instance, curriculum theory—while working to advance that field theoretically.

My assignment, then, is not to make curriculum theory conform to the contours of my own intellectual and political self-interest. Instead of making an argument, I work to create an impression. Rather than devising an "airtight" argument, I deliberately cut "holes" in my argument to enable students to "breathe," to "create spaces and find voices" (Miller 1990). Sometimes polemical, this primer for prospective and practicing teachers asks students to question the historical present and their relation to it, and in so doing, to construct their own understandings of what it means to teach, to study, to become "educated."

What is curriculum theory? The short answer is that *curriculum theory is the interdisciplinary study of educational experience*. Not every interdisciplinary study of educational experience is curriculum theory, of course; nor is every instance of curriculum theory interdisciplinary. Curriculum theory is a distinctive field of study, with a unique history, a complex present, an uncertain future. Discernible in this distinctive field are influences from disciplines across the humanities and the arts, and, to a lesser extent, from the social sciences (primarily social theory).

This interdisciplinary structure of the field, and especially the strong influence of the humanities and the arts, makes curriculum theory a distinctive specialization within the broad field of education, a fragmented field broadly modeled after the social and behavioral sciences. As a distinctive interdisciplinary field (rather than subfield of a single academic discipline such as educational psychology or the sociology of education), curriculum studies may be the only academic discipline within the broad field of education. Several of the social sciences—most prominently academic psychology, but sociology as well—have colonized much of the field of education. Only curriculum theory has its origin in and owes its loyalty to the discipline and experience of education.

In its interest in and commitment to the study of educational experience, curriculum theory is critical of contemporary school "reform." Indeed, "educational experience" seems precisely what politicians do not want, as they insist we focus on test scores, the "bottom line." By linking the curriculum to student performance on standardized examinations, politicians have, in effect, taken control of what is to be taught: the curriculum. Examination-driven curricula demote teachers from scholars and intellectuals to technicians in service to the state. The cultivation of self-reflexive, interdisciplinary erudition and intellectuality disappears. Rationalized as "accountability," political socialization replaces education.

The present historical moment is, then, for public-school teachers and for those of us in the university who work with them, a nightmare. The school has become a skill-and-knowledge factory (or corporation); the education professoriate is reduced to the status of supervisory personnel. While in the schools, millions live the nightmare each day, too few seem to realize they are even asleep. As the great curriculum theorist Dwayne E. Huebner recognized more than 25 years ago, we educators are lost, submerged in present circumstances. As Huebner's opening words suggest, many of us seem to have forgotten the past, and we are unable to imagine the future. This submergence in the present is not unique to educators; historian Christopher Lasch argued that Americans generally have become "presentistic," so self-involved in surviving the present that, for us: "To live for the moment is the prevailing passion—to live for yourself, not for our predecessors or posterity" (Lasch 1978, 5).

While Lasch's (1978) portrait of what he termed "the culture of narcissism" is overdrawn (as is his caricature of progressive education in that book, as I note in chapter 7), it is, in my judgment, largely accurate. "The intense subjectivity of modern work, exemplified even more clearly in the office than in the factory," Lasch (1978, 102) observed, "causes men and women to doubt the reality of the external world and to imprison themselves . . . in a shell of protective irony." Retreating from a public sphere that no longer seems meaningful and worthy of their investment, Americans retreat into the apparent safety of private life where, they discover, there is no safety either. "On the contrary," Lasch (1978, 27) notes, "private life takes on the very qualities of the anarchic social order from which it supposed to provide a refuge."

With no place to hide, Americans retreat into—and, Lasch argues, become lost in—themselves. The psychoanalytic term for this personality disturbance is *narcissism*, not to be confused with egoism or selfishness (see Lasch 1984, 18). Recoiling from meaningful engagement in the world, the privatized self atrophies—Lasch (1984) uses the term *minimal* to denote that contraction of the self narcissism necessitates—and becomes unable to distinguish between self and other, let alone participate meaningfully in the public sphere. The past and future disappear in individualistic obsession with psychic survival in the present. As Lasch (1978, xvi) suggests, "The narcissist has no interest in the future because, in part, he has so little interest in the past."

Because the public sphere—in our case, the classroom—has become so unpleasant for so many, not a few teachers have retreated into the (apparent) safety of their own subjectivities. But in so doing, they have abdicated their professional authority and ethical responsibility for the curriculum they teach. They have been *forced* to abdicate this authority by the bureaucratic protocols that presumably hold them "accountable," but which, in fact, render them unable to teach. (Instead, they are supposed to "manage learning.") As a field, traditional curriculum studies—in the past too often a support system for the school bureaucracy—was complicit with this presentistic capitulation to the "reform" *du jour*. As distinguished curriculum historian Herbert Kliebard (1970) made clear, the ahistorical and atheoretical character of traditional curriculum studies disabled teachers from understanding the history of their present circumstances.

My work in curriculum theory has emphasized the significance of subjectivity to teaching, to study, to the process of education. The significance of subjectivity is not as a solipsistic retreat from the public sphere. As Lasch (1978, 9) points out, subjectivity can be no refuge in an era when "[t]he possibility of genuine privacy recedes." The significance of subjectivity is that it is inseparable from the social; it is only when we—together and in solitude—reconstruct the relation between the two can we begin to restore our "shattered faith in the regeneration of life" (Lasch 1978, 207) and cultivate the "moral discipline . . . indispensable to the task of building a new order" (Lasch 1978, 235–236). Our pedagogical work is simultaneously autobiographical and political.

The reconstruction of the public sphere does not mean remaking the world (or our part of it, the school) over in our own image. The reconstruction of the private sphere does not mean remaking our subjectivity to coincide with the social. Self-understanding is not "self-improvement" so we might "get ahead." Nor is it a defensive response of self-withdrawal. "Confronted with an apparently implacable and unmanageable environment," Lasch (1984, 58) suggests, "people have turned to self-management . . . a technology of the self."

The method of *currere*—the infinitive form of curriculum—promises no quick fixes. On the contrary, this autobiographical method asks us to slow down, to remember even re-enter the past, and to meditatively imagine the future. Then, slowly and in one's own terms, one analyzes one's experience of the past and fantasies of the future in order to understand more fully, with more complexity and subtlety, one's submergence in the present. The method of *currere* is not a matter of psychic survival, but one of subjective risk and social reconstruction, the achievement of selfhood and society in the age to come. To undertake this project of social and subjective reconstruction, we teachers must remember the past and imagine the future, however unpleasant each domain may be. Not only intellectually but in our character structure, we must become "temporal," living simultaneously in the past, present, and future. In the autobiographical method I have devised, returning to the past (the "regressive") and imagining the future (the "progressive") must be understood (the "analytic") for the self to become "expanded" (in contrast to being made "minimal" in Lasch's schema) and complicated, then, finally, mobilized (in the "synthetical" moment). Such an autobiographical sequence of ourselves as individuals and as educators might enable us to awaken from the nightmare we are living in the present.

The first step we can take toward changing reality—waking up from the nightmare that is the present state of public miseducation—is acknowledging that we are indeed living a nightmare. The nightmare that is the present—in which educators have little control over the curriculum, the very organizational and intellectual center of schooling—has several markers, prominent among them "accountability," an apparently commonsensical idea that makes teachers, rather than students and their parents, responsible for students' educational accomplishment. Education is an opportunity offered, not a service rendered.

In Part I, I review the markers of the present, focusing, in chapter 1, on the remaking of the school as a business, a scheme in which teachers first became factory workers. More recently, we have been "promoted" from the assembly line to the corporate office where we serve as "managers of student learning." "Never have corporate values reigned in the United States so supremely as they do today," Daniel Noah Moses (1999, 89) rightly observes, "when an overarching corporate metaphor has invaded all aspects of American society, including academia." While the "invasion" of the public schools is long over and "corporatization" is triumphant, in many of the nation's colleges and universities the struggle is ongoing.

In chapter 2, I outline the autobiographical method of *currere*, a method focused on self-understanding. Such understanding, I believe, can help us to understand our situation as a group. The revolutionary potential of autobiography becomes obvious in African-American practices of the genre, among them slave narratives and post-Emancipation autobiography and fiction.

While a vast body of work, this glimpse (in chapter 2) into African-American autobiography may inspire us to "talk back" to those politicians, bureaucrats, and parents who populate the nightmare that is the present. Of course, our situation cannot be compared to centuries of slavery, segregation, and racial discrimination. But the heroic self-understanding, self-affirmation, self-mobilization, and collective action of African Americans—evident in African-American autobiography—may inspire us mostly white middle-class teachers to protest our present professional subjugation. African-American autobiographical practices can inspire us to carry on despite our degradation, by witnessing to subjective suffering in public, by becoming our own, more modest, versions of the private-and-public intellectuals—such as Ida B. Wells (chapters 2 and 4)—who spoke of their own subjective experience of racism in order to protest and mobilize against it.

To help us understand the present, I invoke the psychoanalytic notion of "deferred action" (*Nachtraglichkeit*), a term Freud employed to explain how the experience of trauma is deferred—and, I would add, displaced—into other subjective and social spheres, where it is often no longer readily recognizable. In Part II, I argue that the "trauma" of the Cold War in the 1950s and the 1954 Supreme Court decision to desegregate the public schools (coupled with the primacy of students in 1960s civil rights struggles) was "displaced and deferred" onto public education. In the aftermath of these traumas, public education was racialized and gendered in the American popular imagination. Bluntly stated, we can understand the nightmare that is our subjugation in the present only if we appreciate that we are the victims of displaced and deferred misogyny and racism.

In arguing that racism and misogyny have been "deferred and displaced" into public education, I am not suggesting that they have been *absorbed* there. Racism and misogyny remain pervasive in America today, and while teachers also suffer from deferred and displaced versions of them, white racism in America remains corrosive and endemic, especially (but not only) in the South, now the political epicenter of American presidential politics (Black and Black 1992). Indeed, my argument here regarding the "deferred and displaced action" of racism and misogyny underlines how these forms of social hatred and prejudice intensify as they mutate.

Nor am I arguing that the subjugation of public school teachers is *only* racialized and gendered. It is classed as well. In contrast to elite professions such as medicine and, less so, law, public school teaching has long been associated with the lower middle class, and not only in salary. Public-school teaching has historically required a shorter and less rigorous credentialing period. Moreover, many teachers have been—in the popular imagination if not always in fact—the first members of their families to complete higher education. (One hundred years ago, public-school teaching rarely required a college degree.) The political problems of public education are, in part, class-based, but they are, I suggest, straightforwardly so. There is little that is deferred and displaced about the class-based character of the political subjugation of the teaching profession.

Moreover, the nightmarish quality of teachers' present subjugation—its peculiar intensity and irrationality—cannot be grasped by class analysis alone. While class conflict in the United States has produced strong political reaction, it has not tended to produce the vicious contempt teachers and *their* teachers—the education professoriate—have encountered. To grasp this "overdetermined" reaction, one must invoke models of racial prejudice and misogyny, wherein complex and convoluted psychological structures and processes intensify emotion well beyond rhyme or reason. We must move to the sphere of psychopathology to grasp the history of the present of public education in America.

We glimpse this phenomenon of deferral and displacement in chapter 3 (the first "regressive moment") where, relying on the scholarship of Robert L.

Griswold, we study the gendered character of the Kennedy Administration's educational response to the Cold War, specifically its embrace of physical fitness in 1960 and 1961. This was roughly the same period during which the National Curriculum Movement was launched. The National Curriculum Reform Movement was dedicated to aligning the secondary school subjects with the academic disciplines as they exist at the university and, in so doing, establishing academic "rigor" in the schools. To accomplish this curricular alignment, the control of curriculum had to be taken from teachers. The continuing legacies of Cold War curriculum politics structures the deplorable situation in which we teachers find ourselves today. Starting then, we began to lose all control over the curriculum, including the means by which students' study of it is assessed.

While 1960s curriculum reform—the genesis of our nightmare—was gendered, it was profoundly racialized as well. It was 1954 when the Supreme Court ruled that public schools must be desegregated, but in the South this did not occur until the late 1960s and early 1970s, under the presidential administration of Richard Nixon. (Desegregation has never occurred in the North, as primarily white suburban school districts ring primarily black urban ones.) As schools became racial battlegrounds and the pretext for white flight, and as college students fought to desegregate other public spaces (perhaps most famously lunch counters and public transportation), racial anxiety began to intensify among European Americans, an anxiety right-wing Republican presidential candidate Barry Goldwater worked to exploit in his 1964 campaign against Democratic President Lyndon B. Johnson. It is the same white racism Alabama Governor George Wallace tried to exploit in his 1968 and 1972 presidential campaigns (Black and Black 1992). While this pervasive and intensifying (white) anxiety—not limited to the South—was focused upon the public schools, it echoed through the culture at large, as broader issues of racial justice and, indeed, of the American identity itself (was this still, or even primarily, a European-identified nation?) were stimulated by the desegregation of the nation's schools. Public education—in the North especially in the urban centers, in the South everywhere—became racialized.

No doubt intensifying the racialization of education in the American popular imagination was the very visible and aggressive roles played by (especially university) students in the civil rights movements of the late 1950s and the 1960s. To illustrate students' participation in the civil rights movement, we glimpse the civil rights activism of the Student Nonviolent Coordinating Committee (SNCC), including the Committee's establishment of "freedom schools." These schools and the student activism they reflected and expressed were located in the Deep South, the epicenter of the segregated nation's racial crisis.

It was in the Deep South where the political struggle for control of public education was most explicitly, most outrageously, localized. Without right-wing exploitation of white southerners' racial fears, the 30 years of "conservative" presidential politics since the 1960s—and the school "reform" that has accompanied it—could not have occurred (Black and Black 1992). In chapter 4, we focus on three of the cultural and political problems—problems of race, class, and gender—which the South has still not worked through, which the (white) South has, in fact, declined to work through. In its reactionary repudiation of progressive racial and gender politics, the (white) South has forced—with the considerable and continuing assistance of "conservatives" nationwide, especially in the Far West and the Mid-West—the nation far to the right.

The political problem of teachers today—our scapegoating by politicians and by uninformed parents, our loss of academic freedom (the very prerequisite for our professional practice)—cannot be understood apart from right-wing politicians' manipulation of public education as a political issue. As seen in chapter 3, this political manipulation was first successfully employed in the 1960 Kennedy presidential campaign. In subsequent campaigns, the tactic was appropriated by the right, enabled all along by white reactionaries in the Deep South (Black and Black 1992).

From this regressive moment—an evocation of the past in the present—I move to the progressive moment, in which we focus on futuristic conceptions of education as primarily technological. In this future screens—television, film, and, especially, computer screens—seem everywhere, prosthetic extensions of our enfleshed bodies, dispersing our subjectivities outward, far from our concrete everyday communities into abstract cyberspace and a "global village." In this prosthetic extension of the everyday ego we took ourselves to be, the self seems to evaporate. Subjectivity itself mutates, and the "self" autobiography purports to identify and express distends into hypertextual personae, ever-changing cyborg identities. New forms of subjectivity and sexuality appear as the natural world threatens to become "virtual." In today's politics of public miseducation, the computer becomes the latest technological fantasy of educational utopia, a fantasy of "teacher-proof" curriculum, a fantasy of going where "no man has gone before."

But, as curriculum theorists have long appreciated, the exchange and acquisition of information is not education. Being informed is not equivalent to erudition. Information must be tempered with intellectual judgment, critical thinking, ethics, and self-reflexivity. The complicated conversation that is the curriculum requires interdisciplinary intellectuality, erudition, and self-reflexivity. This is not a recipe for high test scores, but a common faith in the possibility of self-realization and democratization, twin projects of social and subjective reconstruction.

After considering the future in the present during the progressive moment, we turn to the first analytic moment. There we face the facts, namely the profoundly anti-intellectual conditions of our professional labor. These are conditions both internal and external to the schools, to the university-based fields of curriculum studies and teacher education. The challenge of education in this profoundly anti-intellectual historical moment is made, contrary to expectation, *more* difficult by our situation in the university, where our arts and sciences colleagues—as we term them more hopefully than accurately— too often mistake academic vocationalism and their own budgetary self-interest for interdisciplinary, socially critical, subjectively focused education.

Due to the anti-intellectualism of American culture generally, due to the deferral and displacement of racism and misogyny onto public education more specifically, and due to the anti-intellectual character of (white) southern culture and history now politically hegemonic in the United States, the field of education has (understandably) remained underdeveloped intellectually. Indeed, in part for reasons not our own, we, too, are guilty of anti-intellectualism. But, as chapter 7 makes clear, there are reasons internal to the field, reasons for which we are responsible, that we suffer our subjugation today. We cannot begin to respond to the displaced and deferred racism and misogyny we suffer today until we face the internalized consequences of our decades-long subjugation, namely a pervasive and crippling anti-intellectualism.

Whatever our fate—given our betrayal by government and by powerful professional organizations, the future is not bright—we must carry on, our dignity intact. We must renew our commitment to the intellectual character of our professional labor. We can do so, first, by engaging in frank and sustained self-criticism, as I initiate in chapter 7. There I discuss the deep-seated and pervasive anti-intellectualism in the field of education, obvious in teacher education, and expressed in the anti-theoretical vocationalism found not only in that field. The problem we face is hardly helped by the anti-intellectual hostility of some arts and sciences colleagues—Richard Hofstadter is but one historic example—and it is only intensified by the scapegoating of public schools and the education professoriate by politicians. Despite these assaults on the profession, we cannot retreat into a defensive posture that keeps us from facing frankly the anti-intellectualism built into the field, and from taking steps, both individually and as a professional collectivity, to correct it.

Accompanying frank and ongoing self-criticism must be the reinvigoration of our commitment to engage in "complicated conversation" with our academic subjects, our students, and ourselves, as I assert in chapter 8. Such complicated conversation requires the academic—intellectual—freedom to devise the courses we teach, the means by which we teach them, and the means by which we assess students' study of them. We must fight for that freedom as individuals in classrooms and as a profession: At both "sites" we are under assault by government and by at least two of the professional organizations pretending to representing us.

While the concept of complicated conversation is here a curricular idea and not an instructional one, pedagogical considerations are hardly irrelevant, as curriculum understood as complicated conversation is structured, in part, by teaching. As the analysis in chapter 7 makes clear, the anti-intellectual "barriers" to complicated conversation are numerous and profound (see Huebner 1999). Just how complicated curriculum as conversation is we glimpse in psychoanalytic reminders of structural self-deception, the contradictions of communication, and the fantasmatic character of the public sphere (Britzman 1998; Ellsworth 1997). Still, "complicated" does not mean "impossible," and we must continue the project of intellectualization, both individually and organizationally, if we are to take back our profession as teachers, not technicians.

After these moments of reflection and self-understanding that the analytic phase provides, in the synthetic moment (see chapters 9 and 10), we mobilize ourselves, both as individuals and as a profession. After the "shattering" (or "evaporation") of the ego that regression to the past and contemplation of the future invites, we return to the present, mobilized for pedagogical engagement in the reconstruction of the private and public spheres in curriculum and teaching, what James B. Macdonald (1995) termed the study of how to have a world. Public education structures self-formation and social reconstruction while, in many of its present forms, it blocks both. Teachers ought not be only school-subject specialists; I suggest that they become private-and-public intellectuals who understand that self-reflexivity, intellectuality, interdisciplinarity, and erudition are as inseparable as are the subjective and the social spheres themselves.

It is long past time for us to "talk back" to those politicians, parents, and school and university administrators who misunderstand the education of the public as a "business." Mobilized, we must enter "into the arena" and teach our fellow citizens—including uncomprehending colleagues and self-aggrandizing administrators—what is at stake in the education of children, an education in which creativity and individuality, not test-taking skills, are primary. In our time, to be intellectual requires political activism.

Within our profession, we must repudiate those professional organizations and those legislative actions by government—such as the Bush Administration's "Leave No Child Behind" legislation—that destroy the very possibility of education by misconstruing it as a "business." While we struggle as intellectuals reconstructing the private and public spheres of curriculum and teaching in schools, we must, especially among ourselves, keep hope alive. We can recapture the curriculum, someday. Without reclaiming our academic—intellectual freedom—we cannot teach. Without intellectual freedom, education ends; students are indoctrinated, forced to learn what the test-makers declare to be important.

Nightmares often refer to waking life, and so we must remember the broader political context and historical moment in which our efforts at self-understanding and social reconstruction occur. We live in an American nation in which the (white reactionary) South has culturally and politically triumphed. Only when the South is (finally) reconstructed can the nation resume a progressive course toward democratization. I propose the educational reconstruction of the South through a "curriculum as social psychoanalysis," schooling that speaks to persisting problems of race, class, and gender, not only in the South but nationwide.

Such a "complicated conversation" illustrates a curriculum in which academic knowledge, subjectivity, and society are inextricably linked. It is this link, this promise of education for our private-and-public lives as Americans, which curriculum theory elaborates. If we persist in our cause—the cause of public education—someday the schools and those of us who work in them can deflect displaced and deferred racism. When we do, schools will no longer be knowledge-and-skill factories, not academic businesses but schools: sites of education for creativity, erudition, and interdisciplinary intellectuality. Someday—if we remember the past, study the future, analyze, then mobilize in, the present—education will permit the progressive pursuit of "new modes of life, eroticism, and social relations." For you, let this someday begin today.

I

THE NIGHTMARE THAT
IS THE PRESENT

1

The Miseducation
of the American Public

I
RECONSTRUCTING THE SUBJECTIVE AND SOCIAL
SPHERES IN CURRICULUM AND TEACHING

All too often, however, in the history of the United States,
the schoolteacher has been in no position to serve as a model
for an introduction to the intellectual life.
—Richard Hofstadter (1962, 310)

As we enter the new century, society's agreement on what defines
an educated person, what constitutes essential knowledge and
common discourse, has essentially collapsed.
—Frank H. T. Rhodes (2001, B7)

In any case, it is absurd to expect the public . . . to rise above the
intellectual level of its average constituents.
—John Dewey (1991 [1927], 60)

If public education is the education of the public, then public education is, by definition, a political, psycho-social, fundamentally intellectual reconstruction of self and society, a process in which educators occupy public and private spaces in-between the academic disciplines and the state (and problems) of mass culture, between intellectual development and social engagement, between erudition and everyday life. While the education of the public draws extensively upon the academic disciplines, it does not necessarily coincide with them.

In this time of pervasive vocationalism, including academic vocationalism, when the curriculum is assumed to be courses of study leading to competence in the academic disciplines, curriculum theory testifies to the progressive insistence that education have value for society and the "self," that its end is not only itself, but, rather, that it must engage and extend the interests—intellectual, psychological, social—of students (Dewey 1916). Such engagement is not a matter of seducing stubborn young minds into the school subjects, especially as these are aligned with their more sophisticated parent disciplines as these are currently compartmentalized and bureaucratized in colleges and universities. Rather, teaching—from the point of view of curriculum theory—is a matter of enabling students to employ academic knowledge (and popular culture, increasingly via the media and the Internet) to understand their own self-formation within society and the world (see, for instance, Daspit and Weaver 2000).

Such understanding is both individual and social, "local" and "global," historical and futural (terms with blurred boundaries, as each is embedded in the other). Its contextualization in the ongoing self-formation of students in anticipation of their participation in the public sphere not yet formed requires that we teachers communicate the social, ethical, and political potential of what in the current curricular regime sometimes seems rather "ivory-tower" indeed. Curriculum theory is, then, about discovering and articulating, for oneself and with others, the educational significance of the school subjects for self and society in the ever-changing historical moment. As a consequence, curriculum theory rejects the current "business-minded" school reform, with its emphasis on test scores on standardized examinations, academic analogues to "the bottom line" (i.e., "profit"). It rejects the miseducation of the American public.

That the American school reform movement is dominated by business thinking and is thereby obsessed with the "bottom line" comes as no surprise to any serious student of American curriculum history. Despite the rhetoric of Horace Mann (whose reputation as the founding father of the public schools is, Christopher Lasch [1995, 158] suggests, "well deserved") and late-19th-century U.S. Commissioner of Education William Torrey Harris, both of whom emphasized the virtue-building aspirations of the common school (see Cuban and Shipps 2000), the truth is that, in general, the schools have inculcated not virtue but bourgeois respectability, competition, instrumentality, and Eurocentric monoculturalism. Despite the heroic efforts of millions of teachers, the schools have been—are today—complicit in the miseducation of the American public.

Acknowledging the "moral fervor and democratic idealism" that animated Horace Mann's arguments on behalf of a public school system, Christopher Lasch (1995, 144) locates failure of American public education in Mann's "educational vision" (1995, 148). "The great weakness" in Mann's educational theory, Lasch (1995, 151–152) argues, was his assumption that "education takes place only in schools." While the bureaucratization of public education—academic vocationalism specifically, the mistaking of busy-work for academic work more generally—intensifies after Sputnik, Mann's conception of public education as conflated with schooling established the institutional conditions that made its bureaucratization inevitable.

Despite early-20th-century progressive fantasies of the school as a laboratory for democracy, the truth is that the American public schools have functioned to make immigrants into "Americans" and to prepare all citizens for jobs in an industrial—now largely postindustrial—economy. The private sector did not want to pay for this vocational education; it "persuaded" the public sector to pay. On this issue, little has changed in the last 100 years, even in the administration of schools. As David Tyack (1993, 1–2) observed: "In the Progressive Era, for example, business leaders wanted to centralize control of schools, emulating the consolidation of vast corporations; today they urge 'restructuring' or decentralization, citing business in each case as a guide to reform in schooling." The schools are still assumed to exist for the sake of job preparation, despite continuing, if largely empty, rhetoric linking education with democracy and a politically engaged citizenry.

In one sense, then, it is a patriotic commitment to make the United States live up to its rhetoric that animates many curriculum theorists to insist upon relationships between education and democracy, relationships just as rhetorical today as when John Dewey (1916) insisted that educational experience provided the bridge between "self" and society, between self-realization and democratization. In such a relationship between the subjective and the social spheres, curriculum becomes a complicated conversation, "a political process as well as a search for subjectivity" (Slattery and Rapp 2003, 89). Curriculum development involves "public intellectual leadership" (see Henderson and Kesson 2001).

While a consequence of the American preoccupations with business and religion (as historian Richard Hofstadter [1962] has documented), the closure of complicated conversation in the current regime of power can also be traced to American pragmatism as well. John Dewey's pragmatist predecessor—William James—was, David Simpson (2002, 98) reminds us, "consequence oriented," concerned with the "practical cash value" of experience. The significance of experience—of thought, action, and event—becomes its effect on a particular situation. As Simpson (2002, 98–99) notes, James' "faith in instrumentalism" provided a "green light" for applied social science with its emphasis upon measuring outcomes quantitatively.

From the inception of the nation, Americans have been obsessed with "the practical cash value" not only of experience, but of practically everything. While situated in early-20th-century Europe, Robert Musil's character Ulrich's statement (to Agathe) in the novel *A Man Without Qualities* speaks to those cultural and historical conditions in America in which the common school became first a factory and now a corporation, but always a business.

> Our age drips with practical energy anyway. It's stopped caring for ideas, it only wants action. This frightful energy springs solely from the fact that people have nothing to do. Inwardly, I mean. . . . It's so easy to have the energy to act and so difficult to find a meaning for action! There are very few people who understand that nowadays. That's why the men of action look like men playing ninepins, knocking down those nine lumps of wood with the gestures of a Napoleon. It wouldn't even surprise me if they ended up by assaulting one another, frantic at the towering incomprehensibility of the fact that all their actions will not suffice. (Musil 1979, 87)

In what sometimes seems an increasingly predatory American culture, assault—both domestic (recalling the sniper attacks around Washington, D.C. in October 2002) and international (during summer 2002 President George W. Bush asserted the military "right" to "preemptive strikes")—characterizes the context in which American children go to school.

II
"UNTIMELY" CONCEPTS

> *[T]he possibility of resistance is located in the disjunction at the very center of the historical formation—in the rift between the forms of visibility and the forms of signification.*
> —Ewa Plonowska Ziarek (2001, 19)

> *The best hope . . . appears to lie in a creative tension between separation and union, individuation and dependence.*
> —Christopher Lasch (1984, 177)

> *[T]o assume one's language of desire implies more than apprehending the futural nature of the past.*
> —Kaja Silverman (2000, 66)

Since the 1960s—when the leadership of public-school curriculum development was assumed by university colleagues in the various academic disciplines—many curriculum specialists have been left with working bureaucratically to implement others' materials and content. In the post-Reconceptualization period (see Pinar et al. 1995, chapter 4), we who are positioned in the universities have been working to understand how the curriculum-in-place functions, politically, racially, in terms of gender, subjectivity, and "the global village." We have focused on how ideas generated in other fields or discourses—such as phenomenology or postmodernism or aesthetics—might help us understand the curriculum as a multifaceted process, involving not only official policy, prescribed textbooks, standardized examinations, but as well the "complicated conversation" of the participants. We have reconceived the curriculum; no longer is it a noun. It is instead a verb: *currere*.

In curriculum studies generally, there has been, since the 1970s,

1. a shift from focus on social engineering and the business model to the project of understanding, which involves the concept of curriculum as conversation,
2. the establishment of an intellectually independent—that is to say, not tied to specific pieces of legislation (such as the *No Child Left Behind Act* of 2001)—and academic field dedicated to understanding, and based primarily on research and theory in the humanities and the arts, not upon the social and behavior sciences, and
3. a shift from the emphasis on teaching (especially the technology of instruction) to curriculum, especially interdisciplinary configurations such as African-American studies, Women's and Gender Studies, and cultural studies.

The sharp shift to cultural studies (for a brief history, see Edgerton 1996; for a strong example, see Dimitriadis and McCarthy 2001) during the 1990s has, perhaps, been too abrupt for a field that, just 20 years earlier, was fundamentally reconceptualized (see Pinar et al. 1995, chapter 4). The disciplinary throughline from, say, the 1940s Tyler Rationale (which established the basic procedure that reduced curriculum to objectives measured by examinations) through Madeleine R. Grumet's stunning theoretical synthesis in *Bitter Milk* (1988) to contemporary work in cultural studies in education—on subjects as varied as Disney (Giroux 1999), Barbie (Steinberg 1997), and McDonald's restaurants (Kincheloe 2002)—needs to be articulated, and I hope that this book contributes to that collective and critical conversation.

In moving to cultural studies curriculum specialists are asking, as we once did, what knowledge is of most worth. This is a question that must be asked constantly; the answers we provide will change according to project, person, nation, and the historical moment. As university-based scholars of education, we take from extant academic knowledge to devise mosaics that point to the educational significance of academic knowledge for the individual, situated subjectively, socially, historically, a gendered, racialized and too often tragically human creature.

As curriculum theorists, and, more broadly, as educators (understood not as bureaucrats or technicians but as intellectuals), we decline to conceive of our professional obligation as devising efficient means to deliver knowledge others—with their own agendas (business productivity, academic vocation-alism)—have directed us to deliver. Of course, we must continue to teach the school subjects, the academic disciplines: Those are our passions, not to mention contractual obligations. But the point of such pedagogical labor cannot be only improved test scores on standardized examinations (to establish bragging rights for politicians), not only to prepare students for success in college classrooms, although no educator can be opposed to that.

For those prospective and practicing teachers for whom teacher education has been primarily an introduction to the instructional fields—the teaching of reading or mathematics or science—curriculum theory may come as something of a shock, if only due to its emphasis on "what" one teaches, rather than on "how." Of course, *how* one teaches remains a major preoccupation of curriculum theorists, but not in terms of devising a "technology" of "what works," not as a form of social engineering designed to produce predictable effects (i.e., "learning"), too often quantified as scores on standardized exams. The late-19th-century black feminist (and public-school teacher) Anna Julia Cooper was clear on this point:

> We have been so ridden with tests and measurements, so leashed and spurred for percentages and retardations that the machinery has run away with the mass production and quite a way back bumped off the driver. I wonder that a robot has not been invented to make the assignments, give the objective tests, mark the scores and chloroform all teachers who dared bring original thought to the specific problems and needs of their pupils. (cited in Lemert and Bhan 1998, 235)

Although one can hardly be opposed to higher test scores, it is self-reflexive interdisciplinary intellectuality—the cultivation of "original thought"—that constitutes curriculum theorists' aspiration for the process of education.

Curriculum theory is, then, that interdisciplinary field committed to the study of educational experience, especially (but not only) as that experience is encoded in the school curriculum, itself a highly symbolic as well as institutional structuration of (potentially) educational experience. As Grumet (1988) observed, curriculum is what the older generation chooses to tell the younger generations. The school curriculum communicates what we choose to remember about our past, what we believe about the present, what we hope for the future. Curriculum debates—such as those over multicultural-ism and the canon—are also debates about the American national identity.

Because it is highly symbolic, the theorization of curriculum requires situating it historically, socially, and autobiographically (i.e., in terms of life history and self-formation). Sectors of curriculum scholarship and research include efforts to understand curriculum racially, politically, theologically, autobiographically, and historically, in terms of gender, popular culture, phenomenology, postmodernism, poststructuralism, psychoanalysis, and the arts, all situated locally and in the global village (see Pinar et al. 1995). Echoes of these categories can be heard throughout this avowedly singular articulation of curriculum theory.

Curriculum theory, then, is a complex field of scholarly inquiry within the broad field of education that endeavors to understand curriculum across the school subjects and academic disciplines. While school subject specializations within the field of education (such as the teaching of English or mathematics) tend to focus on teaching strategies within single teaching fields, curriculum theory aspires to understand the overall educational significance of the curriculum, focusing especially upon interdisciplinary themes—such as gender or multiculturalism or the ecological crisis—as well as the relations among the curriculum, the individual, society, and history.

Such an aspiration means that we understand the project of *public education* as the *education of the public*, an understanding that requires us to question—and perhaps reject—the current public school curriculum as it is ritualistically aligned with the academic disciplines as they exist in most colleges and universities. To educate the public requires us to teach academic knowledge, but configured around faculty and student interests, addressed to pressing social (including community and global) concerns. To educate the public suggests that we teach popular culture as well, not only as a pedagogical lure to engage students' interests, but, through the curriculum, to enable students to connect their lived experience with academic knowledge, to foster students' intellectual development, and students' capacities for critical thinking.

To automatically align the public school curriculum with the current curriculum of higher education is, I suggest, an abnegation of our professional obligation to educate the public. It renders the curriculum self-enclosed, abstract, split-off from those everyday lives not only students live, but also from those lived by their parents and those in their communities, their nation, on the earth (Riley-Taylor 2002). The current curricular configuration amounts to the miseducation of the American public. Our professional obligation is the reconstruction of the public sphere in education.

We cannot do so without also reconstructing what I term the *private sphere* in education. Since the 1970s I have argued that the sphere of the subjective is where teachers and students connect academic knowledge to their self-formation, a connection made in historical time, embedded in regional, national, and diasporic cultures. In calling for autobiography in education, I have been asking teachers and students to reconstruct themselves through academic knowledge, knowledge self-reflexively studied and dialogically encountered. The reconstruction of the public sphere cannot proceed without the reconstruction of the private sphere.

In the subjective and social spheres—split off from each other in the current curriculum—the labor of curriculum theory becomes political and psychological as well as intellectual. Especially in this time of pervasive anti-intellectualism, not only inside the broad field of education but across American society and specifically in government, theoretical research becomes a political undertaking. Akin to Gilles Deleuze and Félix Guattari's characterization of philosophy, curriculum theory is the creation of "untimely" concepts in Nietzsche's sense of this term, by "acting counter to our time, and thereby acting on our time and, let us hope, for the benefit of a time to come" (1983a; quoted in Patton 2000, 3). Optimistic by profession, innocent by design, we teachers resist facing the fact that the historical present is an educational nightmare haunted by right-wing reactionaries and business-enamored politicians.

In acknowledging the historical present, we curriculum theorists do not imagine that we represent the vanguard of a movement which foreshadows social change. Even if significant social change seemed a possibility, the position of the vanguard is a discredited one, implying, as it does, an intellectual and political elite who "knows better" than their fellow citizens and colleagues. The labor of curriculum theorizing today can be understood more precisely by invoking Deleuze's conception of theory as a relay of practice, a conception, as Paul Patton points out, that is closer to the idea expressed by Nietzsche's distinction between academic philosophers in uncritical service to the State, and those "true" philosophers who must remain "private thinkers" (see Nietzsche 1983b; Patton 2000, 5).

To remain a private thinker means that one's scholarship, one's thinking, teaching, and writing, are engaged in self-overcoming, the surpassing of the historical, sedimented "self" one has been conditioned and, perhaps, required to be. In working to overcome the "self" conceived by others, one "works from within," from one's interiority, which is a specific configuration of the socius and therefore, by definition, a public project as well. This apparent paradox—that one's private self is necessarily public—is clarified in Patton's characterization of Jean-Paul Sartre, in many ways the preeminent private-and-public intellectual of the 20th century, at least in the West. Patton (2000, 5) describes Sartre "as a modern paradigm of the private thinker who spoke and acted on his own behalf rather than as the representative of a political party or social class." Such thinkers "seek to align themselves with the unrepresentable forces that introduce disorder and a dose of permanent revolution into political and social life" (Patton 2000, 6). Such thinkers I designate, then, as "private-and-public" intellectuals. They are private in Nietzsche's sense of self-overcoming while publicly declining to employ their intellectual labor in unquestioning service to the State and in complicity with the political status quo. They work from "within." Curriculum theory, then, constitutes a public and political commitment that requires autobiographical excavation and the self-reflexive articulation of one's subjectivity in society.

Private can imply isolation from historical forces and social movements. Such an implication would be mistaken here, as I am suggesting that historical forces and social movements are both the sources of interiority and the provocations of theorizing and teaching. But a certain solitude—a "room of one's own" in Virginia Woolf's famous phrase—is a prerequisite for that "complicated conversation" with oneself without which one disappears onto the social surface, into the maelstrom that is the public world. Without a private life, without an ongoing project of autobiographical understanding, one's intellectual "practice" too often tends toward the miming of what is fashionable or profitable. A public intellectual who is not also a private intellectual risks the convoluted expression of private emotion projected onto the social surface, as interiority not self-reflexively grasped can disappear into, and be misrecognized as, "the world." An "organic" intellectual's relation to the "multitude" (Hardt and Negri 2000, 61) necessarily includes one's relationship with one's self, one's self-reflexive articulation of one's subjectivity. It is through subjectivity that one experiences history and society, and through which history and society speak.

III
"TOO LITTLE INTELLECT IN MATTERS OF SOUL":
ON THE EDUCATION OF TEACHERS

Teaching is essentially social, moral, and political.
—Landon Beyer, Walter Feinberg, Jo Anne Pagano, and Tony Whitson (1989, 19)

To the devil with the practical sense, which leads only to the
temporary success of one's own egotistical purposes.
—Wassily Kandinsky (September 9, 1905; quoted in Izenberg 2000, 173)

We do not have too much intellect and too little soul,
but too little intellect in matters of the soul.
—Robert Musil (1990 [1922] 131)

Curriculum theory understands teacher education as engaging prospective and practicing teachers self-reflexively in interdisciplinary study, study often located at the intersections of self and society, the local and the global, the school subjects and everyday life. Examples of such interdisciplinary study include autobiography, multiculturalism, women's and gender studies, postcolonial studies, popular culture, postmodernism, psychoanalytic theory, cultural studies and those scholarly efforts to understand globalization.

Moreover, both schooling and education (intersecting but hardly identical terms) are studied at their organizational and intellectual center, the curriculum. They are also studied historically, in part to enable teachers to appreciate how they came to be working under current conditions, among them diminished academic freedom, including the loss of control over the means by which teachers assess students' study and academic accomplishment.

Curriculum theory understands teacher education not as learning a new language for what teachers already do, although the language we employ to understand what we do structures, as well as represents, professional conduct. After Huebner (1999), we understand the limitations of the language of "learning," embedded as that term is in academic psychology, rather than in psychoanalysis (see Britzman 1998). British-born and -educated Canadian curriculum theorist Robin Barrow (1984, 97) is blunt: "I shall argue, however, that there is very little of importance for educators that can be gained from the study of such things as learning theory, child development and personality."

After Huebner, we appreciate the significance of employing ethical, religious, and aesthetic languages to depict and structure our professional activities as educators. Curriculum scholars are rightly suspicious of rhetorical bandwagons such as "competency-based" or "outcome-based" or "standards" and immediately go to work to situate them historically, in terms of the discourse systems in which they operate, especially in politicians' obfuscating rhetorics.

In studying curriculum theory, then, teachers are not being asked to learn how to do something "new" in the classroom, although their conduct there may well be altered, perhaps even transformed, as a consequence of studying curriculum theory. How it will be altered or transformed one cannot predict, however. We curriculum theorists do not regard our task as directing teachers to apply theory to practice, a form of professional subordination, in positions (as Southern Baptists once described wives' relations to their husbands) of "gracious submission."

Rather, curriculum theorists in the university regard our pedagogical work as the cultivation of independence of mind, self-reflexivity, and an interdisciplinary erudition. We hope to persuade teachers to appreciate the complex and shifting relations between their own self-formation and the school subjects they teach, understood both as subject matter and as human subjects.

Skeptical of "business thinking" (or the business metaphor, "one in which curriculum producers offer something to curriculum consumers" [Aoki in press]) and of military discipline, both of which continue to be invoked as corrective to the supposed lack of "rigor" in schools (a gendered and racialized as well as academic judgment), curriculum theorists appreciate that the profession of teaching requires us—as faculty, that is, as private-and-public intellectuals—to understand and participate collaboratively in the school, including in the governance of the day-to-day life of the institution *and* in the administration of academic matters such as curriculum content, teaching styles, and the assessment of students' study.

Participating in the governance of the school requires us to remain (or to become) self-aware of the multiple functions and potentials of the process of education and of the institutions which formalize them. This means becoming articulate about and exercising influence over curriculum content, including interdisciplinary configurations (such as women's and gender studies), theories of pedagogy, and the various means of assessing student study. How all this gets worked out, including how teachers' already overburdened schedules (too many students and too many classes continue to characterize teachers' underpaid and unprofessional lives in too many schools), is outside the purview of curriculum theory, but its scholarly understanding is not.

Curriculum theory is a form of practical-theoretical reason. As such, it is not subject to the scientific norms of reason and truth (see Kohli 1995). Curriculum theory can be best understood as extension and reconfiguration of theory in the humanities and the arts (including arts-based research [see, e.g., Barone 2000]). Curriculum theory is significantly informed as well by social and autobiographical theory, themselves (as we see in chapter 2) intersecting domains.

Why is autobiographical theory key in social analysis? As Joe L. Kincheloe and Shirley Steinberg (1993, 300) suggest: "Power manifests itself not through some explicit form of oppression, but via the implicit reproduction of the self." I might amend the observation by inserting "only" after "not," but the point is well taken. As Elizabeth Ellsworth (1997, 42) has observed, an exclusive emphasis upon the social in educational research is "impoverished." What is required in teacher education might be the study of what Megan Boler (1999, 142) terms "emotional epistemologies," by which she means "a public recognition of the ways in which the 'social' defines the 'interior' realm of experience, and vice versa."

Curriculum theory, then, is a form of autobiographical and theoretical truth-telling that articulates the educational experience of teachers and students as lived. As such, curriculum theory speaks from the subjective experience of history and society, the inextricable interrelationships among which structure educational experience. The role of language—first articulated by Dwayne Huebner in the 1960s (see his collected works: Huebner 1999)—in such "truth-telling" is key. As the legendary Canadian curriculum theorist Ted Aoki (in press), has warned: "the danger . . . is that we become the language we speak." In psychoanalytic (rather than phenomenological) terms, the point is the same: "[t]here is no language without desire and no desire which is not itself language" (Silverman 2000, 55–56).

If we employ, for instance, that bureaucratic language in which teaching becomes not an occasion for creativity and dissent and, above all, individuality, but, rather, the "implementation" of others' "objectives," the process of education is mutilated. Whatever language we employ, we "become" the language. In "becoming" the language of "implementation," Aoki (in press) notes, "we might become forgetful of how instrumental language disengages us form our bodies, making of us disembodied, dehumanized beings, indifferent to the nihilistic drying out of inspiritedness." "Instead of 'curriculum implementation'," Aoki asks, "how about 'curriculum improvisation'?" Such a shift in theoretical articulation, he notes, "provokes in us a vitalizing possibility that causes our whole body to beat a new and different rhythm."

Such a "new and different rhythm" is very much needed in teacher education, one that makes audible the generative roles of creativity and individuality in teaching. As Elizabeth Ellsworth (1997, 137) has observed: "Our improvisations are performative, they are culture-in-the-making." But teacher education today threatens to become culture-in-the-unmaking as it is deprofessionalized by anti-intellectual interventions by government and by presumably professional organizations such as the National Council for Accreditation of Teacher Education (NCATE) (see chapter 9, sections II and III). In this "business-minded" or "technological" present, theory is severed from practice. In Musil's analysis of European culture, quoted to start the chapter, the problem of the age is the severance of intellect from soul.

When the legendary Ted Aoki recalled working as a public school teacher, his teaching seemed to reflect, rather than challenge, this cultural crisis in which work is split off from play, mind from body, soul from intellect (where it is, presumably, merely a matter of "faith"). "What I was teaching," Aoki concludes, reflecting on his own practice as a public school teacher for 19 years, "was a way of life that sees thinking as theorizing and doing as practicing." The title of the textbook he used to teach reading—*We Think and Do*—represents, he suggests, "a mundane version of what could be entitled *We Theorize and Practice*." "For educators," he notes, "it is a way of life that regards teacher preparation in education curriculum and instruction courses as theorizing and the practicing of theories as *practicum*."

"Must we be caught up totally in the linearized form of from theory into practice? Aoki (in press) asks? Must we? The answer, in the United States at least, is "yes," as government and its enforcers—such as NCATE—position teachers and those of us who teach teacher into positions of "gracious submission." This subjugation—rationalized by a rhetoric of "accountability" that, judged by the Enron and WorldCom scandals of 2002, even American business does not practice—is presumably in service of "learning."

Presumably. But, as Linda McNeil (2000, xiv) understands, "by increasing bureaucratic controls, these reforms inadvertently strengthened the very forces that are known to undermine teaching and learning, as teachers and students react against controls by limiting their own work." "Accountability" is not about "learning," but about controlling what we teach to our children. It is about controlling the curriculum. To achieve this control—which is, finally, control of the mind—the public schools are severed from both the social and the subjective. Teachers are reduced to technicians, "managing" student productivity. The school is no longer a school, but a business.

IV
THE SCHOOL AS A BUSINESS

No doubt there is a certain measure of inherent dissonance between business enterprise and intellectual enterprise.
—Richard Hofstadter (1962, 233)

We may say, of course, that it is a primitive view of life, which thus confuses intellectuality and business ability.
—Jane Addams (2002 [1902], 15)

The various institutions of modern society should be viewed as an archipelago of factories of subjectivity.
—Michael Hardt and Antonio Negri (2000, 195)

While the point of the American public schools has not changed much over the past 100 years, the economy schools were designed to support has. The consensus view is that the American economy is less and less industrial and more and more "service oriented," strongly "information based," increasingly organized around technological developments, including the Internet. It is said to be international or global in character. Rather than the assembly line of the early automobile factory, the major mode of economic production today is semiotic (i.e., production of signs, symbols, and other information), and it occurs not in factories but in committees and in front of computer screens in corporate offices.

Most American schools, however, still tend to be modeled after the assembly-line factory. Modeling schools after the contemporary corporation (that "profoundly undemocratic institution" [Lasch 1984, 51]) represents, presumably, an improvement. So-called "smart schools" tend to be versions of the corporate model (Fiske 1991). In this corporate model, however, the economic function of schools remains unchallenged, and the modes of cognition appropriate to even corporate schools are fewer and narrower than intelligence more broadly understood.

Because the organization and culture of the school are linked to the economy and dominated by "business thinking," the school and the American curriculum field have traveled different paths over the past 30 years. For the foreseeable future, most teachers will be trained as "social engineers," directed to "manage" learning that is modeled loosely after corporate work stations. Certainly some segment of the American curriculum field will devote itself to assist in the design and implementation of this corporate school curriculum. However, those of us who labored to reconceptualize the atheoretical, ahistorical field we found in 1970 have always seen a more complex calling for the field. The theoretical wing of the reconceived field aspires to ground itself not in the pressured everyday world of the corporate classroom but in worlds not present in the schools today, in ideas marginal to the maximization of profits, and in imaginative and lived experience that is not exclusively instrumental and calculative (see Pinar 1999a).

In its press for efficiency and standardization, the factory model tends to reduce teachers to automata. In designing and teaching the curriculum in units that presumably "add up" to a logical even disciplinary "whole" (like products on an assembly line), the factory-model school achieves social control at the cost of intelligence, intelligence broadly understood as including problem solving, critical thinking, and creativity as well as memorization and calculation. As Linda McNeil (2000, 3) has observed: "*Standardization reduces the quality and quantity of what is taught and learned in schools.*" Students who tolerate the routinized, repetitious nature of instruction that relies upon recitation and memorization sometimes are able to perform reasonably well on similar tasks, although the "transferability" of these task-specific skills has remained a problem for the factory model.

The corporate model accepts learning the "basics" as the goal of the school. However, this model permits a variety of instructional strategies to be employed in its attainment. Team and peer teaching, small-group work, other forms of so-called cooperative and collaborative learning, even minor curriculum changes are permitted to allow students and teachers to find their own ways to learn what is demanded of them. Moreover, the corporate model tends to acknowledge that intelligence is multiple in nature and function and includes aesthetic, intuitive, and sensory elements as well as linear, logical, narrowly cognitive ones (Gardner 1983). The social character of intelligence is also acknowledged as corporate classroom organization often permits the use of dyadic and small-group activities. The teacher in this scheme is a manager or, in Theodore Sizer's (1984) image, a "coach," a gendered metaphor Nancy Lesko (2002) associates with the remasculinization of the school. While masculinized, these images—*manager* and *coach*—are considerably less authoritarian than those associated with the teacher in the factory school.

Even in the presumably more flexible corporate model, the goal of instruction—the acquisition of that knowledge and the cultivation of those skills deemed necessary for productivity in a postindustrial economy—is not in question. Intelligence is viewed as a means to an end, the acquisition of skills, knowledge, and attitudes utilizable in the corporate sector. The maximization of profits remains the "bottom line" of the corporation as well as that of its earlier version, the factory. I am not suggesting that schools should have no relationship to the economy. Capitalism does require forms of knowledge and intelligence the corporate model of schooling is more likely than the factory model to produce. Nor am I suggesting that we could have publicly supported schools in the United States that would *not* have economic goals, at least for the imaginable future.

Curriculum theory reminds those of us committed to the project of education (which, of course, does not always coincide with what goes on in the schools) that for intelligence to be cultivated in fundamental ways, it must be set free of corporate goals. Such an idea hardly excludes instrumental reason, calculation, and problem solving as major modes of cognition. Intellectual freedom must allow, however, for meditative, contemplative modes of cognition, and for exploring subjects—those associated, for instance, with the arts and the humanities—that may have no immediate practical pay-off and might not be evaluated by standardized examinations.

Intelligence is made narrow, and thus undermined, when it is reduced to answers to other people's questions, when it is only a means to achieve preordained goals. This instrumental and calculative concept of intelligence, while useful to the present form of economic organization—the corporation—is less helpful in investigations of more fundamental questions of human experience, experience that might not lead directly to economic development and increased productivity. To study these questions is to "ride" intelligence to destinations perhaps not listed in the present economic and political agenda. Such a view of curriculum inquiry and research is akin to what in the natural sciences would be termed basic research, wherein destinations are not necessarily known in advance. For us, it might be theoretical research freed of the taken-for-granted demands of everyday problems in schools. To suggest one form such research in the United States might take, let us attend very briefly an emergent category in American curriculum theory. This category—identity—emerged in debates over multiculturalism, but it promises to take us other places as well, including investigations of what it means educationally to be conceived by others (see Pinar 1994).

V
THE FIGURE OF THE SCHOOLTEACHER

The figure of the schoolteacher may well be taken as a central
symbol in any modern society.
—Richard Hofstadter (1962, 309)

What we have is many good people caught in a bad system.
—Linda McNeil (2000, 269)

Educators, beware of the lesson plan.
—Mary Aswell Doll (2000, 36)

The category of identity organizes educational investigations of political, racialized, and gendered experience around questions of self-formation and subjectivity in the public sphere. This notion of "self" is not the bourgeois individual decried by the various Marxisms and embraced by conservatives but rather the vortex of psychosocial and discursive relations theorized by Lacan, Freud, and Foucault. The study of identity enables us to portray how the politics we had thought were located "out there," in society, are lived through "in here," in our bodies, our minds, our everyday speech and conduct. The political status quo is not simply "reproduced," of course. Even when we resist social trends and political directives, we are reconstructing ourselves in terms of those trends and debates and our resistance to them. In studying the politics of identity, we find that who we are is invariably related to who others are, as well as to whom we have been and want to become.

Currently, the American teacher's identity is being reconceived from factory supervisor to corporate manager. It *is* a promotion. However, if loyal to the cultivation of intelligence and the democratic project of education, teachers still face the challenge to become more than they have been conceived and conditioned to be. If we are submerged in identities conceived by others, the cultivation of intelligence is necessarily restricted and undermined. Of course, we teachers must meet contractual obligations regarding curriculum and instruction. However, we need not necessarily believe them or uncritically accept them. Curriculum theorists might assist teachers to avoid the disappearance of their ideals into the maelstrom of daily classroom demands. We might support teachers' identities apart from those constructed by corporatism by proclaiming the existence of other ways of conceiving education, noninstrumental ways of speaking and being with children.

We teachers are conceived by others, by the expectations and fantasies of our students and by the demands of parents, administrators, policymakers, and politicians, to all of whom we are sometimes the "other." We are formed as well by their and our own internalized life histories. These various spheres or levels of self-constitution require investigation. Locating the process of knowing in the politics of identity suggests escaping the swirling waters created by the demands and pressures of others. The capacity to stand calmly in a maelstrom can come only with knowledge of other worlds, with living in other realities, not split off or dissociated from the everyday world of work. "Separate but connected" permits us to enter the work world larger, more complex, than the roles prescribed for us, making less likely that we will collapse upon the social surface, reduced to what others make of us.

We Americans might then model to our children how we can live in this society without succumbing to it, without giving up our dreams and aspirations for education. Teachers can become witnesses to the notion that intelligence and learning can lead to other worlds, not just the successful exploitation of this one. Theory is a "prayerful act" (see Macdonald 1995). But knowledge need not be regarded as a sacred text as in fundamentalist religions or an inviolate procedure as on the assembly line; nor is it only the more complex, sometimes even creative, means to an end as it is in the corporate model. Rather, knowledge and intelligence as free exploration become wings by which we take flight, visit other worlds, returning to this one to call others, especially our children, to futures more life-affirmative than the world we inhabit now. When we sink, submerged in those roles conceived by others, we become aborted possibilities, unable to realize in everyday life, in our relations with others, the politics of our individual and civic identities, the educational dynamics of creation and birth.

What value is American curriculum theory to the American school-teacher? To those teachers hardened by 30 years of conservative reaction, it may seem pointless. To the novice teacher eager to "learn the ropes," it might seem fanciful, interesting perhaps, but with no immediate pay-off. The constituency of American curriculum theorists may not be in schools at this time. However, if we can teach, if we can make friends with some of those struggling in the schools, build bridges between the realms of theory and practice (even while we avoid collapsing one into the other), if we create passages—to borrow Jacques Daignault's (1992) term—to travel from here to there and back again, broadened, deepened, enlivened by the voyage, then we theorists might participate with subtlety and acumen in school reform. Being a theorist, after all, does not mean being dissociated or inefficient.

Being a theorist does not mean being a celibate in terms of everyday practice. It does not mean one cannot function successfully in the corporate school, providing advice and assistance. Being a theorist does mean that the contemporary curriculum organization and the modes of cognition it requires must be bracketed, situated in history, politics, and our own life histories. Such understanding might allow us to participate in school reform in ways that do not hypostatize the present, but rather, allow our labor and understandings to function as do those in psychoanalysis, to enlarge the understanding and deepen the intelligence of the participants. The tragedy of the present is that school reform—as it is currently cast—cannot achieve this.

The pressure upon us is enormous. Through legislation (such as the Bush Administration's *Leave No Child Behind Act*) and through professional organizations such as the National Council for Accreditation of Teacher Education (NCATE) (see chapter 9), the education professorate is being pressured to comply with the political agenda of the right-wing in America with its business rationale. As in other states, Louisiana school reform has included "reform" of teacher education, both a restructuring of university-based teacher preparation programs (and, as such, an incursion upon the academic freedom of university professors), a "breaking of the ed. school monopoly," as right-wing rhetoric would have it. This means, in Louisiana at least, that private providers "compete" with colleges and universities to produce teachers in abbreviated teacher preparation programs. In Louisiana, this proceeds on the assumption that teacher preparation is about the mass production of teachers, understood as school-subject specialists and school employees.

Because political conservatives tend to identify the school subjects with the disciplines, they tend to suspend key curriculum questions, such as: What does the school curriculum have to say to youth culture, specifically youth alienation and violence? How can the school curriculum help us understand terrorism, the ecological crisis, globalization? The conservative tends to focus on instruction and learning, especially the latter, as it is quantified in test scores. In splitting curriculum from instruction, the right-wing turns teachers into technicians. This anti-intellectualism is reflected in the organizational restructuring of a number of Colleges of Education wherein the historical designation "Department of Curriculum and Teaching" (first appearing at Teachers College, Columbia University in 1937) has been replaced with titles such as "Department of Teaching and Learning" or "Department of Instruction and Learning." Because teachers, and education professors, have little jurisdiction over the official school curriculum, it tends to be ignored (except as content to be learned), no longer deemed by many to be a pressing professional concern. Like the public schools, schools of education are forced into positions of "gracious submission."

In colleges and universities most faculty—especially in the humanities and arts—remain clear that curriculum and teaching are profoundly linked, that the curriculum is the intellectual and organizational center of education. Most understand that the performance of their complicated professional obligations as scholars and teachers requires us to retain the academic—that is, intellectual—freedom to choose those texts and topics we deem, in our professional judgment, most appropriate. Most of us appreciate that our professional labor requires that we decide how to examine our students, sometimes by research papers, other times by essay- or short-answer tests, and even, on occasion, by standardized examinations. The situation in higher education is, of course, hardly ideal: The general education curriculum in many public research universities is more a political than thoughtful and informed curricular arrangement—but my point is that the inseparable relation between curriculum and teaching remains intact, more or less, at many universities. Why it was never fully honored in elementary, middle, and secondary schools is a historical and, for me, gendered and racialized issue, as I suggest in chapter 3.

Because contemporary teacher education is about the "delivery" of instruction, many do not appreciate that the study of education is, first and foremost, an intellectual undertaking, and that the field of education is simultaneously an academic as well as professional field. Our profession *is* academic. Too few appreciate the significance of studying the field's history. In some schools of education, especially at prestigious private and public research universities, there has been a tendency to employ faculty with doctoral degrees in fields other than education, but who have claimed an interest in "education." In this scheme, "education" is an academic interest, an "application" of a "true" academic field, such as psychology or sociology or history or physics (see, e.g., Clifford and Guthrie 1988).

Aggressively self-promotional but having reached (for the moment) the physical size its enrollments and grant activities permit, academic psychology has long looked at the field of education as a potential colony. Rarely is academic psychology self-aware of the historical, political, gendered and racial currents in which child and adolescent psychology appeared and were intertwined at the beginning of the 20th century (Baker 2001; Lesko 2000). Self-absorbed, academic psychology focuses, predictably enough, on "instruction" and "learning," as if unmindful of the central role of curriculum in the education of the American public. Ahistorical, imagining itself a "science," academic psychology "retreat[ed] from the challenge of Freud into the measurement of trivia," as historian Christopher Lasch (1978, xiv) succinctly put the matter. Perhaps for that reason, academic psychology has too often imaged itself the central discipline in the broad—and highly bureaucratized— field of education (see Comer 2003).

Rejecting colonization by the hegemonic disciplines such as psychology, curriculum theory explores and constructs hybrid interdisciplinary constructions, utilizing fragments from philosophy, history, literary theory, the arts, and from those key interdisciplinary formations already in place: women's and gender studies, African-American studies, queer theory, studies in popular culture, among others. Employing research completed in other disciplines as well as our own, curriculum theorists construct textbooks that invite public school teachers to reoccupy a vacated "public" domain, not simply as "consumers" of knowledge, but as active participants in conversations they themselves will lead. In drawing—promiscuously but critically—from various academic disciplines and popular culture, curriculum theorists work to create conceptual montages for the public-school teacher who understands that positionality as aspiring to create a "public" space.

Such efforts to reconstitute ourselves from merely school employees to private-and-public intellectuals cut against the grain not only of dominant school reform rhetoric dominated by right-wing intellectuals and politicians, they cut against the grain of traditional teacher education with its neglect of curriculum and its obsession with instruction and learning. There is, as we see in chapters 7 and 9, a pervasive problem of anti-intellectualism both within the profession and "outside" it (in society, in government) that makes radical curriculum reform in the schools unlikely.

Given our conception by others, we are currently unable, as individuals or as a group, to undertake radical reform. Christopher Lasch's point about the political socialization of the young pertains, I think, to many educators as well: "The socialization of the young reproduces the political domination at the level of personal experience. In our own time, this invasion of private life by the forces of organized domination has become so pervasive that personal life has almost ceased to exist" (Lasch 1978, 30). Given the historical moment, we must work from within.

2

Autobiography:
A Revolutionary Act

I
TO RUN THE COURSE

*[I]ndividuality is no longer associated with sovereignty
but instead with subjection and docility.*
—Ewa Plonowska Ziarek (2001, 26)

*Currere is a reflexive cycle in which thought bends back
upon itself and thus recovers its volition.*
—Madeleine R. Grumet (1976, 130–131)

[A]utobiography can be a revolutionary act.
—L. L. Langness and Gelya Frank (1981, 93)

To support the systematic study of self-reflexivity within the processes of education, I devised the method of *currere*. The method of *currere*—the Latin
infinitive form of curriculum means to run the course, or, in the gerund form,
the running of the course—provides a strategy for students of curriculum to
study the relations between academic knowledge and life history in the interest of self-understanding and social reconstruction.

There are four steps or moments in the method of *currere*: the regressive,
the progressive, the analytical, and the synthetical. These point to both temporal and cognitive movements in the autobiographical study of educational
experience; they suggest the temporal and cognitive modes of relation between knower and known that might characterize the ontological structure of
educational experience (Pinar 1994; Pinar and Grumet 1976).

Stated simply, *currere* seeks to understand the contribution academic studies makes to one's understanding of his or her life (and vice versa), and how both are imbricated in society, politics, and culture (Bruner 1996). Influenced by literary and feminist theory, *currere* becomes a version of cultural criticism. "Cultural criticism," Christopher Lasch (1978, 16) notes, "took on a personal and autobiographical character, which at its worst degenerated into self-display but at its best showed that the attempt to understand culture has to include the way it shapes the critic's own consciousness." Due to the dangers of exhibitionism and exposure (De Castell 1999), I have declined to recommend the use of *currere* as an instructional device in the school curriculum.

The student of educational experience takes as hypothesis that at any given moment she or he is in a "biographic situation" (Pinar and Grumet 1976, 51), that is to say, that she or he is located in historical time and cultural place, but in a singularly meaningful way, a situation to be expressed in one's autobiographical voice. "Biographic situation" suggests a structure of lived meaning that follows from past situations, but which contains, perhaps unarticulated, contradictions of past and present as well as anticipation of possible futures.

> I can see that this has led to that; in that circumstance I chose that, I rejected this alternative; I affiliated with those people, then left them for these, that this field intrigued me intellectually, then that one; I worked on this problem, then that one. . . . I see that there is a coherence. Not necessarily a logical one, but a lived one, a felt one. The point of coherence is the biography as it is lived. . . . The predominant [question] is: what has been and what is now the nature of my educational experience? (Pinar and Grumet 1976, 52; quoted in Pinar et al. 1995, 520)

In the regressive step or moment I conceived of one's apparently past "lived" or existential experience as "data source." To generate "data" one free associates, after the psychoanalytic technique, to re-enter the past, and to thereby enlarge—and transform—one's memory. In doing so, one regresses: "One returns to the past, to capture it as it was, and as it hovers over the present" (1976, 55). In the second or progressive step one looks toward what is not yet the case, what is not yet present. Like the past, I suggested, the future inhabits the present. Meditatively, the student of *currere* imagines possible futures.

In the analytical stage the student examines both past and present. Etymologically, *ana* means "up, throughout"; *lysis* means "a loosening." The analysis of *currere* is akin to phenomenological bracketing; one's distantiation from past and future functions to create a subjective space of freedom in the present. This occurs in the analytic moment: "How is the future present in the past, the past in the future, and the present in both?" (Pinar and Grumet 1976, 60; quoted in Pinar et al. 1995, 520).

The analytic phase is not self-scrutiny for the sake of public performance, a self-theatricalizing in which social life becomes a spectacle. As Lasch (1978, 94) points out: "In our society, anxious self-scrutiny (not to be confused with critical self-examination) not only serves to regulate information signaled to others and to interpret signals received; it also establishes an ironic distance from the deadly routine of daily life." The point of *currere* is an intensified engagement with daily life, not an ironic detachment from it.

What is this temporal complexity that presents itself to me as the present moment? In the synthetical step—etymologically *syn* means "together"; *tithenai* means "to place"—one re-enters the lived present. Conscious of one's breathing, indeed, of one's embodied otherness, one asks "who is that?" Listening carefully to one's own inner voice in the historical and natural world, one asks: "what is the meaning of the present?"

> Make it all a whole. It, all of it—intellect, emotion, behavior—occurs in and through the physical body. As the body is a concrete whole, so what occurs within and through the body can become a discernible whole, integrated in its meaningfulness. . . . Mind in its place, I conceptualize the present situation. I am placed together. Synthesis. (1976, 61; quoted in Pinar et al. 1995, 521)

The moment of synthesis—one of intense interiority—is expressed poetically by Mary Aswell Doll (2000, xii): "Curriculum is also . . . a coursing, as in an electric current. The work of the curriculum theorist should tap this intense current within, that which courses through the inner person, that which electrifies or gives life to a person's energy source."

As Megan Boler (1999, 178) appreciates, "the Socratic admonition to 'know thyself' may not lead to self-transformation." By itself and especially as a psychological process, self-reflection "may result in no measurable change or good to others or oneself" (1999, 178). In contrast to psychologistic conceptions of self-knowledge, what Boler (1999, 178) terms "collective witnessing is always understood in relation to others, and in relation to personal and cultural histories and material conditions." As this volume will make explicit, self-knowledge and collective witnessing are complementary projects of self-mobilization for social reconstruction.

The method of *currere* reconceptualized curriculum from course objectives to complicated conversation with oneself (as a "private" intellectual), an ongoing project of self-understanding in which one becomes mobilized for engaged pedagogical action—as a private-and-public intellectual—with others in the social reconstruction of the public sphere. Curriculum theory asks you, as a prospective or practicing teacher, to consider your position as engaged with yourself and your students and colleagues in the construction of a public sphere, a public sphere not yet born, a future that cannot be discerned in, or even thought from, the present. So conceived, the classroom becomes simultaneously a civic square and a room of one's own.

Autobiography is a first-person and singular version of culture and history as these are embodied in the concretely existing individual in society in historical time. In European and European-American culture (in the modernist period especially), scholarly studies of culture and history have expressed disinterested and spectator-like structures of epistemology and knowledge. In contrast to these fictive universalisms are fiction and poetry. What would the curriculum look like if we centered the school subjects in the autobiographical histories and reflections of those who undergo them? The "subjects" in school subjects would refer to human subjects as well as academic ones. Indeed, the academic disciplines are highly systematized, formalized, bureaucratized conversations among human subjects, circulating in specific regimes of reason, sometimes estranged from bodies of knowledge.

Cultural politics cannot be conducted at this time, in this place, without a politics of the individual, and within this subjective sphere the individual himself or herself must be an activist working to democratize one's interiority. The "population" internalized within is the electorate, as it were, and these "citizens" must be recognized, respected, persuaded, not silenced, "othered," deported without a "hearing." Only through a genuine democratization of one's interiorized elements, none of which gets deported (projected, in psychoanalytic terms) to the bodies of others who then become "others," can the body politic be reformed and the public sphere reconstructed. Autobiography is not bourgeois narcissism, as Christopher Lasch (1978, 206) appreciated: "Discussion of personal issues can no longer be dismissed as a form of 'bourgeois subjectivity'." Indeed, autobiography is the pedagogical political practice for the 21st century.

Indirect autobiography—an autobiographics of alterity (Gilmore 1994)—subjectifies intellectually the process of social psychoanalysis. The official story a nation or culture tells itself—often evident in school curriculum—hides other truths. The national story also creates the illusion of truth being on the social surface, when it is nearly axiomatic that the stories we tell ourselves mask other, unacceptable truths. What we as a nation try not to remember—genocide, slavery, lynching, prison rape—structures the politics of our collective identification and imagined affiliation. The pretensions of the Founding Fathers and their colleagues were not only pretensions; they were, as well, aspirations. Perhaps that was our—the white middle-class, 1960s generations of public university students—naiveté and misunderstanding: We believed only the aspirations, in part due to our teachers' and parents' (innocent?) misrepresentation of the nation.

Was it to justify their suffering during the Depression and during World War II and the Korean War and perhaps to thank someone, something—a nation, God, the two conflated for many—for delivering them from economic deprivation and from the threat of military defeat, that our parents and teachers taught us (their post-World War II children) that America was the land of liberty, freedom, equality? The words of the Founding Fathers seemed proof of an indelible and enduring identity.

And so many of us believed them, our parents, our teachers, ourselves. In the 1960s we learned (at university, not in the censored high-school curriculum) that the USA had never been only or, it seemed, mostly about those aspirations. In the midst of cultural revolution, and the intensifying antiwar and civil rights movements, these seemed not sincere aspirations but rhetorical cover-ups to hide the nation's other life, its "other" identity, its hidden curriculum. In the streets, on college campuses, across the South, we learned that, from the genocide of the indigenous peoples to the Boston Tea Party and the slave trade, the United States has always been about low taxation, individual greed, and mass violence. While these are hardly exceptional in human history, these facts did underscore to us that this country is not exceptional in human history, despite politicians' rhetoric and our miseducation.

The Founding Fathers' rhetoric is inspiring but it is not unique; the French Revolution has some rather fancy if puzzling (given the savagery of events, the quick retreat to the national fantasy Napoleon represented) language accompanying it as well. We declare these truths to be self-evident: This nation is built on the backs and bodies of vanquished "others." Does nationalism always represent, in part, a historically specific version of the dynamics of denial?

The educational task is to take the cover stories we as Americans tell ourselves and look to the back pages. We must teach what the cover stories hide, exposing and problematizing the "hidden curriculum." We do so for the sake of truth but not *just* for the sake of truth: Educational confession, including autobiographical confession (Foucault's association of confession and the regulation of the self to the contrary), is for the sake of psycho-political movement, in order to create passages out of and away from the stasis of the historical present.

Not to romanticize marginalized peoples (although there is much to admire), but it is "there"—that is to say, in our fantasies which construct the "other"—that European Americans must look to initiate our passage out of Egypt. Those split-off fantasies constitute (and hide) the blocks to cultural movement and political restructuring. The American dream understood only as wealth is a nightmare; understood symbolically as psycho-social movement and political transformation, it is dream worth waking up to. In educational terms, it is living the progressive dream of John Dewey, Jane Addams, Boyd Bode, and George B. Counts.

Just as serious autobiographical work requires the surfacing and re-incorporation of repudiated elements, cultural progress requires analogous reconstruction. This is not the same old liberal line: One is not trying to assimilate the repressed elements into the self as it exists. Rather, autobiographical labor aims to reconstitute the nation that exists, the nation that exists, as the reincorporated elements redefine the terms of a new deal, new subjectivities, a new nation, and a sustainable planet.

II
THE SOCIAL AND SUBJECTIVE
IN AFRICAN-AMERICAN AUTOBIOGRAPHY

I saw them [African Americans] hedged for centuries by prejudice, intolerance, and brutality; hobbled by their own ignorance, poverty, and helplessness; yet, notwithstanding, still brave and unvanquished. . . . The situation in which they were might have seemed hopeless, but they themselves were not without hope.
—James Weldon Johnson (1933, 120)

Multiculturalism suspends the traumatic kernel of the Other, reducing it to an aseptic folklorist entity.
—Slavoj Zizek (1998, 168)

Our subjectivity is objectively intended.
—Kaja Silverman (2000, 133)

To ask and begin to answer autobiographical questions requires, then, connecting the subjective to the social, and vice versa. There is, perhaps, no more powerful example of such connection that the traditions of African-American autobiography. African-American autobiographical practices racialize, politicize, and historicize self-narration. Racial politics and violence in America have been undergone as subjective as well as civic experience (Pinar 2001). Whereas both white and black literary traditions in the United States begin with autobiographical accounts, black accounts reveal aspects of early American life absent in the early colonial journals of William Bradford, Cotton Mather, and Jonathon Edwards. African-American autobiographies supported psycho-political struggle against a predatory and enslaving white regime. This reverberating fact affects the entire tradition of African-American literature, not to mention the history of the United States (Morrison 1992). African-American identities have been created, in no small measure, in resistance to murdering white masters, and lived, at times, with seemingly unbearable intensity (Butterfield 1974). In the context of racial politics in America, as Stephen Butterfield (1974, 284) observes, "autobiography . . . becomes both an arsenal and a battleground."

Autobiography, Butterfield (1974) believes, has been an especially appealing form to many African-American writers because, as a genre, it inhabits two worlds: history and literature. Many African-American writers, he notes, have also tended to live in two worlds: white and black, "public mask and private face" (1974, 285). Autobiography, Butterfield (1974, 284) suggests, "affords the greatest opportunities to combine the two perspectives because it develops like a village on the crossroads between the author's subjective life and his social-historical life."

Making the case to European-American readers for the significance of this genre, Butterfield (1974) argues that African-American autobiographies fill in many of the blanks of the nation's self-knowledge. They document what has been ignored in American life by many white writers and critics. Further, they show how white critical judgment has been limited, indeed deformed, by racial blind spots. "I have begun to wonder," Toni Morrison (1992, 5) famously writes,

> whether the major, much celebrated themes of American literature—individualism, masculinity, the conflict between social engagement and historical isolation, an acute and ambiguous moral problematics, the juxtaposition of innocence with figures representing death and hell—are not in fact responses to a dark, abiding, signifying Africanistic presence.

It is a powerful point differently made by Leslie Fiedler (1966).

In key ways, the African-American experience informs the American identity; in one sense, it constitutes the cultural "unconscious" of the nation (Castenell and Pinar 1993). African-American autobiographies provide inspiration and hope for all Americans; as Butterfield asserts, African-American autobiographies *are* the American conscience. But among many European Americans, especially among those in the South, a strong if false sense persists that the African-American experience has no point for them, that what happened "before" has nothing to do with the "now." Stephen Butterfield (1974, 4) knows: "Knowledge of the sins of the fathers is a terrible burden for the children of pirates, murderers, kidnappers, rapists, for the children of those who received the benefits of stolen labor and genocide and closed their eyes, perhaps with a humanitarian shudder, to its effects." This is, Deborah Britzman (1998) might say, "difficult knowledge." But, Butterfield (1974, 4) continues,

> The price of ignoring it is to smother the intelligence, with all the consequences this racism implies: to become divorced from one's humanity, to reduce oneself to a thing, a consumer, a machine for generating or appropriating surplus value, an obstacle to the growth of others. But, as so many black autobiographies demonstrate, one is never required to remain a thing. The humanity won

by the slave and his descendants belongs to humanity everywhere. The door of
the white prison is opened, not closed, by his story. If the very worst effects of
oppression have been unable to wipe out intelligence, compassion, honor, faith,
hope, and the courage to resist in the mass of its black victims, then these qualities are preserved for all, including the children of the ruling culture. The slave's
victory is the victory of the best in ourselves.

Whiteness has deprived whites of their history just as it had deprived African Americans of theirs. Whites must work through the defensive assertions
of their (guilt-laden) innocence, assertions which take aggressive counter-
allegations of "black racism" and "discrimination in reverse" when African
Americans make small, long-overdue advances (see Savran 1998). At the
other extreme, whites must avoid being paralyzed by guilt, which results in
nihilism, or slavish imitations of black culture, becoming, in Norman
Mailer's (1957) famous phrase, "the white negro," visible today in white (especially male) suburban co-optation of hip-hop culture. Pummeled by 30
years of white political reaction to the civil rights movement, it sometimes
feels as if the journey has yet to begin. But in the 1960s, it did begin: "there is
more day to dawn. The revolutionary self is but a morning star" (Butterfield
1974, 287).

Possibly more than any other form in African-American letters, autobiography has been acknowledged and celebrated since its appearance. From
slave narratives to contemporary writing, African-American autobiography
has functioned as a powerful means of addressing and contesting social, political, and cultural realities in the United States. In the ante-bellum period,
abolitionists published slave narratives to mobilize northern indignation. Autobiographical narratives of 1960s black revolutionaries compelled many
literary critics to reconsider conventional assumptions about literature's detached relationship to social struggle (Andrews 1993). But black autobiography's engaged relationship with social struggle was established long before
the activists and leaders of the 1960s civil rights struggle, often from prison,
articulated their experience of being in America (see Cleaver 1968; Seale
1978; Cummins 1994).

Slave narratives were often male slave narratives, the best known of which
is Frederick Douglass' masterpiece. While testifying to suffering and thereby
mobilizing abolitionist sentiment in the North, male slave narratives also
functioned to encode masculinity. Valerie Smith (1987) pointed out that "by
mythologizing rugged individuality, physical strength, and geographical mobility, the [slave] narrative enshrines cultural definitions of masculinity."
Smith understands that racial struggle in the United States has been gendered: "the plot of the standard narrative may thus be seen as not only the
journey from slavery to freedom but also the journey from slavehood to manhood" (quoted passages in McDowell 1993, 44). What can it mean than

emancipation was conceived as "manhood"? Was it a fantasy of freedom associated with white male privilege? Did slavery and racism contain a buried and emasculating homoerotic, rendering the gender of racial violence in America, as Katherine M. Blee (1991) perceptively observed, masculine?

In *Ar'n't I a Woman? Female Slaves in the Plantation South,* Deborah Gray White (1985) reads southern patriarchal culture as consolidating its symbolic power over both women and blacks in a single rhetorical move, making, in Michelle Wallace's (1990, 138) fine phrase, a "symbiotic relationship [between] sexism and racism." White concludes her study by narrating an occasion in the life of Sojourner Truth (see 1968 [1878]). In October 1858, Sojourner Truth was speaking in Silver Lake, Indiana. Men in the audience challenged her to prove she was a woman. She responded by baring her breasts. White (1985, 162) comments:

> Truth's experience serves as a metaphor for the slave woman's general experience. . . . Slave women were the only women in America who were sexually exploited with impunity, stripped and whipped with a lash, worked like oxen. In the nineteenth century when the nation was preoccupied with keeping women in the home and protecting them, only slave women were so totally unprotected by men or by law. Only black women had their womanhood so totally denied.

Michelle Wallace (1990, 140) adds that "Truth herself used the occasion to present further evidence of her sexual labor and exploitation; she told the audience that her breasts had fed many a white infant." Moreover, Wallace (1990, 140) suggests, Sojourner Truth understood, after her experience as both slave and abolitionist lecturer, that "the condition known as 'womanhood' was man-made." Sojourner Truth was not alone. Many black women understood the symbiotic relationship between racism and sexism, a relationship most white women would perceive only later, as the case of Jesse Daniel Ames illustrates (Hall 1979).

What possible defenses could black female slaves employ to defend themselves and their children from white abuse? "Sass" and invective functioned as verbal weapons (Braxton 1989). Derived from West Africa, *sass* is associated with the female elements of the trickster, a concept found in Gates' (1988) discussion of African mythology and Lemelle's (1995) discussion of contemporary African-American men. The *Oxford English Dictionary* ascribes the word's origin to the poisonous "sassy tree." A decoction of the bark of this tree was used in West Africa as an ordeal poison in the trial of accused witches. Such women were described as being wives of Exu, the trickster god. In this mythic sense, sass could kill (Braxton 1989).

Webster's Dictionary defines sass as talking impudently or disrespectfully to an elder or a superior, as in "talking back." In *Incidents in the Life of a Slave Girl*—which Hazel Carby (1993) characterizes as the most sophisticated, sustained narrative exposition of womanhood by an African American before Emancipation—whenever Harriet Jacobs (Linda Brent is her pseudonym) is sexually threatened, she uses sass to defend herself (Braxton 1989). Through sass she "returns" a portion of the poison the master has injected into her. When her master hits her, Brent retaliates, not with her fists, but with sass: "You have struck me for answering you honestly. How I despise you." When he threatens to send her to jail, she responds, "As for the jail, there would be more peace for me than there is here" (1987/1861, 39, 40; quoted in Braxton 1989, 31).

In this way sass protects something of her self-esteem, partly by increasing the psychological distance between herself and her white master. Braxton (1989, 32) notes that Linda Brent employed sass as Frederick Douglass did fists and feet, as a means of "resistance." Jacobs/Brent says: "Even those large, venomous snakes were less dreadful to my imagination than the white men in that community called civilized" (1987/1861, 113; quoted in Braxton 1989, 36). No one knew better what "snakes" white men could be than Ida B. Wells.

Ida B. Wells was a larger-than-life figure in the civil rights movement from the 1890s until her death in 1931. She was the chief architect of the anti-lynching movement in the late 19th century, a cause to which she came after a brief but memorable career of militant journalism in the black community. Before working as a journalist, Wells had been a schoolteacher. In my view, Wells remained a teacher, if imagining her classroom more expansively to include the American and British publics. Through her brilliant manipulation of white assumptions regarding gender, race, and civilization, Wells taught European Americans that lynching was barbaric (Bederman 1995).

This was no small accomplishment for a Memphis schoolteacher who had to battle not only white racism, but misogyny and even occasional envy from her fellow black reformers. John Hope Franklin (1970, x) summarizes her accomplishment this way:

> Her zeal and energy were matched by her uncompromising and unequivocal stand on every cause that she espoused. She did not hesitate to criticize southern whites even before she left the South, nor northern liberals, or members of her own race when she was convinced that their positions were not in the best interests of all mankind. She did not hesitate to go to the scene of racial disturbances, including riots and lynchings, in order to get an accurate picture of what actually occurred. She did not hesitate to summon to the cause of human dignity anybody and everybody she believed could serve the cause.

Ida Wells is "a giant of the [autobiographical] form," Stephen Butterfield (1974, 201) asserts. Her autobiography is important for several reasons. First, Wells' *Crusade for Justice* is significant as a historical source. In my study of lynching, for example, I found it essential to quote from it extensively (Pinar

2001). Wells visited the scenes of race riots and lynchings, obtained information from eyewitnesses, and published accounts which corrected racist distortions in the white press. She organized relief and defense efforts for the victims. From Ida B. Wells one learns firsthand not only the intensity of the violence directed at African Americans from Reconstruction on through the second decade of the 20th century, but the intensity of black resistance to that violence as well. Individually and through organizations such as women's clubs, discussion groups, mutual assistance leagues, black-edited newspapers and pamphlets, African Americans contested Jim Crow.

Butterfield (1974) suggests that Wells' style exhibits the righteous force of a mother protecting her children, recalling Joanne Braxton's characterization of Harriet Tubman and Sojourner Truth as "outraged mothers." Given her concern for her brother and for young black men generally (she formed the Negro Fellowship League, in part to deal with problems associated with the migration of southern black men to Chicago), I suggest that her style also exhibits the righteous force of a sister protecting her brothers (see Decosta-Willis 1995; Wells 1970).

Wells' autobiography is the testament of a feminist, an early civil-rights activist, and, most specifically, an anti-lynching crusader. Born a slave in Holly Springs, Mississippi, in 1862, Wells became first a schoolteacher in Memphis, then a journalist, always a woman of extraordinary courage. Imagine investigating incidents of lynching in the postwar South. Imagine yourself a black woman surrounded by, sometimes, thousands of white (mostly) men, asking direct questions about the black man who was being tortured. Wells' forthrightness is evident in the following passage:

> I found that white men who had created a race of mulattoes by raping and consorting with Negro women were still doing so whenever they could; these same white men lynched, burned, and tortured Negro men for doing the same thing with white women; even when the white women were willing victims. (1970, 71; quoted in Braxton 1989, 126)

The unifying symbol of Wells' autobiography and her life, Braxton (1989) suggests, is "crusade," and this motif reflects—as Butterfield also suggests—the outraged mother and sister defending the life of her people. "Crusade" provides the central metaphor for Wells' autobiographical experience, just as "education" functions for Henry Adams. "Carry on alone" is a central motif of the Wells autobiography (Braxton 1989). As powerful women still do, Ida B. Wells threatened her male contemporaries. For instance, Wells' assertive demands for justice were too much for Booker T. Washington, who disassociated himself from her "radical" views (Butterfield 1974, 114).

Taken together, the slave narratives, Henry Louis Gates (1992) has argued, represent courageous attempts to write African Americans into *being*. This *being*, as Ida B. Wells' autobiography underscores, is social *and* subjective. As Ralph Ellison defined the autobiographical project: "We tell ourselves our individual stories so as to become aware of our general story" (quoted in Gates 1992, 57). This idea has been described in musical terms as well. Braxton (1989) compares black autobiography to the blues. Like the blues singer, the autobiographer incorporates communal values into the autobiographical performance, sometimes rising to serve as the "point of consciousness" of her people (Braxton 1989, 5).

Nikki Giovanni has pointed out that black women's autobiographies have been inextricably linked to changing political conditions. Giovanni rejected the idea "that the self is not part of the body politic," insisting, "there's no separation" (quoted in Fox-Genovese 1988, 69). This point is made by Selwyn R. Cudjoe, who, writing about Maya Angelou, argued that African-American autobiography "as a form tends to be bereft of any excessive subjectivism and mindless egotism." Instead, African-American autobiographies tend to present the experience of the individual "as reflecting a much more im-personal condition, the autobiographical subject emerging as an almost random member of the group, selected to tell his/her tale." Consequently, African-American autobiography is "a public rather than a private gesture, me-ism gives way to our-ism and superficial concerns about the individual subject usually give way to the collective subjection of the group" (quoted passages in Fox-Genovese 1988, 70). Such characteristics distinguish black autobiography as collective and political, not narcissistic or socially withdrawn.

Especially European Americans must study African-American autobiography, for expressed in this genre are not only our sins and those of our "fathers," but spiritual and psychological powers of which we are ignorant, which we probably cannot readily (or, perhaps, ever) know in our cultural condition, but the personifications of which we can discern in many black students in public-school classrooms. Those our ancestors chained and later disdained continue to emerge from their time in Egypt. African Americans are not whom we European Americans have taken them to be. "They" are not the "other" (Morrison 1989, 9). We whites must reclaim our projections and fantasies, and in such reclamation reconfigure the subjective and social structures of whiteness, especially white men. Perhaps then we can begin to see ourselves, and then others, more clearly.

In African-American autobiography, we discern not mindless egoism or asocial subjectivism (characteristics sometimes associated with European and European-American autobiographical practices), but, rather, first-person accounts composed by remarkable individuals whose subjective struggles were simultaneously collective ones. In our time of trial and tribulation, teachers might respectfully mime these autobiographical practices, declining politicians' insistence on our "gracious submission," becoming, instead, "outraged mothers," "talking back" in protection of our children, their education, and everyone's future.

Especially during this time when the public sector does not invite our identification, indeed, when it seems to require our cynicism, even bitterness, what possibility there is of being influenced, of influencing—of doing pedagogical/political work—may reside in the subjective spaces of our lives. (In a different context, Dewey [1991 (1927), 50] observed: "In general, behavior in intellectual matters has moved from the public to the private realm.") Under such circumstances, autobiography represents an important strategy of cultural politics and the reconstruction of the public sphere. At this historical moment, autobiography may have more political potential, possibly more integrity, than running for state senate, signing a petition, even voting, although I am hardly opposed to conventional political action. We teachers must begin to "talk back," to ourselves, to colleagues, to politicians, and to parents.

It is we the people—the "multitude" as Hardt and Negri (2000, 47) have it—who make possible even authoritarian regimes; even dictatorships must fall eventually without public support, as the Soviet example reminds. It may take decades, but it seems to me inevitable that the *ancien régime* must collapse without our subjective support, without our identification with it. In this nightmarish historical moment, as education disappears into "business," one must not lose hope, one must remember, one must testify to the world not here, to the world that could be, the world to come. Is our situation worse than those faced by Frederick Douglass or Ida B. Wells (1970)?

Given the hegemonic position of European Americans, and, specifically, of "white men," I suggest that the educational and cultural task is, in part, one of (white male) self-shattering (Bersani 1995; Silverman 1992). The burden of history must be experienced psychologically and individualistically, as well as understood collectively and politically, if we are to move to horizontal planes of difference and dialogue. After the Holocaust, Marla Morris (2001a) counsels a dystopian curriculum, an abandonment of Christian culture's certainty that "the best is yet to come." In this time of political double-think or no-think, when the public sphere is so degraded that anything remotely resembling "authentic" speech would be dissonant to the ear, in this time, the space open to us is not social and public, but individual. The opening may not last long in the United States, as the private sphere continues to evaporate under the intensification of daily competition and sometimes desperate survival strategies (Lasch 1984).

The private sphere itself is occupied by the public, which is to say, it is no longer self-evidently authentic, or dependably trustworthy. Lasch (1978, 30) observes: "As social life becomes more and more warlike and barbaric, personal relations, which ostensibly provide relief from these conditions, take on the character of combat." Psychoanalysis suggests the private life never was safe, but today it is quite clear that the psychological has been fully invaded by the social. In Lasch's (1978, 1984) terms, in its self-protective social withdrawal, the private self withers (or, in his terms, is rendered "narcissistic" and "minimal").

So the historical task of self-shattering and transformation cannot proceed in a politically straightforward or authentically phenomenological fashion, at least not for those psychologically burdened in the present with the conquests of his imperial ancestors. This is no simple matter of guilt but of character structure, although these are not, if we again think of Lasch's (1984) analysis, unrelated. For those in states of marginalization and victimization, progressive possibilities remain, as African-American traditions of autobiography testify.

Too many whites (especially white men) are, in a psycho-cultural sense, their own slaves, trapped by our their internalized masters, bifurcated into sadist and masochist, one self, at once divided and united under God (Savran 1998). How can we escape our own "plantations," how can we find the "railroad" north to freedom when we have no Harriet Tubman to guide us? We cannot simply turn to the black man, as did Huck Finn, and expect to be healed (see Fiedler 1948, 1966). We cannot become black men; they are, as Ellison knew, invisible to us. What we can do is work to recover those split-off fragments of ourselves that white men—no monolithic category to be sure (Pfeil 1995)—have projected onto "others" (especially black men, black women, white women, children, and others) and reincorporate them (see Young-Bruehl 1996). From that re-experienced trauma of self-disintegration we might begin to decipher not "who am I" but "whose am I."

III
AN AUTOBIOGRAPHICS OF ALTERITY

[I]gnorance seems to be mostly a matter of self-ignorance.
—Norman O. Brown (1959, 322)

Liberation also comes from intimacy with the self.
—Victor Brombert (1978, 71)

The possibility of overcoming the subjugating self-reflexivity
emerges from the intensification of the divergence
within the subject.
—Ewa Plonowska Ziarek (2001, 30)

A classically European statement of autobiography was made by Georges Gusdorf. What is Gusdorf's view? He began by noting that autobiography has not always existed, nor does it exist everywhere. He believed autobiography expresses "a concern particular to Western Man" (Gusdorf 1980, 29; quoted in Graham 1989, 94). That concern is an appreciation for experience, for one's own experience, for oneself. In this sense, autobiography represents an economy of the self wherein the narration of one's story functions to preserve oneself. Additionally, autobiography proclaims the self as witness: "he calls himself as witness for himself; others he calls as witnesses for what is irreplaceable in his presence" (1980, 29; quoted in Graham 1989, 94). For Gusdorf, biography sketches the exterior of a person; autobiography provides the possibility of spiritual revolution: "The artist and model coincide, the historian tackles himself as object" (1980, 31; quoted in Graham 1989, 95). In like fashion, Karl J. Weintraub (1978, 822) asserts that autobiography is "concretely experienced reality and not the realm of brute external fact."

In contrast to a painting, Gusdorf continues, autobiography retraces experience over time and place. In contrast to the diarist who may record daily experience without concern for continuity, the autobiographer must distantiate her or himself from him or herself, "in order to reconstitute himself in the focus of his special unity and identity" (1980, 35; quoted in Graham 1989, 95). While he characterizes memoirs as a "revenge on history" (1980, 35; quoted in Graham 1989, 95), autobiographical remembrance is said to be performed for its own sake, to "recover and redeem lost time in fixing it forever" (1980, 37; quoted in Graham 1989, 95).

Gusdorf finds several problems inherent in autobiography. According to Gusdorf, the autobiographer takes the unity and identity of the self for granted, imagining that he can "merge what he has with what he has become" (1980, 39; quoted in Graham 1989, 96). Gusdorf notes that the individual person exhibits latent as well as manifest intention: "Thus the original sin of autobiography is first one of logical coherence and rationalization" (1980, 41; quoted in Graham 1989, 96). Consequently, the significance of autobiography lies "beyond truth and falsity" (1980, 43; quoted in Graham 1989, 96). Gusdorf concludes that the object of autobiography is not to report the events of an individual's life—that project belongs to the historian or biographer. For Gusdorf, the point of autobiography is to reveal the autobiographer's effort "to give the meaning of his own mythic tale" (1980, 48; quoted in Graham 1989, 97).

Robert Graham (1991) notes that Gusdorf's basic point regarding the significance of autobiography seems largely ignored by many literary theorists. Gusdorf is partly to blame, Graham suggests, choosing Narcissus as the metaphoric myth for autobiographical activity. As James Olney (1980) observed: "This shift of attention from bios to autos—from the life to the self—was, I believe, largely responsible for opening things up and turning them in a philosophical, psychological, and literary direction" (1980, 19; quoted in Graham, 97). Rather than Narcissus, Graham offers, Antaeus might prove a more appropriate image for autobiography, as suggested by Gunn (1982). In this image, Graham (1989, 97) writes, "the self that comes to life is not that of Narcissus who drowned reaching for his mirror-image in the pool, but rather the example of Antaeus, who, so long as he remained in touch with the earth, could not be killed." It was Hercules who, after learning Antaeus' secret, suspended him in the air; there, he overcame him. As Gunn (1982) points out: "Understood as the story of Antaeus, the real question of the autobiographical self then becomes where do I belong? not, who am I? The question of the self's identity becomes the question of the self's location in a world" (23; quoted in Graham 1989, 97), a question of "place" (see chapter 4).

The trouble is, as Shari Benstock (1988, 11) observes, that "autobiography reveals the impossibility of its own dream: what begins on the presumption of self-knowledge ends in the creation of a fiction that covers over the premises of its construction." It is exactly these covered-over "premises" that "indirect autobiography" or, after Leigh Gilmore (1994), the "autobiographics of alterity," is conceived to reveal.

For Lacan, the "mirror stage" of psychic development is that time— Nancy Lesko terms it "panoptical time"—the child is initiated into the social community and brought under the law of the Symbolic (which is to say, the law of language as constituted through society). This stage results in a compelling if false image of the child's unified "self." The apparent cohesion of the self is impressed upon the child from the outside (in the mirror reflection). This seemingly unified self is, in Ellie Ragland-Sullivan's words, "asymmetrical, fictional, artificial." Ragland-Sullivan argued that the "mirror stage must, therefore, be understood as a metaphor for the vision of harmony of a subject essentially in discord" (quoted in Benstock 1988, 12).

The "discord" that is transfigured into a unified, identifiable, continuous "self" has been constructed from those images, sounds, and sensory responses available to the infant during the first 6 months or so of his or her life. This sedimented memory of the symbiotic identification with the mother and, for many men, the violence of one's repudiation of that identification— is called the unconscious, from which heteronormative men flee. In one sense, it is the "wake" which follows in the flight of the self from itself, itself as fragmented, partial, segmented, and different or "other." In this view, the unconscious is not the lower depths of the conscious but rather an inner seam, a space between "inside" and "outside." The unconscious is the "space of difference," a "gap" that the drive toward a unified self can never cover over. The unconscious, then, is what Benstock (1988, 12) terms "the space of writing," a space marked by the effects of the false symmetry of the mirror stage.

In a definition of autobiographical process that provides evidence for Lacan's mirror stage, Georges Gusdorf declared: "Autobiography . . . requires a man [sic] to take a distance with regard to himself in order to reconstitute himself in the focus of his special unity and identity across time" (quoted in Benstock 1988, 14–15). The interest in such a distancing and reconstitution is, Bentock (1988) tells us, exactly a consequence of the mirror stage. In the Gusdorf sentence there is a recognition of the space of estrangement within the specular (*le regard* in Lacan's terminology) that leads to the compensatory unification of the reflected self to suture disintegration and self-division (Benstock 1988). The self-dissociated elements become split-off social fragments, projected onto and, in other ways, associated with those who come to stand for what is missing, and must be kept missing, as in the European-American men's certainty of what "blacks" or "women" are "like."

When autobiography is understood phenomenologically, "distancing" and "reconstituting" need not be, strictly speaking, compensatory. These gerunds can also refer to the process of excavation, and to the architectural rebuilding of a self, with materials previously excluded (now excavated), a self more spacious, more inviting, especially to "others," like women, children, African Americans, who become, now, no longer "others" and no longer invisible. Too often the black male body is, for the European-American male, what he, in his self-dissociated imaginary, is "not," that is, "dangerous, athletic, and virile" (Murtadha-Watts 2000, 52).

For Georges Gusdorf, autobiography "is the mirror in which the individual reflects his own image" (quoted in Benstock 1988, 15). In such a mirror the "self" and the "reflection" coincide. This definition of autobiography overlooks the educational potential of autobiography. This potential has to do with the ways in which "self" and "self-image" fail to coincide. Perhaps, as Benstock (1988) suggests, they can never coincide in language. This "failure" is not because certain forms of autobiography are not sufficiently self-conscious. Rather, it is because certain forms of self-writing have no interest in creating a cohesive self, continuous over time. Certain forms of autobiographical writing acknowledge difference and discontinuity over sameness and identity. Such writing occupies the "seam" of the conscious/unconscious where boundaries between internal and external intersect (Benstock 1988).

Benstock's point seems right to me, but there are racial and gender differences that can be usefully acknowledged. For heterosexually identified white men, finding the seams, discovering the traces of rejected fragments, and creating interior spaces may well prove pedagogically useful, potentially self-shattering. As Ewa Plonowska Ziarek (2001, 39) points out:

> Yet, it is the tear, or the separation of the self from its sedimented identity, that enables a redefinition of becoming and freedom from its sedimented identity, that enables a redefinition of becoming and freedom from the liberation of identity to the continuous "surpassing" of oneself.

The task for African-American and women's autobiography may be different. When already on the margins, when testifying to subjective experience the dominant regime fails to recognize, self-writing—think of Ida B. Wells (1970)—may help form a mobilized, coherent self in solidarity with (subjugated) others. For those whose mobilization is taken-for-granted, even overdetermined, whose integration is the consequence of cultural hegemony, then autobiographical writing must indeed seek the seams.

Language itself may function as a defense against unconscious knowledge, Benstock notes. There is no clearly discernible border between conscious and unconscious modes of experience. Lacerated by language, the speaking subject is, in Lacan's view, primordially divided (Benstock 1988). Does this self-division have to be played out imperialistically, as in hegemonic white masculinity? Or is this self-division itself historical and political and gendered and racialized?

I argue that self-division is gendered; it is male, it is, especially, "straight." "The straight mind valorizes difference," Bersani (1995, 39) asserts. He is not conflating sexual preference with cognitive practice, as he adds "[o]bviously don't have to be straight to think straight." The association of compulsory heterosexuality with a hierarchical view of difference can be understood psychoanalytically. Bersani (1995) reminds us that Kenneth Lewes (1988) theorized male heterosexual desire as the complicated consequence of flight to the father following a horrified retreat from the mother. So conceptualized, male heterosexuality is constructed upon and actively requires a traumatic privileging of difference. "The cultural consolidation of heterosexuality," Bersani (1995, 40) writes, "is grounded in its more fundamental, non-reflective construction as the compulsive repetition of a traumatic response to difference." In this regard, "the straight mind might be thought of as a sublimation of this privileging of difference" (Bersani 1995, 40).

Nor is it "playing in the dark" (to recall Morrison's fine phrase [1992]) to see that self-division may be racialized, as European Americans—especially straight white men—tend not to experience a divided self, but, rather, a splitting off of disavowed interior fragments, projecting them onto the social field, creating "others." This self-structure differs from the "dual consciousness" Du Bois (1903) described, as dual consciousness, fashioned in response to racism and white supremacy, does not involve self-dissociation but stereoscopic vision.

On April 20, 1919, Virginia Woolf wrote: "The main requisite, I think on re-reading my old volumes, is not to play the part of censor, but to write as the mood comes or of anything whatever; since I was curious to find how I went for things put in haphazard, and found the significance to lie where I never saw it at the time" (quoted in Benstock 1988, 18). Is this the Lacanian idea that one's objects of desire are often relocated to fool oneself, to hide the "crime," rearranging the clues at the scene? "Haphazard" is smart because it invites the "truth" to inadvertently find its way through the censor. Later, when one's eyes are looking the other way, perhaps one understands the meaning of a misplaced clue. It is an indirect investigation.

Almost 6 years later (March 20, 1926) Woolf comments, "as far as I know, as a writer I am only now writing out my mind," a turn of phrase that suggests multiple relations between "mind" and "writing." On October 29, 1933, she notes "how tremendously important unconsciousness is when one writes" (both passages quoted in Benstock 1988, 19). Benstock (1988) suggests that the relation of the conscious to the unconscious, of the mind to writing, of the interior to the exterior of political systems, imply a problematization of (I would add, especially male) narrative conventions. There is, perhaps, a questioning of the Symbolic law, which might take the form of reconceptualizing narrative form itself. One such reconceptualization might well, it seems to me, be an "autobiographics of alterity," or "indirect autobiography" (after Pier Paulo Pasolini) or "autobiographicality" (Cavell 1994, 10), in which one's views of "others" are taken to be just that. Such notions invite us to understand curriculum as a verb, as *currere*.

Virginia Woolf believed that the "strong emotion must leave its trace." Finding ways to discover and decode these traces becomes both the impetus for her memoir writing and, Benstock (1988) adds, the guarantee of its failure. Woolf must discount memories: "As an account of my life they are misleading, because the things one does not remember are as important; perhaps they are more important" (quoted passages in Benstock 1988, 27–28). She's right, of course. The first things that come to mind are merely that, the first things. One must wait for the second, third, and fourth, until one has found clues pointing to what the first things hide. Virginia Woolf understands: Strong emotion leaves traces, which is to say clues. What one does not remember, or, at least, remember immediately (and that "immediately" can last for decades), is probably more important. That is why the periphery—of one's everyday ego, of the body politic—is so important.

Shari Benstock (1988) contrasts Virginia Woolf's notion of reality with T. S. Eliot's. Woolf does not experience a shock of recognition in the mirror. Rather, reality reveals itself as a linguistic space (a "scene") that conceals and simultaneously seals the gap (the "crack") of the unconscious. Language operates via distinctions and differences, and thereby becomes a medium by which and through the "self" is constructed. "Writing the self" is, Benstock (1988, 29) continues: "a process of simultaneous sealing and splitting that can only trace fissures of discontinuity."

The autobiographical process occurs—here Benstock quotes James Olney—via "the individual's special, peculiar psychic configuration," but it is not an act of "consciousness, pure and simple," as it must refer to "objects outside itself to . . . events, and to . . . other lives"; it must participate in the "shifting, changing unrealities of mundane life"; it is never "atemporal" (quoted in Benstock 1988, 29).

The cultural precondition for autobiography, Georges Gusdorf had argued, is a pervasive concept of individualism, a "conscious awareness of the singularity of each individual life," a self-consciousness that is "the late product of a specific civilization," by which he meant the post-Renaissance western societies (quoted in Friedman 1988, 34). Gusdorf's contributions are undeniable, Susan Stanford Friedman (1988) reminds, especially his appreciation for the fact that autobiographical selves are constructed through the process of writing and therefore cannot replicate exactly the selves who lived.

But there is a fundamental inappropriateness, Friedman (1988) insists, of individualistic models of the self-formation for women and for other "others." It is twofold. First, individualism does not take into account the problems of a culturally imposed group identity for women and racialized minorities. That is to say, the individualism model tends to ignore the social and political configurations of oppression and colonization, the ways that collective suffering can make for solidarity. Second, Friedman continues, the emphasis on separateness ignores important developmental differences in the socialization of male and female gender identity. From both ideological and psychological perspectives, then, individualistic models of the self ignore the roles of collective and relational identities in the individuation process of women and minorities (Friedman 1988), and, I would add, of men as well, however denied these may be for many men. In the United States, the "possessive individual" is a cultural myth, a psychological compensation, a political convenience, an economic rationale, but not a cultural reality.

Psychoanalytic theories of autobiography, Friedman (1988) continues, focus on the development of the self as it forms through intense interaction with others, particularly with the mother, father, and/or caretakers. Such a relational focus differs sharply, she notes, from the theories of Olney and Gusdorf. Freidman is, of course, right that the self is undeniably plural. While it is so that the self is an interactional self, the self is also capable of singularity and solitariness, a "room of one's own." Being in relation to others does not deny singularity. Besides being in profoundly formative relationships with others, one is oneself a shifting configuration of introjected as well as self-dissociated fragments of (past) others, in kaleidoscopic reconfigurations located in place and across time, structured in gendered, racialized ways. I think of William Earle (1972), who argued convincingly that we cannot get ourselves "right" unless we get ourselves exactly, precisely, uniquely "right" as individuals. If individuality were not a developmental possibility, psychoanalysis would be a subfield of sociology.

Also influenced by psychoanalysis, Jeffrey Mehlman (1971/1974) discerns narcissistic and Oedipal phases inscribed in autobiographical narratives. The failures of Narcissus and Oedipus prefigure the impossible task of the autobiographer to find and report a definitively authentic self. Autobiography is, thereby, "necessarily fictive," as it fashions a self whose very coherence disguises its falseness and alienation (quoted in Friedman 1988, 37). To find a "real" self, a definitive or final self, is the autobiographical version of "positivism."

There are moments in autobiographical work, in the regressive phase, when the movement is back from the present, toward the sources, the antecedents, of one's present situation. The regressive moment or step is an effort to get "underneath" the layers where one lives, to earlier layers where one can re-experience what is excluded in the presently constituted ego. Often this process "feels" like reaching more truthful versions: As in geological formations, there is the experience of "discovery," of learning how the particular knot of feeling/thought/action followed in some very specific way from earlier "knots," earlier events (Laing 1970).

There is, I think we can say, a relatively "authentic" self, or selves, or elements of self. This is the person I was conditioned and brought up to be. When I am in touch with that "self," and act in accordance with him or her, I feel congruent, integrated, "right." The regressive phase of *currere* is about uncovering this self, and in psychoanalytic fashion, experiencing the relief of understanding how one came to be psychically, which is to say, socially. For, as in psychoanalysis, bringing to light what was held in obscurity represents, in part, the therapeutic potential and consequence of self-reflective study. It is also the political potential, as one may choose not to coincide with the racialized and gendered creature one's family required one to be.

Of course, transference relationships can function therapeutically, although this transference can be not only with another individual, for instance, one's teacher. Transference can be with/among various fragments of self, excluded from membership in the present ego assemblage, perhaps repudiated by projecting them onto "others." The regressive phase of *currere* is a discursive (hence specifically fictional in Mehlman's sense) practice of truth-telling, of confession, but not to the priest (as in regulative practices of the Catholic Church) or to one's fellow-travelers (as in the solidarity of Alcoholics Anonymous). It is to oneself one comes to practice the autobiographics of self-shattering, revelation, confession, and reconfiguration. Self-excavation precedes the self-understanding, which precedes self-mobilization, although any rigidly linear conceptions of self-reflexivity necessarily reify subjectivity.

The progressive phrase of *currere* may be understood as a kind of free-associative "futuring" during which one seeks the revelation of one's fantasies of what one might be. These imaginings are expressions of who one is not now, of material felt to be missing, sought after, aspired to. The possibility in this phase, at which Mehlman hints, is to discern how who one is hides what one might become. These fictive representations of who I might be, what world I might inhabit in the future, these fictional versions of who I might be someday but am not now allow us to feel our way through the obscurity of the present. They are the means by which we midwife what is not yet born, in ourselves, generated by others. They change where we are, how we feel, what we think; they become, in another sense, discursive passages, what Rorty calls a "vocabulary" by means of which we move into new lived space. We become different selves, and in so doing, we become different in the world that itself becomes transformed by our presence there.

Both one's past and one's fantasies of the future are simultaneously in "the" past and "the" future. The self is profoundly historical, even if this temporal constitution is obscured in the commodification of social relations capitalism compels. The self is gendered and racialized as well, yet these "aspects" do not "add up" to one, total, complete self. There is a subjective, "felt" singularity that comprises, finally, our individuality, that incorporates these social dimensions, renders them a matter of feeling (Boler 1999; see also Jackson 1999).

Now this individuality may be illusory; it may because we are embodied, that we have separate bodies that we also experience the illusion of being singular selves. Is the body "the locus of learning" (Stoller 1997, 13)? For now, let us acknowledge, with Susan Friedman (1988, 38), that serious autobiography is possible only when:

> [t]he individual does not feel herself to exist outside of others, and still less against others, but very much with others in an interdependent existence that asserts its rhythms everywhere in the community . . . [where] lives are so thoroughly entangled that each of them has its center everywhere and its circumference nowhere. The important unit is thus never the isolated being.

Not only are we never isolated, we are not unitary or self-identical. Formed by sociality, in historical time, we are informed by the past that haunts us through dreams and nightmares.

IV
DEFERRED AND DISPLACED ACTION

*The primal scene is always a scene that is
"unknown" and "forgotten."*
—Ned Lukacher (1986, 27)

*Although representing what is most emphatically our own,
the language of our desire consequently remains for most
of us irreducibly Other. In a certain sense, we do not
even speak it; rather, it speaks us.*
—Kaja Silverman (2000, 51)

*If the affect is a wound to thought, how then
is it possible to think the affect?*
—Deborah Britzman (2000, 43)

Curriculum conceived as *currere* requires not only the study of autobiography, history, and social theory, it requires as well the serious study of psychoanalytic theory. There is, perhaps, no tradition of systematic inquiry into the sphere of the subjective, into the processes of self-formation—and their complex and ever-changing relations to the social and historical—that offers us as many provocative conceptual tools as do the various strands of psychoanalytic theory. As Robert Graham (1989, 101) observed: "Autobiography has everything to learn from psychoanalysis." Psychoanalytic theory offers a model of translating private language into the public language and, thereby, enabling the re-symbolization of private and public meaning (Warnke 1993).

Psychoanalysis shares with modern philosophy, literary theory, and criticism, Ned Lukacher (1986) points out, a refusal to forget the question of origin. Psychoanalysis in particular is dedicated to the labor of remembering "the primordial forgetfulness that conceals the origin" (Lukacher 1986, 26). The notion of the primal scene is key to this labor (see also Edelman 1994). Freud formulated the idea while working with his most famous patient, a Russian man named Sergei Pankejev. On the eve of his fourth birthday, Pankejev had dreamed that through an opened window he saw a barren tree in winter in which six or seven white wolves were sitting and staring at him, obviously about to leap in upon him and consume him. He awoke screaming. For the remainder of his long life, Pankejev—named by Freud the "Wolf-Man"—never forgot the terror and the profound impression of reality that the dream created (Lukacher 1986).

In his study of the Wolf-Man's case—*From The History of an Infantile Neurosis*, published in 1918, wherein for the first time appears the concept of "primal scene"—Freud theorizes the relation of the dream to reality. The patient had presented Freud with both a verbal text and a line drawing of wolves sitting in a tree after remembering the dream early in the course of a 4-year analysis. Much of the remaining analysis was devoted to determining the relation of the dream to reality. For nearly 40 years Freud pondered the relation of dreams to reality, without ever reaching a definitive theorization. Does the dream point to the empirical fact of the primal scene, or is it the consequence of a "primal phantasy"? (Recall the controversy surrounding Freud's famous inversion of his theory that many children had been sexually molested by their parents to the theory of infantile sexuality, in which infants are themselves sexual and desire their parents.) The dream suggests something anterior, perhaps something we might characterize as "the origin," but its interpretation does not necessarily bring this actual primal scene into memory (Lukacher 1986).

In the broad field of education—in which curriculum theory is situated—there is a tradition of interest in psychoanalysis. During the Progressive Era there were efforts to theorize a psychoanalysis of education (see Cremin 1961, 209ff.), but those efforts disappeared as business thinking and the political interests dominated school curriculum.

Psychoanalytically, *currere* invites the interpretation of educational experience, scrutinizing manifest and latent meanings, conscious and unconscious content of language, as well as the political subtext of such reflection and interpretation. Madeleine Grumet (1976, 111) explained that *currere* "is what the individual does with the curriculum, his active reconstruction of his passage through its social, intellectual, physical structures." In so doing, the study of *currere* discloses new structures in the process of naming old ones. However, *currere* is not psychotherapy, as Grumet (1976, 115) made clear.

> *Currere* is not a form of therapy designed to treat symptoms. It cannot employ self-reflection to the degree that psychoanalysis does to free the subject from the chains that objectivize him by liberating him from behaviors over-determined by unconscious impulses, defenses or repetition compulsions. Habermas maintains that in the analytic situation the very understanding of the causal connections in one's own life history dissolves them. The self that was the object of its history regains subject status in self-formative process. While *currere* cannot share the magnitude of this claim, it can adopt both its developmental goal and methodological assumptions that by bringing the structures of experience to awareness, one enhances the ability to direct the process of one's own development.

To readers saturated with poststructuralist critiques of the "self" and skeptical of its capacities for self-direction, the work of the important post-structuralist feminist Bronwyn Davies is instructive. Davies (2000, 67) points out that "agency is never freedom from discursive constitution of self, but the capacity to recognize that constitution and to resist, subvert, and change the discourses themselves through one is being constituted." She notes that it is through the intellectual freedom to recognize and critique multiple readings that one can resist being positioned by (more powerful) others. Of course, "agency is never autonomy in the sense of being an individual standing outside social structure and process" (Davies 2000, 67).

At present there is a renaissance of scholarly interest in psychoanalysis in education, led by Deborah Britzman (1998), Stephen Appel (1999), Doug Aoki (2002), Wendy Atwell-Vasey (1998a; 1999b), jan jagodzinski (2002), Peter Taubman (1990 [1992]), and Alice Pitt (2003). It is also evident in a number of important studies not primarily psychoanalytic in orientation, among them Madeleine Grumet's (1988) *Bitter Milk: Women and Teaching*, Alan Block's (1997) study of the school's psychological violence against the child, Elizabeth Ellsworth's (1997) study of teaching as a mode of address, in Marla Morris' (2001a) study of curriculum and the Holocaust, and in Julie Webber's (in press) study of school violence.

We cannot understand the complex relations among subjectivity and learning, teaching, and the curriculum, without serious and sustained attention to psychoanalytic theory. Moreover, psychoanalytic theory can help us theorize the relations between the subjectivity and sociality, between our inner politics and the social structures of the public sphere. Kobena Mercer (1994, 122) noted that "psychoanalytic concepts now float freely in debates on cultural politics, but there is still a stubborn resistance to the recognition of unconscious fantasy as a structuring principle of our social, emotional, and political life."

I employed psychoanalytic theory—a version of object relations theory (see Chodorow 1978)—in my effort to understand the gender of U.S. racial politics and violence and, especially, what I took to be the "queer" dimensions of racial subjugation. I focused on the "white man," no monolithic category to be sure, but a related series of historically situated, classed and gendered "subject positions" from which unspeakable acts of violence were—are still—performed. Psychoanalytically considered, what the white male subject takes himself to be as his "self" has tended to be "other" and fictive, deriving from unconscious, historical, and social sources (Pinar 2001).

One psychoanalytic conceptual tool that was helpful to me in thinking about the problem of racial subjugation is the concept of "fantasmatic," a notion that has been theorized, among others, by Laplanche and Pontalis (1973). They define *fantasmatic* as the unconscious source of dreams and fantasies, the structuring scenario behind social action, especially "overdetermined" (often ritualistic) actions (such as lynching) structured by transferences and other forms of repetitive behavior. For Laplanche and Pontalis (1973, 317), the fantasmatic "shape[s] and order[s]" the subject life "as a whole." In so doing it becomes "public," as Trevor Hope (1994, 215) points out: "[f]antasy is necessarily public, and the public, therefore, has a fantasmatic dimension." In American racial politics particularly, the public sphere has seemed a nightmare of fantasy, desire, and violence.

While psychoanalytic theory laces this introduction to curriculum theory, it is made explicit only briefly in an invocation of Freud's notion of the "deferred action" (*Nachtraglichkeit*), a concept dating from his *From the History of an Infantile Neurosis* (1918). In simple terms, Ned Lukacher (1986, 35) explains, "deferred action is a mode of temporal spacing through which the randomness of a later event triggers the memory of an earlier event or image, which might never have come to consciousness had the later event never occurred." For us, this "later event" we suffer in the present is our political subjugation by politicians. Our "symptom" is anti-intellectualism. While the public school has always been subject to political controversy and influence, such "influence" is, at present, overdetermined. The rhetoric of "accountability" is the politics of subjugation. As Linda McNeil (2000, 10) understands: "Accountability . . . reifies both a resource dependency and hierarchical power structures which maintains that dependency."

Despite the apparently straightforward and commonsensical character of school reform rhetoric (who dares oppose "accountability"), there is something (in psychoanalytic terms) "overdetermined" in politicians' (and more than a few parents') insistence that teachers are responsible for students' test scores. "Overdetermined" suggests that such rhetoric carries more "freight"—has embedded within it a concealed agenda—than it claims to carry. In part, this concealed agenda is simple scapegoating, politicians taking advantage of a relatively powerless, political vulnerable, minority—public school teachers—for their own political advantage. I tell that story in chapter 3—how 1950s Cold War anxieties, intensified by a specific event, crystallized into 1960s national curriculum reform—but there are related concealed stories, gendered and racialized stories that also must be remembered, if we are to understand the plight of the present.

I am not seeking to reduce these interwoven and, even, conflated anxieties (simultaneously military, gendered, and racialized) to their meaning for us educators. In part, I am using the suggestion of their meaning to provide readers who are probably primarily white and disadvantaged by a Eurocentric education with fragments of a "general education" (Penn State 2002). Structured by curriculum theory, teacher education is a version of general education (Penn State 2002).

"The most obvious and immediate effect of deferred action," Lukacher (1986, 35) notes, "is to undermine and divide the notion of linear causality that works in one temporal direction." While earlier events did in fact "cause" later events, these earlier events become also the effects of the later interpretative events. At work, then, is "a double or 'metaleptic' logic in which causes are both the cases of effects and the effects of effects" (Lukacher 1986, 35). In such logic, there is not only *deferral*; there is *displacement* as well. Events in one, say, military sphere—the 1957 Soviet satellite launching, for instance—reverberate in other spheres, in this instance, the Cold War politics of curriculum reform. Action—in this case reaction—was both deferred *and* displaced.

In the 1950s, Cold War military anxieties mixed with gendered and racialized fears, overloading the nation's capacities to assimilate events. While, of course, the civil rights and feminist movements of the 1960s and 1970s must be located within their own histories, their eruption in the 1960s was not unrelated to the (Cold) war of nerves that overheated dangerously during the Cuban Missile crisis of October 1962. The civil rights movement was well underway by 1962, and its example would inspire the future waves of feminist struggle, waves that would inspire present struggles for the civil rights for lesbians and gay men. "The principal target of the religious right has been displaced from abortion to homosexuality," Bersani (1995, 15). Before abortion was race.

While studying each wave separately is required to begin to understand these important movements in American history, studying them as interwoven, even conflated, events enables us to appreciate how military, gendered, and racialized anxieties became *deferred* and *displaced* as anxieties over public education. Those anxieties cannot be understood *only* as displaced and deferred racial and gendered anxieties associated with the Cold War period. By reconstructing the convoluted genesis of our present plight, I labor to understand not only the present but the past as well, and in ways, I hope, that contribute to reparation for us. As becomes clear in chapter 10, this is a call for self-understanding, self-mobilization, and social reconstruction through the education of the public.

Toward that end I will disrobe bodies of knowledge that might function, like a psychoanalytic remembrance, to reconfigure the pattern of the present in which we teachers find ourselves. By reviewing certain African-American autobiographical practices (see section II of this chapter), I hope not only to participate in a pedagogy of witness and testimony (see Eppert 2000; also Simon, Rosenberg, and Eppert 2000). I do so as well to inspire us to continue to think and converse as colleagues connecting curriculum to society and history and, in so doing, enabling the younger generations to reclaim and enact the dream of an American democracy. Despite our professional subjugation by politicians seduced by "business" thinking, with its obsession over the "bottom line" (test scores), we must not succumb in spirit. We must remember that education is not a business, that it cannot be measured by test scores, that it is too important to be left to either politicians or parents.

I focus on the origin of the present by emphasizing curriculum politics in the late 1950s and early 1960s, a period in which contemporary patterns of gendered and racialized demands upon teachers and students become imprinted (chapter 3). Their imprinting influence upon the present would not have occurred apart from the ascendancy of the political Right in the United States after the Left's defeat in the late 1960s, and that ascendancy cannot be understood apart from the political and cultural role of the American South in that triumph (chapters 4 and 10). By deferring and displacing racism into "conservative" causes, white southerners—in alliance with reactionary Republicans nationwide—have ensured the election of "conservative" Presidents who have allowed or led the continuing and intensifying assault on public education.

Why? Because public education was the site on which racial struggle often occurred (especially in the South), because the public school curriculum also became the site where the gendered Cold War anxieties were focused, can we be surprised that "conservatives" have focused their effort to control the public sphere in America on the school and, in particular, the curriculum? Frustrated by those they deride as "tenured radicals" (Kimball 1990) from winning the "culture wars" in the university curriculum, conservatives have refocused their efforts, concentrating now on the curriculum of the public schools. By linking curriculum with "outcomes" (scores on standardized examinations), conservatives disguise their political agenda with commonsense business rhetoric.

The university-based, academic, field of curriculum studies has responded to this conservative assault on academic—intellectual—freedom in the public schools by reconceptualizing the very concept of curriculum, postulating it as a "complicated conversation," a conception that insists that school texts are also pretexts to conversations whose character and destination cannot be known in advance, whose value cannot be reduced to student performance on standardized examinations, self-reflexive conversations that engage erudition, animate creativity, and cultivate independence of mind. But we university professors have no jurisdiction—and little influence—over the schools, now gripped in a vise of right-wing business-minded ideologues. Such is the nightmare that is the present.

II

THE REGRESSIVE MOMENT:
THE PAST IN THE PRESENT

3

The Primal Scene:
"Mortal Educational Combat"

I
GRACIOUS SUBMISSION

*Today, many Americans have become conscious, not just of the
practical virtues of education, but of its content and quality. . . .
Unquestionably, there has also been a surge of awareness born
of ours sense of imperiled national security. The Soviet Union's
conquests in space, its capability of producing not only
powerful weapons but also an effective industrial society,
have shaken American complacency.*
—Jerome Bruner (1977 [1960], 74–75)

*[T]he post-Sputnik educational atmosphere has quickened the
activities of those who demand more educational rigor,
who can now argue that we are engaged in mortal
educational combat with the Soviet Union.*
—Richard Hofstadter (1962, 358)

*[T]he Cold War would spark the most furious textbook
controversies that America had ever seen.*
—Jonathan Zimmerman (2002, 80)

The "combat" to which Hofstadter refers (above), turned out to be a civil,
rather than foreign, war, one in which public-school teachers and professors
of education were soundly defeated. In less militaristic prose, Richard Elmore (1993, 39) has pointed out: "[S]ince the 1960s, reformers usually agree
that educators are not to be trusted, any more than another parochial special-

interest group, with major decisions about the direction or content of public education." Today, multiple "stakeholders" (not the least among them politicians and textbook publishers) have created something that may look like curriculum consensus but is more like curriculum "gridlock," in which the process of education is grinding to a halt.

Genuine (not just rhetorical) reforms—let alone revolutions, such as suggested by the Progressive Education Association's Eight-Year Study (see Pinar et al. 1995, 133–139)—are unlikely. Certainly they are unlikely to be led by university-based curriculum scholars and researchers. This is not to say that we in the university have lost interest in teachers or in schooling, or that we had been seduced by subjects more interesting and exciting (although some students of popular culture might seem to be saying so).

The simple, if for some, unassimilable truth is that education professors' influence has diminished during the past 30 years, not only due to a more complicated and contentious political and cultural terrain in which curricular issues are now situated, but, as well, due to a devaluation of education professors generally, following, in part, from those attacks by arts and sciences professors in the 1950s and the 1960s, among them Richard Hofstadter. Suddenly finding their classrooms flooded with World War II veterans who before the war might never have attended university but who were now financially enabled to do so due to benefits associated with the so-called G.I. Bill, some number of arts and sciences faculty became indignant over their new students' inadequate academic preparation.

One of the early and most vocal academic critics of public school education was Arthur Bestor, a graduate of Teachers College's experimental Lincoln School at Columbia University, a historian at Teachers College and the University of Illinois, and leader of the Council for Basic Education (Clifford and Guthrie 1988; see Hofstadter 1962, 358). Anticipating Richard Hofstadter's even more influential attack a decade later, Bestor (1953, 14) charged that public education suffered from anti-intellectualism:

> The nation depends on its schools and colleges to furnish this intellectual training to its citizenry as a whole. Society has no other institutions upon which it can rely in this matter. If schools and colleges do not emphasize rigorous intellectual training, there will be none.

After the Kennedy Administration mobilized to make public education more "rigorous," Bestor would be joined by Harvard's former president, James B. Conant, who published *The Education of American Teachers* in 1963 and James D. Koerner, who published *The Miseducation of American Teachers* the same year (Clifford and Guthrie 1988).

Bestor had also been critical of schools of education, complaining about what today critics call "the ed. school monopoly." Bestor complained about the "interlocking directorate" of influential figures in schools of education, state departments of education, public school administration, and the United States Office of Education, who together (presumably) decided the quality and character of schooling. To break the stranglehold of "educationists" on schooling meant to intervene in the training, licensing, and employment of teachers (Clifford and Guthrie 1988). Soon after the 1957 Sputnik satellite launching, Bestor would be joined by military critics, among them Vice-Admiral Hyman Rickover (1959; 1963).

In *Education and Freedom*, Rickover (1959) accused the American public of indifference to intellectual achievement and excellence. He insisted that Americans valued athletic over academic accomplishment, a point with which few curriculum scholars would take issue, but which would be roundly ignored by the soon-to-be-elected Kennedy administration, as we see later in this chapter. Like Bestor, Rickover was sure that a curricular reconfiguration was the answer to the military crisis: "Our schools must return to the traditional task of formal education in Western civilization—transmission of cultural heritage, and preparation for life through rigorous intellectual training of young minds to think clearly, logically, and independently" (Rickover 1959, 18). While complaining about the American preference for muscles over mind, Rickover's call conflates the two, echoing those 19th-century classicists who believed that the mind was a muscle (see Pinar et al. 1995, chapter 2).

Christopher Lasch divides these critics of public education into two groups. Bestor, he suggests, belongs to those who attacked public education as "anti-intellectual and undemocratic" (1978, 139). Rickover, James B. Conant, and Vannevar Bush were critical because schools failed to produce enough scientists and high-level technicians, the reason, they insisted, why the United States lagged behind the Soviet Union in the arms race. These critics, Lasch (1978, 139) tells us, "did not question the school's function as an instrument of military and industrial recruitment, they merely sought to make the selection process more efficient."

Lasch (1995, 76) singles out Conant for redefining the Jeffersonian notion of democracy. From a notion (which, Lasch suggests, Abraham Lincoln shared [see 1995, 69]) in which education was to be encouraged among all citizens for the sake of intelligent and engaged civic life, education merely replacing European aristocracies of wealth with an American aristocracy of talent, not to weaken the principle of aristocracy itself. Lasch (1995, 76) comments: "In the name of the 'Jeffersonian tradition,' which envisioned a community of intelligent, resourceful, responsible, and self-governing citizens, Conant proposed merely to ensure the circulation of elites."

The specific event that led to the intensification of criticism of public education—and its conflation with upward mobility—was the launching of the Soviet satellite Sputnik in 1957, a traumatizing event which suggested to many that the United States no longer enjoyed military superiority over the

Soviet Union. Given the terrible tensions of the Cold War—millions of public school students practiced air raid drills weekly—the Sputnik satellite launching set off a national reaction that 1960 presidential candidate John F. Kennedy exploited in his campaign promise to "Get America Moving" again. Significantly, the Kennedy campaign exploited American anxieties not only over military competition and space exploration, but its tacticians sensed that education—hitherto a local matter—could be exploited as a national campaign issue.

Contra common sense, then, politicians, academicians, and military men argued that the Soviets' satellite success cast doubt on the quality of the American *educational* system. Had American schools been strong, they demanded to know, would the Soviets have defeated us in the space race, jeopardizing America's military superiority? Historian Richard Hofstadter (1962, 5–6) observed:

> The Sputnik was more than a shock to American national vanity: it brought an immense amount of attention to bear on the consequences of anti-intellectualism in the school system. . . . Cries of protest against the slackness of American education, hitherto raised only by a small number of educational critics, were now taken up by television, mass magazines, businessmen, scientists, politicians, admirals, and university presidents, and soon swelled into a national chorus of self-reproach.

The alleged consequences of "slackness in the school system" would change from military to economic concerns over the next 40 years, but the political exploitation of public education would continue and intensify.

In the preface to the re-issued *The Process of Education* (summarizing the proceedings of the 1959 Woods Hole Conference which set the academic agenda for 1960s national curriculum reform), Jerome Bruner reflects on how his book functioned in three nations. In the Soviet Union, he tells us, the book was seized as "a weapon" in the struggle against ideological dogmatism in the school, and the academic-discipline-based curriculum the book demanded as supporting "more independence of mind" (Bruner 1977, x). In Japan, the book functioned to challenge the emphasis upon rote memorization in traditional education. In Italy, Marxists attacked the book as a form of epistemological (i.e., bourgeois) idealism while classicists condemned it as an assault on scholasticism and humanism. "In all of these confrontations," Bruner (1977, xi) observes, "it was quite plain that debate about education was not just about education but about political ideals and ideology." What Bruner fails to note is that the same was true in the United States.

In the United States, Bruner's book—and the curriculum reform movement it rationalized—functioned in favor of academic vocationalism, against progressivism, as a means to "strengthen" and make more "rigorous" or "muscled" young (especially European-) Americans' educational experience and to discipline (through education, also offering opportunities to) rebellious African Americans, while defending the Eurocentric and, especially, scientific knowledge. Apparently "liberal" during the Kennedy–Johnson years, academic vocationalism would become explicitly "conservative" then "reactionary" after the election of Richard Nixon in 1968, as right-wing extremists began the process of appropriating "school reform" to their own ideological ends.

During the Reagan Administration the presumably "lax" condition of American schools was alleged to place the nation "at risk." Republican tax cuts had created budget deficits that imperiled the stability of the American dollar, especially vis-à-vis the German and Japanese currencies. But the crisis manufactured by the Reagan administration in the early 1980s was not only economic. Aggravated by its aggressive foreign policy initiatives there was, as Lasch (1984, 73) observes, a "deterioration of Soviet-American relations," an "escalation of the arms race," and a "revival of the Cold War." But it was not fiscal irresponsibility or military aggressivity that was to blame for the state of the nation: schools were (see the National Commission on Excellence in Education 1983).

During the Bush and Clinton administrations the economic competitiveness of the nation—especially during the latter's administration—presumably imperiled America's ability to compete in the "global marketplace" in the "new millennium." Although few educators would dispute the significance of public education for the fate of the nation, politicians' exploitation of public education as a national political issue—onto which a myriad other issues, especially military and economic ones, were grafted—has been disingenuous at best, diverting public scrutiny from the politicians themselves onto a largely passive professional sector unlikely to aggressively mount a countercampaign. America's public school teachers have been and remain, politically speaking, "sitting ducks."

The consequences of this politicization of public education have been numerous and continuing. The first has been to focus curriculum discussions and funding on science, mathematics, and technology, marginalizing (further) programs in music and in the visual and performing arts. The current hype about the computer occurs within this national fantasy—fabricated and articulated by politicians—that education is too important to be left to the teachers (and education professors). It is, clearly, too important to be left to politicians and parents.

There is a gendered dynamic at work here. Legislators (who are overwhelmingly male) feel entitled—compelled—to intervene in teachers' (coded female, certainly in the American popular imagination) domain of professional activity, as if "mother" cannot be trusted to raise "father's sons" properly. There is a long history of male suspicion of women's primacy in childcare, a suspicion that women's dominance in young men's lives may imperil their very manhood (see Kimmel 1994; 1996; Tyack and Hansot 1990; see also Cannella 1998; Steinberg 1999). In the next section we glimpse this dynamic at work in the Kennedy administration's obsession with "physical education," especially the education of the adolescent male body.

The gendered character of teaching, fueled as it is by popular (male) imagination, is grounded in fact. Geraldine Clifford and James Guthrie (1988, 328) characterize public school teaching as "a feminized occupation," noting that, at the time of their writing, women comprised two-thirds of the nation's teachers. This "feminization of teaching" (Grumet 1988) has been the case for a century. By 1870, Richard Hofstadter reports, women comprised approximately 60% of the teaching force, a percentage that increased in the decades following. By 1900, more than 70% of teachers were women, and in another quarter of a century the percentage peaked at more than 83% (see Hofstadter 1962, 317). Jane Addams (2002 [1902], 87) appreciated this gendering of the profession: " 'Teacher' in the vocabulary of many children is a synonym for women-folk gentry, and the name is indiscriminately applied to women of certain dress and manner."

"In 1953," Hofstadter (1962, 320) writes, seemingly in stunned disbelief, "this country stood almost alone among the nations of the world in the feminization of its teaching: women constituted ninety-three percent of its primary teachers and sixty percent of its secondary teachers." The gender politics of Hofstadter's critique of public education becomes even clearer when he imagines the problem male public-school teachers face from other (presumably more masculine) men:

> But in America, where teaching has been identified as a feminine profession, it does not offer men the stature of a fully legitimate male role. . . . The boys grow up thinking of men teachers as somewhat effeminate and treat them with a curious mixture of genteel deference (of the sort due to women) and hearty male condescension. (Hofstadter 1962, 320)

Within the field of education this gendered assault on public education, with its "hearty condescension" toward public school teachers, has left professors of education indignant and protective. Criticism of the schools from the academic field of education has been nearly suspended; declarations of support have been unending, not that all teachers have been appreciative. This gendered relationship has also been vexed within the academic field of curriculum studies, as several have attacked theory as a failure to fulfill professional obligations to direct teachers' daily practice (Wraga 1999).

With the school curriculum now increasingly tied to standardized examinations (many teachers feel they must "teach to the test" and many are directed by administrators to do so), general "curriculum development" has ceased to be a primary professional concern. In light of these changed circumstances, the academic field of curriculum studies was reconceptualized from a primarily bureaucratized, school-based field focused on "curriculum development" to an academic field devoted to scholarly "understanding" (see Pinar et al. 1995, chapter 4). For those who formulate theory (faculty associated with the university, specifically with curriculum theory) to acknowledge that those who "practice" (teachers associated with the school) are no longer able or willing to accept or follow their dictates and advice, is also a gendered admission that "women" are no longer in a dependency relation to "men." This vexed gendered dynamic has provoked anti-intellectual assaults on theory by a few who seem fixated on "the good old days" before Sputnik (Hlebowitsh 1993; Wraga 1999).

To suggest that (especially white) men have lost their historic position of privilege and influence with schools, that now both scholars and practitioners must reflect together on curriculum—in theoretically informed ways—implies an equality of partnership between men and women that is yet to be realized in American society at large, and not yet in American curriculum studies. Some resort to the Old Testament, citing 19th-century legislation that, presumably, consecrates men's position as head of the (school)household. They inspire presumably crestfallen readers with tales of preaching to the masses, converting them, by the power of the word, to new life (see Wraga 1999). This ongoing "crisis of masculinity" is by no means limited to the educational sphere (see Pinar 2001, chapter 19).

Behind these responses to changed circumstances is a reassertion of traditional sex roles and, in particular, the privileged location of the heterosexual white male, as this gendered subject position is encoded professionally and intellectually in the theory–practice relationship. Democratization is a gendered as well as political and pedagogical aspiration. When we speak of the relation of theory to practice, let us imagine a day when traditional and unjust divisions of labor are memories only, when men regard women not as practice to be guided—in positions of "gracious submission"—but as equal and respected colleagues engaged together in that complicated conversation with our children that is the curriculum.

These contemporary gender politics in education became imprinted during the post-Sputnik era, and especially in the administration of President John F. Kennedy. During that time men's long-standing suspicions of women's influence on children, specifically on boys, were stimulated as the nation—in many men's minds gendered masculine—was imperiled. Never mind that it was men in the Eisenhower administration and in the military establishment specifically who were responsible for this heightened sense of peril, having lost to the Soviets the race to launch the first satellite in space. Intuitively, it would seem, other men—in this case, the Kennedys—sensed the political dividends to be paid should they convince an uneasy American public that public education was to blame.

The origin of the convoluted present is not only gendered; it is deeply (if also covertly) racialized. The racialization of public education, begun in the South 100 years earlier, intensified during the Cold War era as the Supreme Court mandated desegregation and white flight (in the North to the suburbs, leaving urban cores painted black) followed. The Civil Rights movement—animated by student-led organizations such as the Student Nonviolent Coordinating Committee (SNCC)—intensified the racialization of education in the (white) public mind, where desegregation was fought both in school buildings and in school textbooks.

The educational architect of the 1960s national curriculum reform movement, Jerome Bruner, came close to realizing that the national concern over curriculum was not strictly "educational" in nature. In the preface to the 1977 edition of *The Process of Education* (first published in 1960), Bruner (1977, xi) suggests that curriculum reform as a "means of cultivating intellect" was "swamped" by "deep social forces," among them, the Civil Rights and the anti-Vietnam War movements. I would add the "cultural revolution" to his list, as millions of Americans, especially European Americans, expressed their skepticism of cultural conventions, especially sexual and racial conventions.

I would supplement Bruner's verb choice—*swamped*—with another, *expressed*. Although I do not doubt the sincerity of those who participated in the 1960s national curriculum reform movement, I do think that movement was not only swamped by deep social forces, it *expressed* them, including the (white and, especially, male) public's resistance to them (and, specifically, the gendering and racialization of public education). It did not *only* do that, but curriculum reform did—and school reform would thereafter—express deep social forces, among them gendered and racialized forces and, especially, white and masculinist reaction to them. This point will, I trust, become clear in the sections to follow.

II
THE RACIAL POLITICS OF CURRICULUM REFORM

Not until the 1960s would black Americans rise up
en masse against racist history, compelling the rest
of the country to take heed.
—Jonathan Zimmerman (2002, 53)

Antiblack racism is . . . intimately connected to misogyny.
—Lewis Gordon (1995, 125)

History has always provided me a way to reshape
the future through reimagining the past.
—Petra Munro (1998, 264)

As early as 1913, the historian William Dodd complained that "two distinct histories are taught in the schools" (quoted in Zimmerman 2002, 34). One was taught above the Mason-Dixon Line, the other below it. While the racialization of the public school curriculum—in the public (especially in the male and European-American) mind—would intensify after the Supreme Court's 1954 decision, in *Brown v. Board of Education*, to desegregate the public schools, the racialization of the curriculum had begun at least 100 years earlier. But in the years surrounding the 1957 Sputnik incident, this racialization intensified and took the form of curricular control, which is to say an effort at intellectual control.

Pressured by public intellectuals and activists such as W. E. B. Du Bois and Carter Woodson, the NAACP convened in 1932 a textbook committee to coordinate the efforts of local branches to examine history, literature, and civics schoolbooks, and to protest those that misrepresented the facts. It reissued this recommendation in 1938 and again in 1939, publishing a pamphlet entitled *Anti-Negro Propaganda in School Textbooks* as a guide for community activists. NAACP officials visited publishers to demand revision of their textbooks, while calling on the students themselves to join the fight (Zimmerman 2002).

While the school curriculum reproduced the white racism of the nation at large, many hoped that correcting the curriculum might influence the larger society. To illustrate this hope, historian Jonathan Zimmerman (2002, 49) quotes a black Kansas City newspaperman: "I do not say that a change in our anti-Negro text-books will kill prejudice, but I am convinced it is a major step in that direction." Zimmerman points out that as Du Bois came to reject the NAACP's commitment to racial integration, he also came to doubt whether "integrated" textbooks could temper white racism. Carter Woodson remained committed to mixed-raced schools *and* to specialized black history courses in African-American schools (Zimmerman 2002).

The Cold War attack on textbooks was animated at first, and foremost (at least initially) by the paranoid anti-Communism of the right-wing. From elitists like William F. Buckley Jr. to low-brow anti-Semites like Allen A. Zoll, thousands of Americans converged on local school board and classrooms to protest textbooks' allegedly "communistic" bias toward public housing, progressive taxation, and other markers of presumed left-wing subversion (Zimmerman 2002).

Zimmerman points out that the three themes of right-wing assaults on textbooks in the 1950s—communism, internationalism (especially the United Nations), and sexual depravity—came to include, by mid-decade, a fourth one: race. Across the country, right-wing critics pressed publishers and school boards to omit any mention of the Ku Klux Klan, lynching, or segregation. Teaching the truth about the racial violence in the United States amounted to complicity with the Communist plot, as such information

would presumably foment what was then commonly called "racial agita-
tion." In Georgia, Zimmerman points out, the mere mention of black poverty
in Magruder's *American Government* textbook provoked threats of white ret-
ribution. Magruder "should be shot as a traitor to our Country," one citizen
proclaimed in 1950. "This type of stuff might be expected in the Harlem district of New York, but that it should be taught in the Public Schools of Georgia is unthinkable" (quoted passages in Zimmerman 2002, 88).

When in 1952 Alabamians discovered that one of their textbooks included
a chapter on the Fair Employment Practices Committee and other efforts to
fight racial injustice, they demanded that the publisher delete the entire chapter. To "protect" Alabama school children against further "subversion," the
state legislature passed a law requiring all subsequent textbooks to carry a
statement confirming that neither the author nor the people quoted had been
members of a communist or "Communist-front" organization. This very
broad and ambiguous designation was used whenever it suited right-wing
fanatics. In this instance, Zimmerman tells us, the law was directed at the
NAACP, considered by white southerners a "Red" organization. Given
the NAACP's bitter and expensive fight with the Communist Party USA over
the legal defense of the "Scottsboro Nine"—young black men falsely con-
victed of raping white women in 1930s Alabama—one wonders how any
southerner could entertain such nonsense (see Pinar 2001, chapter 12).

Right-wing assaults on school textbooks were most intense south of the
Mason-Dixon Line. The regional difference became apparent, Zimmerman
suggests, in the controversy surrounding the 1948 publication of *Brainwashing in the High Schools* by E. Merrill Root, a former English professor
and right-wing activist. Root alleged that studying subversive textbooks in
high school had led to American prisoners' vulnerability to communist in-
doctrination during the Korean War. The allegation was greeted with widespread ridicule in the North, where critics quickly pointed out that 18 of the
21 "traitors" had not even completed high school, making their study of the
textbooks in question unlikely (Zimmerman 2002).

In the South, however, Root's fantasy was treated as fact. Southern lawmakers hired Root to analyze supposedly subversive texts in their high
schools. No segregationist, Root was of little help to southerners. Despite his
acknowledgment, in a report to Mississippi legislators, of his own support for
voluntary racial integration, Root's rabid anti-communism proved useful to
southerners in their segregationist cause. Zimmerman points out that Root's
list of "Reds" who were cited—or worse, celebrated—in "collectivist" schoolbooks included William O. Douglas, Eleanor Roosevelt, and other advocates
for racial justice. After Root (1948) condemned 12 Mississippi textbooks for
the "pink political fog," lawmakers immediately demanded that schools remove them (see Zimmerman 2002, 104). The color of his visual image is not
incidental; right-wing fanatics often linked political betrayal with gender be-

trayal. In the decade to follow, "Pinko-Commie-Fag" was hurled at more than one long-haired Vietnam War protester.

Perhaps compensating for the treason of their Confederate ancestors, many southerners embraced the anti-intellectual attacks on school textbooks by patriotic societies. Apparently inspired by Root's *Brainwashing in the High Schools*, Zimmerman tells us, the Daughters of the American Revolution issued a list of 170 objectionable texts in 1959. Unlike Root, whose diatribes were limited to history textbooks, the DAR went after literature, biology, music, and even arithmetic textbooks. Like Root's book, Zimmerman reports, the DAR list was taken seriously only south of the Mason-Dixon Line.

In Mississippi, segregationist governor Ross Barnett criticized southerners for failing to take seriously enough the communist threat in school textbooks. Taking control of the state's text-selection system, Barnett promised all textbooks adopted by Mississippi would defend "the Southern and true American way of life" (quoted in Zimmerman 2002, 106). Originating in the North as a campaign to defend America's "free enterprise system" from "creeping collectivism," Zimmerman points out, the assault on textbooks became a southern assault on the prospect of racial integration.

Civil rights movement activists were not silent in the face of (white) southern intransigence. In 1961 a NAACP resolution demanded that school textbooks "properly present the contribution of the Negro to American culture"; in 1963 Urban League officials called for a "nationwide struggle" against "all-white" textbooks; and in 1965 the Congress for Racial Equality condemned "stereotypes and distortions of the roles of Negroes" in school textbooks (quoted passages in Zimmerman 2002, 112). That same year, Zimmerman (2002, 112) tells us, the Urban League convened a "tense" meeting between black leaders and representatives of the publishing industry. While claiming allegiance to responsible racial representation, most of the publishers present cautioned against "moving too fast," fearing that white school boards would refuse to adopt "integrated" textbooks. Publishers should produce "what people ought to know, not just what will sell," Urban League Whitney Young pointed out. "Don't approach integration like castor oil," Young told the publishers. "For once, look at something not as a problem but as an opportunity. . . . Your job as human beings is do what is right. Take a position" (quoted passages in Zimmerman 2002, 112).

Civil rights activists knew they could not rely on publishers to place ethics over profits. Like other civil rights struggles in the sphere of public education, the textbook battle would be won or lost "on the local level," school district by district, school by school. In addition to identifying racist schoolbooks, then, the NAACP also asked local affiliates to organize against them. Across the country, thousands of African Americans responded, demanding racial justice in the school curriculum (Zimmerman 2002).

Activists used two basic arguments, both connected to the era's civil rights movement. First, activists pointed out that accurate history textbooks might help persuade stubborn (especially southern) whites to revise their racist views. Second, activists pointed out that if the school curriculum texts continued to misrepresent African Americans and their experience in America, black children would suffer "feelings of separateness and inferiority," as several Philadelphia activists wrote in 1965 (quoted in Zimmerman 2002, 114). On this point they were in agreement with the theories of Kenneth B. Clark and other "damage" theorists, whose ideas were influential in *Brown v. Board of Education.* If physical segregation was harmful to African Americans, "segregated" textbooks were damaging as well (Zimmerman 2002). Martin Luther King Jr. employed both arguments; he pointed out that biased school curricula supported both "white supremacy" and "the Negroes' sense of worthlessness" (quoted in Zimmerman 2002, 114).

White liberals brought federal power to bear on the matter. On occasion, they used the "bully pulpit," as when Vice President Hubert Humphrey condemned the "Negro history gap" in American schools (quoted in Zimmerman 2002, 115). On other occasion, liberals used legislation. Under the Elementary and Secondary Education Act of 1965, $400 million was allocated to schools and libraries for the purchase of "multi-racial" and "multi-ethnic" books (quoted in Zimmerman 2002, 115). Such actions on behalf of an "integrated" school curriculum were—like actions on behalf of integrated school buildings—were often contested, especially by southern whites (Zimmerman 2002).

While white resistance and recrimination were hardly limited to the South, it was especially widespread and intense there. Southern whites insisted that racial integration was unacceptable, whether in classrooms or in textbook illustrations. As late as 1969, in Birmingham, Alabama, whites blocked the adoption of a textbook that alluded to the church bombing that killed four black girls in the city in May 1963. In truth, Zimmerman (2002, 116) points out, the authors of the textbook "bent over backward to appease local sensibilities," attributing the crime to lower-class "white extremists," thereby absolving Birmingham's political and economic elites. Even through the early 1970s, Zimmerman (2002, 116) notes, "*any* reference to racial violence, hostility, or prejudice often spelled the removal of a textbook."

Even the most modest mention of distinguished African Americans in the textbooks of time was met by white protest in the South. In Florida a teacher who used a text showing black Union soldiers during the Civil War found the tires of her car slashed and warnings scrawled across the windows. Other critics objected to the mention of even Frederick Douglass simply because such mention implied criticism of racist whites. "For God's sake," demanded one white Virginian in 1970, "give us some history to be proud of" (quoted in Zimmerman 2002, 116). By resisting the inclusion of important African

Americans in school textbooks, these same European Americans were insuring that America would have no future of which to be proud.

Racists in the North and West tended to be less direct than those in the South. There they tended to make their objections to integrated textbooks in class rather than in explicitly racial terms. Rarely, Zimmerman (2002) points out, did northern white resistance to integrated textbooks—or, for that matter, to integrated classrooms—employ long-discredited arguments concerning inherent differences between blacks and whites. Rather, racists in the North complained that liberal elites were smearing hardworking, patriotic Americans (Zimmerman 2002). "Of course, we do have much of which we are not proud," acknowledged one Californian, "but why play up our mistakes, downgrade our heroes, and please our enemies?" (quoted in Zimmerman 2002, 117–118)

That Californian, and millions of other European Americans, might have profited by studying James Baldwin's March 1968 testimony before Congress on behalf of a proposed National Commission on Negro History and Culture. While endorsing the Commission's interest in promoting greater study and awareness of black history, Baldwin pointed out that this study must occur as part of *American* history. After all, he pointed out, "my history and culture has got to be taught. *It is yours*" (quoted in Zimmerman 2002, 129).

III

STUDENTS AND THE CIVIL RIGHTS MOVEMENT

> *But we all know that each generation has its own test.*
> —Jane Addams (2002 [1902], 5)

> *[F]or a while all of us seemed to go crazy with hope*
> *for another kind of America.*
> —Audre Lorde (1982, 172)

> *Optimism about democracy is to-day under a cloud.*
> —John Dewey (1991 [1927], 110)

While the physical integration of public schools and the intellectual integration of the public school curriculum provided the major occasion for the racialization of public education in the white American mind, it was not the only occasion. Recall that the struggle for civil rights generally was, in no small measure, conducted by students. True, these were college and university students, but in the "public mind" such distinctions faded into one conflated impression. To further appreciate this phenomenon of racialization in which 1960s curriculum reform was initiated, let us review, briefly, moments in the history of one of the major civil rights organizations in the 1960s, the Student Nonviolent Coordinating Committee (SNCC).

I choose SNCC because it was the most student-affiliated wing of the civil rights movement. Born during a period of extensive student protest activity, SNCC was widely regarded as the "shock troops" of the civil rights movement. SNCC activists established projects in areas such as rural Mississippi considered too dangerous by other organizations. Over time, the SNCC's activities shifted from racial desegregation to political rights for African Americans, and its philosophical commitment to nonviolent direct action gave way to a secular, humanistic radicalism influenced by Marx, Camus, Malcolm X, and, concretely, by the SNCC organizers' own horrifying experiences in southern black communities (Carson 1981).

SNCC's founding conference was held April 16–18, 1960, in Raleigh, North Carolina, called by the Executive Director of the Southern Christian Leadership Conference, Ella Baker. The initiating role of the Southern Christian Leadership Conference (SCLC) might have signaled the widening control over the southern black struggle by Martin Luther King, Jr., and those ministers associated with him. However, Baker understood the psychological significance of independence for student activists, and she resisted efforts to undermine their autonomy. Students at the conference affirmed their commitment to the nonviolent doctrines advocated by King, yet they appeared to be drawn to these ideas due less to their association with King and because they provided an appropriate rationale for student protest. The founding of SNCC was, as Clayborne Carson (1981, 19) points out, "an important step in the transformation of a limited student movement to desegregate lunch counters into a broad and sustained movement to achieve major social reforms." Not only the public school was at stake, it seemed to many (especially southern) whites, it was the public sphere itself.

SNCC appeared to outsiders and even to many black student leaders as merely a clearinghouse for the exchange of information about localized protest movements. To SNCC leaders, it was potentially an organization for expanding the struggle beyond its campus base to include all classes of blacks. At a fall conference in Atlanta on October 14–16, 1960, SNCC attempted to consolidate the student protest movement through the establishment of an organizational structure and by clarifying its goals and principles. In brief, the movement's goals were "individual freedom and personhood" (quoted in Carson 1981, 27).

At the end of 1960 SNCC was still a loosely organized committee of part-time student activists who were uncertain of their roles in the southern struggle. Their political orientations could be said to be more-or-less conventional. Yet within months, SNCC would became a cadre of full-time organizers and protesters. Its militant identity was forged during the "freedom rides," a series of assaults on southern segregation that for the first time brought student protesters into conflict not only with white southern legal officials, but with the Kennedy administration itself. SNCC's militancy was further deepened by the experiences of student activists in Mississippi jails during the summer of 1961. It had been after attending a Congress of Racial Equality (CORE) workshop in December that a few students decided to remain in jail after being arrested rather than posting bond. Imprisonment, many decided, constituted a crucial learning experience (Carson 1981).

The freedom rides not only contributed to the desegregation of southern transportation facilities, but they accelerated the formation of a self-consciously radical black student movement which would soon direct its militancy toward other, even more controversial issues, including the good faith of the federal government. Increasingly, SNCC charged the federal government with hypocrisy, as it failed to act forcefully to achieve domestic civil rights for African Americans while self-righteously proclaiming democratic values abroad (Carson 1981). This understanding would provide the foundation for a coalition with mostly white student groups opposing the war in Vietnam.

SNCC sent representatives—as did other civil rights organizations—to a meeting with Attorney General Robert Kennedy on June 16, 1961. (Kennedy's concern with the state of American manhood becomes coded, in light of his complex and volatile relationship with black activist groups, as racialized.) At that 1961 meeting Kennedy suggested that the freedom ride campaign be refocused toward the goal of registering southern blacks who had been disenfranchised through violence, intimidation, and more subtle techniques such as literacy tests and poll taxes. Students affiliated with SNCC were divided over whether to become involved in voter registration work. While they understood that this was an important activity, many were reluctant to abandon the direct action tactics that had placed them at the forefront of the civil rights struggle (Carson 1981).

The black-dominated southern civil rights movement would have profound effect on the white student left. Without the knowledge of the nonviolent tactics and organizing techniques developed by SNCC in the South, white student activism would probably not have expanded as quickly or as successfully as it did. Tom Hayden and other leaders of the student-led anti-Vietnam War movement learned much from their experiences in the South. Students for a Democratic Society, the northern radical student movement, as well as other predominantly white student organizations, attracted students whose induction into political activism had occurred during their engagement in the struggle for civil rights in the South (Carson 1981).

The pace and scope of protest in the years following accelerated and expanded, respectively, intensifying white southerners' sense of emergency. During 1963, Southern Regional Council researchers estimated that 930 public protest demonstrations took place in at least 115 cities in 11 southern states. More than 20,000 persons were arrested during these protests, in contrast to approximately 3,600 arrests in the period of nonviolent protests prior to the fall of 1961. In 1963, 10 persons died in circumstances directly related to racial protests; at least 35 bombings occurred. Those SNCC activists who were engaged in mass protests became aware of a militancy, especially among urban African Americans, that surpassed their own. This militancy among the people compelled them to reassess their own convictions regarding nonviolent protest (Carson 1981).

IV
FREEDOM SCHOOLS

[E]very subject finds herself obligated to search
for the future in the past.
—Kaja Silverman (2000, 49)

I have often wondered why the farthest-out position always feels
so right to me; why extremes, although difficult and sometimes
painful to maintain, are always more comfortable than on a
plane running straight down a line in the unruffled middle.
—Audre Lorde (1982, 15)

Love is the central motif of nonviolence. Love is the force
by which Gods binds man to Himself and man to man.
—SNCC Statement of Purpose
(quoted in Carson 1981, 24)

During this period of increased student militancy, plans were developed for a "freedom school" program. The idea for the school program had been conceived by SNCC worker Charles Cobb in the fall of 1963. Cobb had recognized the inadequacy of public education in Mississippi, due, in part, to its "complete absence of academic freedom" and its repression of "intellectual curiosity and different thinking." He proposed that schools be established to "fill an intellectual and creative vacuum" in the lives of young black Mississippians. He was especially interested that teachers "get them to articulate their own desires, demands and questions." Cobb proposed that teachers be employed from the hundreds of northern college students who would be arriving in Mississippi during the summer: "These are some of the best young minds in the country, and their academic value ought to be recognized, and taken advantage of" (quoted passages in Carson 1981, 109).

The curriculum for the freedom schools was developed in March 1964 at a meeting of educators, clergymen, and SNCC workers in New York. The curriculum was to include the usual school subjects, plus courses on contemporary issues, cultural expression, and leadership development. This last course would teach the history of the civil rights struggle (characterized in those heady days as the black liberation movement), including the study of political skills. Staughton Lynd, a white radical intellectual teaching at the time at Spelman College in Atlanta, became director of the freedom school program (Carson 1981).

Mississippi children and parents responded favorably to the freedom schools. While encouraging, the innovative educational program only partially removed the barriers of distrust and fear that separated white teachers from black residents. SNCC had conducted educational programs before, preparing black residents for Mississippi's voter registration test. In 1963 SNCC's Maria Varela had established an adult literacy project in Alabama. Despite these precedents, the freedom schools were SNCC's first comprehensive educational program designed for a large number of black youngsters. A statewide enrollment of about 1,000 students had been expected for the freedom schools, but more than twice that number attended classes in 41 schools. Participation was greatest in those areas where there had already been civil rights activities. In Hattiesburg, Mississippi, for example, more than 600 students enrolled (Carson 1981).

In plantation areas participation was much lower. The reasons were not only ideological. A teacher in Shaw explained that black youngsters in that plantation community attended public schools during the summer so as to be available to pick cotton in the fall (Carson 1981). After leaving public school in the afternoon, many youngsters preferred to sleep rather than going to the freedom school to study "in the blazing heat of the Mississippi sun and dust" (quoted in Carson 1981, 120).

Freedom school teachers tended to ignore traditional classroom routines, employing innovative teaching methods in an effort to encourage the free expression of ideas. A curriculum guide developed for boycotting students in Boston was adapted for use in the Mississippi freedom schools. As part of the leadership training, students discussed the role of freedom schools and, specifically, the educational importance and political necessity of preserving and advancing African-American culture. Uncritical assimilation to white culture must cease (Carson 1981).

Students were offered courses in creative writing, drama, art, journalism, and foreign languages. There were evening classes in literacy, health, and typing. Many students attended performances of the Free Southern Theater, a touring company organized as part of the freedom schools by John O'Neal at Tougaloo College. The Theater performed *In White America*, a play written by (white) historian and, later, queer theorist Martin Duberman, depicting the history of American race relations from slavery to the murder of the three civil rights workers at the beginning of the summer (Carson 1981).

Freedom school teachers were both encouraged and frustrated by their experiences during the summer. The students "hardly trust whites," a volunteer in Indianola wrote, "and there is a lot of 'Yes Ma'am' and constant agreement with what you say." Overcoming the students' reticence was, Carson reports, the schools' major accomplishment. Another teacher described her delight when students discovered they could "translate ideas into concrete written words. After two weeks a child finally looks me in the eye, unafraid, acknowledging a bond of trust which 300 years of Mississippians said should never, could never, exist" (quoted passages in Carson 1981, 120).

The schools represented one of the first attempts by SNCC to replace existing institutions with alternative ones. As Howard Zinn (1965, 10) noted, these schools represented a challenge to American education, embodying "the provocative suggestion that an entire school system can be created in any community outside the official order, and critical of its suppositions." For Zinn, the freedom schools raised questions regarding the future of American education. Could teachers and students work together "not through the artificial sieve of certification and examination but on the basis of their common attraction to an exciting social goal?" Could teachers teach values "while avoiding a blanket imposition of the teacher's ideas?" Would it be possible for teachers "to declare boldly that the aim of the schools is to find solutions for poverty, for injustice, for race and national hatred, and to turn all educational efforts into a national striving for those solutions?" (Zinn 1965, 10).

Few SNCC workers were involved directly in the operations of the freedom schools after the Summer Project of 1965. However, the schools continued to be characterized by SNCC's anti-authoritarianism. They constituted important if unacknowledged models and testing grounds for later alternative schools and tutorial projects throughout the nation (Carson 1981; Lomotey and Rivers 1998).

By 1965, SNCC had become, in the eyes of supporters as well as critics, not simply another civil rights organization. SNCC was very much a part of the New Left, that amorphous body of young activists seeking ideological alternatives to conventional liberalism (not to mention conservatism, which had become even more disturbing due to the Goldwater presidential campaign of 1964 and its exploitation of southern white racism). Some observers have attributed SNCC's ideological radicalism to the presence of white leftists in the southern struggle. The truth is, Carson (1981) asserts, that SNCC is more accurately understood not as derivative from white student radicalism, but, rather, as a *source* of insights and inspiration for the New Left. Just as its unique and often spontaneous style of unstructured, rebellious activism broke through decades of southern black accommodation, SNCC helped transform those pervasive patterns of political and cultural conformity exhibited by white college students in Cold War America.

While FBI Director J. Edgar Hoover did not include SNCC in the FBI's Counterintelligence Program (COINTELPRO) until 1967, concerted FBI surveillance of SNCC's activities had begun several years earlier. As early as October 1960, the FBI was receiving reports on SNCC activities. In 1965, Hoover received permission of Attorney General Nicholas Katzenbach to institute wiretaps on SNCC's phones. None of the FBI reports during the period from 1964 to 1967 presented evidence that any member of SNCC's staff was or had been a member of the Communist Party (Carson 1981). Despite the facts, Hoover persisted.

On August 25, 1967, Hoover ordered FBI field officers to begin a new effort "to expose, disrupt, misdirect, discredit, or otherwise neutralize the activities of black nationalist, hate-type organizations and groupings, their leadership, spokesmen, membership and supporters, and to counter their propensity for violence and civil disorder." Among the groups identified for "intensified attention" in this extension of COINTELPRO were the Deacons for Defense and Justice, Nation of Islam, the Congress for Racial Equality (CORE), the Southern Christian Leadership Conference (SCLC), and SNCC. FBI offices were instructed to "establish" the "unsavory backgrounds" of "key agitators" to discredit them. FBI agents were reminded that these projects were to be kept secret. No actions were to be taken without prior Bureau authorization (quoted passages in Carson 1981, 262).

In a COINTELPRO proposal submitted on July 10, 1968 to Hoover, it was recommended that:

> [c]onsideration be given to convey the impression that [SNCC leader Stokely] Carmichael is a CIA informer. One method of accomplishing [this] would be to have a carbon copy of informant report reportedly written by Carmichael to the CIA carefully deposited in the automobile of a close Black Nationalist friend. . . . It is hoped that when the informant report is read it will help promote distrust between Carmichael and the Black Community. . . . It is also suggested that we inform a certain percentage of reliable criminal and racial informants that "we have heard from reliable sources that Carmichael is a CIA agent." It is hoped that these informants would spread the rumor in various large Negro communities across the land. (quoted in Churchill and Wall 1988, 49)

Approved the next day, the proposal also contained a report on an earlier COINTELPRO directed at Carmichael: "On 9/4/68, pretext phone call was placed to the residence of Stokely Carmichael and in absence of Carmichael his mother was told that a friend was calling who was fearful of the future safety of her son. It was explained to Mrs. Carmichael, the absolute necessity for Carmichael to 'hide out' inasmuch as several BPP [Black Panther Party] members were out to kill him, and it was probably to be done sometime this week. Mrs. Carmichael appeared shocked upon hearing the news and stated she would tell Stokely when he came home." One result of this governmental deformation of Carmichael's reputation may be detected in this statement of Minister of Defense of the Black Panther Party, Huey P. Newton, on September 5, 1970, that "We . . . charge that Stokely Carmichael is operating as an agent of the CIA" (quoted in Churchill and Wall 1988, 49).

Hoover moved to initiate similar operations against the growing civil rights movements in the southeast, placing Martin Luther King's name in Section A of the Reserve Index (one step below the Security Index) on May 11, 1962. He directed the Atlanta field office of the Bureau that King should be added to their "pickup list for handling" under the provisions of the Detention Act in the event of a national emergency (Churchill and Wall 1988, 54). The agency's assault on SNCC and other civil rights organizations would anticipate the broader and continuing governmental and judicial assault on the civil rights of racial and sexual minorities that continues to the present day.

V

THE GENDER POLITICS OF CURRICULUM REFORM

The body is . . . a mirror of our hopes and fears,
our needs and desires.
—Robert L. Griswold (1998, 339)

Athletics and a masculinizing school firmly legitimate the
reign of white hegemonic masculinity, with its dominance
of girls, students of color, and less-masculine boys.
—Nancy Lesko (2001, 179)

Desire has a powerful influence upon intellectual beliefs.
—John Dewey (1962 [1934], 22)

In this section I report the research of Robert L. Griswold (1998), scholarship which makes clear the gender politics underwriting the national curriculum reform movement in the 1960s. In particular, Griswold's insightful review of the Kennedy Administration's emphasis upon the body—especially, I argue, the young *white* male body—discloses how Cold War anxieties were grafted onto the bodies of the young. That "grafting" not only expressed a generalized worry over the fate of the nation. It expressed as well, through innuendo, that women—mothers and schoolteachers—were blameworthy in allowing American youth, specifically white male youth, to go "soft."

Such a characterization recalls centuries-long male anxieties over women's "threat" to boys' maturation into men, both in the school (where, for instance, in the late 19th century, debates raged over coeducation animated by fears that not only that boys would be softened, but that girls would be masculinized, threatening the "natural" order of gender and sexuality) and in the home (where father's absence and mothers' tendencies toward over-protection presumably risked feminized boys).

In the United States, this ongoing concern for manhood has been ra-cialized as well. What historians—not without controversy (see Carnes and Griffen 1990)—have characterized as the "crisis of masculinity" has oc-curred, in part, in reaction, to civil rights successes of African Americans (see Pinar 2001; Savran 1998). In 1960, with the Soviets in space and the fate of the nation at hand, once again "gender and race [would] conflate in a crisis" (Gates 1996, 84).

These gendered and racialized conflations of mind and body, of physical and intellectual well-being, became focused as (white) men's worries over young (white) men's bodies, at the same time sublimated into concerns for "rigorous" schooling: the 1960s national curriculum reform movement. While never explicitly racialized, as Griswold's account indicates, one can surmise that the Kennedy Administration's campaign for physical fitness was not concerned over the physical condition of young black men's bodies. Those bodies—given the aggressivity of black student activism, not to men-tion the continuing white fear of black male rape—seemed to many Euro-pean Americans hard enough.

Griswold (1998) cites John F. Kennedy's "The Soft American," which ap-peared in the December 26, 1960, issue of *Sports Illustrated*, as the beginning of the President-elect's campaign to persuade Americans to become physi-cally vigorous. Christopher Lasch (1978, 101) found Kennedy's pronounce-ments on physical fitness "tiresome." Kennedy invoked standardized tests to "prove" the presumably dramatic decline of strength and fitness among American (white, especially male) youth. "Our growing softness, our increas-ing lack of physical fitness, is a menace to our security" (quoted in Lasch 1978, 101). Did he mean "psychological" as well as "national" security?

Kennedy praised the ancient Greeks' conviction (but not their sexual pref-erences) that physical excellence and athletic skill were "among the prime foundations of a vigorous state" and suggested that intellectual ability could not be separated from physical well-being (quoted in Griswold 1998, 323). This restatement of 19th-century "faculty psychology"—namely, that the mind was a muscle—left Kennedy worried over the state of young Ameri-cans' minds, as their bodies were, presumably, in terrible shape: "A single look at the packed parking lot of the average high school," wrote Kennedy, "will tell us what has happened to the traditional hike to school that helped to build young bodies" (quoted in Griswold 1998, 323). The future of America was imperiled by a military/space race in which the Soviets, by virtue of the 1957 Sputnik launching, had moved ahead. Intensifying the nation's crisis, Kennedy worried, was the flabby condition of American youth, especially American boys (Griswold 1998). Especially, I would add, white boys.

With the *Sports Illustrated* article, Kennedy and his new administration launched a school-based program that soon had millions of children exercising the prescribed minimum of 15 minutes per day. Many took a battery of tests that stretched abdominals, flexed biceps, and challenged lung capacity in the 600-yard run. What was at stake? Was Kennedy only concerned about physical fitness? Griswold (1998) suggests that embedded in the fitness campaign were anxieties over morality, postwar consumerism, masculinity, and the survival of the nation itself. Griswold quotes Kennedy, who once again restates the conflation of mind and body:

> We are, all of us, as free to direct the activities of our bodies as we are to pursue the objects of our thought. But if we are to retain this freedom, for ourselves and for generations to come, then we must also be willing to work for the physical toughness on which the courage and intelligence and skill of man so largely depend. (quoted in Griswold 1998, 323)

The concepts—*freedom, toughness, courage*—are, Griswold notes, classic Kennedy rhetoric. Kennedy had molded his own body on the playing fields of Hyannisport, Choate, and Harvard, had tested it in World War II in the Solomon Islands. In his *Sports Illustrated* essay, Kennedy pointed out that young men in America had always been willing and able to fight for freedom but, he warned, that the strength and stamina needed for battle did not come of their own: "These only come from bodies which have been conditioned by a lifetime of participation in sports and interest in physical activity." He warned that "our growing softness, our increasing lack of physical fitness, is a menace to our security" (quoted passages in Griswold 1998, 324). While Kennedy may have been thinking only of the Soviet "menace to our security," for especially white male southern listeners, that phrase—"menace to our security"—reverberated as a racial threat as well.

In the fitness crusade of the Kennedy administration, the bodies of young white men—schoolboys specifically—became the "repository" (Griswold 1998, 352) for anxieties about the Cold War. The obsession with physical fitness was about, Griswold (1998, 235) asserts, "redeeming manhood." Griswold focuses on manhood because, although the fitness campaign included both boys and girls, it emphasized boys. Why?

The answer, Griswold suggests, has to do with the historical moment. He points out that the 1960s physical fitness movement occurred during a period of considerable and, I would add, ongoing (see Pinar 2001, 1139–1152) cultural anxiety regarding the status and future of American manhood. Psychiatric disorders associated with World War II, lingering anxieties about the absence of fathers during that war and the Korean conflict and postwar adjustment problems of veterans were all on the public mind. These anxieties became racialized in the mid-1960s in the Moynihan Report, which diagnosed racial disadvantage and educational underachievement specifically as functions of absent black fathers (see Pinar 2001, 889–895). Despite the "domestic revival" of the 1950s—in which father-led, heteronormative families were, for many, the only option—many men worried about what they imagined to be overly protective mothers, who, they feared, were rendering American manhood impotent (see Pinar 2001, 895–899). Feminized boys and men seemed an imminent danger (Griswold 1998).

The 1948 Kinsey Report on male sexuality, Griswold reminds, had shocked many Americans with its report of widespread homosexuality. In the 1950s the homosexual "menace" terrified not only parents but politicians as well. The McCarthy witch-hunt for Communists targeted not only "gender inverts" but also "egg-sucking phony liberals," East Coast intellectuals, and emasculated "pinks, punks, and perverts." The United States government had been infiltrated, in the words of one of McCarthy's aides, had become "a veritable nest of Communists, fellow travelers, homosexuals, effete Ivy League intellectuals and traitors" (quoted phrases in Griswold 1998, 325). In the grip of such gendered panic, a sex-crimes panic swept America in the late 1940s and early 1950s, reaching even into "the heartland" in the infamous "boys of Boise" scandal (Gerassi 1966). Even comic books—especially "Batman and Robin"—posed, presumably, a threat to young "red-blooded" American boys (see Torres 1996; Wertham 1953/1954).

Press reports were lurid and widespread. Outraged citizens and terrified parents held mass meetings, security programs at schools were beefed-up, and in 15 states government commissions were established to study the threat to children posed by "sexual degenerates" (Griswold 1998, 326). Many psychiatrists and government officials criticized overbearing mothers and passive fathers as the root of the problem and pleaded with teachers, clergymen, and police to watch for boys who were becoming effeminate. Conflating effeminacy with homosexuality and assuming that both were spread like STD's, suspicious boys should be directed to guidance centers for psychiatric counseling (Griswold 1998). Right-wing fanatics in America might have been surprised to learn that the Communist Fidel Castro was also worrying about the masculinity of young men, sending effeminate Cuban boys to "camps" for gender reprogramming (Leiner 1994, 28–29).

Animating American paranoia, Griswold suggests, was the Cold War itself, specifically the anxiety that a military encounter with the Soviet Union was inevitable. A series of gendered terms was commonly used to describe the crisis: "brinksmanship," "massive retaliation," and "flexible response" (quoted in Griswold 1998, 326). The fitness campaign occurred within this general panic; it was an effort to rescue manhood by rescuing the body; to teach boys, as one participant put it, to use the body in "forceful and space-occupying ways" (quoted in Griswold 1998, 326). It would also seem to offer a strategy for sublimating an evidently omnipresent homosexual desire, as sublimated "hard" bodies were imagined as prerequisites to the development of "normal" male identity (Griswold 1998). Programs of physical fitness conflated bodies with minds, and in so doing, would reinvigorate "manhood" so that "we" would defeat the Communist threat to national survival. The threat could not be met with "soft bodies" (Griswold 1998, 326).

The Cold War stimulated numerous anxieties, nearly all of which, Griswold (1998, 326) emphasizes, found their way onto the "bodies of the young." Among these were materialism, conformity, maternal overprotection, parental neglect, government paternalism, moral corruption, and sexual excess, most notoriously expressed in the appearance of the "beats," "rebels without a cause" (Savran 1998), even "the white negro" (Mailer 1957). The consequence was an America "at risk," although that phrase would not be used for another 30 years, and then used to allege "malpractice" in the nation's public schools (National Commission on Excellence in Education 1983).

That national security was at stake was a point made by Attorney General Robert F. Kennedy in a speech in January 1961 at the "Coach of the Year Dinner" in Pittsburgh. Kennedy asserted that since the end of World War II—a war in which "we had proved we had the mental genius, the moral certitude and the physical strength to endure and conquer"—America had been on a precipitous downward moral and physical slide" (quoted in Griswold 1998, 330). Like his brother, Robert Kennedy saw a direct correlation between this national decline and the softening of the (white male) body. Saving the nation, Kennedy seemed to imply, was up to the coaches. It was these older men who could "exert a tremendous influence for good in this country. . . . You, who participate in football, who have played well and have trained others to play well, symbolize the needs of the Nation" (quoted in Griswold 1998, 330).

Robert Kennedy's reference to football was no accident, Griswold points out, as it disclosed the administration's focus upon the bodies of boys and young men. Given a pervasive fear about the state of American manhood throughout the postwar years, a rough sport like football—Oscar Wilde (quoted in Simpson 1994, 90) once quipped that "football is all very well as a game for rough girls, but it is hardly suitable for delicate boys"—reproduced a gendered hierarchy of that elevated the muscular athlete over the limp-wristed sissy-boy, the (straight) stud linebacker over the gay artist (Griswold 1998). Physical force and toughness were combined to reproduce what gender theorists have termed "hegemonic masculinity" secured by "the heterosexual matrix" (Butler 1990, 1993; Disch and Kane 1996; Silverman 1992). In this gender system men presumably project strength, power, aggressiveness, morality, and superiority while "inferiorizing the other," that is, women and less manly men (Griswold 1998, 331).

Historically, American football has functioned to forge male solidarity around a beleaguered ideal of sovereign and powerful masculinity (see Lesko

2000; Pronger 1990). One hundred years ago masculinity was widely perceived to be in "crisis" (Carnes and Griffen 1990; Filene 1998). Michael Kimmel (1990, 57) has argued that the emergence of the sport in the late 19th century was prompted by a "perceived crisis of masculinity" among white middle-class males whose illusions of manly character and autonomy were compromised by profound political, economic, and gender shifts. Then the "crisis" was precipitated by the closing of the American frontier, by the mechanization and routinization of labor that erased economic individualism and autonomy (except for a few robber barons), by black political progress, by the rise of the women's movement (secular as well as Christian feminism and the campaign for women's suffrage), by the massive influx of immigrants into the industrial centers of the United States, by the end of "romantic" friendship and the appearance of "homosexuality" (see Pinar 2001, chapter 6). In the 1960s, it was the Cold War from which radiated a multitude of gendered, racialized, and educational anxieties.

In the 1960s physical fitness crusades and the process of "inferiorizing the other" were expressed in gendered terms. Griswold points out that sports and exercise had different meanings for girls and boys, at least in the minds of fitness advocates. For boys, fitness leaders emphasized competition (i.e., winning the game, running the fastest, completing the most sit-ups). For girls, experts emphasized friendship, health, and becoming sexually appealing to boys. Griswold (1998, 331) cites Dr. Benjamin Spock's public doubts about the appropriateness of competitive sports for girls. Sports were "really invented by boys, for boys." If add the modifier "straight," queer theorists would agree, if for different reasons: "It might be argued that with their homosexuality completely (or mostly) desublimated they have no need for them; for gay men team sports are experienced not as sexualized aggression, just aggression" (Simpson 1994, 90).

Fitness advocates focused on the ways physical exercise enhanced girls' sexual attractiveness to young men. Some suggested that some of girls' "workouts" might also include watching the boys compete, thus enabling girls, as one writer put it, to "admire the boys for their [physical fitness] achievements" (quoted in Griswold 1998, 331). (Today, heterosexual girls might watch boys as sexual objects.) Girls could also use sports as a strategy to meet boys, a point made by *Seventeen* magazine when it suggesting that walking a mile in 11 minutes would be made more palatable if accompanied by "a boy from the track team!" (quoted in Griswold 1998, 331).

A movie sponsored by the American Dairy Association and the President's Council on Physical Fitness made clear that fitness, drinking milk, and sexual attractiveness went hand-in-hand, a strategy replicated in the 1980s and 1990s by milk advertising campaigns in which nearly naked boys and girls swam across a lake, emerging from the lake with glistening bodies to the announcer's simple declaration: "milk!" In the 1960s, one newspaper publisher speculated that fitness "will make teen-age girls appear glamorous to teenage boys," and, later in life, support woman's "true destiny" (quoted in Griswold 1998, 331) by creating "healthful, vital, feminine women who can mother a vigorous generation" (quoted in Griswold 1998, 332).

Although the fitness crusaders publicly praised multiple forms of physical activity, it is clear, Griswold (1998, 332) notes, that many pinned their hopes on football, that manhood would be "reborn" on the nation's playing fields. "Rough sports" would make boys' bodies hard, capable of enduring pain, and restore masculinity itself. "Except for war," Robert Kennedy asserted, "there is nothing in American life which trains a boy better for life than football. There is no substitute for athletics—there can be no substitute for football" (quoted in Griswold 1998, 332). More than any other sport associated with the 1960s fitness movement, football engaged the imagination of politicians and the public alike. Here was a sport that turned boys into men (Griswold 1998).

In hardening his body, the young man's masculinity would, presumably, also be reinvigorated. Now his mind and body would be strong, resilient, tough; now both could be placed at the service of his country. Speaking to a New York City audience, Robert Kennedy emphasized that sport was key to the fate of the nation. Football was fun, of course, but the patriotic significance of contact sports was that they built healthy bodies and promoted "stamina, courage, unselfishness, and most importantly, perhaps, the will to win." And without the will to win, added Kennedy, "we are lost" (quoted passages in Griswold 1998, 333).

Hot bodies and cold wars seemed to go together, at least in the mind of Robert Kennedy. Griswold tells us that he, his brother, and many others believed that physical fitness would prepare the male body for war. Nothing less than national survival was at stake in the bodies of young men; they constituted a flesh-and-blood barometer of national supremacy or decline. To make the young man's body strong and virile was to restore the nation's power and vitality. America could secure its future only if a vigorous fitness program could first transform the (white male) body. (Never mind that nuclear annihilation made the hardness or softness of bodies irrelevant.) If the soft, feminized bodies of boys could be hardened, Kennedy felt sure, then there was a chance to discipline their minds (Griswold 1998).

But bodies were foremost, or so it seemed, as Robert Kennedy pledged to physical education teachers that the administration was committed to fitness. Minds would come soon enough, as science and mathematics curriculum would be "toughened" as well in the national curriculum reform initiatives. (Mathematics and science functioned in the mid- and late-20th-century curriculum debates as Latin and ancient Greek had in 19th-century debates; like physical exercise, mental "discipline" also made the mind/muscle hard.) Robert Kennedy emphasized hard bodies, noting that mathematics and science curriculum reform would amount to little if American youth lacked the bodily strength to make use of their knowledge. After all, Kennedy asserted, even technological warfare requires American soldiers and technicians to walk to the silos to push the buttons: "If we are sick people; if we are people that have difficulty walking two or three blocks to the engineering labora-tory, or four or five blocks to the missile launching site, we are not going to be able to meet the great problems that face us in the next ten years" (quoted in Griswold 1998, 336).

Robert Kennedy concluded his New York speech by praising Americans as a "tough, viable, industrious people" who do not "search for a fight" but are "prepared to meet our responsibilities." Evidently, as Griswold points out, pull-ups, sit-ups, and sprints in school gym classes constituted the first line of defense in the Cold War. "We cannot afford to be second in any-thing—certainly not in the matter of physical fitness," he insisted, using a logic that would be applied to standardized test scores 30 years later. Before the nation's strength was sapped further, Americans must implement a na-tionwide, systematic program that would make American youth strong, a "program that, in the defense of our freedoms, will enable them to pass any test, any time, any place in the world" (quoted passages in Griswold 1998, 336).

Griswold notes the echo here of late-19th-century efforts to resuscitate a masculinity in "crisis" (see Pinar 2001, chapter 6). Then the causes were mul-tiple, but in the 1950s, it was, above all, the Cold War that left youth in crisis, especially white male youth, now softened by the sins of indulgence and com-fort. Presumably "[t]he future of manhood and of the nation itself hung in the balance" (Griswold 1998, 336). And while the Cold War dominated the rhet-oric of fitness, it was not the only issue, Griswold reminds. Profound shifts in race, work, and community, all agitated by fears of male homosexuality and women's assertiveness rendered the young man's body symbolic not only of continued male dominance, but of heterosexuality itself, linked—through U.S. Senator Joseph McCarthy's association of the Communist threat with homosexual traitors—to national supremacy. Like the nation's schools, by the late 1950s the young white male body seemed at risk. Like the public school curriculum, the young man's body required—so the nation's leaders insisted—a national response. Only such a massive intervention could restore the vigor and strength of both.

The Cold War came to represent several issues. As Griswold (1998, 337) asserts, "boys' bodies" would be hardened not only to reassert the dominance of "men over women and less manly men," but to stand firm against the threats of the age. One threat of the age was military; another was politically ascendant African Americans, who, just 6 years earlier, had gained legal ac-cess to previously all-white schools in the 1954 Supreme Court ruling in *Brown v. Board of Education*. Of course, actual access would come slowly—as of this writing (autumn, 2002), the desegregation suit in Baton Rouge, Louisiana, has still not been settled—but the sense of threat, Griswold emphasizes, was then not only military, but gendered. It was, I suggest, racialized as well.

It was gendered and, specifically, masculinized. By lifting weights and participating in athletic competition, boys would, presumably, learn to become men, and only men could learn to become the fierce soldiers the Cold War presumably demanded. As Griswold notes, the re-masculinization of the American male body required the male body at war, and it would not be long after the Kennedy Administration took office before American foreign policy would provide an opportunity. The Vietnam War would become a shattering experience, not only for American military hegemony, but for American manhood as well (Savran 1998).

As Nancy Lesko (2002, 178) observed in another context, "schools are masculinizing institutions." While that has almost always been the case, since the politicization of public school reform in the 1960 Presidential election and its conflations of military, racial, and gendered anxieties, school reform and masculinization have been like twins in the same womb. Because they share the same "maternal body," their "birth" parallels the ontogeny of the individual boys in a patriarchal society, namely the repudiation of maternal identification and the exaggerated cultivation of separation, struggle, and competitiveness (Chodorow 1978; Gilmore 1990, 2001).

The price for those who do not, or cannot, conform is high, as the disciplinary society becomes (almost) totalizing in its regulation of academic rites of passage. "In the United States," Lesko (2001, 151) points out, "the remasculinizing of schools includes a number of features: the spread of competitive sports; higher standards through increased testing; a more rigorous curriculum; zero-tolerance policies; and redoubled efforts in math, science, and technology." Nowhere is this reactionary and racialized remasculinization more obvious than in the American South.

4

The Significance
of the South

I
CURRICULUM-IN-PLACE

*Today, one looks at the South and sees America. There is
abundant reason to pay close attention to future political
developments in the South, for it now shapes the trends and
sets the pace of national political outcomes and processes.*
—Earl Black and Merle Black (1992, 366)

*The work of mourning, of memory, requires that the mourner work
through her or his own impulse to idealize the lost object, to split
off the affect from the fact of loss, and hence attempt to bring
back as unchanged and familiar what can no longer exist.*
—Deborah Britzman (2000, 33–34)

We are creatures of the cruelties we witness.
—Paul Monette (1992, 37)

As we have seen, the American nation became mobilized after Sputnik as politicians exploited multiple anxieties and attached them to the education of the young. Accompanying the Kennedy Administration's emphasis upon the young (white male) body and its hardening was an emphasis upon science and mathematics to "toughen" the mind. As recent studies of "internationalization" and "globalization" make clear (see Pinar 2003a) curriculum is embedded in national cultures. It is also embedded in regions, and nowhere in the United States is that fact more obvious than in the Deep South. The

American South is a "place" with a distinctive history, distinctive cultures, and distinctive problems, but given its political ascendance since 1968, its problems plague the nation as a whole (see Black and Black 1992, chapter 12).

"Place" has been a concept largely absent in traditional curriculum scholarship, predictably so. From its conception as a specialized field in the early 20th century, curriculum studies have tended toward the formulation of principles of curriculum development applicable anytime and anywhere (Tyler 1949). In this chapter, I situate curriculum regionally, that is, in the "South," and suggest in chapter 9 a program of study appropriate to this region. Such a curriculum not only represents a *place*, it also becomes *place*, a curricular embodiment and contradiction of peculiarly southern experience, taught in ways appropriate to the reconstruction of that experience, toward the end of demystifying southern history and culture. As *place* or *ground* in Gestalt terms, this curriculum is a form of social psychoanalysis; it permits the student to emerge as "figure," capable of critical participation in a historical present widely ignored and denied. The educational, economic, and cultural development of the region—and the nation—requires both.

Tendencies toward curriculum standardization mirror tendencies toward cultural homogenization in the United States generally, despite the tip of the rhetorical hat toward "diversity." Indeed, Linda McNeil (2000, xxvii) argues, "*[e]ducational standardization harms teaching and learning and, over the long term, restratifies education by race and class.*" Now in the service of racial and class stratification, 100 years ago curriculum standardization meant cultural assimilation. Standardization developed, in part, as a response to the mass entry of immigrants to the United States during the period 1890–1930, and, as well, to the "great migration" of southern blacks north, in search of economic opportunity and to escape lynching (Spring 1986; see Pinar 2001; Pinar et al. 1995, chapters 3 and 5).

While primarily in the service of cultural homogeneity, then, curriculum standardization also developed due to the circumstances of the middle class. The evolution of an industrial civilization into an increasingly corporate and postindustrial one required increasing mobility, especially among the managerial classes. As one commentator on the significance of "place" and locale in southern experience has noted, a nomadic people tends to de-emphasize place as significant (Dabbs 1964). There are those who argue that regional or sectional differences are inconsequential, given the rise of the New South (clearly a South "newer" in, say, Virginia and North Carolina, than in Louisiana and Mississippi). The presidential politics since the 1960s suggests otherwise.

The notion of a New South is a century old (Ayers 1992; Genovese 1968). While referring to actual demographic, economic, and cultural shifts, the concept also functions to obscure the considerable extent to which the specific history of this region echoes in the lives of its present inhabitants. This denial is psychological, as students of the South as varied as W. J. Cash (1941) and Lewis Simpson (1983) have described. To bring this denial to individual and collective awareness is a pedagogical priority, as the consequences of this denial include distortions in several psycho-social spheres. These include, but are not limited to, the domains of race, class, and gender. I will review these spheres and suggest the thematic outline of an interdisciplinary public-school curriculum of Southern Studies that might function to both articulate and surpass them.

Every region has its history, of course. Why might studying the history of the South for southerners be more important than studying the history of, say, the Midwest for midwesterners? The reasons are two. One involves the southern history of slavery, segregation, violence, and (relative) poverty. Lewis Simpson pointed out that southerners responded to this legacy by "forgetting" it. Simpson argued that both history and memory were lost in the aftermath of the Civil War and Reconstruction. Like Joel Williamson (1984), Cash argued that southerners retreated from the facts of their history to fictions and fantasies. This phenomenon of denial and flight from reality involves, unsurprisingly, distortions in several spheres, distortions that undermine the South's efforts to develop culturally, even economically.

For such development to occur, the South must avoid efforts to merely "Northernize" it (Clement 1983). The South must experience (multi)cultural reconstruction on its own terms (terms which do involve the North, of course). Reconstruction, however, for those estranged from their own histories, requires a social psychoanalytic process the curricular elements of which I will sketch here. Suffice to say now that the South differs from the Midwest, the West, or New England in its particular history and, perhaps, more important educationally, in its response to that history. Moreover, the power of place as a category of social and individual experience is strong in the South. Students of the South from various disciplines testify to the power of *place* in southern political and literary history. Historian David Potter (1968, 15) once observed:

> It was an aspect of this culture that the relation between land and people remained more direct and more primal in the South than in other parts of the country. (This may be more true for the Negroes than for the Whites, but then there is also a question whether the Negroes have not embodied the distinctive qualities of the Southern character even more than the Whites.)

An intensified relation to place and a psychological denial of the facts of the southern experience underline the appropriateness of attention to southern history. As Potter's remark implies, this history, this place, is a fundamentally African-American place.

II
RACIAL AND SEXED BODIES

One cannot disregard racial and sexed bodies
as the location of historical struggles.
—Ewa Plonowska Ziarek (2001, 16)

[T]he Negro's body was exploited
as amorally as the soil and climate.
—Ralph Ellison (1995, 28)

Racial hatred, then, is carnal hatred. It is sexualized hatred.
—Calvin C. Hernton (1988 [1965], xiii)

Since the slave trade began, Europeans and Europeans in America wondered whether or not the African "species of men" were capable of creating formal literature, could ever master the arts and sciences. If they were capable, Africans could be said to be human in the European sense. If not, they were not, and there could be no substantive objections to the practice of slavery. Determined to discover the answer, several Europeans and Americans undertook pedagogical experiments in which young African slaves were tutored and trained alongside white children, the first integrated schools one might say (Gates 1988; Jordan 1968). As Gates (1988) points out, Phillis Wheatley was just such an experiment.

Wheatley was not alone, however. A Jamaican named Frances Williams took the B.A. degree at Cambridge before 1750. Someone named Jacobus Capitein earned several degrees in Holland; the doctoral degree in philosophy at Halle was conferred upon Wilhelm Amo. Ignatius Sancho, who published a volume of *Letters* in 1782, was also a subject of pedagogical experiments. The published writings of these black men and one woman, who wrote in Latin, Dutch, German, and English, were used both by pro- and antislavery proponents to justify their arguments (Gates 1988).

The European debate over the humanity of the African between 1730 and 1830 was extensive; it would not be until the Harlem Renaissance that the work of black writers would be as scrutinized as it was during the 18th century (Hull 1987; Lewis 1997 [1979]). Phillis Wheatley's reviewers included Voltaire, Thomas Jefferson, George Washington, Samuel Rush, and James Beatty, among others. Francis Williams' work was examined by David Hume and Immanuel Kant. In his *Philosophy of History*, published in 1813, Hegel pointed to the absence of an African literature as the sign of Africans' innate inferiority. The list of participants in this debate amounts to a "Who's Who" of the French, English, and American Enlightenment (Gates 1988).

The publication of Phillis Wheatley's poetry in 1773 marks the birth of the "Afro-American literary tradition" (Gates, quoted in McDowell 1993, 56).

Phyllis Wheatley died poor and malnourished in 1784. Her verse was republished in 1838 by abolitionists eager to prove that black slaves could write poetry, that is, that they were "culturally human" (Christian 1985, 120).

In contrast to the sentimentalized view of American slavery expressed in popular fiction like Margaret Mitchell's *Gone with the Wind*, slave historians debate just how inhuman the system was, on its own terms and compared to other systems of slavery. Stanley Elkins' (1959) controversial study suggested that the racial stereotype of "Sambo"—ignorant, innocent, and loyal—had an empirical basis in the actual experience of slavery. Employing Harry Stack Sullivan's (1965) psychosocial theory of "significant others," Elkins worked to reconstruct a process of mass infantilization, a process of destruction of the slaves' personalities. In Elkins' view, the child-like Sambo represented the mutilated fragment of human personality remaining after the slave system crushed the kidnapped Africans. Elkins likened the American slave system to the Nazi extermination camps of World War II.

While not dissenting from the general view of slavery as bestial, other students of slavery see a more complicated picture. For instance, Eugene Genovese criticized the "onesidedness" of Elkins' study, calling it deterministic. In reducing all aspects of slave life to the mass infantilization model and the concentration camp parallel, Elkins ignored the slaves' struggles to undermine the slaveholders' authority, as well as the slaves' creation of culturally self-affirmative rituals and behaviors. Genovese views slaves and slaveholders as culturally and politically intertwined. So understood, the concept of "South" is a fundamentally black as well as white concept (Genovese 1968).

Also emphasizing the slaves' capacity for rebellion, Wilmore (1983) contests the conventional view of Christianity as politically emasculating. Instead, Wilmore suggests, Christianity played a central role in slave rebellion. He traces recent expressions of African-American radicalism to these rebellions. In particular, many 19th-century black women were inspired by their religious experience to teach and preach and agitate against seemingly overwhelming odds, as the cases of Ida B. Wells, Sojourner Truth, and Anna Julia Cooper, among others, testify. However, at least one historian of the civil rights movement believes that historians have exaggerated the importance of the black church in racial politics (see Fairclough 1999, 71).

By reducing slaves to their bodies—that was their economic as well as sexual value—whites blurred the boundaries between themselves and those they exploited. By forcing slaves to act "happy" and by pretending that slaves were part of the family, by taking the black body as property to be used at will, whites erased black suffering as they inflated white pleasure (Hartman 1997). In so doing, the "whiteness" became invisible (it was "reality") and the white male body disappeared into imagined black ones. Part of the task of antiracist antisexist education is to return white men to themselves so that they might in fact "hear" when the subaltern speaks.

The extent to which slavery was a moral issue in the political crisis that became the Civil War (or the Southern War for Independence, as more than one southern writer has characterized it), has been debated extensively in the scholarly literature. Not surprisingly, southern historians tend to view the issue as primarily political, involving in a central way the issue of "states rights" (Cooper 1978). Whereas the moral issue was paramount for the abolitionists, Lincoln and others used the slavery issue as a political and, during the War, military lever. Furthermore, it is clear that the North profited indirectly from slave labor (Genovese 1968). Further undermining the view of the North as morally superior in this conflict is the experience of those escaped slaves who joined the northern army. These soldiers faced humiliating racial prejudice, despite which, by all accounts, many performed bravely.

While there was a legal decommodification accompanying "Emancipation," Robyn Wiegman (1993, 1995) notes, in the white male mind the black body remained firmly fixed, commodified as "body." Indeed, in *The Gender of Racial Politics and Violence in America* I argue that the historical throughline from the Middle Passage to the present is a continuing commodification and de-subjectification of the black body as whites struggle to keep it in its place, a place in the white imaginary (Pinar 2001). As Saidiya V. Hartman (1997) shows, racial subjugation means the white occupation of the black body. That body remains commodified today, if remunerated, as athlete, entertainer, laborer. It remains today a sexualized body.

Like whiteness, the North is invisible to itself, except, perhaps, to imagine itself as morally superior to the South. Episodes like the Trent Lott scandal (December, 2002) confirm northern smugness. But as African Americans' experience in the North suggests, this sense of moral superiority is not warranted. Moreover, as Black and Black (1992) make clear, the South did "rise again," and, in fact, dictates—in collusion with "conservatives" nationwide—those national policies all Americans must follow. In mass culture in the South there remains an aggressive defensiveness regarding race, including a denial of guilt and responsibility for enslavement and consequent segregation, disenfranchisement, prejudice, and violence, including white male rape of black female slaves and that other form of sexualized racial violence known as lynching.

III
"AMERICA'S NATIONAL CRIME"
—WELLS-BARNETT (1977 [1901], 30)

*[T]he atrocity of lynching has left an indelible
mark on American life.*
—W. Fitzhugh Brundage (1993, 259)

Is not the lynching of the Negro a sexual revenge?
—Frantz Fanon (1967, 159)

[C]astration is also an inverted sexual encounter
between black men and white men.
—Robyn Wiegman (1993, 458 n.)

Between 1882 and 1927, an estimated 4,900 persons—nearly all the victims were young black men—were lynched in the United States, although other estimates, including the Tuskegee Institute archival records, place the number slightly lower (Brown 1975; Hall 1979, 141; Harris 1984; Zangrando 1980, 4). James Elbert Cutler (1905) estimated that 3,837 human beings were lynched between 1882 and 1903. Contemporary sociologists Stewart Tolnay and E. M. Beck (1995) limit their estimates to the "lynching era," encompassing the five decades between the end of Reconstruction and the beginning of the Great Depression, 1882 through 1930. During these years they estimate that there were 2,108 separate incidents of lynching in which at least 2,462 African-American men, women, and children met their deaths at the hands of white men. Approximately 14% of the 2,018 black lynching incidents involved more than one victim.

Of the 2,462 black victims Tolnay and Beck count, 3% (74) were female. Tolnay and Beck assert that there are no "hard data" for the 5-year period between 1877 and 1881, or for the Reconstruction period from 1865 to 1877, even though there were certainly black lynchings before 1882, especially during the early period of Reconstruction. George C. Wright (1990) agrees; he argues that more lynchings occurred in the 15-year period from 1865 to 1880 than during any other 15-year period, even the years from 1885 to 1900, which most scholars and contemporary observers characterize as the zenith of lynching. Perhaps it is this knowledge upon which former slave and antilynching activist Ida B. Wells relies when she estimates more than 10,000 black lives were lost to "rope and faggot" (see White 1929).

Lynching statistics are not comprehensive, of course, as they report only recorded lynchings. Estimates of the number of prevented lynchings range from 648 during the years 1915–1932 (Raper's [1933] estimate) to 762 for the 1915–1942 period (Jessie Daniel Ames' [1942]—see Hall 1979). Although the exact number is not known, these figures suggest that between one-half and two-thirds of threatened lynchings failed, usually due to the active intervention of the authorities (Griffin, Clark, and Sandberg 1997). When one takes into account how many lynchings were prevented, one can only guess how widespread the practice of lynching actually was (Zangrando 1980).

In the popular imagination, lynching was a response to black male rape of white women. On occasion black men did assault white women, but, as Robert Zangrando (1980, 4) points out, "neither that nor the greater frequency of rape and sexual harassment inflicted on black women by white and black men accounted for mob violence." The gendered and specifically queer character of the practice is suggested in Hazel Carby's (1998, 76) lyrical and lingering question:

> We must ask if the ritual of dismemberment and sadistic torture of black bodies is, in fact, a search to expose, and perhaps an attempt to claim, an essence of manhood that is both feared and desired, an essence of the possible which escapes its pursers as the blood pours from their hands and soaks the earth.

Although they constituted a minority of all lynchings, some victims were lynched for even the most trivial "violations," including breaches of conduct such as "insulting a white woman," "grave robbing," or "running a bordello" (Tolnay and Beck 1995, 103). Young black men were lynched for any reason at all, including "for just acting troublesome" (Zangrando 1980, 4). The fact that most victims were tortured "suggests the presence of sadistic tendencies among the lynchers" (Raper 1969 [1933], 1). Indeed, over the history of the phenomenon, "lynching . . . seems to have become increasingly sadistic: emasculation, torture, and burning alive replaced the hangman's noose" (Hall 1979, 133). As the nationwide campaign to end the practice intensified, lynchings were slowly replaced by "legal lynchings," a phrase used to describe the mockery of the American judicial system that enabled whites to murder blacks "legally." Nearly all scholars acknowledge that only rarely—if indeed ever—did African Americans receive fair trials, especially in the South (Wright 1990).

Walter White (1929) notes that the rape myth apparently did not exist before 1830. Given that the first slaves were brought to North America in 1619, for more than two centuries charges of rape against African Americans were virtually unknown. White (1929, 88–89) emphasizes economic motives for lynching, commenting that "such accusations [of rape] were made only after a defective economic system had been upturned and made enormously profitable through inventions and in doing so had caused slave-labor to become enormously more valuable." Some 40 years earlier, after the lynching of three businessmen, Ida B. Wells had perceived that economic motives were at work: "[t]hey [the three lynched men] had committed no crime against white women. This is what opened my eyes to what lynching really was. An excuse to get rid of Negroes who were acquiring wealth and property and thus keep the race terrorized and 'keep the nigger down' " (Wells 1970, 64). No doubt economic motives were at work, but there were other motives at work as well.

What was a typical lynching like? As Fitzhugh Brundage (1993) points out, there was no "typical" lynching. Sociologists Tolnay and Beck (1995, 23) report: "Although most lynchings were straightforward, albeit illegal, executions with little ceremony or celebration, many went far beyond a mere taking of a human life. At times lynchings acquired a macabre, carnival-like aspect, with the victim being tortured and mutilated for the amusement of onlookers." While not in fact, there was a *typical* lynching in fiction, in the white male imagination, and not infrequently, this fiction became fact (see Baldwin 1998 [1965]; Harris 1984; Wiegman 1993, 1995).

After a precipitating event occurred (murder was the most common, but anything could be a pretext for violence, including nothing at all), white men assembled, determined to take revenge. Whether the "crime" was imaginary or real did not matter; a "guilty party"—usually a young black man—was "identified," and the "manhunt" was on. Once captured, public notices were circulated usually a day or two in advance of the lynching event itself. Sometimes the notices were distributed to distant communities. Sometimes trains made special trips, adding extra cars to meet the demands of crowds wishing to travel in order to watch the spectacle (Harris 1984). (Anna Julia Cooper [quoted in Lemert and Bhan 1998, 210] recalls: "Excursion trains with banners flying were run into place and eager children were heard to exclaim: 'We have seen a hanging, we are now going to see a burning!' ")

The number of spectators on one occasion reached 15,000. The lynching itself was sometimes preceded by hours of physical torture and sexual mutilation, often climaxed by what whites euphemistically called "surgery below the belt." Those parts of the victim's body that had been dismembered were sometimes photographed for picture postcards, later to be sold as souvenirs. The remains were usually burned. The leaders of lynchings were often well-known and seen by thousands. But nearly everyone, including law enforcement officers, participated in a conspiracy of silence; invariably the coroner would declare that the lynching was committed by unknown persons (Brown 1975; Bulhan 1985; Harris 1984).

Lynching reverberates throughout American culture today, faintly but unmistakably. In January 2000 more than 60 photographs of lynchings as well as antilynching pamphlets and newspaper reports went on display at the Roth Horowitz gallery on the Upper East Side of Manhattan. Part of the permanent Allen-Littlefield collection at Emory University in Atlanta, these photographs depict charred corpses which were mailed in the thousands as mementos and sometimes as warnings. Not until 1908 did the postmaster general of the United States forbid the mailing of such material.

The American public was reminded of lynching some 10 years ago during the confirmation hearings of Clarence Thomas. That drama was reported live over network television, cable, and radio between October 11 and October 13, 1991, reaching an estimated 27 million homes, or 80% of the television viewing audience. The hearings and their aftermath were widely debated in the popular and academic press (Bystrom 1996; Roper, Chanslor, and Bystrom 1996; see Ragan, Bystrom, Kaid, and Beck 1996). The testimony of Anita Hill challenged Thomas' claim to be qualified to serve as Supreme

Court Justice. Many agreed that the turning point in the proceedings occurred when Thomas likened the hearings to a "high-tech lynching." More than any other statement, that image was pivotal in reversing perceptions of who was on trial and what the trial/hearings themselves were about (Wood 1996).

In March 1996, a black rapper known as Wise Intelligent produced a CD entitled "Killin' U for Fun." On the back cover was a photograph of a charred body, collapsed over a mound of coals, with a group of white men and boys in the background, some of them smiling and laughing. The image was so haunting and horrible that the *Washington Post* printed it, along with a short description of the lynching, which occurred in Coatesville, Pennsylvania, in 1911, near the Worth Brothers Steel Company. "It's a black man being burned on the stake, crucified," Wise Intelligent told the *Post*. "And there's the Establishment looking on, loving the destruction of the black man in this picture" (quoted in Worth 1998, 65).

To Robert Worth (1998, 65) this was no faint historical echo: "I read those words with a jolt of recognition because my great-grandfather owned and ran the steel mills that employed the victim and many of the men who burned him to death. The extended Worth family still lives indirectly on the profits from those mills, but few of us knew anything about the lynching." Thirty or forty years ago, Worth reflects, there might have been some public political point in acknowledging that the Coatesville lynching was an act of barbarism. "By the time I came of age in the 1980s," he continues, "that rhetoric had begun to sound forced. After reading through the grand-jury documents and the old newspaper coverage of the lynching, I couldn't avoid the feeling that an apology . . . no matter how eloquent, would no longer mean much" (Worth 1998, 76).

Perhaps not. But by remembering we can see through layers of scar tissue that deform not just the skin but the entire body of the American nation. Why recall such *unpleasant* material? The answer, of course, has to do with memory. Those of us committed to antiracist education accept Jane Flax's (1987, 106) affirmation that " 'new' memory" is "a powerful impulse toward political action."

Still a fundamental "American dilemma" today, racism requires political and pedagogical action. "The reason we remember the past at all," Maxine Hong Kingston pointed out in an interview, "is that our present-day life is still a working-out of a similar situation"; to "understand the past changes the present. And the ever-evolving present changes the significance of the past" (in Rabinowitz 1987, 179). Toni Morrison too has spoken of the "ways in which the past influences today and tomorrow" (quoted in the *Los Angeles Times*, October 14, 1987); she has referred to her writing in general as a way of "sorting out the past," of identifying "those things in the past that are useful and those things that are not" (Le Clair 1981, 75–76).

To understand white racism today, we must deliberately work to remember precisely that which we feel compelled to forget, to force our repression to fail, to engender regression. We must return to lynching, that "peculiar" form of vigilante law, social control, and gendered violence that reached its zenith during the last decade of the 19th century, a decade of gendered, political, and economic crisis. Often sexualized violence, lynching was a mangled form of interracial homosexual rape, rationalized by a white male fantasy of interracial heterosexual rape. Lynching was parallel to white men's rape of black women (see Pinar 2001).

IV
WHITE TRASH: CLASS IN THE SOUTH

The terrorization of black men, the abuse of white women of the lower classes, and the conflation of politics and sex were interlocking elements in the broader sexualization of politics in the Reconstruction South.
—Martha Hodes (1993, 412)

[T]he poor reputations of a certain class of white women render[s] their rape a lesser crime even if their rapists are black.
—Susan Brownmiller (1993 [1975], 221)

This obsession of dependency is what makes white Americans, in general, the sickest and certainly the most dangerous people, of any color, to be found in the world today.
—James Baldwin (1985, 478)

The myth of a southern aristocracy is just that. As Cash (1941) and others have pointed out, a true aristocracy does not choose to travel an immense ocean and settle a primitive frontier. Those who came to the South sought economic opportunity and escape. The immigrants' creation of slavery and plantation life was hardly an extension of a genteel life lived in Europe. Relatively few in number, the early plantation owners were often "rough and ready types" whose capacity for alcohol consumption and violence was enormous. (Historically, levels of violence have tended to be higher in the South than in any region [see Ayers 1984].)

Many more whites were "yeomen," small landowners with fewer than five slaves or with no slaves at all. The profound class difference between these yeomen and the planter class was obscured by the presence of black slaves who provided a permanent class "floor" to southern white society. As well, the personalism of an agrarian culture in which many inhabitants of a particular county or parish were indeed members of the same extended family, numbed working and poor whites to the sharp social and economic inequities the political economy of slavery (and the post-Emancipation systems of sharecropping and convict-leasing) guaranteed (Ayers 1984). Within slavery, house slaves tended to assume superior class positions to those who worked the land. Some evidence suggests the former class formed the beginnings of the African-American bourgeoisie (Genovese 1964).

Despite white fantasies of interracial sex, such occasions were rare and usually class-linked. Certainly no white women in the planter class were imagined as desiring black men. But white men did imagine that lower class white women tended toward a certain sexual depravity, quite capable of illicit liaisons, including unthinkable (for "respectable" white southerners) liaisons with black men. Indeed, white male fantasies regarding lower class female sexuality were as strong as their obsession over black male sexuality (Hodes 1993).

Class played a role in the practice of lynching. For some white southerners, the experience of the mob crystallized a sense of group belonging, especially for poor, socially fragmented whites; it provided a "safe" outlet for the diffuse but intense frustrations that could not be readily expressed against those responsible, namely other whites more highly placed in the socioeconomic and political hierarchy. For rich whites, lynching not only enacted, in dramatic fashion, the racism of the region but provided a means of deflecting lower class white anger away from them. In death as well as life, blacks remained central to the psychological, economic, and political life of whites (Zangrando 1980).

Stewart E. Tolnay and E. M. Beck (1995) employ Bonacich's (1972, 1975) division of rural postbellum southern white society into three major classes: the dominating white planters and employers; a class of white day laborers, sharecroppers, and tenants; and a class of black landless workers. Planters and employers were dependent on the cheap labor that subjugated and exploited African Americans provided, but poor white laborers were threatened by the competition from the cheaper black labor force. Although the economic interests of the two classes of whites diverged in many important respects, Tolnay and Beck (1995) speculate that periods of economic stress may have created a potential for convergence, at least as expressed in racial violence. When cotton profits were low or nonexistent, whites across class may have resorted to intensified racial hostility and mob violence (Tolnay and Beck 1995).

There were times when the white elite benefited from intensified racial antagonism and the violence that expressed it. These were times when elite whites worried over a possible coalition between black and white labor. Such a coalition was perhaps the greatest threat to the social, economic, and political hegemony that the southern white elite enjoyed, as the Populists would discover in the early 1890s. Antagonism and rivalry between black and white men served the interest of the white elite, who on more than a few occasions acted to create conflict between black and white laborers. Tolnay and Beck (1995) quote Raper (1933) on this point: "Lynchings tend to minimize social and class distinctions between white plantation owners and white tenants" (47). They quote Shapiro (1988) as well: "When those committed to racial subordination saw the possibility of blacks and whites coming together for common purposes, their responses most often was to reach for the gun and the rope" (219). The threat of coalition between black and white laborers seemed most real, Tolnay and Beck conclude, when cotton prices were under stress.

Class may have been at work in the composition of some lynching mobs. Social psychologist Roger Brown (1965) reminds that scholars have distinguished between "Bourbon" (Cantril 1941) or "vigilante" (Myrdal 1962 [1944]) lynchings. In vigilante or mob lynching (Myrdal 1962 [1944]), there was little concern with the guilt of the victim; the innocent were not protected, and the leaders were not exactly "respectable" citizens. The Bourbon lynching was led by leading citizens with the knowledge of law enforcement officers and other community leaders. Their objective, presumably, was the punishment of a specific crime, and, also presumably, there typically was some interest in establishing the guilt of the accused, and innocent black men were even sometimes protected (Cantril 1941).

The Bourbon lynching was planned and "orderly" and at times so "institutionalized" that Roger Brown (1965) was not sure it belongs in his discussion of collective behavior. In its orderliness and community support such lynchings were directly linked to the lynching practices of Revolutionary and frontier days (which were not racialized and did not often result in death). I suspect there is some classism at work in this distinction, and that relatively few lynchings could be so neatly categorized. Historian Joel Williamson (1984) suggests that upper-class southern whites were eager to portray lynching as a lower class phenomenon. Were Bourbon lynchings always orderly and crime-specific authorized by community-support? In what sense could any lynching seem "reasonable"?

The truth is that, regardless of class, there was an element of unpredictability in whites' reactions to alleged black crime. For reasons that are not clear, whites did not interpret every attack by an African American as a provocation for lynching. But even trivial confrontations between white law officers and blacks were volatile, a fact that became clear to all Americans during the 1960s, when southern police officers often responded brutally to black protest, events captured on TV. Even when an African American defended him- or herself, not to mention challenged or attacked an abusive policeman—"the caretaker of the color line and defender of the caste system" (quoted in Brundage 1993, 76)—a violent response was forthcoming. Perhaps only the rape of a white woman by a black man could match the power of black disrespect toward white policemen to mobilize whites into lynching mobs. Certainly during (but also beyond) the 1960s in many areas of the

South, police brutality enjoyed a degree of (white) community sanction that mob violence no longer could summon (Brundage 1993).

While too many African Americans remain in the underclass in the South today, some upward mobility is visible. Despite progress, still noticeably absent in the South are the assertiveness and willingness to contest racism observable among some African-American citizens living in the North. Southern African Americans know that southern whites fought and died to keep them enslaved, then devised systems of segregation and fought violently to retain them. Northern African Americans know that the nonracist claims of northern whites are often just pretense, and understandably respond to them with indignation. In both instances, white antagonism is related not only to racism but also to perceived economic competition, increased by federal antidiscrimination legislation and long-term contraction in the manufacturing and industrial sectors.

In the South, there is a persisting issue of class, intertwined as it is with race. Condemned by many whites to a permanent underclass status due to "race," African Americans' economic and cultural emergence undermines the white-defined class structure of the South. Poor whites have allowed their racial prejudice to keep them politically complacent. No matter how poor whites are, their view is that there remains a class underneath them, a fantasy exploited by ex-Ku Klux Klansmen David Duke in his bid for the U.S. Senate and Governor's office in Louisiana in 1988 and 1990, respectively. William Faulkner (1946) portrayed in powerful ways the self-destructiveness of the southern racial and class system for poor and working whites, as well as for African Americans.

V
WHITE LADIES AND BLACK WOMEN

*[H]ow do we integrate the study of gender within the
framing of racialized culture?*
—Sandra Gunning (1996, 141)

*[B]ourgeois sexuality and racialized sexuality [are] not ... distinct
kinds ... but ... dependent constructs in a unified field.*
—Ann Laura Stoler (1995, 97)

*[T]here is an automatic and natural patriarchal alliance among
men (of different classes and cultures) against women.*
—Mervat Hatem (1986, 252)

As the previous sections suggest, the domains of race, class, gender converge and conflate in southern culture and history. Nowhere is that more obvious than in the social construction of the southern (white) "lady." The socially constructed character of the role was precisely what southerners denied, insisting that "good breeding" was the only cause (and consequence) of this peculiarly southern accomplishment. As Drew Gilpin Faust (1996) observed, "lady" denoted both whiteness and class privilege as well as gendered refinement. Moreover, a lady's elite status required the existence of "gentlemen," as well as slaves, black men and women whose daily labor and suffering propped up white delusions of gentility, exclusivity, and civilization (Faust 1996).

During the Civil War, as Faust's superb study makes clear, this construction was contested by circumstances. Before the war there had been few occupations that "respectable" women could enter and remain respectable. Such vocations as teaching or shop-keeping, considered suitable for middle-class women in the North, had remained in the South the almost exclusive domain of men (Stowe 1987). The Civil War changed all that, and as women suddenly began to perform jobs only men had performed before, southerners across the Confederacy remarked on the phenomenon with curiosity, even amazement. In 1862 Lila Chunn of Georgia alluded to the development as part of the news from home in a letter to her husband, Willie, stationed at the front:

> Ladies keep the stores here now . . . their husbands having joined the army. It looks funny in Dixie to see a lady behind the counter, but it would be natural if we were in Yankeedom as it has always [been] the custom there, a custom however I do not like. The idea of a lady having to face and transact business with any and everybody. It is alone suited to the North[ern] women of brazen faces. But I say if it's necessary, our ladies ought to shopkeep and do everything else they can to aid in the great struggle for Liberty. (quoted in Faust 1996, 81)

One of the first professions to which women turned was teaching, a vocation that has seemed to many to parallel women's traditional responsibilities as mothers. In the North, a "feminization of teaching" was well underway, but the ante-bellum South had not yet encouraged women to enter classrooms (Grumet 1988). In North Carolina in 1860, for instance, only 7% of teachers were women. During the war, however, this percentage changed significantly, until by 1865 there were as many female as male teachers in the state (Faust 1996).

When New Orleans—the South's largest city—fell to Union forces in April 1862, Major General Benjamin Butler took on the challenging task of governing a furiously unfriendly civilian population. Not exactly ready to play the role of the defeated and submissive, the residents of New Orleans declined to comply with orders from the newly arrived Yankees. They gathered in unruly mobs, threatening the safety of Butler and his troops. Forced to govern by force and threat of force, Butler reluctantly gave up any thought of conciliation. Crowds refusing to disperse were met by Union artillery. Shopkeepers who refused to do business with the occupying troops found their stores seized and sold. A man destroying a Union flag was sentenced to death. Those pastors who declined to pray for the United States were sent North (Faust 1996). "Very soon," Butler recorded, "there was no uncivil treatment received by our soldiers except from the upper class of women" (quoted in Faust 1996, 209).

The ladies of New Orleans took for granted that they could not be treated in the same harsh ways as New Orleans men had been, and so they continued to treat northern soldiers with contempt. The more mild-mannered among them registered their feelings by immediately and sometimes dramatically fleeing churches or streetcars if Union soldiers entered. But others chose to spit in the faces of northern soldiers struggling to be polite; still others did not hesitate to empty chamber pots on the war-weary men. In countless ways subtle and outrageous, the ladies of New Orleans sought to convey their complete contempt for their conquerors. Butler was uncertain what to do in response to these outrages. The perpetrators were often young, even "pretty and interesting" he noted, frequently socially prominent, the class of ladies who, if treated badly, would immediately become martyrs (Faust 1996). Even so, Butler knew he had to do something, for "a city could hardly be said to be under good government where such things were permitted" (quoted phrases in Faust 1996, 209).

On May 15, Butler issued the infamous General Order No. 28, what Faust (1996, 209) characterizes as "an astute invocation of prevailing assumptions about class and gender" designed to force the ladies of New Orleans to stop their hostilities:

General Order No. 28

As the officers and solders of the United States have been subject to repeated insults from the women (calling themselves ladies) of New Orleans . . . it is ordered that hereafter when any female shall, by word, gesture, or movement, insult or show contempt for any officer or soldier of the United States, she shall be regarded and held liable to be treated as a woman of the town plying her avocation. (quoted in Faust 1996, 209)

Butler's order shrewdly exploited the ambiguities in white southern women's identities, Faust notes. "By their behavior shall ye know them," he was saying, not by their categorical pretensions to the privileges and shelters of ladyhood. Those women who acted with the vulgarity of prostitutes would be treated as if they were prostitutes; if they showed no sign of appropriate feminine delicacy and self-restraint, they would see no sign of that masculine protection men accorded true ladies. Unlike many other northern commanders, Butler was determined not to be manipulated by southern ladies' simultaneous use and abuse of their feminine status. "I did not carry on war with rose-water," he recorded. Butler rightly predicted that almost all the ladies of New Orleans would want to cling to the title of "lady," and would therefore conform to the day-to-day conduct of civility he wished. The idea that one might be treated as a "woman of the town" was so intolerable, the threatened loss of status so unimaginable, that no Yankee officer ever had to enforce the measure (Faust 1996). As Butler had predicted, the order "executed itself." Horrified at the prospect of being identified as whores, the ladies of New Orleans immediately resumed being "ladies" (quoted passages in Faust 1996, 209–210).

The ladies of New Orleans may have been tamed, but "chivalrous" men, south and north, were outraged by the news. Not only the southern press described him in less-than-human terms—a "beast" was not an uncommon descriptor applied to the Union officer—even the *New York Times* criticized him. In London, both the press and Parliament were contemptuous of Butler's "intolerable brutality" (quoted phrases in Faust 1996, 210). These criticisms took their toll. After facing additional difficulty in subduing the locals, combined with crises regarding the rights of foreign nationals in the city, Butler was replaced in December 1862 by Nathaniel Banks. Instructed to conduct a more conciliatory administration of the troublesome city, Banks was immediately challenged by residents who decoded his generosity as weakness. The ladies of New Orleans once again began to insult northern soldiers and to make public declarations of their Confederate patriotism (Faust 1996).

By the final months of the War many women were expressing their newfound self-interest, sometimes boldly, and, from a Confederate point of view, not very patriotically. Especially middle- and lower-class women—those who experienced the war's deprivations most severely—were not just keeping husbands and brothers at home; they were forbidding them to join the crumbling Confederate army. Other women were actively urging men already serving the Confederacy to desert. The risk of execution and the certainty of shame must have seemed to these women an acceptable price to pay in the face of almost certain injury, if not death, at the front. Desperate Confederate leaders recognized the influence that Confederate women exercised in persuading soldiers to give up the fight. One military officer recommended to the secretary of war that he censor the mails, for, he insisted, "the source of all the present evils of Toryism & desertion in our country is letter writing to . . . the army." As a Confederate official in North Carolina declared, "Desertion takes place because desertion is encouraged. . . . And although the ladies may not be willing to concede the fact, they are nevertheless responsible . . . for the desertion in the army and the dissipation in the country" (quoted passages in Faust 1996, 243). As war-exhausted southern white men fought off complete defeat to the hated Yankees, southern white women were busy making their own contributions to just that conclusion to the lost cause (Faust 1996).

Not only household chores occupied white women after the war. Without slave labor generating wealth, many once wealthy families now struggled to make ends meet, often requiring "ladies" to work outside the home. No longer able to afford considerations of respectability, many turned to teaching. By 1880 the majority of southern schoolteachers would become female for the first time. The necessity for increasing numbers of middle- and upper-class women to find employment prompted southerners to restart the wartime conversation regarding women's education. By the 1890s the president of a southern women's college would observe that nearly a quarter of his graduates now supported themselves. This fact, he explained, moved students to study with far greater earnestness and diligence than had their antebellum predecessors. Several southern state universities introduced coeducation in the 1880s, and women's colleges, such as Sophie Newcomb at Tulane University in 1886, were established to offer women educational opportunities nearly equal to those of men (Faust 1996). By the 1890s a Vanderbilt researcher found that economic necessity had led to the "growing respectability of self support." Few seemed nostalgic about the loss of the ornamental character of antebellum white female life; indeed, one applauded the erosion of prewar beliefs in "the nobility of dependence and helplessness in woman" (quoted passages in Faust 1996, 251).

Black women had no political power after "Emancipation," but that fact did not mean defeat or submission. A black woman who had been born a slave would make the first memorable intervention in the white-male compulsion to mutilate the black male body. That black woman was Ida B. Wells, a Memphis schoolteacher and journalist. Her moral courage, pedagogical brilliance, and political acumen mark her as one of the greatest Americans to have ever lived. Thirty years later, a white woman understood that lynching—presumably a practice conducted for white women's sake—had nothing to do with them: Jesse Daniel Ames (see Hall 1979; Pinar 2001).

A public schoolteacher like Anna Julia Cooper, Ida B. Wells found her true calling in protesting with the pen and she became a militant journalist and antilynching activist. For whites and some black men, Wells was, as Carby (1987) reminds, an "uppity" black woman with a strong analysis of the relations among political terrorism, economic oppression, and conventional codes of sexuality and morality. For Carby (1987, 108), Wells' analysis "has still to be surpassed in its incisive condemnation of the patriarchal manipulation of race and gender." Carby finds the influence of Wells' work in the writing of black women from Pauline Hopkins to June Jordan and Alice Walker who, like Wells, have labored to understand how rape and lynching were used as interlocking tools of political, social, and economic oppression.

The literature of black women at the beginning of the 20th century is, Mary Helen Washington (1987, 73) writes, "a literature frozen into self-consciousness" by the necessity for defending black women and men against those vicious and omnipresent stereotypes that typified 19th-century European-American culture. Minstrel shows, for instance, caricatured African Americans as ignorant, lazy, childlike, cowardly. Plantation literature, written by defeated, embittered proslavery advocates, created the stereotypes of the contented slave, the tragic mulatto, the noble savage, the hypersexualized "buck" or whore, the submissive Christian. The "buck" was portrayed as a brutal rapist, the whore as a treacherous mulatto, the submissive Christian in fact as a corrupt politician. Washington (1987, 73) comments:

> While most of these stereotypes were aimed at black men, the most common attack on the image of black women was to portray them as immoral women, licentious and oversexed, whose insatiable appetites were responsible for the bestial nature of the black man. At a time when the popular literature of the day attempted to create for white women an idealized "true woman," chaste and loving, in the center of the sacred trinity of marriage, home, and family, black women were exploited as sexually promiscuous, so base as to be disinclined toward the virtues of true womanhood.

Not 40 years out of an enslavement that denied legal marriage or protection against rape, the black woman, commented Fannie Barrier Williams, was the only woman in American for whom virtue was not an ornament but a necessity. So common was this stereotype, that those black women who wrote fiction felt obligated to defend themselves and black women everywhere against these fantasies (Washington 1987). In her 1897 speech to the Society of Christian Endeavor entitled "The Awakening of the Afro-American Woman," Victoria Earle Matthews expressed her rage at these defamations by the same white men who had instituted slavery to demoralize "this woman who had stood upon the auction block possessed of no rights that a white man was bound to respect, and none which he did respect" (quoted in Washington 1987, 74).

Williams and Matthews expressed outrage at a white patriarchy that first enslaved, then raped black women. Their arguments implied that, having been degraded by slavery, black women could hardly be expected to copy the qualities of virtuousness expected of white women. Speaking before a mostly white Society of Christian Endeavor, Matthews commented on this sense of past disgrace: "What a past was ours! There was no attribute of womanhood which had not been sullied—aye, which had not been despoiled in the crucible of slavery. . . . It had destroyed, more than in men, all that a woman holds sacred, all that ennobles womanhood" (quoted in Washington 1987, 74). Washington (74) comments: "With a race to uplift and every poisonous slander against its women and men used to justify continued oppression, black women race leaders could hardly be expected to reject the ideals set up for 'true womanhood' for what they were: a fanatical method of sexual repression prescribed by white men to oppress and control women."

African-American women are still victimized by white fantasies, often expressed as negative sexual stereotypes. Patricia Collins (1991, 77) argues that the image of the sexually aggressive "Jezebel lie[s] at the heart of black women's oppression" by the dominant culture. Supplementing the image of the Jezebel is the black matriarch, symbol of the "bad black mother" who emasculates black men because she will not permit them to assume roles as black patriarchs (see Collins 1991, 72, 78). Black matriarchs have been held responsible for black men's low educational achievements, inability to earn a living for their families, personality disorders, and delinquency (King 1973; Moynihan 1965). More recently, fantasies of the domineering black matriarch have been expressed into stereotypes of aggressive, career-minded black women. These women are maligned as "egotistical career climbers, better paid, better educated and more socially mobile than [their] male counterparts" (Ransby 1992, 169–170). In her Congressional testimony during the Clarence Thomas confirmation hearings in 1991, Anita Hill was subject to these same stereotypes (Roper, Chanslor, and Bystrom 1996).

The racial chasm between black and white women in the segregated South was a topic Toni Morrison (1971) discussed in a *New York Times Magazine* article. The article was actually about the signs that marked segregated public facilities. "These signs," Morrison (1971) wrote, "were not just arrogant, they were malevolent: 'Whites Only', 'Colored Only', or perhaps just 'Colored', permanently carved into the granite over a drinking fountain." The bathrooms were a special case: "But there was one set of signs that were not malevolent: in fact, rather reassuring in its accuracy and fine distinctions: the pair that said 'White Ladies' and 'Colored Women.' The difference between white and black females seemed to me an eminently satisfactory one" (quoted in Wallace 1990, 164). One is reminded of the San Francisco theater group named "Ladies Against Women."

Sara Evans (1979) records interviews with women who either grew up or studied at college during the time when segregation was enforced between black and white. She describes how many of these women moved from an awareness of injustice against black people to a sense of their own struggle for equality:

> Twice in the history of the United States the struggle for racial equality has been midwife to a feminist movement. In the abolition movement of the 1830s and 1840s, and again the civil rights movement of the 1960s, women experiencing the contradictory expectations and stresses of changing roles began to move from individual discontents to a social movement in their own behalf. Working for racial justice, they gained experience in organizing and in collective action, an ideology that described and condemned oppression analogous to their own, and a belief in human "rights" that could justify them in claiming equality for themselves. In each case, moreover, the complex web of racial and sexual op-

pression embedded in southern culture projected a handful of white southern women into the forefront of those who connected one cause with the other. (24; quoted in Ware 1992, 32)

As the 1960s progressed and the anti-Vietnam War and civil rights movements gained momentum, black and white women working within male-dominated protest groups—among them the Students for a Democratic Society (SDS) and the Student Non-Violent Coordinating Committee (SNCC)—began to express their frustration with their own situation of powerlessness. Many white women experienced this as a discovery of a cause with which they could identify completely: Instead of supporting someone else's struggle against oppression they could fight for themselves (Ware 1992). Sara Evans (1979, 25) stresses that the rebellion by mainly young white women against racism had powerful implications:

Within southern society, "white womanhood" provided a potent cultural symbol that also implied little practical power for women. The necessity of policing the boundaries between black and white heightened the symbolic importance of traditional domestic arrangements: white women in their proper place guaranteed the sanctity of the home and the purity of the white race. As long as they remained "ladies," they represented the domination of white men.

Ellen Willis (1984) recalls how, during the 1960s, she sided with the "feminists" (against the "politicos"), arguing that male supremacy was a systematic form of domination, requiring a revolutionary movement of women to challenge it. "Our model of course was black power—a number of early radical feminists had been civil rights activists." Despite being dismissed by the leftist men as bourgeois and antileft, the majority of feminist women allied themselves with various leftist causes. Ellen Willis writes that "with few exceptions, those of us who first defined radical feminism took for granted that 'radical' implied anti-racist, anti-capitalist, and anti-imperialist. We saw ourselves as expanding the definition of radical to include feminism" (93; quoted in Ware 1992, 33).

Leslie Cagan remembers that she felt "torn apart" by the distinction between "politicos" and "feminists." Although she was quickly caught up in the early women's groups and was committed to the idea of feminism, her involvement in other political struggles made it hard for her to jump one way or the other:

At the same time, deep in my heart of hearts I felt that we couldn't separate ourselves totally. We had to deal with the fact that Panthers were being shot down, we couldn't ignore the war in Vietnam. I didn't know how to do it, how to pull it together. So I felt and acted as if I were several different people all at once; I was an anti-war activist; I was a Panther support person; I was a feminist and my women's groups had the biggest impact on me. (quoted in Ware 1992, 33)

For Cagan, the problem in 1968 was to remain in both camps without feeling rejected by either one. Active involvement with other liberation movements in the following months taught her the importance of combining a feminist perspective with an internationalist and leftist one. She describes a particular incident which for her illustrated the significance of "organic" connections among protest movements.

In 1970 Cagan was one of a group of white women who campaigned to raise bail money for Joan Bird, a 19-year-old student nurse who had been arrested with 20 other members of the Black Panther Party on a false charge of conspiracy. For the women in the campaign, the issue was both that she was a woman and that she was an activist with the Black Panthers fighting racism; they wanted to stress those facts in the campaign literature. At that time many men did not believe that women's issues were legitimate parts of political struggle and the women were worried that their support for Bird would not be accepted by the Panthers (Ware 1992). To their surprise, they were greeted with "a beginning of what seemed like mutual respect. We weren't just coming as some sort of guilty white people who wanted to help the poor Panthers. We were saying that we had a struggle too and we thought there was some way to connect the two" (in Cluster 1979, 244–245; in Ware 1992, 34).

VI
COMPLICATED EYES

For southern men, defeat meant a kind of gendered humiliation—
the southern gentlemen was discredited as a "real man."
—Michael Kimmel (1996, 77)

After slavery ended, black men were constructed as feminine by
white supremacist rhetoric that insisted on depicting the black
male as symbolically castrated, a female eunuch. In resistance
to this construction, black males cultivated and embraced
the hypermasculine image.
—bell hooks (1994, 131)

The black male body, hypersexualized and criminalized, as always
functioned as a crucial and heavily overdetermined metaphor
in an evolving national discourse on the nature of an
multiethnic, multiracial American society.
—Sandra Gunning (1996, 3)

The Civil War experience of southern white women left many with profound doubts about themselves and their men. The structure of ante-bellum sex roles became unraveled in the absence of white men, but the opportunities— in teaching, nursing, plantation management—left white women questioning the desirability of such freedom and autonomy. It was hard work and many southern women felt they had failed to achieve what they might have. But the bittersweet taste of war-time independence persuaded few to go back, even if they could have, to being gendered ornaments in a male world. In that world they had traded public freedom for male protection; the war taught they could no longer rely on their men for such protection. Their men had failed. Still, they were the only men they had, and so in 1865 they cast their lot with them once again. This complicated and ambivalent result of the War would influence southern assertions of female power in the late 19th and 20th centuries (Faust 1996). As Faust (1996) points out, the "burden of southern history" (Woodward 1960) is also a peculiarly gendered, specifically women's, burden.

The determination and optimism that characterized the movement for women's rights elsewhere was not discernible in the South. Many southern women active as leaders in the southern suffrage movement, for instance, expressed a disdain for men and a need to defend the interests of women and children that can only be understood by remembering their wartime experience. As Faust (1996, 256–257) observes:

> Invented from necessity and born of disappointment and desperation, southern female assertiveness grew from different roots than that of their northern sisters. The appeal, the character, and the extent of southern feminism has been shaped by women's sense of their own limitations. Southern women, like their men, had learned to think of success as elusive; their own experience made it difficult for them to identify with the confidence of Susan B. Anthony's much quoted rallying cry, "Failure is impossible."

In this experience, then, is the origin of feminism's very limited appeal in the South, even into the present time, and with a southern popular wisdom that takes for granted a paradox of strength and frailty in white southern women. The pathway, as Faust (1996, 257) puts it, "from Altars of Sacrifice to Steel Magnolias" requires further research, but thanks to her research, and that of other women historians, it is clear that the Civil War left a mark upon southern women, a distinctive and complex mark that remains discernible even today (Faust 1996).

The Civil War left marks of contradiction and ambivalence upon southern white women; it devastated southern white men. Many returned home wounded, many missing limbs, all crushed by the utter destruction, yes of the landscape, of their homes and cities, but crushed too by the destruction of their dreams of independence and autonomy. These latter dreams were civic and political dreams, but they were, as Faust points out, gendered dreams as well. For in men's eyes, the fortunes of war were very much dependent upon the virility of one's manhood. The battles of the Civil War had demonstrated not only northern military superiority, but northern superiority as men as well. "Johnny Reb" had been sure he was twice the man any "damned Yankee" pretended to be—why the latter's inability to control his women was proof of that. Those northern "poofs" would be put in their place in short order, my darling. And that "darling" was the other object of the white man's gaze: He must demonstrate his manhood not just to the Yankees, to his friends and to himself, he must demonstrate it to his wife, mother, and daughters. He would uphold the ante-bellum promise of protection in return for the masculine presumption of superiority. When the Confederacy lay in ruins in 1865, it was most literally and blatantly a military defeat, but it was less obviously but perhaps equally profoundly a gendered defeat. Michael Kimmel (1996, 77–78) summarizes:

> Southern soldiers returned to a barren and broken land of untilled farms, broken machinery, gutted and burned buildings, and a valueless currency. Schools, banks, and businesses were closed, unemployment was high, and inflation crippling. For the rest of the century and well into the twentieth century, southern manhood would continually attempt to assert itself against debilitating conditions, northern invaders (from carpetbaggers to civil rights workers), and newly freed blacks. The southern rebel, waving the Confederate flag at collegiate football games, is perhaps his most recent incarnation.

The southern white man, if alive, was shattered, often physically, always, I suspect, psychologically. That shattered self was a gendered self, and it was his manhood that had also been the casualty in his inability to establish his independence and defeat those "poofs" from the North. The image of the President of the Confederacy trying to flee in women's clothes delighted northern men—who in their victory felt ever so much more manly—and further crushed southern white men. By the Victorian period that distinctive southern version of manliness evident in studies of the ante-bellum era had become increasingly unacceptable and had begun to fade (Hughes 1990).

It is clear from Faust's compelling study that, at war's end, southern white women faced their husbands, brothers, and sons with complicated eyes. There must have been thrilled tears at the return of those one loved. But there must have been, maybe only for a moment, in the corner of that eye, disappointment, even resentment, a look southern men had never seen—or noticed—before. It was a look that felt strange, but more than strange, less accommodating, less respectful, less admiring, perhaps even slightly chilly. Southern white men had placed their ladies on pedestals, but when they had looked at them with the pride of possession, they were not looking up, but down. For if their gender subordinates were well placed, they (the white gentlemen of the South) were even higher, and their fall—at the hands of Yankee men—was all the greater. No wonder this self-shattering trauma lasted, in political terms, for only a year or two, before the support of women and the attempt by the North to "reconstruct" the South in American not Confederate terms swelled the southern phallus once again. He would rise again, the South would rise again, the Yankees would be chased away.

How did southern white women and men regard the freed people, those whose slave labor had made white southern wealth possible, whose subjugated bodies had been, against their will, sexually as well as economically exploited? Feeling betrayed by their husbands' inability to perform their manly responsibility to protect and provide for them after the Civil War, many southern white women may have displaced their anger onto black men, as Gail Bederman (1995) suggests. By colluding with white men in the fantasy of the black male rapist, white women expressed their contempt for their husbands' failure to perform their manly responsibilities while at the same time making common cause with white men over the issue of racial privilege (Bederman 1995; Faust 1996; Whites 1992).

Historical throughlines are discernible today. In behavior and in musculature, southern men and women exhibit more masculinized and feminized characteristics respectively, than do many in the North. Stylized versions of masculinity and femininity, while hardly restricted to the South, did accompany the slave system and plantation life. The myth of the (white) southern woman can be traced to these developments—highly feminized, vulnerable yet resourceful, always the lady—as can the myth of the (white) southern man—masculine, invulnerable, masterful, always the gentleman. The plantation owner so mythologized "his lady" (the myth of purity implies sexual inaccessibility) that he turned regularly to African-American slave women (and, sometimes, men) to satisfy his often violent desires. His fear that many African-American men schemed to rape white women was untrue, a fantasy, in which the former's presumed sexual prowess was threatening to the masculinity of the latter (Williamson 1984). There was a powerful homoeroticism at work here, because it was denied, was projected onto white women. As Freud postulated, paranoia can be inverted desire (Pinar 2001).

If gender binaries are associated with specific historical periods and forms of economic production (Pinar 1994), then the South's agrarian past and present, the relative recentness of industrialization and corporatization, make intelligible contemporary gender patterns in the South. While relatively hypermasculinized and feminized, they are mediated by the mass culture industry, wherein some sexual ambiguity and somewhat altered gender relations are regularly presented. Thus the present situation, while overtly layered with antiquated gender forms, is approaching greater fluidity but not instability. This is suggested in the South's reactionary gender politics, including a virulent homophobia. As Elisabeth Young-Bruehl (1996, 317) appreciates: "Hypermasculine and hyperfeminine behaviors designed to forge an identity have as their corollaries prejudice against homosexuals, who represent the feared possibility."

Articulations of gender, and in particular articulations of the status of women in the South, become more urgent, while institutional support for such work, say in women's and gender studies programs, remains woefully inadequate. This willful inadequacy of response originates not only in the ignorance of gender, that is, in its taken-for-grantedness, but also in willful efforts to conserve "traditional" gender arrangements. As well, the South's tendency toward reactionary gender politics resides in the particular ways that gender and family configurations in the South resisted institutionalization generally (Genovese 1968). To this issue we turn next.

VII
SEPARATE SPHERES: PRIVATE SPACE
AND THE PUBLIC DOMAIN

*[T]he fetishization of the black male body as the object of a
white mob's fury divorced the notion of blackness
from any association with domesticity.*
—Sandra Gunning (1996, 78)

*Although the domestic or separate spheres ideology defined women
and men as well as the home and marketplace oppositionally,
these antipodes were actually less distinct.*
—Carolyn A. Haynes (1998, 91)

*The geography of protest plainly identifies the Deep
South as the core of the white revolt.*
—Earl Black and Merle Black (1992, 172)

Few would dispute the observation that the public domain remains underdeveloped in the South, with attendant underdevelopment of the constituent institutional forms of that domain, including public education. This retreat from the public sphere, while perhaps national and historic (see Lasch 1978, 1984), has specific antecedents in the South. In the 19th century, the "separate-spheres" ideology was certainly gendered, as (white) women were to remain home caring for children while men engaged other men in the public sphere. But these separate spheres were not only gendered; they were racialized as well. Black men were disenfranchised and all African Americans were relegated—in the Jim Crow South—to separate and unequal spaces in the public sphere, including schools.

The plantation system was pre-capitalistic (although it participated in capitalism) and pre-bourgeois in class structure. The social structure of three centuries of slavery are summarized by Gilberto Freyre (1963), who characterized the power of planters as feudalistic and patriarchal, unrestricted by civil law. The plantation owners owned all: wives, children, and slaves. They established the laws of everyday life, and in so doing usurped the role of public institutions, including legal ones. Law and its enforcement remained particularized and embodied in the person of the landowner, extending feudal social organization well into the 19th century. The articulation of "states rights" in the southern rationale for secession can be understood as a political expression of patriarchy and its projection into the public sphere (Haynes 1998; Phillips 1963). Indeed, the public sphere was often viewed as an extension of private space.

The Civil War changed all that, severing the public sphere from the private. The divorce between the two is evident, for instance, in wartime New Orleans where, by the end of 1863 (the second year of occupation), it had become clear to the occupying Americans that many whites in New Orleans—where, in 1841, free public schools for white children had been established—dismissed the public schools as "federalized" and thereby no longer suitable for Confederate children. In 1863, a mandate from the headquarters of U.S. General Nathaniel Banks (commander of the Department of the Gulf and successor to Benjamin Butler), required "the singing of National airs in our schools and the inculcation of Union sentiments by the teachers" (quoted in Mitchell 2000, 34). The Confederate response was civil disobedience: Half of the enrolled students were kept home for several days by their parents in protest. By 1864, only 12,511 of the city's 37,665 school-age children attended public schools, while private schools, always important in New Orleans due to its large Catholic population, grew in both size and number (Mitchell 2000).

Rebel "flight" and the politicized character of the city's private schools alarmed the occupation forces and its appointed educational officials. In July 1864, General Banks created a commission to visit the schools to look for evidence of seditious activities, which were, unsurprisingly, widespread. The commission found teachers pledging allegiance to the Confederacy in various ways, including the singing of "Dixie" (Mitchell 2000). Occupation forces responded by insisting on expressions of loyalty to United States. The consequence, Ted Mitchell (2000, 38) observes, was that "schooling, during occupation and reconstruction, became a direct instrument of central state policy." The effect was to render the public school, and to an extent the public sphere, a federalized, and later, racialized sphere, from which white southerners withdrew. W. E. B. Du Bois (1975 [1935], 727; quoted in Mitchell 2000,

39) understood precisely: "Public education for all at public expense was, in the South, a Negro idea."

After the destruction of plantation life in the Civil War, whites recoiled from a public sphere suddenly controlled by African Americans and northerners. The concept of the public school, ante-bellum in origin but introduced on a mass scale during and after Reconstruction, was viewed as antagonistic to southern social organization and to "the southern way of life." That way of life conceived the public sphere as an extension of the private one. No longer controlling the public domain, whites did more than withdraw from it; they both passively and actively resisted its development.

The establishment of schools for the freed people was to continue the unmaking of Confederate loyalties, but the textbooks functioned less to reconstruct the South than to attempt to enslave black subjectivity (Hartman 1997). Despite the racism of textbook writers, however, the very fact of Freedmen's schools established a precedent for the assertion of national interest over the interests of states and localities that would prove instrumental in the mid-20th-century effort to desegregate southern schools and public places. For postbellum southerners and northerners alike, the education of African Americans was decoded as a post-military imposition upon the defeated South by the victorious Union (Mitchell 2000).

As the Freedmen's Bureau was to discover, the South was defeated militarily but not politically. A system of schools that was forced on the South could be maintained only by force, as the bureau superintendent in Louisiana made clear in an 1867 report: "it would be impossible" to sustain schools in "several parishes"; they would simply "not be tolerated and could only be carried on as guarded by United States troops" (quoted in Mitchell 2000, 42). It would take United States troops in the 1950s to desegregate some southern schools.

In New Orleans, where Banks had worked hard to eradicate treasonous conduct from the schools, the return of Confederate sympathizers to power in 1866 brought about an early end to Reconstruction and the near destruction of the city's school system. Testimony taken by congressional investigators following the New Orleans riots in 1866 revealed that 110 teachers had been dismissed for pro-federal sentiments (Mitchell 2000). As Mitchell (2000, 48) points out: "Reconstruction marks a decided turning point in the history of education, for it was the Reconstruction, and in particular the work of the Freedmen's Bureau, that brought the nation-state into active agency in creating and maintaining educational programs."

But this precedent would not be employed meaningfully for another 100 years. In the meantime, black disenfranchisement, black impoverishment, and lynching would signal that while the Confederates lost the war, they had won the peace. "Reconstruction," Mitchell (2000, 34) notes, recalling the title of historian Eric Foner's (1988) study, was "America's Unfinished Revolution." It remains unfinished today. Southern intransigence and reactionary politics were reinvigorated by the 1950s and 1960s Civil Rights movement and the federally mandated desegregation of public places. The residue today is under-investment in the public domain. (This fact varies of course; public investment tends to be greater in the Upper South than in Deep South.) Indeed, public monies have been viewed as opportunities for private gain, as the corrupt political history of Louisiana, for instance, indicates.

Many forms of institutional life remain underdeveloped today in the South. To reclaim the public as an American, not residually Confederate, space will require reclaiming the history of its disclaiming. No simple memorization of the facts of southern history will permit the psychological and intellectual "working through" that is necessary now. A social psychoanalytic curriculum of interdisciplinary southern studies might. To that subject I turn in chapter 10.

Despite the efforts of Americans living outside the region to deny its centrality to the political formation of the present, we must recognize that it is the South that made possible the restoration of the Right in the United States after 1968. It is not possible to understand the plight of public education today without appreciating its appropriation first by a liberal Democratic President, then by successive Republican ones. As the 20th century came to close, right-wing politicians have become increasingly eager to employ the racialized and gendered domain of public education as a distraction from the failures of their own reactionary regimes. We are still at (Civil) War.

III

THE PROGRESSIVE MOMENT: THE FUTURE IN THE PRESENT

5

The Evaporation of the Ego
and the Subjectivity of Cyberculture

I
DREAM, THOUGHT, FANTASY

*It is the purpose of curriculum, I argue, to engage the imagination,
such that it is possible to think more metaphorically,
less literalistically, about one's world and one's
presuppositions about that world.*
—Mary Aswell Doll (2000, xi)

*Always ambivalent, technologies project our emotions,
intentions, and projects into the material world.*
—Pierre Lévy (2001, xv)

*[F]utures in curriculum are not "out there" waiting
for us to arrive. We must visualize them here, now.*
—Noel Gough (2002, 18)

That was the past (in the present). What of the future? In an autobiographics of alterity, the progressive moment of *currere* may not elicit fantasies of the future in a literal sense, just as the regressive phase may not recall remembrances of the subject's personal past. As I have done here, one might focus on one's professional and political past, a past shared, each in his or her own way, by us all. That collective past structures our present, as individuals and as a collectivity, as teachers.

The progressive phase of *currere* is distinguished in one of two ways, although in these chapters it will be, on occasion, both. The first is stylistic.

Through stylistic experimentation one might disrupt the somnolence of linearity, as in hypertext, which, relying on George Landow, I will discuss momentarily. It can be as well the use of fiction and poetry, those modes—although very different from each other—can be said to resemble dreamwork, supporting the simultaneity and the juxtaposition of primarily imagistic material (see, e.g., Dunlop 1999). Again, we are in the sphere of deferred and displaced action.

I am thinking of the dreamlike work of Avital Ronell (1992a), who has suggested that literature can sometimes produce the effects of lived experience. Curriculum theory might likewise work to produce the effects of education, in the present case, a movement of the ego toward the futural as that future is imagined in the present: "[I]t is the way in which we understand our past which determines how it determines us. But this understanding is itself intimately related to our orientation towards the future" (Sarup 1992, 38).

The second mode of the progressive phase of *currere* is thematic. The progressive represents an exploration of what is imagined as futural. In one sense, by imagining the future, the future becomes the present. Each section in this chapter explores such a futural subject, a subject absent in the regressive phase but, I am suggesting, nonetheless present, if split off as "future." Here I use theory to invoke these split-off subjects, in hopes of dissolving what blocks us from moving "forward" toward a future not yet present, a present opened out to the not-yet, in Deleuzian terms, an inside folded into the outside. "In this way," Deleuze (1986, 89) explains, "the outside is always an opening on to a future: nothing ends, since nothing has begun, but everything is transformed." The obsession with the computers-in-the-classroom might be deferred and displaced into technologies of self-mobilization and social reconstruction.

Certainly the obsession with computers-in-the-classroom functions as a distraction from educationally engaging the cultural and political problems of the nation. In this sense, it displaces reality. Oscar Wilde wrote to W. E. Henley: "Work never seems to me a reality, but a way of getting rid of reality" (quoted in Pine 1995, 193). But Wilde's observation has a different, less dismal, point for us. Busywork may distract from the facts we fact, but educational work can change reality.

In the progressive phase of *currere* one writes to become other, that which has been split-off, denied. In the fall of 1983 Foucault remarked to an interviewer: "One writes to become someone other than who one is. There is an attempt at modifying one's way of being through the act of writing" (quoted in Miller 1993, 33). Of course, not any writing can achieve this. One must listen to one's silence, observe the shadows among which one moves. One must identify the ghosts who haunt us now; one must "talk back," to oneself as well as to those who will listen. Theory so understood becomes a passage out of the knotted present, into the seams, the unraveled past, embedded in fantasies of the future.

Through remembrance of the past and fantasies of the future, I am suggesting, we educators might write our way out of positions of "gracious submission." Not in one fell swoop, not without resistance (both inner and outer). But creating passages out of the present is possible. We know that. That is why we believe in education; we see how powerfully schooling crushes it, and yet, still, there *is* education, despite the schools. There is God despite the church, justice despite the government, and love despite the family. We educators must prepare for a future when the school is returned to us and we can teach, not manipulate for test scores.

For some, only the future provides access to a reconfigured present. Paolo Fabbri (1994, 79) agreed: "That is, you have to return to the present from the future." In the *Concept of Dread*, Kierkegaard argued that "in a certain sense, the future signifies more than the present and the past; for the future is in a sense the whole of which the past is a part, and in a sense the future may signify the whole" (quoted in Taylor 1980, 177). Merleau-Ponty (1966, 441) described the future almost like a tornado coming one's way: "the future is not prepared behind the observer, it is a brooding presence moving to meet him like a storm." Lyotard imagined the future itself as fictional, as disguising the compulsion to relive the past:

> Now this idea of a linear chronology is itself perfectly "modern." . . . The very idea of modernity is closely correlated with the principle that it is both possible and necessary to break with tradition and institute absolutely new ways of living and thinking. We now suspect that this "rupture" is in fact a way of forgetting or repressing the past, that is, repeating it and not surpassing it. (Lyotard 1993, 76)

The most intimate acts of naming, knowing, and experiencing, Mark Ledbetter (1996) tells us, occur through the metaphors of the human body, itself laced with memory and fantasy. N. O. Brown (1959, 163) elaborates: "The more specific and concrete mechanism whereby the body-ego becomes a soul is fantasy. Fantasy may be defined as a hallucination which cathects the memory of gratification; it is of the same structure as the dream, and has the same relation to the id and to instinctual reality as the dream." And the relations among dreams, fantasy, and thought? In his astonishing study of Flaubert, Sartre (1981, 214) tells us: "The time is not far off when Gustave will say, 'My life is a thought'." Is this the project of the early Sartre, in which the individual creates a life through aesthetic engagement in the world? Or does "thought" mean something more imaginary, closer to "hallucination"?

Dream, thought, fantasy: these are the modes of releasing the imagination, as the legendary Maxine Greene (1995) depicted the process of education. Releasing the imagination means moving into the future, at least as the contents of dream, thought, and fantasy are split-off fragments of self and society blocking the present. Like the regressive, the progressive phase or moment in the method of *currere* is an effort to sidestep the ego, to find a passage to material the ego has covered up, denied, evaded.

Just as the free-associative method supports the inclusion of material that the everyday, rational, defended ego is committed to exclude, reverie and fantasy both provide information and means to escape a present formed, maintained, and occupied by the everyday ego. Georges Bataille (1991, 11) once suggested that "the reasons for writing a book can be traced back to a desire to modify the relations that exist between a man [*sic*] and his fellow-creatures." It can also be written to modify the relations that exist between a "man" and himself, thereby altering his or relations with "others," including gendered and racialized others.

Fantasy can perform several functions. It can "negate" what is by symbolizing the literal, by pointing simultaneously to a mythic and idiosyncratic future. As Norman O. Brown (1959, 167) observed: "Fantasy, as a hallucination of what is not there dialectically negating what is there, confers on reality a hidden level of meaning, and lends a symbolical quality to all experience." While it can seem fragmentary, ambiguous, illusory, fantasy can confer upon everyday events autobiographical, and mythic, significance. Post–World War II Italian poet, novelist, essayist, and filmmaker Pier Paolo Pasolini understood the political and psychological potential of thinking mythically in an age when meaningless materialism renders individual lives pointless (see Greene 1990).

Against audience expectations, Pasolini rendered the mythic (by definition "unreal") centerpiece of *Oedipus Rex* in a realistic fashion. Yet, as Naomi Greene (1990, 156) points out, the lyrical, silent prologue in that film is "wraithlike and hallucinatory . . . a remembered dream." "The intense lush green of the meadow," Pasolini explained, was presented as "an aestheticizing and fantastic element" (quoted in Greene 1990, 156). The progressive phase of *currere* is in this sense hallucinatory, rendering the futural present, if immaterial. The progressive is like a "remembered dream," where the future seems cast as already past, as now. Norman O. Brown (1959, 166) suggested: "[T]hey [fantasies] do not exist in memory or in the past, but only as hallucinations in the present, which has no meaning except as negations of the present." In terms of text as well as time, Roland Barthes imagined text as an intertext, that is, a space to be perceived simultaneously forwards and backwards, without progressional assumptions (see, e.g., Barthes 1981; also Burke 1992; Hasebe-Ludt and Hurren 2003). The progression is hallucination. Perhaps it is true that "[p]resence [itself] is hallucinatory" (Deleuze 1993, 125).

Fantasy can lead not only to the future, but outward, as it were, to culture, to the public world. Psychoanalytically, fantasy represents a mode of sublimation, and as such, is projected into daily life, underwriting ritual, constructing social reality. Norman O. Brown (1959, 168–169) theorized:

> After the castration complex the ego loses the body but keeps the fantasies. . . . Fantasies, like everything else, exist only in the present, as hallucinations in the present, and must be attached to objects in the present . . . after their detachment (in Freud's blunt style, after masturbation is given up) they are projected into reality, forming that opaque medium called culture, through we apprehend and manipulate reality.

To re-enter the moment of castration, underneath, scarred over, forgotten, taken-for-granted in heteronormativity, to re-enter the oedipal drama so as to have a different outcome, requires a certain self-shattering, a "vaporization" of the ego. We return to the future in order to reincorporate those fragments denied then projected outside subjectivity to create the "other." Reality is not only manipulated by hallucination; it is, in a certain sense, created by it, co-terminus with it.

Subjectivity is cultural, and the cultural is subjective. Fantasy is private but public; it is through ideas expressed in specific traditions one can engage the private fantasies of another: our students, for instance. Brown (1959, 7) asserts: "[I]t would be more correct to say that repression deals with the emotions, but these are comprehensible to us only in their tie-up with ideas." Conceived this way, fantasy leads to curriculum theory as cultural studies: "It becomes plain that there is nothing for psychoanalysis to psychoanalyze except those projections—the world of slums and telegrams and historical and cultural analysis" (Brown 1959, 170–171).

The serious student of autobiography appreciates that the "slums" that must be reconstructed are also internal, that the politics in which one engages are intrapsychic and imaginary (Anderson 1991 [1983]; Berlant 1991). Richard Rorty (1991, 121) understood the role of fantasy in culture, specifically in intellectual culture: "[M]any transfigurations of the tradition . . . begin in private fantasies. Think, for example, of Plato's or St. Paul's private fantasies—fantasies so original and utopian that they became the common sense of later times."

But making "common sense" is not the point of the progressive phase of *currere*, a phrase in which the movement of fantasy enacted through sublimation to culture is reversed back to oneself, to the subjective processes of self-formation: self-shattering and self-mobilization. One writes for oneself, not for culture, more precisely, in Ronell's (1992a, 107) phrase, for "no one. Still, writing for no one to no address counts for something; it is the writer's common lot." There may be no concrete other, but there is an Other to whom one is speaking; it is the other that is oneself denied, repressed, split-off. It is a self that can only be imagined; it is culture not yet conceived.

In fantasies of the future there are "fear and trembling" as well as hope and excitement. Pasolini understood that one's fondest dreams and dreaded nightmares were derived from the same fabric: "In my films, barbarism is always symbolic: it represents the ideal moment of mankind [*sic*]" (quoted in Greene 1990, 129). Fantasy can be "barbaric," can reproduce the violence of subjectivity's structuration. "[T]he essence of society is repression of the individual and the essence of the individual is repression of himself," Brown wrote (1959, 3) too simply, if understandably, given that that he was working toward the end of Eisenhower's second term. In re-experiencing the intrapsychic violence structuring subjectivity, one might experience what is affirmative, in Nietzschean terms what is noble, what in Pasolini's antimodernist symbolism, is barbaric, what is dystopian, as Marla Morris (2001a) theorizes.

Toward the close of the 19th century appeared Herbartianism, Bernadette Baker (2001, 463) explains, "in the vicinity such fears [of racial amalgamation in the late 19th century]," fears that were simultaneously racial and gendered (Pinar 2001, chapter 6). Herbartianism contested classical curriculum theory, insisted that the figure of the "child" evolved and developed, and not just as a muscle. Rather, in the life history of the individual was the collective history of the species: ontogeny recapitulates phylogeny. Brown elaborates the idea that surfaced in curriculum theory just before being reformulated in psychoanalysis, just before being displaced by quantitative behavioral science:

> Freud abstains from adopting Jung's term but says, "The content of the unconscious is collective anyhow." Ontogeny recapitulates phylogeny (each individual recapitulates the history of the race): in the few years of childhood "we have to cover the enormous distance of development from primitive man of the Stone Age to civilized man of today." From this it follows that the theory of neurosis must embrace a theory of history; and conversely a theory of history must embrace a theory of neurosis. (Brown 1959, 13)

Not only the thematic content of fantasy is noteworthy; so is its narrative structure, including its sequence, character, its tone. Discussing Pasolini's *Oedipus Rex*, Naomi Greene specifies a number of that film's qualities which also illustrate the character of fantasy one might experience in the progressive phase of *currere*:

In this atmosphere of baroque instability, narrative divisions take the shape of striking ruptures and sudden metamorphoses. The abrupt cuts Pasolini had always favored—as he went, without transition, from close-ups to long shots, or from one close-up to another—fragment the narrative itself as it slashes across time and space, the known and the unknown, legend and imagination. By virtue of a cut, a baby born in Fascist Italy becomes the mythical Oedipus. (Greene 1990, 150)

In this sense, writing autobiographically is working on the cutting-room floor. "After this hallucinating process, which is quite simply called experience" (Sartre 1981, 252), one stitches the frames together, perhaps (after Pasolini) in abrupt, transition-less, moves, as I am attempting here. Such a composition might suggest the structure of futural fantasy, might encourage in the reader something akin to hallucination and dream. The progressive phase of *currere* might aspire to be like Pasolini's "cinema" which resides underneath every "film," the psychic-historical-social substrata of everyday life. "Releasing the imagination" (Greene 1995) can provide opportunities to become clear about the intellectual "objects" and processes of identification and disidentification (Munoz 1996).

Robert Musil understood the temporal complexity of what is "not yet." He would dislike my making a method of it, its "splitting off" (he would also eschew psychoanalytic language) into a stage or phase of the autobiographical study of educational experience. I am a teacher (certainly in the traditional sense of always working to make an esoteric subject accessible); perhaps that is why I constructed "steps" to take in a method. Musil reminds me that, in an important sense, the regressive-progressive-analytic-synthetic does not occur in discrete temporal or conceptual units, but simultaneously:

[W]hat in the distance seems so great and mysterious comes up to us always as something plain and undistorted, in natural, everyday proportions. It is as if there were an invisible frontier round every man. . . . What originates outside and approaches from a long way off is like a misty sea of gigantic, ever-changing forms; what comes right up to any man, and becomes action, and collides with his life, is clear and small, human in its dimensions and human in is outlines. And between the life one lives and the life one feels, the life one only has inklings and glimpses of, seeing it only from a far, there lies that invisible frontier. . . . (Musil 1955, 159–160)

For Musil the process of education is, in part, self-revelation, a process in which outer events provoke inner transformations one cannot easily perceive, certainly not initially. Only in retrospect does the movement, texture, and structure of experience become evident. Writing about the young

Torless (a student at a *fin-de-siecle* residential Prussian military academy), Musil tells us:

> There was within him now something definite, a certainty that he had never known in himself before. It was something mysterious, almost like a dream. It must, he thought, have been very quietly developing under the various influences he had been exposed to in these last weeks, and now suddenly it was like imperious knuckles rapping at a door within him. His mood was that of a woman who for the first time feels the assertive stirring of the growing child within her. (Musil 1955, 116)

Such imagery is not uncommon in Musil. "Her" presence is not only metaphoric, either. Torless feels "girlish," and not only emotionally, but bodily:

> Today for the first time he felt something similar again—again that longing, that tingling under the skin. It was something that seemed to partake simultaneously of body and soul. It was a multifold racing and hurrying of something beating against his body, like the velvety antennae of butterflies. And mingled with it there was that defiance with which little girls run away when they feel that the grown-ups simply do not understand them. . . . Torless laughed quietly to himself, and once again he stretched luxuriously under the bed-clothes. (Musil 1955, 129)

Butterflies, bed-clothes, body and soul: the juxtaposition not only alliterates, but recapitulates a dream sequence, and perhaps not only for young Torless. Before we dream of a future, before we stretch out (luxuriously? anxiously?) over (under? through?) the Internet, let us get out of "bed" and go "outside." Is that where we might "wake up"?

II
"LET THEM EAT DATA"
—BOWERS (2000)

> *Environmentalism is unpopular, in part, because it rejects the frontier psychology and the dream of unlimited expansion.*
> —Christopher Lasch (1984, 86–87)

> *The ecological crisis, in effect, now confronts us with the challenge of reconstituting our guiding ideological and epistemological frameworks.*
> —C. A. Bowers (1995, 38)

> *Let us call these [technological teaching aids]*
> devices for vicarious experience.
> —Jerome Bruner (1977 [1960], 80)

For many—especially politicians—the future of education seems to depend on technology, specifically the computer. "This myth," C. A. Bowers (1995, 4) asserts, "is predicated on an anthropocentric view of the universe and the further assumption that our rationally based technology will always enable us to overcome the breakdowns and shortages connected with the natural world." More specifically, Bowers (1995, 12) argues "that the cultural orientations amplified through educational computing are the very same cultural orientations that have contributed to destroying the environment in the name of progress."

In *Let Them Eat Data*, Bowers (2000, 22) questions "whether computers lead us to substitute decontextualized ways of thinking about the world for the sensory encounters with the natural world that intertwine our lives." Probably that "substitution" occurred several hundred years ago; perhaps it is intensified by "cyberspace." Time will tell. If he and other eco-analysts are right, time is what we do not have. The point of "no-return" in the degradation of the planet may have already occurred, although it will take decades for our fate to become obvious.

Bowers is surely right to criticize those (especially politicians who spend enormous sums on computerizing the schools while neglecting teachers' work conditions, among them salary, class size, and scheduling) who naively accept "Western myths that represent change as linear, progressive, and evolutionary" (Bowers 2000, 8). But it seems to me he overstates his case when he asserts "the inescapable reality is that computerization commodifies whatever activities fall under its domain" (Bowers 2000, 8).

Commodification is pervasive in capitalism and cannot be ascribed causally only or even primarily to "computerization." In terms of the struggle for ecological sustainability, computers might, in fact, be helpful, at least in the dissemination of information regarding the crisis. While "computers provide us a window (information) for recognizing the early warning signs of over stressed ecosystems," Bowers (1995, 13) allows, "they also mesmerize us into thinking this is the primary form of knowledge we need for correcting the problem."

Perhaps, but it seems also true that in the conceptualization of the "biosphere" (Bowers 1995, 1) individuality (not "individualism," its parody) disappears, as Lasch (1984, 19) suggests: "The minimal or narcissistic self is, above all, a self uncertain of its own outlines, longing either to remake the world in its own image or to merge into its environment in blissful union." Bowers (2000, 58) acknowledges "the breakdown in the distinction between our private and public lives," but appears to reinscribe this immobilizing state of affairs in his embrace of "the biosphere."

For me, Bowers' (2000, 12) strongest point is that "our ecological crisis is essentially a crisis of cultural beliefs and values," as such, it is a problem, in part, of education. It is culture—in our context, American culture—that must be reconstructed. While Bowers sees little reason for hope in the institution of schooling at any level (because it remains embedded in capitalism and Enlightenment mythology [see Bowers 2000, 56]), schooling remains the only official site of public instruction.

Bowers is alarmed that computers represent the lynchpin in the cultural crisis that threatens to destroy the very conditions of sustainability of the species. There is some truth in his summary of these conditions, namely that

> the subjectivity of cyberspace expresses all the attributes of the individualism of the Industrial Revolution: a natural attitude toward being a rational, self-determining individual who looks on both past and present in terms of immediate self-interest; a view of the environment as a technological and economic opportunity; an expectation that change leads to a personal enlargement of material well-being; and a view of the world's other cultures as evolving toward the rootless individualism that can easily adapt to the rapidly changing routines of technologically intensive modes of production. (Bowers 2000, 41; see also Bowers 2000, 106)

But it is also true, as we will see momentarily, that cyberspace reconfigures subjectivity, dispersing the cult of "individualism," rendering rationality sensate, even unrecognizable in its modernist manifestations. The commodification of the natural environment, the obsession with material self-advancement, and cultural imperialism: well, these are hardly new and, as Pierre Lévy's reverie suggests, cyberspace may well prove not altogether hospitable to them.

Certainly Bowers (2000) is right in expressing skepticism toward the current obsession—he terms it "addiction" (see 177)—with computers in schools, with what, in a different context, Christopher Lasch (1978, 217) termed a "grandiose vision of a technological utopia." (Likewise, Ted Aoki [in press] speaks of our "intoxication" with technology and science.) Lasch (1984, 33) worries that: "By holding out a vision of limitless technological possibilities—space travel, biological engineering, mass destruction—it removes the last obstacle to wishful thinking. It brings reality into conformity with our dreams, or rather with our nightmares."

The current obsession with the computer in schools is part of the nightmare that is the present. The history of technology in the schools (see Pinar et al. 1995, 704–719) counsels only caution and sobriety. While the introduction of computers into classrooms and the provision of access to the Internet will not, in themselves, raise test scores (let alone simplify the lived complexities of education), there are educational possibilities associated with these developments that portend a culturally different future. We begin our futural fantasy (in the present) with hypertext.

III
HYPERTEXT

Technoliteracy, for us, is the challenge to make a historical
opportunity out of a historical necessity.
—Andrew Ross (1991, 132)

[T]he outcome of such an experimental praxis aiming to surpass
the historical limits of bodies, language, and sexuality cannot be
predicted in advance because it opens up a relation to a future
that can no longer be thought on the basis of the present.
—Ewa Plonowska Ziarek (2001, 41)

Behind the great hypertext teems the
multitude and its relationships.
—Pierre Lévy (2001, 142)

The first computers (preprogrammed calculators) appeared in England and the United States in 1945, employed by the military to perform scientific calculations. The civil use of computer technology expanded throughout the 1960s to include its employment in scientific calculations, government and business statistics, and large-scale administrative functions such as payroll, accounting, etc. (Lévy 2001). Today computers are pervasive, indispensable, prostheses for a cyborg species (Haraway 1991).

Hypertext was coined by Theodor H. Nelson in the 1960s, George Landow reminds. It refers, he continues, to a form of electronic text, a radically new information technology, and a mode of publication. "By 'hypertext,' " Nelson explained, "I mean non-sequential writing—text that branches and allows choices to the reader, best read at an interactive screen. As popularly conceived, this is a series of text chunks connected by links which offer the reader different pathways" (quoted in Landow 1992, 4). Hypertext is text comprised of blocks of text, what Roland Barthes termed a *lexia*, and those electronic links that connect them (Landow 1992).

Barthes' description of "ideal text" elaborates the multiple and unstable character of this notion of hypertext. "In this ideal text," wrote Barthes (1974, 5–6), the networks [*réseaux*] are many and interact, without any one of them being able to surpass the test; this text is a galaxy of signifiers, not a structure of signifieds; it has no beginning; it is reversible; we gain access to it by several entrances, none of which can be authoritatively declared to be the main one; the codes it mobilizes extend as far as the eye can reach, they are indeterminable . . . ; the systems of meaning can take over this absolutely plural text, but their number is never closed, based as it is on the infinity of language.

Landow points out that, like Barthes, Michel Foucault, and Mikhail Bakhtin, Jacques Derrida uses terms evocative of hypertextuality, terms such as link (*liaison*), web (*toile*), network (*réseau*), and interwoven (*s'y tissent*). Unlike Barthes, who emphasizes the readerly text and its nonlinearity, Derrida emphasizes textual openness and intertextuality, a political as well as epistemological position (Egéa-Kuehne 2001). Distinctions drawn between inside and outside a particular text are illusory (Landow 1992). "*Il n'y a pas de hors-texte*," Derrida (1967, 227) famously asserts. While Marxists have insisted that thought derives from the forces and modes of production, Landow (1992) notes, few discuss the most important mode of literary production, that mode dependent upon the *techne* of writing and print.

Derrida employs the word assemblage for cinema, which he perceives as a rival to print (Landow 1992). Pasolini left print for cinema, after writing award-winning books of poetry and fiction, precisely because he judged cinema epistemologically superior to print (Greene 1990). Is the book as an object the body bleached of desire, a mummified body, Cleaver's (1968) "omniscient administrator"? Is film—with its pornographic visuality—the medium of Cleaver's "menial"? I think not only of the visibility of the skin, but of the cultural primacy of the imagistic and, as well, the faint linearity of (especially Pasolini's) film, its free associative but still very (psycho-) logical structure. Is this why cinema (and television, its poor cousin) constantly threatens to replace the book? Can the book be rewritten as an imagistic object, partly by the use of iconography but, more subtly, by a certain nonlinear progressivity, a sense of logic that is more psycho(logical), dreamlike, and suggestively imagistic than it is specifically cognitive?

Is the book a mummified abstract version of the author's body? Bringing the book to your nose, does it smell of paper and glue and embalming fluids? True, the embalmed fibers of the wooden body—the tree—is now in your hands. Take the book to your chest, hold it there, now breathe. I am in your hands. Are you in mine as I write? I am in your lungs; am I in your mind? If you can let yourself go, can you rest against the presence embedded in the words, succumb to the point of view in the text, if for only a moment? Are you now "six feet under"?

Put me down, please. Put other books on top of me, hide me from view, books like bodies stacked in a morgue, ah your library. Is it true, as Mark

Ledbetter (1996, 144) suggests, "there is a sexual relationship between reader and text"? "Nakedness," he asserts, "is an appropriate metaphor for how we should approach a text, confessionally" (1996, 144). Naked bodies lying on top of each other, ideas flowing like blood, types A and O and others without categorizing capital letters. Nonlinear intertextual writing is like fiction without a throughline.

A hypertext system, Landow (1992) writes (too hopefully, it seems to me), permits the individual reader to choose his or her locus of investigation and experience. He says that Derrida understood that electronic computing and other changes in media have eroded the power of the linear text. The book is no longer a culturally dominant form, but was it ever? "The end of linear writing," Derrida (1976, 86) declared, "is indeed the end of the book," even if, he continues, "it is within the form of a book that the new writings—literary or theoretical—allow themselves to be, for better or worse, encased." Is that the meaning of being "bookish": encasement, entombement, maybe in a spaceship floating toward, or a frozen chamber waiting for, the future?

Sometime in the future, Landow (1992) believes, all individual texts can be electronically linked to one another, thereby creating "metatexts" and "metametatexts" of a scale and type only partly imaginable at present. That would seem to be John Willinsky's fantasy, as we will see momentarily. At present, more modest forms of hypertextuality have appeared. These preserve the linear text, including its order and fixity, then append various texts to it, including critical commentary, textual variants, and chronologically anterior and later texts (Landow 1992). Is hypertextuality materialized intertextuality; if so, does it suggest a futuristic form of curriculum?

Derrida calls for a new "pictographic writing" (Landow 1992, 43) as a way out of logocentrism. Hypertext, Landow (1992) believes, provides such writing. It redefines not only beginnings and endings of the text but also its borders. Hypertext escapes what Gérard Genette termed a "sort of idolatry, which is no less serious, and today more dangerous" than idealization of the author, "namely, the fetishism of the work-conceived of as a closed, complete, absolute object" (quoted in Landow 1992, 60). Is this a queer model of text, a textual space like the old (early 1970s) gay bathhouses, wherein bodies without social identities caressed and copulated? Is writing like sex? Mark Ledbetter (1996, 145) would seem to think so: "Yet to expose myself is not to be from the posture of presenting a norm or standard for what ought to be privileged but rather to offer myself, passively, to be seen, read and perhaps changed by another narrative, another race and another gender than my own." Why another gender? He continues:

> In fact, I would suggest that we have taught a generation of readers to read as though there were a heterosexual relationship between reader and text, subtly and perniciously requiring a woman to assume a male role in order to discover

"meaning" in a text. Could we not opt for a homosexual relationship between reader and text and therefore provide a whole series of new and important metaphors besides and along with words like, enter, penetration, inside, and so on? . . . I suggest that to stand "naked" before the text is to offer the possibility of assuming a sexual identity other than my own, and in doing so discover new ways of reading and being read by the text and therefore, of understanding the text. (Ledbetter 1996, 146)

Is reading, in this sense, an opportunity for transgendering? Do homosexual relationships portend futural forms of sociality, as Leo Bersani (1995) suggests?

Heterosexist prose uses the "other" to create the "child," the procreative moment in which through argumentation (or in the case of child-study, through observation [see Baker 2001]) one occupies or repositions (recontextualizes for Richard Rorty) the body of the Other. Does this heterosexual conception of reading require the conceptual subjugation of the Other, into womb, "wife," "mother"? Is homosexual prose, in contrast, promiscuous? Can we find the multiple ways bodies of knowledge can be juxtaposed, and in these positionings, are new pleasures and loves and knowledges created? Is my labor as scholar not to find inadequacies of others' positions—how I can out-sex them by my superior intelligence or skill or size—but how I can sleep with bodies of knowledge to produce new pleasures, new knowledge? Is my work to adore the other, to be entered by and/or enter the other, our bodies co-mingling, producing a third thing: pleasure, knowledge, the future. "Those who do not become wild beasts when they write, who write to please, write nothing that has not already been written, teach us nothing, and forge extra bars for our cage," Helene Cixous (1992, 42) asserts. Even inside the cage—the prison-cell—there are beasts (see Pinar 2001, chapters 16 and 17).

With its built-in bias against "hypostatization" and against privileged descriptions as well, hypertext embodies the approach to philosophy that Richard Rorty takes, Landow (1992) believes. For Landow, hypertext represents the convergence of poststructuralist conceptions of textuality and electronic embodiments of it. It undermines certain aspects of the authoritativeness and autonomy of the text. In so doing, hypertext reconfigures the author, Landow asserts, presumably by dissolving his or her unitary cohesion.

Certain conceptions of textuality emphasize participation without autonomy (although "agency" need not be a casualty [see Davies 2000, chapter 4]). Landow (1992) thinks of Lévi-Strauss's presentation of mythological thought as a complex system of transformations without a center. So understood, mythological thought becomes a networked text. This is not surprising, continues Landow, given that the network functions as one of the main paradigms of synchronous structure. Next Landow quotes Edward Said, who observed that:

> two principal forces that have eroded the authority of the human subject in con-
> temporary reflection are, on the one hand, the host of problems that arise in de-
> fining the subject's authenticity and, on the other, the development of the disci-
> plines like linguistics and ethnology that dramatize the subject anomalous and
> unprivileged, even untenable, position in thought. (1975, 293; quoted in
> Landow 1992, 75)

No longer, Said points out, can we (does he mean Europeans and European Americans?) imagine:

> the human subject as the grounding center for human knowledge. Derrida,
> Foucault, and Deleuze have spoken of contemporary knowledge (*savoir*) as
> decentered; Deleuze's formulation is that knowledge, insofar as it is intelligible,
> is apprehensible in terms of nomadic centers, provisional structures that are
> never permanent, always straying from one set of information to another.
> (1975, 376; quoted in Landow 1992, 77)

After Derrida, Landow (1992) suggests that those linear habits of thought associated with print technology force us to think in particular ways. These particular ways tend toward narrowness, decontextualization, a certain at-tenuation of the intellect. The main issue for Landow seems to be linear-ity. By its very structure, he suggests, linearity separates a quoted passage from other, apparently irrelevant, passages, and in so doing reconfigures its meaning.

Hypermedia systems provide an environment in which exploratory or discovery learning may flourish, Landow believes. He asserts that "the his-torical record reveals, however, that university teachers have fiercely re-sisted all educational technology and associated educational practice at least since the late Middle Ages" (Landow 1992, 13). To illustrate, he notes that in "fourteenth-century universities, private silent reading [was] forbid-den in the classroom" (quoted in Landow 1992, 163). Was this a Catholic resistance to Protestantism?

Certainly the opposite appears the case for elementary and secondary-school teachers. At least rhetorically, there has been an uncritical embrace of educational technology, from the filmstrip to the radio (in the 1920s and 1930s), to educational television in the 1960s and now the computer (see Pinar et al. 1995, 704–719). As we have seen, C. A. Bowers detests computers, as he worries they reproduce the worst features of modernist thinking, think-ing devastating to the ecosystem: "Computers are, in effect, simply the ampli-

fiers of Western traditions that we currently associate with modernization,"
he writes (Bowers 1995, 84). In so doing they "obscure the way in which language thinks us as we think within the language" (Bowers 1995, 86).

Landow disagrees, viewing the computer as a kind of prosthesis. According to the *American Heritage Dictionary*, Landow (1992, 170) observes, the
term *prosthesis* has two closely related meanings: (1) the "artificial replacement of a limb, tooth, or other part of the body" and (2) "an artificial device
used in such replacement." Landow (1992, 170) notes that "prosthesis" is associated with language and information, since it derives from a late Latin
word meaning "addition of a letter or syllable," which in turn comes from the
Greek for "attachment" or "addition, from *prostithenai*, to put, add: pros-in
addition + *tithenai*, to place, to put."

Suspicion of the artificiality of such devices is echoed in many contemporary humanists' attitudes toward technology, Landow (1992) suggests. This
suspicion does not seem to include what Landow allows may be the single
most important technology human creatures have devised: writing. Landow
quotes Walter J. Ong's reminder that writing is technology; Ong considers its
artificiality desirable:

> To say writing is artificial is not to condemn but to praise it. Like other artificial
> creations and indeed more than any other, it is utterly invaluable and indeed es-
> sential for the realization of fuller, interior, human potentials. . . . Alienation
> from a natural milieu can be good for us and indeed is in many ways essential
> for full human life. To live and to understand fully, we need not only proximity
> but also distance. (Ong 1982, 82; quoted in Landow 1992, 171)

Like McLuhan, Landow notes, Ong claims that "technologies are not mere
exterior aids but also interior transformations of consciousness" (1982, 83;
quoted in Landow 1992, 171). It was writing, Ong argues, that created human
nature, thought, and culture as we know them.

Like other technologies, writing possesses a logic, but it can produce different, even contrary, effects in different social, political, and economic contexts. Landow quotes Marshall McLuhan's remark on its multiple, often opposing effects: "if rigorous centralism is a main feature of literacy and print,
no less so is the eager assertion of individual rights" (1962, 200; quoted in
Landow 1992, 173). Landow (1992) notes that historians have long appreciated the powerful and conflicting roles played by print in the reformation and
in the savage religious wars that followed. "In view of the carnage which en-
sued," Elizabeth Eisenstein observes,

> it is difficult to imagine how anyone could regard the more efficient duplication
> of religious texts as an unmixed blessing. Heralded on all sides as a "peaceful

art," Gutenberg's invention probably contributed more to destroying Christian concord and inflaming religious warfare than any of the so-called arts of war ever did. (1979, 319; quoted in Landow 1992, 173).

One reason for these conflicts, Eisenstein suggests, has to do with the fact that when fixed in print—recorded, that is, in black and white—"positions once taken were more difficult to reverse. Battles of books prolonged polarization, and pamphlet wars quickened the process" (1979, 326; quoted in Landow 1992, 173).

Because hypertext diffuses selfhood and complicates authorship by its intertexuality while it embeds both in textuality generally, Landow (1992) argues that hypertext implicitly discredits mainstream notions of pluralism. Such notions require a political and/or cultural center, he points out, not a diffused, complicated, textualized notion of diffuse power flows. Hypertext, Landow (1992) continues, functions to destabilize the very conception of a permanent center, or the center as any but a traveling, momentary focus of attention. In so doing, it resists the political co-optation implicit in theories of pluralism. Describing his theory of theater, Pasolini asserted: "Where there are the ears and mouths of single individuals . . . there can be no mass culture. It is for this reason . . . that the 'theater of the World' affirms it real democracy, as opposed to the false democracy of the communications media that address the masses" (quoted in Friedrich 1982, 104).

In the age of the Internet we appear to have entered an era in which state regulation of communication is difficult, but whether that fact foreshadows greater democratization is not clear to me. As we will see in the work of Pierre Lévy, there are reasons to believe that the diffusion of the individual ego Landow ascribes to hypertext will occur across the species, that the Internet and computer access to it will enable "complicated conversation" governments and corporate entities cannot control.

Certainly that is the intention of Renee Fountain and Jacques Daignault, designers of the Website for the International Association for the Advancement of Curriculum Studies (www.iaacs.org). In the preamble to the constitution of the International Association for the Advancement of Curriculum Studies, I underlined the importance of diffusion and difference:

> The Association is established to support a worldwide—but not uniform—field of curriculum studies. At this historical moment and for the foreseeable future, curriculum inquiry occurs within national borders, often informed by governmental policies and priorities, responsive to national situations. Curriculum study is, therefore, nationally distinctive. The founders of the IAACS do not dream of a worldwide field of curriculum studies mirroring the standardization and uniformity the larger phenomenon of globalization threatens. Nor are we unaware of the dangers of narrow nationalisms. Our hope, in establishing this

organization, is to provide support for scholarly conversations within and across national and regional borders about the content, context, and process of education, the organizational and intellectual center of which is the curriculum. (www.iaacs.org)

To support such aspirations, the computer must not become just another screen on which we project private prejudice and national hubris. It must, as Landow suggests, diffuse and democratize.

6

"Sex Times Technology Equals the Future"

SCREENS

I prefer to contemplate life as a cyborg identity than
death in a tenured position.
—Noel Gough (1994, 67)

Through the displacement of excitation away from one memory
to a perceptual stimulus or another memory, the latter
comes to have the perceptual "charge" of the former.
—Kaja Silverman (2000, 91)

The death of God has left us with a lot of appliances.
—Avital Ronell (1992b, 5)

If the computer is a prosthesis, what is the television? After all, their similarity is unmistakable: both are screens. Avital Ronell (1992b) suggests that television is related to the law, that it is located at the site of trauma. The television is not so much a panopticon—not yet at least, Ronell notes—as it is a super-egoic surveillance of free-circulating desire: crime, for instance, or politics, or automobile ads or sports. Television is also a drug, Ronell (1992b) asserts, a tranquilizing force, absorbing while administering "hits" of violence. She recalls that Alfred Hitchcock would doze off in front of the television after a hard day's work on *Psycho*. Unlike film, television was, he said, soporiferous. Alternately stimulating and tranquilizing, ever anxiety-reducing-inducing, television must, Ronell (1992b) argues, be subsumed in the larger domain of drugs. Recall, she says, that the Rodney King event—television par excellence, with the help of a camcorder—began with a false but necessary start: Everyone involved in the car chase assumed they were pursuing a PCP suspect.

In order to mobilize themselves, the police had to imagine that its suspect was on PCP. What does it mean, Ronell (1992b) asks, that the police were hallucinating drugs? In this sense, she suggests, the Rodney King event was a metonymy of the war on drugs. This war, as Ronell (1992a) has argued elsewhere, constitutes an act of ethnocide by "hallucinating mainstreamers." Not unrelatedly, the Rodney King event was also, Ronell suggests, an eruption of the Gulf War. Television coverage of the War eroded our sense of horror into a blank stare, whiting out the Gulf War. On the freeways of Los Angeles, nomadic video "flashed a metonymy of police action perpetrated upon a black body" (Ronell 1992b, 4).

"The death of God," Ronell (1992b, 5) quips, "has left us with a lot of appliances." No longer do we watch the skies for the second coming; we watch television instead. "Without recourse to any dialectic of incarnation," she continues, "something yet beams through, as though the interruption itself were the thing to watch" (Ronell 1992b, 5). Is this the trauma of taboo, of murdering the son who was the father, leaving his body nearly naked on a cross for all the world to watch? Is Law the penalty we pay for the rape of Noah and the murder of God (Pinar 2003c)? Because we saw his nakedness, does His dead/absent body haunt us as the forever sealed, simulated body: television? The "original" (not-so-good) news is erased by religious ritual and masculinized posturing, but the trauma persists in the continuing sense of a permanent ongoing urgency: "breaking news."

This permanent sense of emergency—the daily threat of nuclear annihilation during the Cold War and the daily threat of terrorism now—is textualized in the unpredictable serialization of television images. This imagistic series suggests, Ronell continues, that television is a mode of reading in which interruption of the text re-enacts the original rupture of the species and of individual life history. Does ontogeny recapitulate phylogeny? With newsflashes—"we interrupt our regular programming"—television communicates, Ronell suggests, the residue of the "good news," attempting in its narrative structure, its interrupted discourse, to re-experience and anesthetize, the originary rupture. Is this the separation from the mother we call "birth," the originary violence which reverberates through boys to men? Mother mother, why have I forsaken thee?

The Rodney King event, Ronell (1992b) argues, forced a repressed image back on the screen. The Rodney King beating broadcast that which was unpresentable during the War, namely that the black body was under attack by a massive (white) force. The Rodney King beating, Ronell (1992b) announces, showed what would not be shown in its global form, namely the American police force attacking helpless brown bodies in Iraq. What we could not bear to see globally we could bear, indeed, demanded to see locally.

In a haunting way, Ronell (1992b) suggests, the image comes to inhabit the amnesiac subject. Total recall, she points out, is not the same as memory or recollection. It can be total only to the extent that it expresses the need for a prosthetic technology that would produce a memory track. Certain contemporary films, Ronell (1992b, 14) explains, are providing a means of transport, modalities of "getting higher," and in so doing the difference between drugs and electronics fades. Both film and TV produce amnesia as we surf through "blank zones of trauma" (Ronell 1992b, 14).

The laceration of the television image, Ronell suggests, split into sometimes parodic, at other times self-canceling, bits of meaning, thematized into mutilated segments of *Dasein*—assembled into a "sitcom"—both erase the originary wound and re-present the scar tissue as image. Prosthesis as unconscious, the television becomes the hypertext of a civilization throwing up on itself. Pasolini advocated banning it. In her stunning study of Franz Kafka, Elizabeth Boa (1996, 229) discusses the "hyptertextuality" of the pornographic screen.

> In both flagellation and voyeurism the active organ of intercourse is displaced from the penis to the whip or the eye. The flesh being whipped and the object of the gaze are the locus of sensuality whereas the whip, not a bodily organ at all, and the eye, which is not touched and so does not feel as the penis does, become pure instruments of power.

There is, Boa believes, a double taboo at work in which the penis is alienated from the male organ onto the abstract phallus. At the same time, the sensual body is rendered shameful. Like Susan Bordo (1993), Boa (1996) points to that dualistic metaphysics that demands absolute difference between the sovereign mind and the enslaved body, between "man" as the transcendent universal subject and "woman" as dependent natural object. "The body to which something is done," Boa (1996, 229) concludes, "even if only writing or painting it, thereby becomes effeminate while the act of writing takes on sadistic meaning so turning the writer's sado-masochistic imagination into the scene of narcissistic self-exhibitionism to the punishing eye and of self-abandonment to the sadistic pen."

There were ancient Greeks who, evidently, understood these dynamics of writing and reading, even if they tended to add "boy" to "woman" in this calculus of voyeurism, exhibitionism, penetration, and sado-masochism (Halperin 1990). Is the reader/ TV viewer today like the young Greek boy of yesterday, as Lyotard (1993, 132) suggests?

He lets his voice be occupied, appropriated, not by the words of another, but by words that were already there, without belonging to anyone. This is an important moment, for the intrusion experienced by the reader precipitates a sudden awareness of the self as this self is in fact invaded. It is not irrelevant to recall that some very early Greek inscriptions equate the process of reading with anal penetration.

Reading, watching television, and being entered anally all require a certain openness to the other, an interest in being occupied and transformed by sensation and intellection. When Norman O. Brown (1959, 191) asserts that "anal eroticism has not been renounced or abandoned but repressed," is he providing us an embodied understanding of contemporary anti-intellectualism?

II
WHERE NO MAN HAS BEEN BEFORE

If the cyborg is anything at all, it is self-difference.
—Donna Haraway (1991, 22)

[C]ertain kinds of postmodernist fiction—especially in such genres as cyberpunk science and fiction and feminist tabulation—are particularly helpful in developing and renewing specific educational discourses and practices.
—Noel Gough (1998, 95)

We certainly do need to change our bodies and ourselves, and in perhaps a much more radical way than the cyberpunk authors imagine.
—Michael Hardt and Antonio Negri (2000, 217)

All this talk of decentering, diffusion, and de-regulation can make one queezy, even queer. Is there not now—especially after September 11, 2001—a sense as well that the "metanarrative of the present as the decisive conclusion of history ('apocalypse now') . . . structures what postmodern theorists celebrate as the cessation of all such narratives" (Pask 1995, 182)? Is not Kevin Pask's epistemological point simultaneously a temporal one? Has the future disappeared or only materialized when we have concluded there is only now? If the future has slipped away (into the present), what do our fantasies of the future mean? Writing about cyperpunk, Pask (1995, 183) asks: "If the present is also the future, what is the role of science fiction in imagining what present-future?" Like any imagining of the future, Pask points out, science fiction necessarily reflects the historical moment of its production. He notes that Jameson has argued that the function of the genre is "not to give us 'images' of the future . . . but rather to defamiliarize and restructure our experience of our own present, and to do so in specific ways distinct from all other forms of defamiliarizaton" (quoted in Pask 1995, 183).

In this sense, Pask (1995, 183) suggests, the optimism of early science fiction was derived from the confidence accompanying early industrial capitalism, what he terms "an epistemic progressivism" shared by both capitalism and socialism. While embarrassed by its genesis, Pask continues, cyberpunk too reflects the dystopian character of the present. We might ask: Is Noel Gough's (1998) embrace of science fiction as curriculum research an expression of the current dystopian moment? Is any other posture ethically legitimate in the post-Holocaust period? Marla Morris (2001a, 9) argues: "Under the sign of a dystopic curriculum, memories emerge not as a promise of hope, but as a testament to despair and truthfulness."

Juxtaposing, as Pask (1995) does, Donna Haraway's insistence in her "Manifesto for Cyborgs" (first published in 1985) that "the boundary between science fiction and social reality is an optical illusion" (quoted in Pask 1995, 184) with the opening declaration of *The Terminator* is clarifying. From the latter: "The machines rose from the ashes of the nuclear fire. Their war to exterminate mankind had raged for decades, but the final battle would not be fought in the future. It would be fought here, in our present. Tonight" (quoted in Pask 1995, 184). The paradoxical temporal logic of the film, Pask suggests, undermines European culture's fantasy regarding the individual's capacity for autonomy, to make change, to construct the present-future.

J. G. Ballard's succinct formula for recent science fiction is "sex times technology equals the future" (quoted in Pask 1995, 184). Pask (1995) recalls that Haraway's "Manifesto," the crucial text for most recent celebrations of cyborg sexuality, is an explicitly socialist one. She locates "cyborg feminism" in the international division of the labor. The burden of exploitation is borne by women, third-world women (184).

Cyborg identity became possible at the end of the 20th century, Leigh Gilmore (1994) argues, due to the breakdown of identity structures that rendered the very notion of identity knowable and stable. The boundaries that have been fractured, she suggests, include the human/animal boundary, the human-animal/machine boundary, and the physical/nonphysical boundary. Racial boundaries too have blurred, at least crossed-over, certainly to many middle-class white boys who listen to hip-hop while driving their oversized trucks, ripping off (through identification with and/or desire for) black hypermasculinity for themselves. But these guys remain "white boys," not exactly the cyborg identity Donna Haraway imagines: "a cyborg identity, a potent subjectivity synthesized from fusions of outsider identities" (quoted in Bordo 1993, 230).

Technocultural feminism construes technologies, Linda Howell (1995) asserts, not as inanimate machines, but as enlivened, historically formative, and highly social actors. They are both laborers and boundary transgressors; cyborg bodies constitute a monstrous, perverse, primarily peaceful collectivity, which Haraway describes as "a kind of disassembled and reassembled, postmodern collective and personal self" (quoted in Howell 1995, 201). Haraway's cyborg imagery and "rhetoric of blasphemy" (201) emphasize the materiality of apocalyptic discourse.

Structured like hypertext, like Derridean discourse, amidst disappearing distinctions between fantasy and belief, the cyborgs of Haraway's manifesto ground postmodern discourses of the body in the "materiality of everyday life" (Howell 1995, 201). That is to say, in the materiality of life at home, in school, at the workplace, in church, and in clinics and hospitals, we experience, Howell (201) suggests, "eroding distinctions" between public and private, production and reproduction, work and leisure in a technological world.

To pose homoerotic pornography as a possibly progressive tactic for gaining authorial recognition challenges, Howell (1995) points out, the assumption that pornography is universally demeaning to women. Penley's (1991) description of so-called K/S writing challenges such a universalizing conception. She claims that these women's writing constructs a "unique hybridized genre" in which romance, pornography, and utopian science fiction converge (1991, 137). In these stories, Kirk and Spock "overcome the conditioning that prevents them from expressing their feelings" (1991, 156), and "slashers" avoid the well-worn formula of masculine dominance and feminine submission.

By choosing a relationship between the two adventurers as their focus, these writers imagine possibilities for remaking masculinity without accepting the wimpy "sensitive man" of the eighties (1991, 155). Howell (1995, 204) comments: "Running parallel to their commitment to accessible technologies in practice is a commitment to retool the masculine psyche in conscious affinity with gay men." In the K/S world there is a "comprehension of the fact that all men (and women) must be able to recognize their own homosexual tendencies if they are to have any hope of fundamentally changing oppressive sexual roles" (Penley 1991, 156).

Constance Penley (1991) emphasizes that female *Star Trek* fans, especially the "slash" fans, have defined technology very broadly to include the technology of the body, the mind, and everyday life. This is a expansive notion of technology that extends to nearly everything in the world, as well as out of it. Sex is also a technology, as we hear in this exchange between Kirk and Spock. While reflecting on *Star Trek*, Kirk tells Spock that Gene was wrong about one thing: " 'Space isn't the final frontier. . . . You are!' The Vulcan replies, 'Indeed. Then perhaps, Jim,' he suggested, leaning closer to whisper softly into one ear, 'we should . . . boldly go . . . where no man has gone before' " (quoted in Penley 1991, 151). This erotic exchange is embedded in the realization, as Penley (1991, 151–152) explains:

that they must return to the future so that they can have existed to be able to back into the past to make sure that Star Trek gets produced, the world gets saved, and humans go into space. (Kirk has a hard time following this, but fortunately the more intellectual Spock grasps the intricacies and paradoxes of time travel.) The novel ends with their dramatic rescue by the female security officer of the *Enterprise*.

There is an appreciation of the fact, Penley (1991) suggests, that everyone must be able to recognize their own homosexual potential if we are to have any hope of fundamentally transforming the oppressive sexual reality of the present time. That term of endearment and devaluation that is "fag-hagging" obscures, Penley (1991, 157) insists, the very real appreciation these female fans have for gay male challenges to heteronormative masculinity, as well as "their feelings of solidarity with them insofar as gay men too inhabit bodies that are still a legal, moral, and religious battleground."

Constance Penley's account of "slash" fashion illustrates, Howell (1995) argues, three key points about cyborg cultural politics made in Haraway's (1985, 205) manifesto. The first is that new technologies provide new possibilities for resistance, especially when they combine, as in the slashers' hybridization of romantic pornography. Second, these new technologies of resistance are not necessarily expressed or articulated in the traditional terms of feminism and the Left, but may, in fact, be conveyed in what appear to be regressive or reactionary forms. Third, issues of sexuality and gender are simultaneously blended intensified, blurring distinctions, deferring and displacing originary desire with new objects, and vice versa. In K/S, for instance, male homosexual desire is the complicated consequence of female heterosexual desire.

When marginalized aspects of our identities (racial, gendered, ethnic, sexual) are expressed in the central arenas of culture, Susan Bordo (1993) believes, they are themselves transformed, and are transforming. She is thinking particularly of the workplace, that central location of our working lives—for some of us the central location of our lives—which can seem exempt from profound political and cultural questions. Bordo (1993) warns that if we do not struggle to inform our work and workplaces with our embodied experience, we collude in the cultural reproduction of dualisms, among them, of course, are the public/private divide, male/female, black/white, gay/straight. Do these binaries become altered under the rainbow sign? Poet James Merrill (1993, 142) remembers an afternoon spent with poet Elizabeth Bishop:

My accord with the author [Elizabeth Bishop] of "Exchanging Hats" came to a head, as it were, one day in Brazil, when she and I were being driven through sunny red-and-green hillsides sparkling from a recent downpour. Just ahead squatted a small intense rainbow we seemed about to collide with before, leaping out of our path, it reappeared round the next bend. Something Elizabeth said in Portuguese set the fat black driver shaking with laughter. "In one of the northern provinces," she explained, "they have this superstition: if you pass under a rainbow you change your sex."

Are transsexuals cyborgs? Cyborgs foreshadow, Noel Gough (1994) asserts, the real possibility of a posthuman condition. They are, he writes, "what humans might be becoming in the late twentieth century. Unlike many of the other creatures of SF, cyborgs are both narrative and material constructions" (Gough 1994, 65). So imagined, "cyborgs not only violate ontological boundaries in a metaphorical sense but also materialize and embody the human capability to transform and transcend such boundaries with our own imaginative and material resources—without the intervention of Others or otherness" (Gough 1994, 66). Does the exchange of hats qualify?

"If the cyborg is anything at all," Haraway (1991, 22–23) writes, "it is self-difference." She goes on to say:

> Feminist embodiment, then, is not about fixed location in a reified body, female or otherwise, but about nodes in fields, inflection in orientations, and responsibility for difference in material-semiotic fields of meaning. Embodiment is significant prosthesis; objectivity cannot be about fixed vision when what counts as an object is precisely what world history turns out to be about.

The body, then, is not something apart from text; it *is* text. We can discern this in the *bishonen* comics where, Sandra Buckley (1991) explains, androgynous figures are drawn, wrapped in each other's arms, naked in bed, passionately making love, gazing longingly into each other's eyes, and kissing each other on the cheek. These images of the young lovers kissing are within the *bishonen* genre. A scene of a man kissing another man on the lips, Buckley (1991, 175) tells us, is portrayed as being "more sensuous than any bed scene."

The word *jiyu* (freedom) occurs again and again in the pages of the *bishonen* comics. The feature story of the July 1989 edition is headlined "All My Life" and follows the gradual shift of the old male protagonist's love from his girlfriend to a beautiful young boy (Buckley 1991). Ewa Plonowska Ziarek (2001, 219) points out:

> [F]reedom in this sense means not only the task of resistance to multiple forms of domination but also the creation of new modes of being, eroticism, social relations, and, ultimately, new models of democracy. This shift of emphasis from the liberation of repressed identities to the creation of new configurations of power relations stresses the radical futural dimension of democratic politics.

By the 1980s, Buckley (1991) tells us, the market for the *bishonen* comics had expanded far beyond the original readership of pubescent schoolgirls. Now it included gay men and women, heterosexual male university students, and young heterosexual women, in particular young *okusan* (housewives— literally, "the person at the back of the house"). The *bishonen* comics, Buckley (1991) suggests, would seem to represent a denial of (hetero)sexuality among teenage girls, but such a reading of these *manga* risks denying the sexual awareness and curiosity of the millions of teenage girls who purchase these comics.

What is being denied or rejected by the readership of the *bishonen* comics, Buckley (1991) believes, is the strict regulation of gender and sexual practice in postwar Japanese society. Buckley (1991, 180) suggests that the *bishonen* comics offer young men "a fantastical space for the exploration of sexual desire outside the closed circuit of the oedipal theater of the family but on the familiar territory of the homosocial formations of their youth." Such homosocial formations, she continues, structure the social relationships of the Japanese men throughout his life, echoes of the mythology of the "comrade samurai" lived out in the contemporary workplace.

These comics [*manga*] function, Buckley (1991) speculates, to transform events associated with everyday experience—she lists commuting, eating, golf clubs, tea ceremony utensils, baseball bats, food processors, secretaries, bosses, plumbers, and much more—into eroticized objects of fantasy. In the Edo-period woodblock prints of the phallus was everywhere, Buckley (1991) reports. In contemporary pornographic comic books the penis does not appear; it is nowhere. Yet, it is everywhere. The penis is present in its absence. The current legal requirement that the penis be absent has led, Buckley tells us, to graphic innovations that communicate the Lacanian idea that the phallus is not equal to the penis. The phallus, in Lacan and in these Japanese comic books, transcends the anatomical, signifying the power that is the privilege of the creature whose identity is inseparable from that organ. Does the organ that is the computer degender the phallus? Is the "World Wide Web" a masculinized frontier or a feminized inner "outer space"? What is the gender of cyberculture?

III
CYBERCULTURE

The social and cultural movement that underlies cyberspace . . .
is converging not toward any particular content but toward a form
of communication that is unmediated, interactive, community
based, non-hierarchical, and rhizomatic.
—Pierre Lévy (2001, 112)

More information does not necessarily lead to greater wisdom.
—John Willinsky (1999, 30)

Clearly, the machine is not going to replace the teacher.
—Jerome Bruner (1977 [1960], 84)

Curiously, while Pierre Lévy (2001, 5) asserts that "we cannot, in effect, speak of the sociocultural effects or the meaning of technology in general," he does just that. Given "the global interconnection of computers," he writes, "the extension of cyberspace continues unabated" (Lévy 2001, 6). He posits "collective intelligence" as "one of the principal engines of cyberculture" (Lévy 2001, 10), a metaphor strangely stuck in a presumably earlier, industrial, period.

The development and commercialization of the microprocessor (a device for performing logical and arithmetical calculations, lodged on a single small electronic chip) stimulated, starting in the 1970s, numerous macro economic and social processes, including the emergence, Lévy asserts, of cyberculture. The first and fundamental aspect of cyberculture, he asserts, is globalization, which, in turn, has led to the creation of a space wherein humanity is virtually present to itself. Virtualization is the second key aspect of cyberculture; Lévy (2001, 29) suggests that "virtuality and actuality [are] nothing more than two different modes of reality." "The virtual is an infinite source of actualization," he (30) continues, and, presumably, vice versa. The extension of cyberspace is cause and consequence of what he terms "a general virtualization of the economy and society" (Lévy 2001, 31).

While this phenomenon has been stimulated by commercial interests, Lévy acknowledges, it is its democratic potential that interests him. Cyberspace is less interesting as a global shopping mall than as a site of "collective intelligence," "a single and unique virtual world, one that is immense, infinitely varied, and perpetually changing" (Lévy 2001, 88). For him, this is "the essence of cyberculture," what he characterizes as "universality without totality" (91).

Lévy (2001, 94) predicts that "the elements of cyberspace will continue toward integration, interconnection, and the establishment of increasingly interdependent systems that are universal and transparent," a development, he suggests, not unique to cyberspace, but evident in extant technological systems, among them aviation, automotive engineering, and the production and distribution of electricity. This movement toward integration and interconnection is, for Lévy, the value of cyberculture, namely its universality, its interconnecting of people, machines, and information.

Where Landow sees parallels between hypertext and the technology of writing, Lévy discerns differences. He asserts that the World Wide Web constitutes a different order of universality than that established by writing. He imagines that universality as characterized by "meaning that remains unchanged by interpretation, translation, transference, diffusion, conservation" (Lévy 2001, 96), a view hermeneutics, for instance, would seem to dispute. "The signification of the message," he overstates, "must be the same in all places and at all times" (96). But then he modifies this exaggeration, terming it "an attempt at semantic closure" (Lévy 2001, 96). This is a less extravagant claim but still, from the point of view of literary art, for instance, clearly inaccurate. He insists that writing amounts to an "effort of totalization" and, as such, strives for "decontextualization" (Lévy 2001, 96). Except for certain strands of logical positivism in philosophy and science, his claim is certainly false. Writing does not, despite Lévy's assertions, insert the same meaning into every locale, some would say not even in forms of science (Weaver, Appelbaum, and Morris 2001).

While still exaggerating to make his point, Lévy (2001, 96) may be closer to the truth when he names the mass media—the press, radio, cinema, and television—as functioning to create the illusion of universality and totality. Ronell's analysis of the Rodney King incident implies as much. Television, in particular, may create "a plane of emotional existence that reunites the members of society in a kind of fluctuating, amnesiac, rapidly evolving macrocontext" (97). But in cyberculture, contrary to the virtual world television and other media create, Lévy thinks that we—as social actors—will ultimately construct the macro-culture together.

Lévy (2001, 98) argues that "cyberspace dissolves the pragmatics of communication, which, since the invention of writing, has conjoined the universal and totality." In so doing it brings us back to a "preliterate situation," certainly a fair judgment to my mind, given the intellectual quality of much that exists on the Web. But Lévy has another point in mind, namely that the on the Web "real-time interconnection and [the] dynamism of on-line memory once again create a shared context, the same immense living hypertext for the participants in a communication" (98–99). Every message, he asserts, is connected to other messages, comments, and sites. He pictures messages as fragments of text that pass unnoticed through hypertext until they connect with other textual fragments, and there become "reciprocal, interactive, uninterrupted communication" (99). This would seem to be the case with writing as well—recall Landow's citation of Derrida in which writing and hypertext seem two words for the same communicative and representational process—but Lévy is determined to draw the distinction.

In official writing, he asserts, the reader is required to mime the text, then submit the performance for judgment by officials and institutions, among them churches and schools. He has a point, if overdrawn. Especially in school, students must be authorized to make formal expressions and representations. But if Foucault is right about the subjectivation of disciplinarity, it is not clear how we are suddenly set free once we go on line. For Lévy, it is not the politics of subjectivity he has in mind, rather the "immanent networking of all the machines on the planet," a fact which for him guarantees that there are almost no messages " 'out of context,' separated from an active community" (2001, 99), an odd claim given the junk email many of us receive every day, especially in private email accounts, despite the presence of "filters." "Virtually," he continues, undaunted, "all messages are plunged into a communicational bath that is teeming with life, including humans themselves, and cyberspace will gradually emerge as its heart" (99). Given Lévy's earlier (but not discussed here) invocation of the biblical flood, it is not obvious to me we contemporary Noahs should be pleased to be included.

Rather than focusing on the pervasive commercialization and vulgarization of the Web, Lévy focuses instead on the "desire for reciprocal communication and collective intelligence" (2001, 104). Three "principles," he suggests, are discernible in the initial growth of cyberspace: "interconnectivity, the creation of virtual communities, and collective intelligence" (107). Changing metaphors from that of the "communicational bath," Lévy asserts that all cyberspace will become an "interactive channel." Given this view, perhaps it is predictable that he asserts that in virtual communities there is an ethics an "reciprocity" (Lévy 2001, 108), but this seems to me assumed, not elaborated. "With certain exceptions," Lévy (2001, 109) insists, "freedom of speech is encouraged, and users are uniformly opposed to any form of censorship." Issues of "communicative competence," after Habermas (1970, 1979), seem for Lévy somehow resolved in front of the computer screen. Even the prejudices (see Young-Bruehl [1996] on the use of the plural) disappear: the "two essential values," he asserts, include "autonomy and openness toward alterity" (Lévy 2001, 112).

IV
INTELLECTUAL TECHNOLOGIES

Knowledge as flow, work as a transaction of the understanding,
and the new technologies of individual and collective intelligence
profoundly change the data used for education and training.
—Pierre Lévy (2001, 138)

Too much knowledge in the Age of Information?
Do we name our ages by our excesses?
—John Willinsky (1999, 35)

The Great Community, in the sense of free and full
intercommunication, is conceivable.
—John Dewey (1991 [1927], 211)

Cyberspace supports what Lévy (2001, 137) terms "intellectual technologies" that increase, externalize, and otherwise modify a number of human cognitive functions, among them memory (he lists databases, hyperdocuments, binary files), imagination (he names simulation), perception (he lists digital sensors, telepresence, virtual reality) and reasoning (he lists artificial intelligence, modeling complex phenomena). These intellectual technologies, he asserts, support: (1) new forms of access to information, including what he terms the "navigation" of hyperdocuments, the multiplication of search engines to locate information, and (2) what he believes to be novel forms of reasoning and understanding, by which he means "simulation, an industrialization of thought that is based neither on logical deduction nor on experience-based induction" (2001, 137).

Qualifying as an example of such a new intellectual technology is, I should think, curriculum theorist John Willinsky's (1999, 2001) proposal for public access to scholarship and research in the human sciences. This proposal, which Willinsky (1999, 20) calls the "Automata Data Corporation," is, in one sense, an elaborate curriculum design. It would create a site on the Web at which those interested in specific issues or problems (Willinsky cites as an example the phonics–whole language debate in reading instruction) could access readable summaries of relevant research. Designed to improve public access to academic scholarship and knowledge, Willinsky's Automata Data Corporation would also facilitate debate and dialogue over research on contentious topics. He writes:

> The Automata Data Corporation amounts to an experiment in the public value of a certain kind of knowledge. More specifically, it is about the difference that might come of improving public access to social science research. It is intended to test what I have been calling the public value of the social sciences, by affording social scientists a new way of serving public interests. . . . (Willinsky 1999, 153)

One assumes this site would also make available scholarship in education conducted in the research traditions of humanities, scholarship such as Willinsky's (1998) own historical and theoretical analysis of colonialism and curriculum. As Elizabeth Ellsworth (1997, 11) points out, "few" schools of education provide students with knowledge of research traditions in the humanities.

What makes Willinsky's proposal feasible—certainly it is sensible and, in the tradition of curriculum design proposals, brilliant—is the existence of new intellectual technologies such as navigation, what Willinsky (1999, 25) terms "data mining." The improved structuring of and access to information, Willinsky (1999, 27), notes, "[m]ight . . . provide the public with far more helpful and comprehensive picture of what has been studied and what has been found." A sophisticated curriculum theorist, Willinsky has no illusion that technology per se can solve persisting educational problems: "Whatever hope we hold out for the benefits and consolation of knowledge lies not with the machines but in our hands and heads, in what we come to expect of this knowledge and the ends to which we turn it" (Willinsky 1999, 29).

That acknowledged, Willinsky is clear that the new intellectual technologies do offer opportunities to advance our understanding of curriculum design as well as to improve public access to academic knowledge. Given the number and complexity of research studies on a given topic, facts which intensify the fragmentation that divides and subdivides disciplines (themselves divisions of the larger knowledge enterprise), the establishment of structures such as the Automata Data Corporation might function, Willinsky (48) theorizes, "as countervailing forces. These structures should be directed not at seeking the unity of all knowledge but at mapping the diversity, the ways of knowing, so that one can find a bridge."

That sentence distinguishes Willinsky from educational technologists who too often uncritically concern themselves with "application" and "practice" only. In that sentence Willinsky brings to bear on the complex relationship between education and technology the curriculum theorist's expertise, namely the pedagogical concern for configurations of knowledge, in this instance, its structural interrelationships and its relationships to the public. On this last point Willinsky (1999, 49, 40) asserts his hope

> that the social sciences can mount a more concerted effort at identifying with or against the public "what we really want to understand," before the research community is called, once too often, on those obfuscating research clouds. . . . [I] hope to see through a device such as Automatic Data the full range of research inquiry made available as a public resource, without sacrificing the social sciences' own democratic play of ideas about knowledge and its purposes.

For Willinsky, this amounts to nothing less than "a renewed social contract" (1999, 95).

Willinsky's commitment to democracy and education represents an extension and revival of the progressive project associated with John Dewey (1916). Willinsky is committed to the democratization of knowledge, including democratic dialogue over the public uses of specialized academic knowledge. Willinsky (1999, 149) makes this point explicit: "[T]his project of renewing the social contract of the social sciences is not about technology, but a determination, a determination to use whatever tools are available to do a better job of creating a public resource out of the research enterprise." "Still," he continues, here anticipating Pierre Lévy, "I cannot close this chapter on democracy without recognizing the enthusiasm for how certain forms of technology can develop new levels of public engagement and community, in a coda that offers its own resistant notes from the underground within the new networked age of information" (1999, 149).

The increased circulation of knowledge—what Lévy (2001, 138) terms "knowledge as flow"—as well as this potential for "democratic" participation in collective as well as individual understanding may function to reconfigure the processes of education. "What must be learned can no longer be planned or precisely defined in advance," Lévy (2001, 138) notes, making, without knowing it, an old argument in curriculum theory. Skills and specialized knowledges are singular, less and less able to be programmed into courses useful for everyone. "We need to construct new models of the knowledge space," he asserts (2001, 138).

Lévy is skeptical of traditional organizations of education into graded steps, what he terms a pyramid model with "higher" forms of knowledge accessible only by taking step after step in a linear sequence leading to the "top." In contrast, he employs the metaphor of space to imagine knowledge—not unlike Willinsky's proposal—as "open, continuous, in flux, nonlinear . . . where each participant occupies a singular and evolving position" (Lévy 2001, 138). This requires models of "collaborative" and "individualized" instruction that allow for singular strategies and journeys, and to destinations not planned by teachers or textbook companies, not unlike progressive organizations of the school subjects according to "project" (see Pinar et al. 1995, 114).

Like so many others, Lévy (2001, 138) lists "open distance learning" as the first of the two major educational reforms required at this time. His sense of "distance learning" seems, however, comparatively sophisticated; it includes hypermedia, interactive networks, and other intellectual technologies of cyberculture. "But what is essential," Lévy (2001, 138) asserts, "is a new style of pedagogy which promotes both personalized learning and cooperative networked learning. In this context, the teacher inspires the collective intelligence of groups of students rather than directly dispensing knowledge." Unmindful of Paulo Freire and Maxine Greene and Dwayne Huebner and much of the curriculum theory of the past 100 years, Lévy states the obvious, obvious to those of us who work in the academic field of curriculum studies, but opaque to politicians and other such school (de)form advocates.

Despite his naiveté regarding education and his exuberant embrace of cyberspace, Lévy does sketch a futural possibility in the present that could support "complicated conversation" across and within culture, class, and place. The intellectual technologies he describes and that Willinsky proposes provide forms of communicational infrastructure that can enable students and scholars in curriculum studies worldwide to create new organizational structures toward the intellectual advancement of the field, a movement underway now in the United States, signaled by the inauguration in 2001 of the International Association for the Advancement of Curriculum Studies and its American affiliate, the American Association for the Advancement of Curriculum Studies. It is signaled as well by the appearance of the first international handbook of curriculum research (see Pinar in press-a).

As part of what, as of this writing, Willinsky terms the Public Knowledge Project, is the *Open Journal Systems* (OJS). This online journal management and publishing system is part of the Public Knowledge Project's research initiative to make scholarship accessible to various publics worldwide. Open Journal Systems enables editors to manage, publish and index peer-reviewed journals over the Internet on an open access or free-to-read basis, increasing readership dramatically. Able to be installed on web-servers anywhere and requiring few if any technical skills from editors, Willinsky suggests that OJS will make journals far easier, far more efficient, and less expensive to produce. (1. To read more about OJS as well as to see a demo journal, go to http://pkp.ubc.ca/ojs 2. To take OJS for a "test drive" and see what online management is all about from the inside, go to http://research2.csci.educ.ubc.ca/pkp/ojs/demo2)

Considerations of communicational infrastructure raise concerns about the processes of worldwide cultural imperialism and economic standardization subsumed under the term *globalization*. Others foresee a different, less dismal, even exciting future. Edouard Glissant (2002) employs the French phrase *tout monde* to evoke his sense of a new but not-yet global totality, a totality, he imagines, without totalitarianism, a world of endless multiplicities, described by the word "globalness," not globalization. Glissant evokes Deleuze and Guattari's (1987) phrase "lines of flight" in a poetic image of a flock of birds flying over an African lake. In this image he is not suggesting that earthlings are like a flock of birds, but, rather, that our movements in the emerging *tout monde* are creative, unpredictable, ever-shifting, not unlike the movements of birds in flight. The phrase "lines of flight" also invokes the infinitude of our relationalities. "We are the world," Glissant asserts, "but not one type or identity. Rather, we are 'multiplicities.' " He rejects any notion of reified identities, whether these be cultural or nationalistic, embracing, instead, ever-changing relational identities in a new human history. Like Lévy, Glissant is millennial; he declares that we are at the moment of genesis of *tout monde*.

Considerably more ambivalent about the future, I have been reluctant to use any derivative of *globalization*, worrying, for instance, that my call for an international association—realized as the International Association for the Advancement of Curriculum Studies—would be recoded as a call for standardization in curriculum studies worldwide (Pinar 2003b). In anticipation of that concern and to underscore that curriculum studies are very much embedded within nations and regions, I chose the word *internationalization* to thematize the next phrase of the field's development (see Pinar 2003b). (After Reconceptualization comes Internationalization.) The term is still worrisome, insofar as it appears to accept uncritically the historical and problematic concept of "nation," a concept David Held and his colleagues suggest "may need to be rethought and recast" (Held et al. 1999, 450).

In Chinese, the notion of *internationalization* supports a more democratic conception of the future, of *tout monde*. In Chinese, Hongyu Wang (2002b) reports, internationalization translates into Chinese as "between/country/ change (process)." "Globalization," she continues, translates as "whole/ world (planet)/change (process)." For Wang "it is the inter-space that is more interesting." "Conversation" occurs at the boundaries and between spaces. That is why Donna Trueit (2002, 278 n. 2) prefers "conversation" to "dialogue," a term, she worries that may imply an element of the notion of "agenda," a term associated with "control (and power)." For Wang, "internationalization," in this Chinese sense, represents a challenge to the centralizing control and power of nationalism, due to its tendencies toward the realignment and destabilization of traditional, now ever-shifting, borders. For me, Wang's translation represents a welcome revision of internationalization, in that it protects locality while taking flight toward Glissant's "globalness."

"If East-West conversation in curriculum is to be authentically East-West dialogue, if North-South conversation is to be authentically North-South dialogue," Ted Aoki (in press) suggests, then "such conversation must be guided by an interest in understanding more fully what is not said by going beyond what is said." Aoki is using a phenomenology of language—and specifically its depth imagery—to remind us that the social surface of speech is precisely that. Authentic conversation requires "going beyond" the surface to take into account "unspoken" and "taken-for-granted" assumptions, including "ideology," what Aoki characterizes as "the cultural crucible and context that make possible what is said by each in the conversational situation."

Aoki reminds us that "authentic conversation is open conversation," never "empty," always one in which the participants engage in a "reciprocity of perspectives." Invoking one of his favorite metaphors, Aoki (in press) tells us: "I understand conversation as a bridging of two worlds by a bridge, which is not a bridge." Conversation is a passage from here to there and elsewhere, but it is not "here" or "there" or "elsewhere," but in the conjunctive spaces in-between. Perhaps in such conjunctive spaces, we can create a "complicated conversation" worldwide. As Michael Hardt and Antoni Negri (2000, 49) remind us, "There was a time, not so long ago, when internationalism was a key component of proletarian struggles and progressive politics in general." May it become so again, especially so for us, engaged in our various locales in the project of understanding education within and across national borders.

IV

THE ANALYTIC MOMENT: ANTI-INTELLECTUALISM AND COMPLICATED CONVERSATION

7

"Something Sound and Important": Interdisciplinarity, Erudition, Self-Reflexivity, and Intellectuality

I
ANTI-INTELLECTUALISM

The school has been considered the real space
and the university the theoretical space.
—Bernadette M. Baker (2001, 41)

To what extent able students stayed out of teaching because of its
poor rewards and to what extent because of the nonsense that
figured so prominently in teacher education, it is difficult to say.
—Richard Hofstadter (1962, 318)

[C]ulture is nothing other than a suffocating process
of repetition, of the stereotype.
—Michael Moriarty (1991, 142)

In the regressive moment we discovered how public education has been racialized and gendered in the American popular imagination. Now we understand that our positions of "gracious submission" to politicians and, secondarily, to parents (who imagine themselves "consumers" of "services") are covert racialized and gendered positions in which the academic—intellectual—freedom to develop the curriculum and devise the means of its assessment has been usurped by politicians in the name of "accountability." As Linda McNeil (2000, 7) has pointed out: "[t]he conservative transformation of American public education [has occurred] through the use of technicist forms of power." Accountability is the face of fascism in America today.

163

Using a business model, politicians and others have made the common-sensical (if anti-educational) argument that all that matters is "the bottom line"—scores on standardized tests—and in the process converted the school into a business, a skill-and-knowledge factory (or corporation), but a busi-ness—not an educational institution—nonetheless. Again, McNeil under-stands these issues precisely. Speaking of Texas school reform, an antecedent (for former Texas Governor) George W. Bush's presidential educational agenda, McNeil (2000, xxiv) points out that "incipient in the [these] reforms was the shifting of control over public schooling away from 'the public,' and away from the profession, toward business-controlled management account-ability systems."

Employing a classic "blame the victim" tactic, politicians have insisted that we educators are to blame, and not just for what they judge to be low test scores. In the 1950s and early 1960s we were to blame for jeopardizing the American military position vis-à-vis the Soviet Union and, in the early 1980s, for U.S. currency devaluation. Now we are held "accountable" for America's economic performance in the "new millennium," distracting the public from the unethical and unprofitable practices of many American businesses, the most spectacular instances of which are Enron and WorldCom. "Account-ability" would seem to be nothing more than a "projection" onto educators of what many businessmen and politicians themselves lack.

Much of this is simple scapegoating, but it has occurred and succeeded as a tactic in the "conservative" restoration of the last 30 years, a political phe-nomenon that could not have occurred without active participation of the re-actionary white South. First in the 1964 Goldwater campaign, Republicans discovered they could draw upon reactionary (white) southern resistance to (especially) racial justice to animate their broader causes of cultural authori-tarianism and economic elitism. In allegiance with "conservatives" in the Midwest and the Far West, Republicans contained the progressive political potential unleashed during the 1960s civil rights and anti-War movements. Without the reactionary white South, right-wing politicians, business execu-tives, and religious fundamentalists (intersecting categories to be sure) could not have forced their elitist agenda on an increasingly alienated American electorate.

This coalition of business, religious, and cultural reactionaries have fo-cused on the schools, where they have forced teachers—through so-called "school reform" initiatives—to do their bidding. It had been students and professors who had animated the 1960s revolt against racial injustice and U.S. imperialism abroad, and it would be educational institutions where "conservatives" would focus their attention in the decades following. By ty-ing the curriculum to student performance on test scores, teachers are forced to abandon the intellectual freedom to choose what they teach, how they teach, and how they assess student learning.

While historically public-school teachers have not taken advantage of their academic freedom to the extent their colleagues in the university some-times have, at present they do not have the opportunity to do so. Curriculum theory is that interdisciplinary field in which teacher education is conceived as the professionalization of academic freedom, including intellectual dissent, creativity, and self-reflexive, interdisciplinary erudition.

The marginalization of curriculum theory in American teacher education is, in part, a reflection of the anti-intellectual vocationalism of mainstream teacher education. Too often teacher educators have colluded in preparing teachers to accept their positions of gracious submission in the school. While victims of anti-intellectualism in government, in the university (as we will soon see) and of anti-intellectualism in the culture at large, the field of educa-tion, too, has embedded within it destructive anti-intellect tendencies, in large part *due* to these external influences.

That there is in American culture—in which the American field of curricu-lum studies is thoroughly embedded—a profound and persistent anti-intellectualism has been documented by, among others, the distinguished his-torian Richard Hofstadter (1962). By definition, culture tends toward the conservative. This tendency positions intellectuals (and artists), often dedi-cated to cultural experimentation and progress, oppositionally in those cul-tures in which they live and work. For Americans, this anti-intellectualism is historic and specific; Hofstadter (1962) identifies it with business and relig-ious zealotry. Christopher Lasch (1978, 52) points out that, in America, the two intersect: "According to the myth of capitalist enterprise, thrift and in-dustry held the key to material success and spiritual fulfillment."

In addition to business and religion, Hofstadter also associates anti-intellectualism with "us," that is, with teachers and especially teachers' teachers, the education professorate. In his *Anti-Intellectualism in American Life*, Hofstadter's main target is life adjustment education, that post–World War II amalgamation of earlier progressive and social efficiency move-ments in education (see Pinar et al. 1995, 146). Hofstadter (1962, 343) de-clares that the life-adjustment movement "was an attempt on the part of educational leaders and the United States Office of Education to make completely dominant the values of the crusade against intellectualism that had been going on since 1910," a "crusade" he associates with the child-centered wing of progressivism.

Hofstadter appears to hold John Dewey responsible for this crusade, which he describes in the following terms: "the central idea of the new educa-tional thought [was] that the school should base its studies not on the de-mands of society, nor any conception of what an educated person should be, but on the developing needs and interests of the child" (Hofstadter 1962, 369). Probably only a minority of child-centered progressives ever held this extreme view, a view which was never the "central ideal of the new educational thought." As for Dewey, he insisted that education and society were inextricably linked, not only together but to the psycho-social and intellectual growth of children as well (Dewey 1916, 1938).

As a professional historian, did Hofstadter mistake the project of professional education—the point of which is to train, in his case, competent historians—for "general education," in which the interdisciplinary study of important ideas is to be linked to society and to students' self-formation? Is that why he was so quick to judge the life-adjustment movement as "anti-intellectual"? Note his response to a passage he quotes from *Life Adjustment Education for Every Youth*, which defines life adjustment as "a philosophy of education which places life values above acquisition of knowledge" (quoted in Hofstadter 1962, 345). Hofstadter (1962, 345) comments: "Repeatedly, life adjustment educators were to insist that intellectual training is of no use in solving the 'real life problems' of ordinary youth."

Now there were, no doubt, life-adjustment educators who held such a view, but his claim does not follow, as Hofstadter implies, from the statement he has quoted. From that quoted sentence there is no reason to believe that those who formulated the idea of life adjustment education devalued the acquisition of knowledge except, possibly, for its own sake. Knowledge acquisition, it is asserted in the passage Hofstadter quotes, must in the service of "life values." Knowledge is obviously valued; it is in the service of "life values."

There were excesses in the life adjustment movement, and historian Christopher Lasch—who, like Hofstadter, provides a caricature, rather than a history, of progressive education—is eager to refer to them. Quoting Joel Spring (1976, 18–21), Lasch (1978, 137) provides surely the most questionable examples of "life adjustment." In Illinois, advocates of life adjustment urged schools to give curricular attention to such "problems of high school youth" as "improving one's personal appearance," "selecting a family dentist," and "developing and maintain wholesome boy–girl relationships." Such socialization into consumption and society as a spectacle—Lasch's point—could become educational were these subjects taught from a critical and intellectual point of view.

Like Hofstader, Lasch makes no argument, supplies no evidence; he only makes declarations in his condemnation of the "democratization of education" (Lasch 1978, 125). Such education, he continues,

> has neither improved popular understanding of modern society, raised the quality of popular culture, nor reduced the gap between wealth and poverty, which remains as wide as ever. On the other hand, it has contributed to the decline of critical thought and the erosion of intellectual standards, forcing us to consider the possibility of that mass education, as conservatives have argued all along, is intrinsically incompatible with the maintenance of educational quality. (Lasch 1978, 125)

While I would be hard pressed to argue that public education has significantly improved critical thought, intellectual standards, and the quality of American popular culture, it is not obvious to me that schooling is specifically to blame for their underdeveloped state.

Moreover, Lasch's allegations contradict his broader argument, in which the school, like the family, sport, politics, and even aging, all become degraded in a "culture of narcissism." He writes: "Institutions of cultural transmission (school, church, family), which might have been expected to counter the narcissistic trend of our culture, have instead been shaped in its image" (Lasch 1978, 141). While he is disinclined to trace this crisis of American culture to one cause, at least in the 1978 book, capitalism seems a likely suspect. In the 1984 book, historical events, among them the Holocaust and the Cold War, join capitalism as contributing to the dissolution of both the public and private spheres.

In his last book, Lasch seems to resolve this contradiction. No longer does he target the school, but, instead, acknowledges that "most of the shortcomings of our educational system can be traced . . . to the growing inability to believe in the reality either of the inner world or of the public world, either in a stable core personal identity or in a politics that rises above the level of platitudes and propaganda" (1995, 186–187). I wonder if this shift, evident too in his generally favorable treatment of Dewey, can be attributed, in part, to the addition to the University of Rochester History Department (now relegated to history by arrogant administrators; see Moses 1999) of Robert Westbrook, who whose important book in Dewey and the politics of progressivism (see Westbrook 1991) may have had influence. Lasch's 1995 book is dedicated to him.

Hofstadter (of whom Lasch is sometimes critical) is more focused in his complaints, targeting progressive education and, specifically, the life adjustment movement. Drawing on Lawrence Cremin (1961), Hofstadter draws a throughline from Dewey's *Democracy and Education* to life adjustment education (see Hofstadter 1962, 361). While he focuses on "the limitations and the misuse of these [Dewey's] ideas," Hofstadter (1962, 359) asks us not to read his account as a "blanket condemnation of progressive education." "Although its reputation suffered unwarranted damage from extremists on its periphery," he judges, "progressivism had at its core something sound and important" (Hofstadter 1962, 359). Hofstadter makes a list:

> The value of progressivism rested on its experimentalism and in its work with younger children; its weakness lay in its effects to promulgate doctrine, to generalize, in its inability to assess the practical limits of its own program, above all in its tendency to dissolve the curriculum. This tendency became most serious in the education of older children, and especially at the secondary level, where, as the need arises to pursue a complex, organized program of studies, the question of the curriculum becomes acute. (Hofstadter 1962, 360)

It would seem that it was the progressives' commitment to public school curriculum as a public issue, that is, linked to society and to students' interests ("life values" in life-adjustment movement rhetoric) which distressed Hofstadter most.

Hofstadter's book was widely read and has been enormously influential, except in mass culture, where the anti-intellectualism of the American preoccupations with business and religion have continued, even intensified, since the book's publication 40 years ago. Probably few present-day university arts and science faculty remember Hofstadter's condemnation of the "life-adjustment" movement, which he associated with progressivism (regarding which, despite his claim to find "something sound and important" at its "core," he is, it seems to me, mostly negative). But his association of academic vocationalism with "traditional education" (Hofstadter 1962, 355)—that is, mistaking professional for general education—serves the political and institutional interests of too many arts and science faculty. What remains most of all, I suspect, is Hofstadter's *ad hominem* hostility to teacher education, uncomfortably evident in this gendered, classed, and scatological diatribe:

> The more humdrum the task the educationists have to undertake, the nobler and more exalted their music grows. When they see a chance to introduce a new course in family living or home economics, they begin to tune the fiddles of their idealism. When they feel they are about to establish the school janitor's right to be treated with respect, they grow starry-eyed and increase their tempo. And when they are trying to assure that the location of the school toilets will be so clearly marked that the dullest child can find them, they grow dizzy with exaltation and launch into wild cadenzas about democracy and self-realization. (Hofstadter 1962, 340)

And this fantasy in a book awarded the 1964 Pulitzer Prize in *non-fiction*! True, this is one of the few pieces of nonsense in the book. Overall, Hofstadter's argument is carefully crafted, perhaps why the anti-intellectualism of his diatribe on teacher education passed for considered and scholarly judgment.

To his credit, Hofstadter understood that, in America, serious intellectual work makes sense only when it leads to wealth, spiritual or material. In America, intellectual work tends to be for, well, eccentrics. Not surprisingly, more than a few Americans consider intellectuals (and artists) as eccentric, or worse. And so our calling as teachers—dedicated, perhaps, to "life values"—tends to position us in tension with, sometimes in opposition to, many, perhaps most, of our fellow citizens, and not a few of their children. It also positions us oppositionally to many of our students, including prospective and practicing teachers who themselves must grapple with a pervasive anti-intellectualism among the American populace (Hofstadter 1962).

Anti-intellectualism is not only an American problem; probably many cultures tend to position its intellectuals (and artists) oppositionally. As university-based scholars, and as public school teachers (although teachers, especially in politically conservative areas, are more vulnerable than university professors), we cannot allow ourselves to be unduly anxious about the skepticism and sometimes hostility of our fellow Americans. Nor can we afford to alienate them either, of course, at least not irrevocably. As teachers we work to keep the bonds that bind alive, in order to be heard, in order to hear, in order to teach and learn. Our interest in our students is, of course, partly parental; we wish them well, independently of our self-interest. We want our students to succeed, even if our ideas of success differ from theirs. When we fight for cultural progress, we do not (only) seek our own narrow political gain; we fight for what we perceive to be in the public's—in the next generation's, the culture's—interest.

In addition to the anti-intellectualism of American mass culture, there is an anti-intellectualism specific to the field of American curriculum studies, embedded as it is in American culture. Because curriculum studies is construed as a "professional" field, an "applied" discipline, it has sometimes been suspicious of scholarship not obviously linked to the workings of schools. Theory and scholarship that seek to understand curriculum (which may, but may not, attend to schools explicitly) have, on occasion, been ignored or contested (Pinar 1999b; Wraga 1999). Partly, this form of anti-intellectualism derives from a genuine (if narrow) loyalty to the schools, and, particularly, to the children and teachers who inhabit them. Partly it comes from pressure from our students (prospective and practicing teachers), who have been conditioned, partly by (mis)understandings of education in popular culture, articulated by politicians and even, on occasion, by university presidents.

One recently appointed university president expressed that form of anti-intellectualism which mistakes vocational practice for professional education. Harvard University President Lawrence H. Summers (2001, 1) informed his colleagues in the Graduate School of Education that he understood how

> "[i]important the work . . . of education" is because "for each of the past seven years in Washington, D.C. . . . on Veterans Day [because federal government employees enjoy a holiday] . . . I have therefore gone and watched my children's classes and sat through a half a day or a whole day in a second grade classroom and then a third grade classroom, and then a fourth grade classroom.

President Summers then told Harvard Graduate School of Education faculty and students that the field must be about, in part, "a rigorous assessment of facts about what works. . . . Figuring out rigorously what works, and spreading it. These are profoundly important missions" (Summers 2001, 4).

One wonders if President Summers presumed to tell his colleagues in English or Physics what the mission of their discipline must be.

Such an admixture of ignorance and arrogance undermines the advancement of the broad field of education, and of curriculum studies, specifically. But we cannot blame only administrators or arts and sciences colleagues or pesky politicians. We must also take responsibility for the problem of anti-intellectualism ourselves, including its expression in popular misunderstandings of our field's mission, namely, that we are to find out "what works" and then "apply it" in the schools. This misunderstanding seems to assume that education is somehow like a complex automobile engine, that if only we make the right adjustments—in teaching, in curriculum, in assessment—that we will get it humming smoothly, and that it will transport us to our destination, the promised land of high test scores. Even Richard Hofstadter (1962, 339) noticed that "the misuse of tests seems to be a recurrent factor in American education."

This misunderstanding of our work—that we are engineers of and thereby responsible for student learning—is circulated not only by university presidents but by many of our own—education—colleagues. It leads to the concoction of funny phrases like "action research" (redundant as that phrase is, and based on a false binary) and to a pervasive (and anti-intellectual) suspicion of theory. This almost institutionalized suspicion toward theory undermines our intellectual movement and the scholarly advancement of our field; it amounts to an anti-intellectualism peculiar to the field of education itself.

II
INTELLECTUAL EVENTS

But a belief in intellectual freedom where it does not exist
contributes only to complacency in virtual enslavement, to
sloppiness, superficiality and recourse to sensations
as a substitute for ideas: marked traits of our present
estate with respect to social knowledge.
—John Dewey (1991 [1927], 168)

[L]earning is a psychic event, charged
with resistance to knowledge.
—Deborah Britzman (1998, 118)

How could there possibly be anti-intellectualism in education, of all fields? I will suggest an initial answer to that question, an answer that I hope will contribute to a sustained and sober reflection on the state of our field, in particular the problem of anti-intellectualism. Before I begin my speculations, I want to emphasize I do not think American curriculum studies is "only" or even "primarily" anti-intellectual.

The 1970s reconceptualization of American curriculum studies was, among other things, a profoundly intellectual event (see Pinar et al. 1995, chapter 4). In the introduction to *Contemporary Curriculum Discourses: Twenty Years of JCT*, I (Pinar 1999a, xi) characterized that decade-long event as an "intellectual breakthrough." Moreover, the field that has followed is characterized by often powerful intellectual preoccupations, among them a continuing interest in theory (see Trifonas 2000). There is much to praise in the intellectual state of the contemporary curriculum field as even a cursory review of recent books makes clear (see Baker 2001; Carlson 2002; Doll 2000; Lesko 2001; Morris 2001a; Trifonas 2000, 2003; Weaver, Applebaum, and Morris 2001).

But it is true, I think, and not only for education faculty, that too often books amount to currency in a careerist system, rendering secondary the intellectual content and scholarly accomplishment of the works. Not often enough does publication constitute the major intellectual event in our professional lives that it ought to be in a field committed to education.

I am not suggesting, of course, that every book or article that appears is a major event. I am suggesting that the books and articles that do appear ought to be our *major* professional anticipation, excitement, and obligation. As scholars based in colleges and universities, the appearance of a book in our field should, at the minimum, merit our attention, and, in general, warrant its purchase, its study, and perhaps its critique and/or incorporation into our own ongoing scholarly work. Again, I am not suggesting that each of us read everything that appears in or is related to the field of curriculum studies.

I am suggesting that if the intellectual life of our field were its key feature, then we would take notice of every book, study as many as we could, and respond to these in serious ways, certainly by reading them, perhaps by taking notes, maybe by critiquing them, in class, in a conference paper, in an article or in a book of one's own. It is an unmistakable symptom of anti-intellectualism in our field that books and articles do not always occupy this key and prestigious position in our professional lives. More than a few of us, I suspect, do not feel professionally obligated to keep up with the scholarly production in our field. Is this another form of "death in a tenured position" (see Pinar 1994)?

For too many, the appearance of books and articles is noteworthy not as intellectual events, but as utilitarian ones: books and articles help with promotion, tenure, and/or a merit raise. Possibly they become eligible for use in a class one teaches. Now I am not suggesting that considerations of promotion, tenure, and merit raises are unimportant. Nor am I suggesting that choosing new texts for teaching is not intellectual labor. But probably too many of us still break copyright laws and photocopy material for class use, rather than ask students to purchase pertinent texts. Presumably such instructors do not want to burden students financially. While that sensitivity is laudable, it is, finally, an unacceptable—unprofessional—reason for failing to require texts (and I use the plural) for serious study in each of our classes, from freshman and other undergraduate classes, through post-bachelors, M.A., Ed.D. and Ph.D. study.

I suspect what often animates faculty sensitivity in the assignment of readings is not so much financial empathy as it is a concern for students' opinion of the class, expressed in their evaluations at the end of the term, evaluations forwarded to department chairs and deans, evaluations which can figure in merit-pay deliberations. Students—especially undergraduate but working teachers as well—can complain when the "easy" education class they anticipated turns out to involve "work." Of course, student evaluations of our teaching are important, as they inform us of student perceptions and allow us to rethink and possibly restructure the courses we teach. I appreciate that they are additionally significant for untenured colleagues. But student evaluations must not drive our curriculum choices, must not dissuade us from assigning numerous and serious texts, and, then, from carefully (if creatively) examining students' study of them.

III
A TROUBLED MARRIAGE

But one thing is certain: there do not appear to be sufficient
data for a theory of instruction in any specific,
coherent and worthwhile sense.
—Robin Barrow (1984, 134)

Habit does not preclude the use of thought, but it
determines the channels within which it operates.
—John Dewey (1991 [1927], 160)

Curriculum exists in our embodied relationships.
—Dennis J. Sumara and Brent Davis (1998, 85)

How can university-based scholars committed to the project of education *not* view intellectual activity as the main index of the field's vitality? The answers I propose to these questions are neither pleasant nor comfortable. The first, simple, and obvious answer is that our students are teachers, prospective or practicing. While certification requirements are, in general, being reduced, some number of required education courses remain in place. I think this arrangement amounts to something akin to a troubled marriage (and a heterosexual one at that), given that the image of the college professor in the American popular imagination tends to be male, while the image of the schoolteacher tends to be female.

Certainly it is an "arranged marriage," although, of course, an arranged marriage is not necessarily a bad marriage, especially in those cultures where marriages are routinely arranged (Viruru and Cannella 2001). But given the American romance with "romance," and the widely held assumption that (especially but not only) life-long relationships ought to be chosen by the participants rather than selected for them, having a relationship "arranged," as they are in teacher education courses, can, and does, spell trouble.

More than a few students in our classes express their resistance to certification requirements by demanding of us a social-engineering expertise (i.e., we are presumed to know "what works"). It is a demand our scholarship (and probably our teaching experience) has taught us is, in principle, impossible to meet. I suspect many of our students know it is impossible too, but many play the "practice" card with determination and skill, not to mention with a thinly concealed hostility. To require students to study curriculum as an intellectual rather than narrowly institutional or practical problem sometimes provokes that hostility.

Because students' enrollment in teacher education courses amounts to "an arranged marriage," and because most bring to their education courses an expectation that they will learn (but cannot possibly learn, given, in part, education professors' remove from the schools) "what works," there is often resistance to serious academic study. Education professors too often capitulate to this resistance, too often confer high grades for coursework that is not always intellectually challenging. While grade inflation is hardly limited to schools and colleges of education—Christopher Lasch (1978, 145) complains about "the ubiquitous inflation of grades"—there are few areas of the university where the problem seems more intractable.

There is, as noted earlier, a gendered element to this resistance, a fact that underlines the second word in the phrase "arranged marriage." Because college professors are coded masculine and schoolteachers as feminine in the American popular imagination, there is a gendered, and specifically heterosexual, structure to teacher education courses, despite the anatomies of those individuals participating. Especially professors in the instructional fields have sometimes directed students how to teach, a hierarchical relationship that has regularly engendered not only resistance but resentment. When teachers complain about education courses, they are sometimes complaining about their positioning as passive, in positions of gracious submission, in those courses.

In complaining about this forced and hierarchical position, students often view education courses as "hurdles" to jump, rather than intellectual opportunities to study the various scholarly efforts to understand curriculum as historical, as political, as racialized, as gendered, as phenomenological, as postmodern, as autobiographical, as aesthetic, as religious or theological, as international, and as institutionalized (see Pinar et al. 1995). Instead, students want to study as little as possible and gain "admission" to their profession as effortlessly as possible, an especially curious demand given that they will soon, or are now (if they are practicing teachers returning for additional coursework) demanding that *their* students appreciate the courses they are teaching as opportunities to understand science, literature, etc.

This unhappy state of affairs is pervasive, I suspect, not limited to particular kinds of institutions (regional public universities versus elite private research universities, for instance). At the University of California at Riverside, for instance, Reba Page (2001, 21) reports just such an "anti-intellectual" student subculture, even at the most advanced stage of study: "For them [doctoral students], doctoral studies seemed to be either a chance to prove the worth of a pet project or an inconvenient but necessary burden they had to put up with to get a degree that would allow them to return to the world of practice with some authority." The education professoriate has been too tolerant of such anti-intellectual careerism among its students. Anti-intellectualism among those claim the title of "teacher" and who are presumably engaged in the process of "education" must be denounced in the strongest possible terms.

Evidently the education professorate does not face this problem alone. If a statement that appeared in the University of Michigan Law School Announcement is any indication, professors of law have also had to face their students' confusion over the distinction between an academic or professional education and a vocational or technical curriculum:

> The Law School is very much a professional school. But it is distinctly not a vocational school. Students are not trained to perform many, or even most, of the tasks that its graduates may be called upon to perform as lawyers, and should not expect to be fully prepared to deliver a wide range of legal services on the day of graduation. Students may acquire or begin to develop some practical or technical skills and may gain confidence in their ability to perform as lawyers. Our practice-oriented courses and clinics provide, however, only an introduction to skills and a framework for practice which can only be defined through years of experience. The majority of our graduates join law firms where numerous opportunities exist for skill development under supervision of experienced practitioners who share with the novitiate responsibility for the quality of service rendered. Michigan, more than many other law schools, seeks to provide students with the intellectual and theoretical background with which an attorney can undertake a more reflective and rewarding practice. It is felt that too much haste or emphasis on vocational skills, without a broader and more criti-

cal view of the framework in which lawyering occurs, runs the risk of training technicians instead of professionals. (quoted in Pinar et al. 1995, 759)

There is no point, of course, in stating a distinction already widely appreciated and encoded in students' expectations.

During the summer of 2002 Columbia University's President Lee C. Bollinger called for the University's School of Journalism to become more "intellectually based." "In contrast to other professional schools, there's a much wider gap between conceptions of what a journalism-school education ought to be," Bollinger said. "There's much more a university can do to educate future leaders in this profession, and it's much more important to leave the teaching of on-the-job skills" to the workplace (quoted passages in *Chronicle* 2002, A9). Too few university presidents—certainly not Harvard's, as we saw—seem as clear as Bollinger that University-based professional schools must "educate" and "leave the teaching of on-the-job skills" to the workplace.

In the field of education, including teacher education and curriculum studies, professional preparation *is* academic education. Yet the instructional fields, with their emphasis upon teaching strategies, distract students from their professional obligation to understand, and not merely manipulate, the processes of education, the organizational and intellectual center of which is the curriculum. *What* we teach is at least as important, if not more important, than *how* we teach it, although, of course, the two domains—the curricular and the instructional—cannot be sharply distinguished and, are, in fact, intertwined.

In addition to the problem posed by forcing teachers to study education (one can hardly be opposed to the practice; after all, by definition teachers are students of education) is the problem that most professors of education are themselves former schoolteachers. In fact, several states require it, as if the schools were not already too influential in the intellectual lives of education professors. The old adage—that we work in schools and departments of education, not schools and departments of schooling—is, evidently, no longer in circulation. The requirement that education professors be former schoolteachers would seem to assume that teaching is akin to a physical skill like, say, horse-shoeing, and that knowledge of it requires prior practice of it. One would think it obvious that the question of curriculum is an intellectual as well as institutional question. Experience as a teacher or an administrator in the schools might position a scholar to more fully understand curriculum. But it might not. In fact, prior experience might make likely a certain submergence in the curricular status quo, a submergence that would make even more difficult the project of critical and scholarly understanding.

As professors of education we should speak of schools sparingly. We should speak of education. Such a distinction does not deny that education sometimes—often—occurs in schools. We should speak to schoolpeople, of course; they are our students, sometimes our friends. We should visit schools and help as we can. But like the drug addict trying to recover, we should sometimes allow the thought of the school to pass through us without engaging us, without prompting us to act. If we always believe what we think and feel, we become trapped in the pointless practice of speaking only about schools. Too many education professors talk about schools like men waiting in a barber shop talk about the weather; it is something beyond our control, something to complain about or appreciate, but about which there is nothing to be done (except to take cover). Too often, the "school" becomes a projective screen without material or concrete or historical specificity, a vague referent for our open wound, a monosyllabic abstraction for our hope. Such a projective screen is pointless, except, perhaps, in barber shops, where it can function to pass the time and avoid genuine encounter.

What does it mean to acknowledge that most of our colleagues are former schoolteachers? (I am, myself, a former schoolteacher.) It is to say, of course, that professors of education are individuals whose first interest was teaching in the public schools. It was not, in general, to engage in original research; it was not necessarily to press back the limits of conventional thought; it was not necessarily to participate, however modestly, in the centuries-old "conversation" that could be said to comprise intellectual life in the West. Most of us, as it is phrased in the vernacular, wanted to teach "kids." Sure, if we were secondary-school teachers, we chose a subject. But that subject was probably chosen less as a life-long medium of intellectual labor than it was a subject to teach "kids."

I do not want to complain much about this fact. Teachers' first obligation must be to the children, although the school reform (and the curriculum reform specifically) of the last 40 years has tended to weaken as it has complicated this ethico-professional obligation, making performance on standardized tests the main thing (as everyone is well aware, ad nauseam). Such right-wing, business-minded reform plus profound political, cultural, and economic shifts—not a one of which seems to make coming of age in America (see Friedenberg 1962) any easier, let alone more intellectual—have led to many more detached, even cynical, teachers, to many more alienated students, to less engaged thinking, teaching, and studying. More than ever—and social engineering has, in general, typified American schools for at least a century—there is the idea that if only we make the appropriate adjustment (in curriculum, in teaching technique, in how teachers are prepared, in testing, etc.), the school engine will then hum smoothly, and those test scores will soar.

At least two teacher union leaders accept this naïve and misleading idea, unsurprisingly perhaps, given its pervasiveness in the research on teaching. In the following newspaper report one observes how the social engineering idea expresses unconcealed hostility toward researchers. United Teachers of New Orleans President Brenda Mitchell told researchers—assembled at the 2002 annual meeting of the American Education Research Association, held that year in New Orleans—that the *Handbook of Research on Teaching* was "hard-to-read and that classroom teachers would not care to curl up with it after a grueling day" (Warner 2002, B-1). While teachers welcome sound research, Mitchell offered, teachers find academic writings "jargon-filled and do not get at the nuts and bolts of what it takes to be a successful teacher" (quoted in Warner 2002, B-1). The factory metaphor (see chapter 1) is evidently alive and well in New Orleans.

At the same session, Bob Chase, president of the rival National Education Association affiliate, told researchers to do more to ensure that their work "targets" issues that preoccupy schoolteachers. Moreover, researchers must be more innovative in how they communicate results. "I am talking about presentation, not content," Chase said, unselfconsciously reiterating the 1960s structure-of-the-disciplines faith that one can teach anything to anybody. (Jerome Bruner [1977 (1960), 33] expressed that faith this way: "[A]ny subject can be taught effectively in some intellectually honest form to any child at any stage of development.") Chase concluded: "The last thing we need is for you to dumb down your research or to lose your appreciation for education's complexity" (quoted passages in Warner 2002, B-2).

Teacher unions have been and continue to be deep disappointments, and not only to teachers, for whom they have, in general, failed to win adequate working conditions, including adequate salaries and appropriate class sizes. By focusing on such traditional union issues as salaries (and failing at significantly increasing these: since 1973, the average teaching salary has increased by only 70 cents a day, after inflation [Gregorian 2001]), and by ignoring pressing professional concerns such as discretion over curriculum content and the means by which its study is assessed, union leaders have failed to mobilize America's teachers or to persuade the American public that quality public education is worth paying for.

While researchers who play the social-engineering game—if you would only teach this way students' test scores will increase—position themselves to be servants of the bureaucracy, assisting school employees to do their job "better" (a view discernible in Chase's comment that researchers should "target" teachers' practical problems, and in language they can readily understand), given education professors' ongoing (if fiscally self-serving) loyalty to public school teachers, those assembled did not, I think, deserve the anti-intellectual aggression Mitchell and, to a lesser extent, Chase expressed.

It is a complicated situation that we professors of education face, live in, and try to find our way through. Our professional work lives have embedded within them, and express many of, these conflicting and too often undermining conditions. There are others. For instance, at some institutions there are seemingly endless meetings, meetings concerning possible reorganizations of the college of education, meetings forced by state intervention in university teacher education curricula, meetings presumably in the service of "institutional maintenance." Given that universities are funded to support teaching, research, and service, the inordinate amount of time devoted to institutional maintenance at some institutions represents a scandalous waste of private and public monies.

Inattention to and the under-appreciation of the educational significance of research (even the social-engineering kind) in many schools and departments of education, except as a contractual obligation and a means of institutional visibility in a commodified academic market (wherein institutions are ranked according to "quality" in news magazines), underlines the too widely held assumption (including among education faculty) that the field of education is not an academic discipline, that it does not construct legitimate and valuable knowledge, and that it is thereby incidental to the main point of departments and schools of education which is teacher training, too often regarded as the induction into a bureaucracy by learning "what works" in classrooms.

Consequently, there are administrators who do not hesitate to call meeting after meeting, reducing sharply the amount of time faculty can devote to the slow and arduous conduct of serious research. I suspect this particular strain of anti-intellectualism explains why so many administrators do not seek senior scholars to replace retiring senior scholars; given that the field is not "really" a discipline and the "business" of education is the production of public school personnel, why hire a more expensive faculty member (whose work possibly advances our understanding) when a less expensive one will do (to generate student enrollment)?

Then there is the somewhat "colonial" relationship we suffer vis-à-vis arts and science professors, vis-à-vis practically everyone else in the university. (Hofstadter's diatribe expressed as well as created the animosity education professors face from many colleagues across the university.) Few hesitate to tell us what the field of education should be, what its inadequacies are, how profound our responsibility is for those educational failures, that is, public-school graduates now college students, to whom our "colleagues" (as we characterize them more hopefully than accurately) try to teach physics or history or mathematics.

Add to this vexed position vis-à-vis arts and sciences colleagues the too-frequent betrayal of our own department chairs and deans whose career advancement (or security) too often seems more important than the scholarly field they are, presumably, hired to represent. With intense pressure from business-minded university presidents, cajoled if not required to enforce business models of teacher education such as that promoted by the National Council for Accreditation of Teacher Education (NCATE; see chapter 9, section II), deans and department chairs (not unlike school principals and super-intendents) are caught between right-wing "reformers" and rightfully resisting, sometimes alienated and discouraged, faculty. Too many protect their jobs, not their fields.

Almost alone is Vartan Gregorian (2001, B7), President of the Carnegie Corporation of New York and former President of Brown University, who pointed out that "treating schools of education as mere profit centers undermines their quality, demeans the faculty, and penalizes students." While it is clear, as he argues, that "teacher education must become colleges' central preoccupation," Gregorian does succumb, in at least one sentence, to NCATE jargon when he asserts that colleges and universities must play a central role in establishing "national standards for what teachers need to know and be able to do, and in organizing teacher education around those standards" (2001, B7). Moreover, Gregorian leaves unquestioned (at least in this article) the correspondence between the secondary school subjects and the academic disciplines.

Add to the caldron the apparent sadism of many central administrators, including more than a few provosts. "Be like arts and science professors!" we are sometimes admonished. "Be like business professors!" "Make the schools better!" "Obtain grants!" "Teach large classes!" "Produce scholarship of quality!" There is a gendered element to this institutional abuse (informally characterized as "ed. school bashing"), as the figure of the education professor tends to be female vis-à-vis her university colleagues (if "male" vis-à-vis his "female" colleagues in the schools). The life of the "transgendered" seems nowhere easy in a patriarchal empire.

IV
WHAT WE CAN DO

Surely the essence of the educated mind is a
breadth of understanding.
—Robin Barrow (1984, 35)

[L]anguage is central to the formation of subjectivity.
—Peter McLaren (1994, xi)

Words "do."
—Mary Aswell Doll (2000, xviii)

Despite these conditions which undermine the intellectual advancement of American curriculum studies, there are scholars who press ahead with the project of intellectual and scholarly understanding. These are sometimes embattled individuals who proceed on their own terms, decline to do what bureaucrats, even arts and sciences colleagues, imagine they ought to be doing, including scrambling after training grants. The project of understanding education—curriculum in particular—proceeds not at an arrogant distance from those in schools, but is in fact inspired by our commitment to those children and teachers who seem trapped in a huge bureaucratic machine, a machine that appears to run on its own, impervious to outside influence. The school seems impervious to our influence, for sure, but obviously not to the influence of politicians and, especially, their insistence that American public education become a business, not just in the accountant's office, but in every teacher's classroom, now structured around the "bottom line" (i.e., test scores).

Certainly education professors exert a limited influence over (and, correspondingly, have a limited liability for) what transpires in American public school classrooms. Perhaps someday we will enjoy more influence, but for now we must move ahead, not wring our hands over lost or wished-for influence. We must work to understand what curriculum is and might be. And this means we must focus on education, not just on schooling. We must labor to remain and/or become intellectuals, not just professors (i.e., employees of increasingly corporatized institutions). In doing so, we must encourage our students—prospective and practicing teachers—to become intellectuals as well, finding in their various locales sites of resistance to top-down business-style reform, opportunities for solidarity with their colleagues and with students, to reassert their academic freedom, their jurisdiction over curriculum content and the means by which its study is assessed.

That does *not* mean intellectual license, of course. No school teacher or college professor can be judged competent who alleges that the Holocaust did not take place, for instance, or that biblical versions of "creation" hold equal intellectual status with evolutionary theory. Complaining about the erosion of intellectual freedom that test-driven curriculum standardization brings, Kevin Kumashiro (in press) makes my point: "By critiquing the standardization of teaching, I am certainly not advocating that anyone be allowed to teach anything in any way—such freedom could mean that some teachers now have license to teach in overtly oppressive ways."

We—*both* university-based and public school-based faculty—must take seriously, above all else, our intellectual lives and the intellectual lives of our students. We must take as our professional obligation (not to mention private pleasure) the scheduling of time each day to read, to take notes, to write, and to incorporate that research into our scholarship as well as our teaching. While we—I am thinking specifically of those of us working in university-based teacher education programs—want to be (and, as a consequence of the importance of students' evaluations, are required to be) popular teachers, we must not structure our courses around only what students easily accept. We must assign texts that press our students beyond their intellectual limits; we must make clear that education coursework is intellectual work, not simply the sharing of personal experiences in the classroom and popular prejudices about "effective" teaching. Like any other academic discipline, to study education requires the cultivation of critical thinking, independence of mind, intellectual courage and, of course, erudition.

Edward Said (1996) underscores certain features of the intellectual many of us already valorize, but which, I think, bear repetition. For me, working in curriculum studies, I am reminded by Said to remain skeptical, not only of mainstream political and social trends, but of American culture itself. I am reminded to remain skeptical toward my own work, including (and perhaps most of all) my apparent successes, to remain in a relation of relative disaffiliation from both my work and my field. For Said, this means the cultivation of a position of exile, an intellectual position from which one is not easily seduced by success or by the solidarity of colleagues. Nor must one allow oneself to be defeated by one's failures. As Dwayne Huebner (1999) understood, to be a teacher requires spiritual courage as well as ethical commitment (see also Quinn 2001; Wang 2002a).

Edward Said reminds us to remain critical of the institutions which employ us. Of course we must fulfill contractual obligations, but Said asks us to remain vigilant toward our enculturation into a teaching profession in which job security is too often valued more than intellectual activism, ethical commitment, and political courage. Said's notion of the scholar as "amateur" is, for me, a powerful idea. In his *Representations of the Intellectual*, Said (1996, 82–83) writes:

> The intellectual today ought to be an amateur, someone who considers that to be a thinking and concerned member of a society one is entitled to raise moral issues at the heart of even the most technical and professionalized activity. . . . [T]he intellectual's spirit as an amateur can enter and transform the merely professional routine most of us go through into something more lively and radical; instead of doing what one is supposed to do one can ask why one does it, who benefits from it, how can it reconnect with a personal project and original thoughts.

Anti-lynching activist Ida B. Wells (see chapter 7 and Pinar 2001) and social activist Jane Addams ("whose carefully crafted essays made her a leading public intellectual" [Elshtain 2002, 25]) remain powerful personifications of the intellectual as Said has described her. In our time, Susan Sontag, Cornel West, Christopher Lasch and, in the field of education, Maxine Greene and Ted Aoki, are among North America's "leading public intellectuals."

To perform the professor as "amateur"—as a private-and-public intellectual—requires us to press against the boundaries of what is safe and respectable inquiry, not for the sake of "dressing" in whatever is, at the moment, intellectually fashionable, but to surpass our own accomplishments and, most

importantly, to advance the field, that "socio-intellectual community" (Pagano 1999 [1981]) in which we work to understand curriculum. Moreover, in
Said's elaboration of the intellectual's autobiographical signature, I hear a
call to regard scholarship as a individuated medium of self-production as well
as the symbolic production of an individuated self. We become our work as
our work "becomes" through us. As such, our scholarship and teaching aspire to become public performances against conformity, uncritical conservatism, and political correctness, against the miseducation of the American
public, against anti-intellectualism, including Richard Hofstadter's kind.

As important as facing the fact of anti-intellectualism as individual university professors is, it is also essential for us to face the problem together, as a
field. What can we do as a field? The panel held on this subject at the 2001
Bergamo Conference was a first step (Asher 2001; Morris 2001b; Weaver
2001). As a field, we must frankly acknowledge the problem of anti-intellectualism and ask ourselves and our colleagues to join together in responding to it. What form might this collective response take?

One possibility is the formulation of a Code of Professional Standards for
the field, one which, above all, supports a conception of our work in intellectual rather than bureaucratic terms, as NCATE standards do. "Standards"
seems another means of assault upon the academic freedom of America's
schoolteachers, but in the university-based field of curriculum studies the assertion of scholarly standards might well constitute a progressive move
against anti-intellectualism. At the first annual meeting (April 2002) of the recently established American Association for the Advancement of Curriculum
Studies (AAACS), I proposed to the membership that an Ad Hoc Committee
on Professional Standards and the Accreditation of Academic Programs in
Curriculum Studies be established to undertake this work (see appendix).

As the name of this now-established committee makes clear, I see as related the labor of elaborating professional standards for graduate study in
the field of curriculum studies as well as stipulating eligibility for teaching undergraduate (as well as graduate) curriculum courses. This could be an opportunity to insist that graduate study in the field incorporate all the major
sectors of contemporary scholarship, not just the specialties of those teaching
the coursework. For instance, in addition to studying the scholarship on
school curriculum (policy, design, implementation, evaluation, technology),
graduate study in curriculum must focus as well as on curriculum theory and
history (see, for instance, McKnight 2003; for an overview, see Kridel and
Newman 2003; Schubert et al. 2002). It is long overdue that graduate programs in curriculum studies require courses in these subjects, as well as serious attention to emerging sectors such as cultural studies and internationalization. The aim is to provide infrastructure for the intellectual advancement
of American curriculum studies. For that to occur, scholars in curriculum
studies need to know the field, the intellectual field, the scholarly field, of cur-

riculum studies, and teach it responsibly, without succumbing to their own ideological or self-interested, self-promoting agendas.

Of course, not all of us face the problem of anti-intellectualism in the same ways and to the same extent. Many believe that anti-intellectualism is not a problem at research universities and elite undergraduate colleges, although, as I well know, there can be what might be characterized as a "country-club" phenomenon at such places, wherein education faculty identify with the status of their prestigious institutional affiliations but produce few substantive intellectual contributions to their fields. Worse, these same faculty sometimes bother reading only scholarship produced at similarly prestigious institutions, yet another, we might say, class-based, form of anti-intellectualism. Others tend to take seriously only the scholarship produced by fellow graduates of the institutions where they did their doctoral work. Moreover, while serving on search committees to fill faculty positions, doctoral graduates of elite institutions sometimes hire fellow graduates even when superior candidates are available from other possibly less prestigious institutions. Such "tribal" networks undermine the intellectual quality and slow the intellectual advancement of curriculum studies while perpetuating "insider" or "country-club" elites within the field.

There are participants in the field who partition the domains of their professional practice, limiting their pedagogical politics to their positions on specific theoretical and institutional issues. How one conducts oneself with one's students and one's colleagues is, I submit, also a major domain of professional practice, wherein ethical and pedagogical considerations, not calculations toward careerist self-advancement, or in the case mentioned above, institutional advancement, should predominate. During my 30-year participation in the field, I have found it curious that there are, for example, left-wing scholars who complain about class hierarchies and inequities in education but who have proven themselves to be among the most elite and the least democratic in their professional practices, especially in their professional relations with colleagues, with colleagues' scholarship, and with their own students. On occasion such scholars teach only their own work or work they deem sympathetic to their work or work that is, in general, ideologically agreeable, eschewing their professional obligation to teach the field as a whole, including points of view which differ from and even contest their own. There is, of course, a long tradition in academe of such practice, but it seems so especially unsuitable for those who claim to be "radical" educators.

Given these dysfunctions and deformations of professional practice, these in-house (if you will) forms of anti-intellectualism, it comes as no surprise that many of the most important scholars in contemporary American curriculum studies work not at prestigious research universities, but at regional and at other, not highly visible, institutions. Given the prejudices accompanying institutional status, some might believe the problem of anti-intellectualism is worse at regional institutions whose commitment to "teaching" is sometimes, admittedly, an evasion of serious academic inquiry in favor of budget enhancement through student recruitment. But as even a casual if critical survey of scholarship produced at the various types of institutions reveals, colleges and universities without national reputations can afford faculty a degree of intellectual freedom prestigious places sometimes do not. Prestigious institutions sometimes exact a "tax" on education faculty who teach there, sometimes in term of lower salaries (trading salary for prestige, presumably), sometimes in terms of excessive committee work and other forms of "institutional maintenance."

On these points generalizations are, of course, just that. Only individuals can know the "institutional press" of where s/he works, only individuals can judge where s/he stands in relation to the cultures of anti-intellectualism surrounding and within the field of education, including curriculum studies and teacher education. Only individuals know where and how s/he might press against one's own limits and those of the institution which employs him/her. As Edward Said suggests, it is the scholar's professional obligation to remain vigilant. Surely our situation in the university is no worse than that faced by many of those we teach, namely those teachers working in the public schools. It is our obligation to them, and to the students they teach, that animates our renewed commitment to professionalism, namely, a commitment to the intellectual advancement of American curriculum studies. Such advancement requires, I would argue, our ethical and disciplined performance—in every domain of our professional practice, especially in research, teaching, and our relations with colleagues worldwide—of the concept of curriculum as complicated conversation, a concept to which we turn next.

8

"Possibly Being So":
Curriculum as Complicated
Conversation

I
COMPLICATED CONVERSATION

*So, imagination is the capacity to think of things as possibly being
so; ... it is not distinct from rationality but is rather a
capacity that greatly enriches rational thinking.*
—Kieran Egan (1992, 43)

*For if the word has the potency to revive and make us free,
it has also the power to blind, imprison and destroy.*
—Ralph Ellison (1995, 24)

We need to move toward a communicative democracy.
—Peter McLaren (1998, 364)

For many practicing teachers, "curriculum" is understood as what the district office requires them to teach, what the state education department publish in scope and sequence guides. For many prospective teachers, curriculum denotes a course syllabus, perhaps only a list of books you to read. After a review of historical and contemporary curriculum scholarship, William Reynolds, Patrick Slattery, Peter Taubman and I acknowledged that curriculum incorporates such literal and institutional meanings, but, it was clear from the research we surveyed, the concept is by no means limited to them. "Curriculum is," we concluded, "a highly symbolic concept" (Pinar, Reynolds, Slattery, and Taubman 1995, 847). In one important sense, school curriculum is what older generations choose to tell younger generations. Whatever the

185

school subject, the curriculum is historical, political, racial, gendered, phenomenological, autobiographical, aesthetic, theological, and international. "Curriculum becomes the site on which the generations struggle to define themselves and the world" (1995, 847–848). It is the symbolic character of curriculum that renders debates over the canon (see McCarthy 1998) struggles over the American identity itself (Castenell and Pinar 1993).

"Curriculum is," we suggested, "a extraordinarily complicated conversation" (Pinar et al. 1995, 848). Because the curriculum as it has been institutionalized in schools today is so highly formalized and abstract, it may not be obvious how we might conceive of curriculum as "conversation," as this term is usually employed to refer to more open-ended, sometimes rather personal and interest-driven, events in which persons dialogically encounter each other (Freire 1968). Just how "complicated" such encounter can be we will glimpse in the final section of this chapter.

That curriculum has become so formalized and abstract, so often distant from the everyday sense of conversation signals, we asserted, how profoundly the process of education has been institutionalized and bureaucratized. Instead of employing school knowledge to complicate our understanding of ourselves and the society in which we live, teachers are forced to "instruct" students to mime others' (i.e., textbook authors') conversations, ensuring that countless classrooms are filled with forms of ventriloquism rather than intellectual exploration, wonder, and awe (Huebner 1999).

Imagining that the best is past, "conservatives" have indeed managed to turn back the clock, and with a vengeance, so that the "crisis of the classroom" identified by Charles Silberman at the end of a decade of national school reform has only intensified. Thirty years of "back to the basics" and "accountability" render Silberman's dated description chillingly current: "It is not possible to spend any prolonged period visiting public school classrooms without being appalled by the mutilation visible everywhere—mutilation of spontaneity, of the joy of learning, of pleasure in creating, of sense of self" (Silberman 1970, 10).

The divorce between school curriculum and public life, between school curriculum and students' self-formation that the current cult of academic vocationalism ensures guarantees profound social alienation and, on spectacular occasion, violence (Webber 2003). As Huebner has remarked, Columbine—school violence generally—is a curricular issue. Is it not strange that the sometimes violent aggression of secondary school students (almost always boys) is not the pretext for interdisciplinary courses on the history of violence, the gender of violence, the psychology of adolescence? Why are teachers not permitted, indeed, encouraged, to show students that academic knowledge is not self-contained, that it often reaches out toward and back from life as human beings live it? Why is not the school curriculum a provocation for students to reflect on and to think critically about themselves and the world they will inherit?

The last 40 years—since the National Curriculum Reform movement associated with the Kennedy Administration—the (especially secondary) school curriculum as been aligned with post-school destinations, primary among them the university and the workplace. Because our university-based colleagues in the academic disciplines have also, since the 1960s, tended toward academic vocationalism and away from interdisciplinary experimentation (except in honors programs and in specific, if too often segregated, interdisciplinary configurations such as African-American Studies, Women's and Gender Studies, and Southern Studies), they tend to project onto the school curriculum the content and purpose of the university curriculum (e.g., the production of disciplinary specialists). This misunderstanding of public education received unfortunately eloquent expression in Richard Hofstadter's (1962) attack on "life-adjustment" education, as we have seen.

Curriculum theorists assert that the point of the public school curriculum is not to make everyone into specialists in the academic disciplines, although few among us would complain if it did. Nor is the point of public school curriculum to produce accomplished test-takers, so that American scores on standardized tests compare favorably to Japanese or German scores, providing politicians with bragging rights. Nor is the *educational* point of the public school curriculum to produce efficient and docile employees for the business sector.

The *educational* point of the public school curriculum is *understanding*, understanding the relations among academic knowledge, the state of society, the processes of self-formation, and the character of the historical moment in which we live, in which others have lived, and in which our descendants will someday live. It is understanding that informs the ethical obligation to care for ourselves and our fellow human beings, that enables us to think and act with intelligence, sensitivity, and courage in both the public sphere—as citizens aspiring to establish a democratic society—and in the private sphere, as individuals committed to other individuals. As feminist theory has shown, the two spheres are not, finally, separable (Grumet 1988).

Once we appreciate that the *educational* point of the public school curriculum is not only itself (knowledge for knowledge's sake, especially at the university, is hardly inappropriate), not the economic, and political goals of others, once we teachers "take it back" for ourselves and our students, we realize we must explore curriculum as a lived event in itself (Aoki in press). That is, as soon as we take hold of the curriculum as an opportunity for ourselves and our students, as citizens, as ethical and spiritual persons, we realize that curriculum changes as we engage it, reflect on it, and act in response to it, toward the realization of our private-and-public ideals and dreams. In *Understanding*

Curriculum we concluded: "Curriculum ceases to be a thing, and it is more than a process. It becomes a verb, an action, a social practice, a private meaning, and a public hope. Curriculum is not just the site of our labor, it becomes the product of our labor, changing as we are changed by it" (Pinar et al. 1995, 848). It is an ongoing, if complicated, conversation.

II
"AN *UNREHEARSED* INTELLECTUAL ADVENTURE"

> *In a conversation participants are not engaged in an enquiry*
> *or a debate; there is no "truth" to be discovered, no proposition*
> *to be proved, no conclusion sought.*
> —Michael Oakeshott (1959, 10)

> *The path of understanding, if it is not to "simplify,"*
> *must be trend gently.*
> —Megan Boler (1999, 175)

> *[E]ducation might be understood as the opportunity of getting lost.*
> —Alan A. Block (1998, 328)

A Fellow of Gonville and Caius College, Cambridge University, and a professor of Political Science in the University of London, Michael Oakeshott (1959, 9, 10) theorized "conversation" as the "meeting-place" where "the diverse idioms of utterance which make up current human intercourse" converge. "Conversation is not an enterprise designed to yield an extrinsic profit," he is clear; nor is it "a contest where a winner gets a prize" (10). Surely he overstates his case when he insists it is not exegesis or inquiry, and when he insists (11) "it is an *unrehearsed* intellectual adventure." Surely it can be prepared for, it can provoke or be the consequence of study, and, of course, it can be spontaneous, perhaps playful. Oakeshott is not guilty of overstatement when he observes that conversation "is impossible in the absence of a diversity of voices: in it different universes of discourse meet, acknowledge each other and enjoy an oblique relationship which neither requires nor forecasts their being assimilated to one another" (1959, 11). Alterity structures and animates complicated conversation.

Oakeshott cannot escape his time or place, and his situatedness in time and place is evident when he asserts that conversation is the appropriate image of human intercourse because it recognizes the qualities, the diversities, and "the proper" (1959, 11) relationships of human utterances. "As civilized human beings," he continues, echoing 19th-century assumptions of civilization and progress that legitimated Empire, "we are the inheritors, neither of an enquiry about ourselves and the world, nor of an accumulating body of information, but of a conversation, begun in the primeval forests and made more articulate in the course of centuries." There are English shades of the German mythology of the *Volk* here (Hannaford 1996). But I can embrace his acknowledgment that this conversation is one "which goes on both in public and within each of ourselves" (11). As the emphasis upon autobiography in this formulation of curriculum theory testifies, the two are inextricably interrelated.

Then Oakeshott seems to acknowledge his earlier overstatement, admitting that "of course there is argument and enquiry and information" (11), but he nicely conceives of these "as passages" in conversation, complaining quickly, as if to honor his ongoing ambivalence regarding the point, these are not the most "captivating" (11) of passages. Once again the echoes of Empire and the Great Chain of Being echo, innocently perhaps, in Oakshott's thinking, as he insists that: "It is the ability to participate in this conversation, and not the ability to reason cogently, to make discoveries about the world, or to contrive a better world, which distinguishes the human being from the animal and the civilized man from the barbarian" (1959, 11).

Oakeshott appreciates the significance of the concept of conversation to understanding education, at least in the Anglo-American tradition: "Education, properly speaking, is an initiation into the skill and partnership of this conversation in which we learn to recognize the voices, to distinguish the proper occasions of utterance, and in which we acquire the intellectual and moral habits appropriate to conversation" (Oakeshott 1959, 11). He appreciates as well the importance of interdisciplinarity to such educational conversation: "[t]he final measure of intellectual achievement is in terms of its contribution to the conversation in which all universes of discourse meet" (11). In conversation, that judgment is both immediate and deferred, present and displaced.

Ted Aoki (in press) notes that the conversation is not "chit-chat," nor is it the simple exchange of messages or only the communication of information. None of these, he suggests, requires "true human presence." Nor is language only a tool by means of which thoughts are recoded into words. Curriculum as conversation, in this formulation, is no conveyor belt of "representational knowledge." It is a matter of attunement, an auditory rather than visual conception, in which the sound of music (for Aoki, jazz specifically) being improvised is an apt example. Given the poetic quality of Aoki's theorization, poetry provides another example of the sound of complicated conversation.

III
THE POETIC SELF

There are doubtless many things which the public would never
demand unless they were first supplied by individual initiative,

> *both because the public lacks the imagination, and*
> *also the power of formulating their wants.*
> —Jane Addams (2002 [1902], 73)

> *[T]he role of the imagination is not to resolve, not to point*
> *the way, not to improve. It is to awaken, to disclose the*
> *ordinarily unseen, unheard, and unexpected.*
> —Maxine Greene (1995, 28)

> *For* all *possibilities reach us through the imagination.*
> —John Dewey (1962 [1934], 43)

Oakeshott is astonished that conversation has survived as a concept and practice in education, given how "remote" (1959, 12) our ideas of education have become from the concept. For me, this remoteness has followed (although hardly created by) the intensifying bureaucratization of curriculum, especially in public schools. Oakeshott (1959, 15) hopes to "rescue" "conversation," by which he means "to restore to it some of its lost freedom of movement," and while he suspects "rescue" is too ambitious an aspiration, he proposes something "more modest." His proposes that we reconsider the "voice of poetry; to consider it as it speaks in the conversation." To do so he considers the nature of the "self."

As he understands it, "the real world is a world of experience within which self and not-self divulge themselves to reflection." He acknowledges that the distinction is "ambiguous and unstable." Even so, it allows him to regard the work of the self as "separating itself from a present not-self: self and not-self generate one another" (Oakeshott 1959, 17). It is difficult not to think of object-relations theory here, and the primal "object" from which, especially, the male child separates itself is the maternal body (Chodorow 1978).

"The self appears as activity," Oakeshott (1959, 17) suggests. Sounding like the Jean-Paul Sartre of *Nausea* and *Being and Nothingness*, Oakeshott (1959, 17) asserts that the "self is not a 'thing' or a 'substance' capable of being active; it is activity." His ontology of the self sounds Sartrean—"this activity is primordial; there is nothing antecedent to it" (17)—but curiously devoid of history, culture, the moment as lived, all aspects of the "situation" in which, for Sartre, the "self-as-activity" finds itself and takes form. The situatedness of the self may be what, by different semantic means, Oakeshott (1959, 17) is describing when he acknowledges that "[o]n every occasion this activity is a specific mode of activity; to be active but with no activity in particular, to be skillful but to have no particular skill, is as impossible to the self as not to be active at all." One must acknowledge that this ceaseless activity may be altered by various technologies of the self, among them psychotherapies, meditation, and other religious regimens, as well as by drugs (see Pinar 2002).

Given the multidimensional complexity of the self-as-activity, it is curious that Oakeshott (1959, 17) decides to settle on one aspect as definitive, "imagining," by which he means the self "making and recognizing images," and "moving among them." Whatever the modality of experience—Oakeshott lists sensing, perceiving, feeling, desiring, thinking, believing, contemplating, supposing, knowing, preferring, approving, laughing, crying, dancing, loving, singing, making hay, devising mathematical demonstrations, and, I would add, making love—each, he asserts, is engaged in the experience of imagination.

There is a powerful and burgeoning literature on visuality and, especially, its complex role in "modernity" (see, for instance, Brennan and Jay 1996; Crary 2002; Jay 1993; Levin 1993; Mitchell 1994). Given that he would not have known this scholarship, Oakshott's apparent participation in the "hegemony of the vision" (Levin 1993) seems unself-conscious. For Oakeshott (1959, 18), "the not-self, then, is composed of images." But not all images are located outside the self: "the self is constituted in the activity of making and moving among images" (1959, 18). Oakeshott's reliance on the image underscores the centrality of the imagination to the educational process (Eisner 1979; Greene 1995; Rugg 1963). Conversation is, Oakeshott (1959, 19) explains, "the meeting-place of various modes of imagining; and in this conversation there is, therefore, no voice without an idiom of its own: the voices are not divergences from some ideal, non-idiomatic manner of speaking, they diverge only from one another."

Oakeshott's characterization of conversation as not conforming to a predetermined end enables us to understand how academic vocationalism—institutionalized through the Carnegie unit requirements for high-school graduation and cemented by the current rhetoric regarding "standards" and by the aggressive use of standardized examinations—cannot easily be a curricular conversation. Classroom conversation, within carefully boundaried school-subject borders, *is* possible and, often, preferable to the lecture as an instructional strategy. But even lively classroom talk directed toward expertise in the school subject as measured on standardized exams meeting national standards is not the practice of curriculum as "complicated conversation." This practice requires curricular innovation and experimentation, opportunities for students and faculty to articulate relations among the school subjects, society, and self-formation. It is not, as Jerome Bruner (1977, ix) summarized the academic vocationalism of the 1959 Woods Hole Conference (which he chaired), learning to "talk physics" with students rather than "talk about" it to them. (Of the 34 Conference participants, only 3 were education specialists; no school teachers were present [see Bruner 1960 (1977), xix].)

Michael Oakeshott accomplishes much more in his essay on "the conversation of mankind," and I recommend that the essay be read in its entirety.

For now, however, let us focus next on the contemporary relegation of "conversation" to "classroom discourse." Even as sophisticated a scholar as Arthur Applebee succumbs to the academic vocationalism that today structures the public school curriculum, and the rhetoric around it.

IV
CURRICULUM AS COMPLICATED CONVERSATION
IS NOT (ONLY) CLASSROOM DISCOURSE

[G]raduates must be more than skilled specialists
or technicians in their fields.
—Frank H. T. Rhodes (2001, B10)

[A] curriculum is like an animated conversation on
a topic that can never be fully defined.
—Jerome Bruner (1996, 116)

But what happens when dialogue as a teaching strategy—
a supposedly neutral carrier of meaning and intention—
is questioned about its own interests and intentions?
—Elizabeth Ellsworth (1997, 48)

It is true that one sense in which the curriculum is a complicated conversation is that the school subjects, often introductions to the academic disciplines as they are organized and advanced at the university, are themselves conversations. While highly regulated and bureaucratized, the academic disciplines "represent . . . an ongoing debate about significant aspects of human knowledge and experience" (Applebee 1996, 10). While this statement is accurate, Arthur Applebee's formulation is here a bit too voluntarist, too rationalistic, especially given that sectors of the academic disciplines—especially the natural and social sciences—are built in response to foundations' initiatives and public funding, that is, to politics (Kuhn 1962). More recent work in the cultural study of science punctures rather completely the fantasy of self-disinterested and high-minded scholars who are immune to social rewards and influence and strictly rationally research "significant aspects of human knowledge and experience" (Weaver, Appelbaum, and Morris 2001; see also A. Gough 1998).

It is true, as Applebee (1996, 10) tells us, "the disciplines exist because thoughtful people care about the traditions of knowing and doing that they represent," but they also exist due to governmental priorities, business interests, and political lobbyists. As a longtime student of autobiography, I will not quarrel with Applebee's (1996, 11) citing of Michael Polanyi (1958) to remind us that even the most "scientific" ways of knowing are finally "grounded in the tacit knowledge of participants in the dialogue out of which the field is constituted." Michael Oakeshott (1959, 27) makes a different but related point, namely that science too is "a universe of discourse," a discipline of the imagination, distinguished by its process (the scientific method) as much as its product (scientific knowledge). Science too, Oakeshott (1959, 28) insists, is a "conversable voice." That is, science is no sacrosanct discourse apart from everyday human affairs, but, rather, a disciplinary form of participation in those affairs.

For Oakeshott (1959, 10) those affairs—what he terms "the diverse idioms of utterance which make up current human intercourse"—are discussed in what he thinks of as a "meeting-place." He adds: "this meeting-place is not an enquiry or an argument, but a conversation" (1959, 10). Surely Oakeshott overstates his case when, in the sentence quoted to open section II of this chapter, he asserts that conversation is not debate or inquiry, but his point is a strong one, namely that scholarly discourses, even scientific ones, must be situated in human affairs and discourse, and that the "meeting-place" for this complex cacophony is "conversation."

When we understand curriculum as conversation, it means, as Arthur Applebee (1996, 20) is right to observe, that the academic disciplines are "living traditions," although this characterization does not speak to the problem of their educational significance, the problem for curriculum theory. What does Applebee mean by "living traditions"? He suggests the matter can be "put simply," that such traditions are of "knowledge-in-action." By that he means such traditions are "dynamic" and "changing," learned through "participation" and focused on the "present and future rather than the past" (20). In contrast, schools too often organize "knowledge-out-of-context," which cast curriculum "in terms of what students should learn about, and in the process they strip knowledge of its most vital contexts" (20). "Action" evidently refers to "classroom discourse," which plays a "critical mediating role between broader traditions and schooled knowledge" (Applebee 1996, 35). But classroom discourse is a means to another, usually predetermined, destination, as "the process of schooling must be a process of actually entering into particular traditions of knowing and doing"(Applebee 1996, 36).

It is this positioning of classroom discourse as mediating between "broader cultural traditions and schooled knowledge" that leads Applebee to think about curriculum as conversation. "Through such conversations," he writes, "students will be helped to enter into culturally significant traditions of knowledge-in-action. In most schools, these traditions will reflect the major academic disciplines—language, history, literature, science, the arts—though they can just as easily be interdisciplinary or cross-disciplinary, or be based on the traditions of home, community, or workplace" (Applebee 1996, 37). While he allows the possibility of inter- and cross-disciplinary "traditions," in general Applebee seems willing to leave the current curriculum unquestioned. What's "new"—as he suggests his approach is (37)—is that kids will talk more in class. Even when he acknowledges that the school subjects are "domains for conversation" (Applebee 1996, 37), he seems to limit classroom discourse to the school subjects as they exist.

To illustrate the notion that education represents an "entry into ongoing cultural conversations about their lives and the world in which they live," Applebee (1996, 39) quotes approvingly Gerald Graff (1992, 77, in Applebee 1996, 39): "In short, reading books with comprehension, making arguments, writing papers, and making comments in a class discussion are social activities. They involve entering into a cultural or disciplinary conversation, a process not unlike initiation into a social club" (77). Doesn't Graff mean "country club"? Such a sentence is not surprising from a sophisticated player in an academic discipline at the university level, and for higher education (especially at the graduate level), the notion makes a certain self-serving sense.

But for a public school curriculum, such "entering" amounts to academic vocationalism, a self-involved self-perpetuation of institutionalized, indeed, bureaucratized, conceptions of the school subjects' educational significance as preparing students to become disciplinary specialists in the academic disciplines. It is *not* a conception of curriculum that directs school knowledge to individual's lived experience, experience understood as subjective *and* social, that is, as gendered, racialized, classed participants in understanding and living through the historical moment. Referring to Graff's conception of the academic disciplines as "social clubs," Applebee confirms my suspicion that his sense of "conversation" is limited to classroom talk: "Curricular conversations are similarly constructed by their participants. The knowledge that evolves is knowledge that is socially negotiated through the process of conversation itself; it is knowledge-in-action" (Applebee 1996, 39–40).

Confined to classroom discourse, curriculum becomes a "domain for conversation" (Applebee 1996, 42), not the conversation itself. These "domains" turn out to resemble the conventional curricular organization of separate school subjects: "domains would represent 'culturally significant' traditions of knowing and doing. . . . [A]ny curriculum is a selection that represents what a community believes is worthwhile" (42). So defined, curriculum also excludes what certain communities believe is unworthy of knowing, such as the study of lynching in secondary school history classes in the Deep South (Pinar 2001).

Having reinscribed the conventional curriculum, Applebee (1996, 44) construes "the problem of curriculum planning, then, [as] the problem of establishing a conversational domain and fostering relevant conversations within it. In a general sense, the conversational domains that are most important in American schools begin with the traditions of science, mathematics." Here he reiterates the taken-for-granted positioning of science and mathematics as central, in the 1960s a military and now an economic restatement of 19th-century classical curriculum theory, founded on faculty psychology: The mind is a muscle and the weightier subjects produce muscles that bulge, minds that are rigorous and disciplined. We glimpsed the gendered politics of 1960s curriculum reform in chapter 3.

Having paid homage to mathematics and science, Applebee (1996, 46) turns to the humanities for an example: "Creating a New Conversational Domain in an Introductory American Literature Course." Here it is again clear that he leaves the conventional curricular structure intact. "Conversation" has now become relegated to teaching and technique, not content. Applebee acknowledges that teachers have little control over what they teach, but rather than complain about this fact, he de-emphasizes the educational significance of "content" in general, declaring that "[i]nstitutional constraints on subjects and materials may be less critical than the teacher's decisions about the conversations in which students will be asked to engage" (Applebee 1996, 50). Of course, the two are inextricably interrelated, but the emphasis upon teacher decision-making risks asking too much of teachers already burdened with the complexities of teaching and the demands of the school as a business.

By Applebee's chapter 5, we are working exclusively in a bureaucratic logic, a fantasy of social engineering, and, predictably, he tells us he can name the "characteristics of effective curricula" (Applebee 1996, 51). He is not speaking of the overall curriculum, but rather "the curriculum of the individual course, which is the level at which curriculum planning and debate usually take place in American middle and high schools" (Applebee 1996, 51). Of course, that is true given that the larger curriculum questions have been answered by politicians, bureaucrats, and eager-to-please textbook companies. He acknowledges that "at the college level, course content is more likely to be the prerogative of the individual professor, and debates about curriculum structure are cast more broadly, about what courses to teach and what relationships, if any, there should be among them" (Applebee 1996, 51), but he fails to see the educational significance of such professional prerogatives, and how damaging to the project of public education the absence of these prerogatives for public-school educators is.

Given the erasure of academic freedom for school teachers, of course "curriculum planning is usually approached as an exercise in domain specification and task analysis" (Applebee 1996, 51). Rather than focusing on inventories of the structure of the subject matter, Applebee (1996, 52) advises that "we begin with a consideration of the conversations that matter—with traditions and the debates within them that enliven contemporary civilization." He appears on the verge of taking the curriculum question seriously, but quickly—as do too many professors of education today—he retreats from curriculum to teaching: "The question then becomes, how we can orchestrate these conversations so that students can enter into them?"

(Applebee 1996, 52) Orchestration means arranging a piece of music for a particular orchestra, an analogy for arranging subject matter for one's students. This very quickly becomes an emphasis on technique (although later he asserts that a "curriculum of conversation is more than just part of a pedagogy in support of knowledge-in-action" [1996, 127]). I would say that the point is to change the official curriculum so that students' entry into intellectually-engaged conversation is made more likely, perhaps even inevitable.

Applebee (1996, 52) quotes Grice, a philosopher of language, to help him name the features of "an engaging and well-orchestrated curricular conversation." Grice notes that effective conversations are guided by "a common purpose or set of purposes, or at least a mutually accepted direction. This purpose or direction may be fixed from the start (e.g., by an initiation proposal of a question for discussion), or it may evolve during the exchange" (Grice 1975, 45; quoted in Applebee 1996, 52). Applebee is now ready to make his list: "A curriculum that is cooperative and effective in a Gricean sense has four important characteristics. . . . [These include] quality, quantity, and relatedness of the topics of the conversations, and the manner in which the conversation is carried forward" (Applebee 1996, 52–53). So curriculum as conversation, for Applebee, is another formula, and one that is too commonsensical to represent an intellectual vibrant experience (Britzman 1998; Ellsworth 1997). If we are determined to list characteristics, I much prefer Bill Doll's (1993, 2002), as they are grounded not in bureaucratization but in curriculum history and theory.

There are issues on which I can agree with Applebee, namely his criticism of the contemporary obsession with testing (1996, 116), his praise of Ted Sizer (1996, 116), his criticism of the melting-pot metaphor and advocacy of a notion of "common culture in which diversity yields richness rather than chaos" (Applebee 1996, 127), and his commitment to conceive classrooms that are more "interesting" (Applebee 1996, 128). But by focusing on classroom conversation on state-mandated school subjects aligned, more or less, with post-elementary and secondary school destinations, whether those be the workplace or the university, Applebee trivializes the concept of conversation and leaves undisturbed the official curriculum.

Until educators—in collaboration with colleagues in higher education, and in conversation with parents and students—exercise greater control over what they teach, and until what they teach permits ongoing curricular experimentation according to student concerns and faculty interest and expertise, school "conversation" will be stilted at best, limited to classroom discourse, disconnected from students' lived experience and from the intellectual lives of the faculty. Understood as the education of the public, complicated conversation *is* our professional practice. William Wraga (2002, 17) reiterates a discredited dualism when he asserts: "But curriculum is more than a conversation; curriculum is a realm of action." In the profession of education, conversation *is* action. Or, as Ted Aoki (in press) put the matter once, "competence" is "communicative action and reflection."

How do we—school teachers and the education professors who teach them—find ourselves in this strange situation in which we have so little influence over what we teach, when politicians and others feel entitled to insult us by suggesting that schoolteachers have not before had "standards" or that education professors have not worried about "outcomes" or that either concept adequately conceptualizes the complexity of education? How is that politicians can speak openly about and pass legislation to "end the ed. school monopoly on teacher education"? The present political situation is a complex confluence of many factors and forces, among them (as we saw in chapter 3), the resounding echoes of the gender and racial politics of 1960s national curriculum reform.

V
MODES OF ADDRESS

> *How might we teach in and through the leaky edges of the*
> *"social outside" of the curriculum, and the "individual*
> *inside" of the psyche?*
> —Elizabeth Ellsworth (1997, 116)

> *[T]he feminist project of radical democracy has to take into*
> *account the sexed body,* jouissance, *and the discontinuous*
> *temporality of becoming, on the one hand, and the ethical*
> *imperative of judgement and obligation, on the other.*
> —Ewa Plonowska Ziarek (2001, 14)

> *Pedagogy as a social relationship is very close in.*
> —Elizabeth Ellsworth (1997, 6)

Just how complicated conversation can be is brilliantly explicated by Elizabeth Ellsworth in her study of "modes of address." An analytical concept employed in film and media studies, "mode of address" asks how films address its audiences. Elizabeth Ellsworth (1997, 8) employs the concept to ask: "How do teachers make a difference in power, knowledge, desire, not only by *what* they teach, but *how* they *address* students?" In asking this question, Ellsworth notes (1997, 11) that much curriculum research has cast the construction of meaning in terms of "social formation and social agency." In her view, such research is "greatly impoverished" (1997, 42).

To emphasize this last point, Ellsworth suggests that even those social roles strongly associated with public life (e.g., citizen, teacher, politicians) are not free of the "inner" life. Even those subjectivities wed to the social sphere of "mutual interaction" "are never disconnected from fantasies, transgressive desires, and 'monstrous' terrors of the kind that surface in dreams" (O'Shea 1993, 504; quoted in Ellsworth 1997, 42).

Ellsworth's critique of dialogue in education—and the work of Nicholas Burbules (1993; see Burbules 2000) specifically—turns on its overidentification with the social, its naiveté toward the intrapsychic, its ignorance of the complexities of conversation and understanding. "Educators constantly invoke dialogue as a means of coming to understanding without imposition in ways more democratic than one-way determination," Ellsworth (1997, 48) writes. Teachers imagine dialogue as a means of "ensuring" open-mindedness, that is, open to having one's mind changed as consequence, presumably, of "rational understanding" (48).

It is as if, Ellsworth (1997, 48) points out, dialogue—as a "teaching practice"—is politically disinterested. Whether understood "simplistically" (49) as a conversation among interlocutors "seeking mutual understanding" or as a theoretically driven transformation of social relations, "dialogue as a form of pedagogy," Ellsworth (48) asserts, is a "historically and cultural embedded practice." "The point," Ellsworth (49) emphasizes, is that "when teachers practice dialogue as an aspect of their pedagogy, they are employing a mode of address." The pedagogy of dialogue is "not neutral," but embedded in particular "networks of power, desire, and knowledge" (49).

"Dialogue in teaching," Ellsworth (1997, 49) continues, cannot function as "a neutral vehicle" conveying speakers' ideas "back and forth across a free and open space between them." It is not neutral and, moreover, "the rugged terrain between speakers that it traverses makes for a constantly interrupted and never completed passage" (49). For these reasons—"the unresolvable crack inside of education itself, its perennial failures to produce desired social outcomes, or to wall off young minds from their own and their society's shadow's through reason, understanding, and dialogue" (52)—that rendered education, for Freud, an impossible profession.

"Teaching is not psychoanalysis," Ellsworth (1997, 70) reminds, "but consciously or unconsciously, teachers deal nevertheless in repression, denial, ignore-ance, resistance, fear, and desire whenever we teach." As a consequence, teachers must cultivate a "third ear" that "listens to the latent contents concealed in the manifest text" that the student speaks (Bollas 1995, 171; quoted in Ellsworth 1997, 71). This means that the teacher responds to both latent and manifest content; the practical effect has less to do with the conceptual content of the teacher's response to the student's statement, interpretation, but in "what the interpretation does" to the student (Felman 1987, 102; quoted in Ellsworth 1997, 69). To illustrate, Ellsworth (73) asks us to imagine a seminar where the focus is not on the explication of the textbook, but on the following:

What happens to my own processes of thinking, my own symbolic constellation when I read this author's words? Where, as I read this author, do I get stuck, do I forget, do I resist? Where, when I listen to a classmate's response to this reading, does my own project of "becoming a teacher" get shifted, troubled, unsettled—why there?

The focus here is on teaching as a structure of address; it is, implicitly, on curriculum as a verb.

To make her critique of dialogue as information exchange, Ellsworth draws on Chang's (1996, xviii; quoted in Ellsworth 1997, 91) charge that "the ideology of the communicative" is the reduction—even erasure—of "difference." When theorists of communicative dialogue reify "*understanding* as the *ideal*, the *telos*, and the *norm* of communicative activities," they exclude "misunderstanding," "equivocation," "ambiguity," "nonsense" (Chang 1996, 174; quoted in Ellsworth 1997, 91). By "excluding 'disorder' at its originary moment," Chang argues, communication theory in fact helps to "legitimate the sociopolitical status quo" (1996, 175; quoted in Ellsworth 1997, 91). Ellsworth (93) underscores that the labor of understanding the "other" is never an "innocent, disinterested reading of the other's message."

Coupled with the politically conservative consequences of understanding dialogue as neutral exchanges among unitary rational subjects is the unfounded confidence that self-reflection guarantees self-transformation. Self-reflection, Ellsworth (1997, 94) points out, "is always in danger of becoming just that—a reflection of the prior, same self." Self-reflection is "always a mirror reflection, that is, the illusory functioning of symmetrical reflexivity, of reasoning by the illusory principle of symmetry . . . that subsumes all difference within a delusion of a unified and homogeneous individual identity" (Felman 1987, 62; quoted in Ellsworth 1997, 94). In this view, Ellsworth (94–95) notes, "what communicative dialogue for understanding may 'change,' in this additive way, are conscious opinions, attitudes, beliefs, values." New information may be added, but the structure of the self does not necessarily change.

The endorsement of dialogue as classroom practice may function, Ellsworth (1997, 95) worries, as guarding against "the breaking of a continuously *conscious* discourse." What the concept of communicative dialogue as rational discourse is, Ellsworth (95) argues, is a prophylactic against "the unconscious, the unmeant, the unknowable, the excessive, the irrational, the unspeakable, the unhearable, the forgotten, the ignored, the despised." It is on this point (among others), that Ellsworth is critical of Nicholas Burbules' (1993) discussion of dialogue, arguing that it lacks "a theorization of the limits of continuity" (1997, 102).

Without such theorization, Ellsworth argues, the issue of persuasion in dialogue is evaded. Referring to Rooney's (1989) *Seductive Reasoning*, Ellsworth (1997, 103) suggests that pluralists' claims that their invitation to communicative dialogue are "inclusive" are, in fact, "seductions" (103). She quotes Rooney: "[U]nderstanding is never the neutral gesture pluralism requires it to be; it can never be evaluated on a simple scale of purity or accuracy. As Derrida points out: it is not a question of true or false but of the play of forces" (1989, 109; quoted in Ellsworth 1997, 103).

Understanding is never neutral and can be disguised as persuasion. When the parties agree on a point, "understanding" is "a reciprocal act" (Rooney 1989, 109). In this sense, "to understand is to be persuaded" (1989, 109; quoted in Ellsworth 1997, 103). But, Ellsworth (103) points out, importantly, "understanding can actually be an act of disagreement. It can be an act of demystification." Such understanding requires a different conception of dialogue, what Ellsworth (115) terms "analytic dialogue."

Analytic dialogue, Ellsworth (1997, 115) suggests, has no investment in an "economy of exchange, continuity, or understanding." In acknowledging the impossibility of full and complete understanding, analytic dialogue "can teach us something, can become itself instructive" (Felman 1987, 79; quoted in Ellsworth 1997, 125). What it teaches us, Ellsworth suggests, is that knowledge is always provisional, textual, multiple and, as such, never finished or complete (see Ellsworth 1997, 126). This means that teaching is paradoxical; it is a call "to participate in the ongoing, interminable cultural production that is teaching" (141–142).

Because teaching is neither a skill nor a technology, Ellsworth (1997, 193) points out, finding out "where, when, and how teaching happens is undecidable." It is also, in some sense, "impossible," in that "*all* modes of address misfire one way or another" (8). That is inevitable given that "I never 'am' the 'who' that a pedagogical address thinks I am. But then again, I never am the who that *I* think I am either" (Ellsworth 1997, 8). "The point," she suggests, "is to explore the meanings and uses of pedagogical modes of address that *multiply* and *set in motion* the positions from which they can be 'met' and responded to" (9). It is a point well taken, including from curricular as well as instructional points of view.

Ellsworth's important research underscores the necessity and complexity of coupling the social with the subjective. There can be no "public intellectual" who is not also a "private intellectual," one who understands the fantasmatic character of apparently public dialogue and debate. Without encountering the complexity of one's life history and biographic situation, one cannot appreciate how to reposition oneself in private-and-public space, or "set in motion," as Ellsworth so nicely phrases it, the subject positions from which one can experience and, perhaps, surpass the present.

For those (especially white male) egos congealed, opaque to themselves, and who imagine themselves as having a stable and unitary "address" from which and to which "messages" can be sent and received, the regressive and progressive phases of the method of *currere* amount to a process of self-shattering (see Silverman 1992). The "same old self" which renders education merely the acquisition of new information is decentered, splintered, rendered "a play of dynamic forces." In one sense, it is a complex process of the "evaporation of the ego." Perhaps the culture of cyberspace can contribute to such dispersal, but I am skeptical. The complex intellectual work provoked by Ellsworth's sophisticated analysis might.

Now we understand the profoundly anti-intellectual consequences of 40 years of "conservative" restoration, of a careerist university system in which "intellectual events"—such as Ellsworth's book—are too often quick cites, rarely studied in the profoundly serious way private-and-public intellectual work requires. Victims of deferred and displaced racism and misogyny, we educators must detach ourselves from those *personae* "hailed" into existence by 40 years of "school reform." In order to depart those positions of "gracious submission," we must, first, perform the inner work psychoanalysis suggests, not in the name of personal therapy, but in the cause of social reconstruction. The latter cannot occur without the former: The subjective and the social are inextricably interwoven with each other. We must face our internalized anti-intellectualism as well as "talk back" to those whose modes of address positions as bureaucrats and technicians doing others' "dirty work." After self-understanding, comes self-mobilization in the service of social reconstruction.

V

THE SYNTHETICAL MOMENT: SELF-MOBILIZATION AND SOCIAL RECONSTRUCTION

9

Reconstructing the Private and Public Spheres in Curriculum and Teaching

I
INTO THE ARENA

Power at the turn of the twenty-first century . . . inheres . . .
in thought itself, in knowledge, in discourse, in the body.
—Bernadette M. Baker (2001, 622)

A pedagogy of discomfort does not assert one right ideology or
resolution. Rather, it is a mode of inquiry and invitation that
emphasizes a historicized ethics and testimonial witnessing.
—Megan Boler (1999, 200)

[T]he goal of democratic struggles is redefined . . . as the
transformation of the existing power relations,
discourses, and subjectivities.
—Ewa Plonowska Ziarek (2001, 219)

The field of education—especially in the United States—is so very reluctant to abandon social engineering. If only we can find the right technique, the right modification of classroom organization (small groups, collaborative learning, dialogue) or teach in the right way, if only we have students self-reflect or if only we develop "standards" or, simply, focus on "excellence," then students will learn what we teach them. If only we test regularly, we will "leave no child behind." Certainly we will leave no child untested.

Tying the public school curriculum to test scores and, then, requiring teachers to engineer improvements in students' test scores: this political maneuver performs cultural authoritarianism for the right wing in the name of "accountability" and, presumably on behalf of "under-served" populations. In this institutional sphere of "displaced and deferred action," the right wing forces teachers to do their political "dirty work." And it does so by invoking commonsense categories, such as "accountability." As Michael Moriarty (1991, 36) has noted in a different context: "Coercion is camouflaged as the statement of the obvious."

As noted in chapter 1, social engineering had its genesis, in part, in American pragmatism, in William James' construal of the significance of thought as its "effects" on situations (see Simpson 2002, 98–99). After psychoanalysis, it is clear that accompanying, indeed informing, the attunement of thought to reality (thought's "effect" on "practical" situations) is an ongoing effort at understanding, yes important in itself, but also important given its "effects" upon the situation. "Understanding" transforms how we discern a situation, and in that transformation, both we and the situation—organically connected—are changed. That change is not necessarily predictable, but it is inevitable.

The American preoccupations with business and religion tend to be anti-intellectual, as Richard Hofstadter has documented (see chapter 7). The "business-minded" are interested in designing "effects" on situations that can be predicted and profitable. In this sense, social engineering is the complement of capitalism. The "religiously-minded" mangle the present by disavowing it ("the best is yet to come") or by employing religious rituals (such as prayer) to try to manipulate present circumstances. In this sense, too (especially), Protestantism and capitalism are intertwined, perhaps most savagely in the American South.

The promise of social engineering—of "if only"—rings repeatedly in the politics of education as well as in much research and teaching in the broad field of education, including teacher education, now focused especially on "learning technologies" such as the computer and "intellectual technologies" such as hypertext. The transmutability hypertext promises contributes to the insubstantial and "fantastic" character of the public sphere. Like those "fantastic mass-produced images that shape our perceptions of the world," hypertext may "not only encourage a defensive contraction of the self but blur the boundaries between the self and its surroundings" (Lasch 1984, 19).

The future we face in cyberspace may exacerbate the cultural crisis that not only imperils the possibility of education but threatens the sustainability of the planet. Technological progress does not necessarily mean material and social progress (see Lasch 1984, 42). Moreover, "technology [can] undermine the self-reliance and autonomy of both workers and consumers" (Lasch 1984, 43), not to mention of teachers and students, as in the documentation and surveillance system known as PASSPORT (see next section).

While curriculum as "complicated conversation" can occur in cyberspace, through computer technologies, the "evaporation of the ego" in cyberspace can just as easily diminish as make more complex the individual self. The mutability and anonymity of cyberspace may only mirror a public sphere reduced to a shopping mall where "niche shopping" means "niche" sociability, where the only meaning of "citizen" is as "consumer." Without a world in which we are grounded and to which we are committed, we can dissolve as individuals and disappear as citizens. As Lasch (1984, 32–33) observes:

> [T]he collapse of our common life has impoverished private life as well. It has freed the imagination from external constraints but exposed it more directly than before to the tyranny of inner compulsions and anxieties. Fantasy ceases to be liberating when it frees itself from the check imposed by practical experience of the world. Instead it gives rise to hallucinations.

"Complicated conversation" is not solipsistic soliloquies, cryptic (too often not proofread) monosyllabic email messages, although it can occur in cyberspace and can be furthered by judicious and thoughtful use of "intellectual technologies," as Willinsky's project makes clear. But, "complicated conversation" makes no promises about raising test scores. As Deborah Britzman, Elizabeth Ellsworth, and Alice Pitt have demonstrated, communication is complex, riddled with intrapsychic crosscurrents and social contradictions; it is, at best, an aspiration, not an empirical fact.

While I cannot link free (or undistorted and unconstrained) speech with social emancipation, I do accept the Habermasian conception of reason as potentially communicative. But we cannot be confident about what complicated conversation will bring; historical transformation—the future—is enigmatic, contradictory, incalculable (Jonsson 2000). While curriculum as complicated conversation in the service of social and self-reflective understanding *will* transform the present, it will not do so in predictable ways, certainly not according to politicians' self-interested agendas. As Martha Grace Duncan (1996, 187) has observed: "[I] believe, as Socrates did, that there is no voluntary evil, only ignorance. It follows that understanding automatically leads to change; more exactly, understanding, in itself, *is* change."

The advancement of understanding can not occur when government intervenes in the intellectual lives of teachers and students, as the Bush Administration is now attempting. To stipulate the intellectual agenda of the nation's teachers and professoriate by specifying not only the *categories* of research to be funded but, in the "Leave No Child Behind" legislation, by the *methodologies* by which research is to be conducted, is profoundly and aggressively anti-intellectual. The Bush legislation is not, finally, many steps away from censorship.

Contrast the situation in the United States with that in Canada, where the Social Sciences and Humanities Research Council of Canada (SSHRC) provides the majority of governmental research grants in education. While

SSHRC periodically targets specific topics for "strategic grants," such as the "new economy" or "valuing literacy," it does so without disturbing its regular grant program. In its regular funding program, decisions regarding the receipt of grants are made by panels of scholars through an extensive peer-review process (in which I have participated). These practices ensure that while governmental interests are represented in the allocation of research funs, the intellectual agenda continues to be set by the research community—as diverse as that is—and not by the political agenda of the government (Willinsky 2003).

Curriculum theory and the complicated conversation it supports seek the truth of the present state of affairs, not the manipulation of them for political purposes, in the present instance, higher test scores on standardized exams. Higher test scores may well result, but they are hardly the motive for a curriculum as complicated conversation. Erudition, interdisciplinarity, intellectuality, self-reflexivity: curriculum as complicated conversation invites students to encounter themselves and the world they inhabit through academic knowledge, popular culture, grounded in their own lived experience. In chapter 2 we saw one powerful example of how the social, the subjective, and the intellectual merged in African-American autobiographical practice, "a *public* rather than a *private* gesture, [in which] *me-ism* gives way to *our-ism* and superficial concerns about *individual subject* usually give way to the *collective subjection* of the group" (Cudjoe 1984, 9; quoted in Fox-Genovese 1988, 70). Self-mobilization and social reconstruction are co-extensive and inextricably intertwined.

Gilles Deleuze expresses, if in different language, a similar sense of the subjective as social, of the autobiographical as a political project, of the inextricability of the private and public spheres. Deleuze speaks of

> the inclination to say simple things in your own proper name, to speak through affects, intensities, experiences, experiments. To say something in one's own name is very curious; for it is not at all when one takes one's self as an "I," a person or a subject, that one speaks in one's name. On the contrary, an individual acquires a real proper name only through the most severe exercise in depersonalization, when he opens himself to the multiplicities that traverse him from head to toe, to the intensities that flow through him, letting himself explore without inhibition an infinite variety of postures and situations. (quoted in Miller 1993, 194–195)

Such is the subjective labor of teacher education in the service of "retrieving public spaces" (see Gaztambide-Fernández and Sears 2004; Sears 2001; Sloan and Sears 2001).

But in contemporary Colleges of Education—Departments of Curriculum and Instruction (or Learning and Instruction) specifically—research is focused on teaching or, as most prefer, "instruction." The dominant interest is in learning how to teach more effectively, so that students can learn more quickly, as measured on standardized examinations. Curriculum theory invites us to return to the former, to curriculum, but, as we have seen, hardly in any traditional sense in which we have devised (bureaucratic) procedures and rationales for "curriculum development" (Pinar et al. 1995, 148). As we saw in chapter 3, the official or institutional curriculum (especially the secondary school curriculum) was settled, more or less, during the early 1960s; it would be directed toward and articulated with post-secondary destinations, primary among them the university and the workplace. It was—and remains—a gendered and racialized rite of (academic) passage.

By the early 1960s, what remained of the progressive dream—education for democratization which meant schooling for psycho-social as well as intellectual development—was past. We whose interest was in the educational significance of the curriculum (i.e., the meaning of the school subjects for self-formation, social reconstruction, and the historical moment) awoke in the aftermath of the 1960s national curriculum reform movement to find that we were "invited" to be, in a word, bureaucrats. Our job was not to think about the complex relations among schooling, society, and subjectivity, but, rather, to accept the conflations of school curriculum with the academic disciplines and the marketplace to ensure that students "learn" what others—politicians, policymakers, university faculty in natural sciences, social sciences, and the humanities—declared to be worth learning. Vocationalism, academic and the literal kind, ruled the day. As Joseph Schwab (1978, 302, 303) acknowledged:

> Of the five substantial high school science curriculums [constituting 1960s national curriculum reform], four of them—PSSC, BSCS, CHEMS, and CBA— were instituted and managed by subject matter specialists; the contributions of educators was small and that of curriculum specialists near the vanishing point. . . . Educators contribute expertise only in the area of test construction and evaluation, with a contribution here and there by a psychologist.

Even Project English and other humanities curriculum projects of the period were conducted under the direction of subject-matter academicians (see Clifford and Guthrie 1988, 176).

Directed by disciplinary specialists, the 1960s national curriculum reform movement was animated by, as Jerome Bruner (1977 [1960], 1) acknowledges, "what is almost certain to be a long-range crisis in national security, a crisis whose resolution will depend upon a well-educated citizenry." Why this "resolution" did not depend also and primarily upon the savvy of politicians and military personnel already in place, is now clear. After Sputnik, politicians searched for a scapegoat. As Bruner (1997 [1960], 1) observed: "One of the places in which this renewal of concern [for national security] has expressed itself is in curriculum planning for the elementary and secondary schools." The crisis in national security was "displaced" onto curriculum planning, in effect, the stipulation and control of what is taught and learned in school.

What became clear was that our task as curriculum specialists was to assist curriculum to be the means to those ends specified by politicians and corporatists and our well-meaning, if narrowly and academically-vocationally-focused, arts and sciences colleagues in the university. We were to help teachers forget their historical (although never realized, in part for gendered reasons) calling to practice academic freedom, to be intellectuals and scholars, not automata or technicians. We curriculum specialists were asked to help teachers become skillful implementers of others' objectives, something like an academic version of the postal service, delivering other people's mail. We were not to participate in what was delivered to the children (except for the sake of its more efficient transmission); our job was to see that the mail—the curriculum—was delivered, opened, read, then learned. "Accountability" was—remains—the Orwellian watchword of the day.

The great private-and-public intellectual (and poet, novelist, and filmmaker) Pier Paolo Pasolini once observed that the obligatory school mandates the "common education, obligatory and mistaken" of late-capitalist "cannibalism," which "pushes us all into the arena." This imaginary public arena is where "free" and "obligatory bread and circus games" are provided. In this sense, Pasolini complained, the culture of the school enforces "carcinogenic structures, at the very roots of the formation of desire and even of needs, infiltrating, like vampirical, caricatural doubles of some primary authenticities, the zones of the psyche though inaccessible to the charms—pedagogies—persuasions set up in the past" (quoted in Allen 1982, 31). "Vampirical, caricatural doubles" are exactly, it would seem, what two "professional" organizations have become.

II
BETRAYAL BY PROFESSIONAL ORGANIZATIONS

Mass production is not confined to the factory.
—John Dewey (1991 [1927], 116)

We become party to our own depersonalization, and to the
thoughtlessness of our students, when we see ourselves as
merely place-holders and low level bureaucrats,
filling out forms and completing procedures.
—William Ayers (1993, 19)

Is this not "education" reduced to a half-life of what it could be?
—Ted T. Aoki (in press)

Evidently even leaders of professional associations become spellbound by politicians' self-interested scapegoating. On January 18, 2002, David G. Imig, President of the American Association of Colleges for Teacher Education (AACTE) informed the College of Education faculty at Louisiana State University that "times have changed," that it is no longer appropriate for individual scholars to pursue individual research agendas. He urged education faculty to "come together" and "sell our services to the schools," which, in the $22+ billion-dollar Bush administration legislation (No Child Left Behind or Public Law 107-110), are funded to purchase such educational "services" (Imig and Earley 2002).

"Twenty-two billion is not enough," Penelope M. Earley (AACTE Vice-President) asserted at the same faculty "retreat," but she did not contest the assumption that the money could or should engineer higher test scores. Because it is stipulated in the Bush legislation, Earley endorsed so-called "scientific" research in education (Imig and Earley 2002). There was no acknowledgment that one of the most persisting and pervasive problems of the broad field of education is that we have been overly sensitive as well as politically vulnerable to rhetorical fashions and political winds, to specific pieces of legislation like the Bush bill (Kliebard 1970, 1975). That day at least, the leadership of AACTE appeared to have completely capitulated to political pressures and financial incentives.

The American Association of Colleges for Teacher Education (AACTE) is not the only professional organization to betray the profession. At a National Council for Accreditation of Teacher Education (NCATE) Clinic for Louisiana colleges and universities disingenuously entitled "A Partnership Approach to Enhancing Teacher Quality and Accountability," NCATE Senior Vice President Donna Gollnick explained to the assembled professors of education from across Louisiana that the new (2000) NCATE standards focus on "how and what" teacher candidates *learn*, not on what they have been *taught*. Gollnick warned those of us in the audience that NCATE accreditation examiners will be asking faculty: "How can you document that what your unit does is efficient and effective?"

Just as public-school teachers are being told they are responsible for student learning (as measured on standardized exams), those Louisiana professors of education engaged in teacher preparation were told that their teaching—its thoughtfulness, inventiveness, one's erudition—is, well, irrelevant. All that matters is that teacher candidates are able to teach "so that students learn," that is to say, so that students can perform acceptably (by politicians' and their appointees' standards) on standardized examinations.

NCATE requires "performance data," Gollnick (2002) continued, a demand that follows, one might suppose, from the real problem of grade inflation in schools of education, but which, in all likelihood, has nothing to do with it. Given the "business" model at work here, in all likelihood teacher educators would be told they are responsible for the "bottom line"—student "learning" as measured by student test scores—whatever their grading practices may have been. Gollnick (2002) assured those assembled in Baton Rouge that NCATE is in accord with the "recommendations" asserted by the United States Department of Education (dominated at this time by the Bush Administration) regarding teacher education, including the conferring of teacher certification based on scores on licensure examinations. NCATE is complicit with the reactionary anti-intellectualism of the Bush Administration.

Gollnick was followed by Charles Hodge, a "NCATE Mentor," who told the audience that NCATE is "committed to teacher competence," apparently something to which, NCATE staff members have evidently concluded, schools of education have not been committed. Teacher candidates, he continued, must be able to work "effectively" in the schools, including in urban schools. NCATE requires "evidence," Hodge explained, that teacher candidates are "doing that" (working effectively in urban settings). By "effective" he meant, I think, that teachers are producing increases in student test scores. There was no acknowledgment that "effective" teachers must attend to critical thinking, creativity, and independence of mind, for example, and that these might not be visible in standardized examination scores.

NCATE dictates—through its Standard One—that every teacher preparation program be organized according to its "conceptual framework." Hodge told us that every faculty member should accept the "conceptual framework." He called it a "road map" because "without it, we're all over the place," thus making intellectual differences and diversity a matter of being disorganized, rather than the very condition for intellectual growth and development. Hodge alluded to the NCATE standard for "diversity," but it was clear that this term did not include intellectual diversity.

Perhaps in anticipation of resistance to the barrage of NCATE jargon, Clinic planners scheduled the Director of the Education Trust, Kati Haycock, to speak on the afternoon of the second day. While her advocacy for children—especially poor children—seemed sincere, Haycock positioned herself within the right-wing assault on teachers and teacher educators by relying exclusively on test scores to gauge educational "improvement." After 20 years of reform, Haycock said, the "results are not very satisfying," disclosing her naiveté regarding the fundamentally political character of this "reform." She noted that "gaps" (in test scores) between groups (she listed "whites," "Hispanics," and African Americans) are stable or growing after 1988, with no acknowledgment that these are not reliable (certainly not comprehensive) indicators of students' educational accomplishment. During the two-day "clinic" there was never *any* acknowledgment of the public and scholarly controversy regarding standardized tests. Nor was there any acknowledgment in Haycock's presentation that deteriorating conditions in the nation's poorest schools might well follow from Reagan–Bush social policies which transferred wealth from the poor and middle classes to the already wealthy, thereby intensifying poverty for the lower classes (see, for instance, Lasch 1995, 32).

Haycock's presumption was that differences in educational achievement are due *only* to teaching. There were constant references to "effective" teachers, a term that was never defined. (If it has a definition, it would seem to be circular: "effective" teachers are those whose "teaching" raises student test scores.) Haycock implied that "effective" teachers might have more experience and more "content" knowledge than others, but performance on test scores seemed to be the main thing. Those students working with "ineffective" teachers—this term was never defined either; presumably it referred to those whose students do not post improvements in test scores—stayed the same or fell behind. "It's not the kids," Haycock declared, contesting racist arguments that black or Latino/Latina or poor kids are genetically inferior, but, at the same, erasing any responsibility for educational accomplishment from the students themselves and/or their families or from the predatory (and intensely anti-intellectual) culture right-wing policies have helped create.

Hancock told us that if students "don't get it," teachers must teach "it" in another way, in "multiple" ways. Yet, curiously, she insisted that "content knowledge"—not pedagogy—is what enables teachers to improvise. Teaching is an "intellectual task," she said, an acknowledgment dissonant with the message of the NCATE speakers who had preceded her. "Teacher education," Hancock informed the Louisiana education professorate, "should be driven by and flow from K–12 standards and learning goals." Whether teacher education should include attention to these "standards" and "learning goals"—even as opportunities to study political meddling in the profession—should, of course, be determined by university and college faculty of education. In her casual stipulation of the teacher education curriculum, Haycock performs her version of right-wing, anti-intellectual, authoritarian dismissals of academic freedom.

Haycock's last "power point presentation" image was: *And there was culture*. She narrated the story of speaking with a Latina principal in Los Angeles who told Hancock about her student teaching experience in an elite school in Palm Springs, California, where her "best lessons" seemed to fail, despite her good intentions, despite her best efforts. She was transferred to a poor school in Indio, California where, with her mentor teacher, she made a home visit. "Home" turned out to be a boxcar where the parents of the child shared their meager meal with the two. These were parents who clearly honored the educators' work. This experience persuaded the Latina educator to work in poor schools. What Haycock failed to conclude from her story was the obvious fact that it matters where one teaches. Perfectly strong teachers—"verbally capable" and with strong "content knowledge" in the Bush Administration's rhetoric (see Paige 2002)—may fail in classrooms for reasons not of their own making, "culture" being one, as illustrated in Haycock's anecdote. The NCATE demand that all teacher candidates perform "effectively" in all schools is political rhetoric, not professional ethics (see Slattery and Rapp 2002).

That academic programs—such as teacher education—ought to undergo rigorous review for accreditation is obvious, but such accreditation cannot be conferred by pseudo-professional organizations in the political service of presidential administrations. Whatever aspirations NCATE may have had to represent the profession have been forfeited in its complicity with the Bush Administration's agenda of scapegoating public-school teachers and the university professors who educate them. In its arrogant ignorance of the complexity of the scholarly field—in which the business model is, overall, *not* taken seriously, especially in curriculum studies—NCATE is itself guilty of anti-intellectualism. In its uncritical acceptance and bureaucratic rearticulation of the Bush Administration's rhetorical game of scapegoating teachers, NCATE is guilty of betraying the profession it claims to represent.

By making the NCATE accreditation "process" labor intensive (this point was emphasized throughout the two-day "clinic"), the quality and quantity of research and teaching in schools of education will be negatively impacted, as the busywork performed in anticipation of NCATE site visitations will siphon off faculty energy and consume already limited faculty time. In this regard, the effect of NCATE amounts to the higher education version of public school teachers' deskilling. With the diminished intellectual quality of teacher preparation programs NCATE accreditation reviews guarantee, schools of education will be made even more vulnerable to the Bush Administration's (through U.S. Secretary of Education Rod Paige [see Paige 2002]) agenda to dismantle schools of education (Munro 2002).

By insisting on a "shared vision"—intellectual homogeneity—the NCATE standard concerning the "conceptual framework" of the "unit" (any notion of an academic department disappears) produces the "de-intellectualization" of schools of education, exacerbating the problem of anti-intellectualism discussed in chapter 7. Petra Munro (2002) points out that this assault can be understood as part of the larger process of "corporatization" of educational institutions (see also Molnar 2002) in which faculty are reduced to institutional employees. No longer are we scholars whose academic—intellectual—freedom makes education possible. Moreover, the NCATE standards guarantee a "de-intellectualization" by "de-democratizing" schools of education (Munro 2002). Significantly, the NCATE "standard" concerning "governance" nowhere mentions the centrality of academic (i.e., intellectual) freedom to the educational process. Rather than representing university education faculty and teacher candidates, the National Council for Accreditation of Teacher Education (NCATE) ensures their de-legitimization and de-professionalization.

The Professional Accountability Support System (PASSPORT) is an elaborate documentation and surveillance system developed in Louisiana to solidify the grip of NCATE on teacher education in Louisiana. (Education professors in Louisiana were "invited" to undergo a five-hour PASSPORT training session; I did so on January 17, 2003.) Making more a general point, C. A. Bowers appreciates the reactionary politics at work in "technical" systems like PASSPORT:

> [A]ll technological experiments with the culture are viewed as inherently progressive in nature and thus not requiring any sort of questioning attitude. Basically, the capacity of computers to collect, store, and retrieve massive amounts of data is turning American society into a Panopticon culture. (Bowers 1995, 88)

In sync with NCATE's anti-intellectual and thereby de-professionalizing agenda, PASSPORT accustoms prospective teachers to never-ending busywork, increasingly the fate of public-school teachers now being held "accountable." (We have seen how "accountability" schemes disable teachers from, in fact, performing their profession.) This intricate record-keeping system increases the faculty's bureaucratic workload (not to mention that of students) while reducing educational coursework to record keeping. Forced to employ PASSPORT, Louisiana education professors are pressed to become an academic version of Internal Revenue Service (IRS) agents, employed to enforced bureaucratic regulations devised by politicians. By making less likely the appearance of more intellectual and erudite teachers in Louisiana's public schools, PASSPORT will help ensure that the state remains at the bottom of national surveys of educational accomplishment.

Obvious in the AAACTE and NCATE events, and in the Bush legislation informing them, is the assumption that university-based schools of education exist to prepare teachers to do a specific job, namely to teach the school subjects as dictated, in ways that presumably ensure student learning (as measured on standardized exams). Indeed, teachers are to be held "accountable" for student learning (as measured on standardized exams), and education professors are to be held accountable for their graduates' success as teachers in raising student test scores. Imagine business school professors being held responsible for the financial success of their graduates or law school professors for the ethical conduct of theirs! There is a gendered and racialized dynamic at work in the politics of "school reform." Professors of business and law are coded "masculine" in the American popular imagination, while professors of education are coded feminine. Therein lies the difference in how these professions are treated, even by their own professional organizations.

What can be done? Colleges, schools, and departments of education must repudiate NCATE and its anti-intellectual agenda. Accreditation of teacher education programs must be an intensely intellectual experience, not a bureaucratic and behavioral enforcement of business rhetoric (rhetoric business itself does not always take seriously). Probably education faculty can not count on many deans and provosts to take leadership in this repudiation; probably we faculty must rely on ourselves to teach administrators why NCATE has disqualified itself as an organization capable of conferring professional accreditation.

Given the contentious character of this pedagogical action, probably tenured senior faculty need to take leadership in the repudiation of NCATE, if only to protect untenured faculty from administrative reprisals. Senior faculty must be willing to take leadership not only in persuading provosts and deans that NCATE is no longer a credible organization for teacher education program review, but in starting new, or making use of existing, organizations (those close to the research and scholarship of the field such as the American Educational Research Association, the American Educational Studies Association, or the American Association for the Advancement of Curriculum Studies) to assess the *intellectual* quality of teacher education. Undertaking this pedagogical action will likely be unpleasant work, but the betrayal of the profession by NCATE leaves us no choice.

III
BETRAYAL BY GOVERNMENT

The search for cheap teachers was perennial.
—Richard Hofstadter (1962, 319)

*Fantasy in politics is a subject that has
been insufficiently explored.*
—Elizabeth Wright (1996, 146)

*And yet politics, and surely American politics,
is hardly a school for great minds.*
—Anna Julia Cooper (1998 [1892], 114)

At the same NCATE "clinic" for Louisiana education professors described in the previous section, Counselor to the U.S. Secretary of Education Susan K. Sclafani (2002) told Louisiana university and college professors of education that the Bush Administration's *Leave No Child Behind* legislation was designed to make all American schoolchildren "proficient" by 2014. (Presumably "proficient" means achieving certain scores on standardized examinations. Probably it does *not* mean political literacy.) Sclafani claimed that the Bush legislation was aimed at neglected populations, especially at the poor and at African Americans. In making this claim, Sclafani and the Bush Administration (for which she was an apologist) have targeted new scapegoats. Blaming the (black and poor) victim is, apparently, no longer politically profitable, even for Republicans. The new targets are public-school teachers and those who prepare them.

Like Haycook (2002), Scalfani demanded "alignment" between teacher-training programs and standards-based reforms. Academic freedom disappears in "An Aligned System" which requires that "coherent instruction" be aligned with the "standards," with "rigorous assessment" based on these standards, and with an acknowledgment of the "value of testing" (as if teachers have not been testing all along). Sclafani construed the "public" construed as consumers; she noted they "have a right to know how we're doing" (as if tests provided that information). In the Bush scheme, the school is to be the unit of accountability, not individual teachers and students whose individual commitment and hard work disappear into the collective in this conversion of the school into a business.

In Sclafani's speech, the workplace and the university were the only destinations of public school curriculum. "We cannot accept the levels of performance we've accepted in the past," she announced, as if it was the moral laxity (or professional ineptitude) of teachers that has produced the alleged educational crisis. "If our mantra is my [the teacher's] students will leave the year improved," she declared in a naive mix of volunteerism and common sense, "then we have a first-rate system." In a diatribe disguised as rational argument, Sclafani ascribed the total responsibility for education to teachers. Listening to these words in the Deep South, they sounded more like those of a "plantation" rather than a "business" manager.

"We're going to close the achievement gaps" between the poor and other groups by improving teaching, Sclafani announced, as if leading a moral crusade rather than political assault. Education's "dirty little secret," she continued, is that teachers are teaching subjects in which they have inadequate training. By using the phrase "dirty little secret" she implies that the profession has been "getting away" with something, when, in fact, professional educators and their administrators have been fighting this problem—created by poor working conditions, among them inadequate salaries (which Sclafani never mentions nor has, evidently, any intention to correct)—all along.

"We worry about our grandchildren going to the public schools," Sclafani concluded, indulging now in straightforward teacher bashing (and silent racial profiling). She wants "everybody on the same page," making explicit the political authoritarianism of the Bush Administration's educational initiatives. After tipping her hat to the humanities, arts, and social sciences,

Sclafani underscored that math and science are most important subjects because jobs in the "twenty-first century require high proficiency in them." There is not even academic vocationalism here, just vocationalism. The country needs "worker bees," she is asserting, not an educated and politically astute citizenry.

And these "worker bees" are to be produced by teachers, not exactly "queen" bees in this scheme, more like domestic help. By positioning teachers as responsible for the (re)production of able workers/students, Sclafani is exploiting the gender of the public-school teaching profession. As Patti Lather (1994, 245) has observed: "teaching has come to be formulated as an extension of women's role in the family: to accept male leadership as 'natural' and to provide services that reproduce males for jobs and careers, females for wives and mothers and a reserve labor force."

Sclafani's remarks derived from U.S. Secretary of Education Rod Paige's (2002) "annual report on teacher quality." Declaring that the system is "broken," Paige (2002, viii) points out the *No Child Left Behind Act* demands that, by the end of the 2005–2006 school year, every classroom in America have a teacher who is "highly qualified" (Paige 2002, iii). He notes that that the states will have to move quickly if they are to align their certification requirements with those of the *No Child Left Behind Act*. In order to comply with the new law, states and universities will have to strengthen requirements for coursework in the academic disciplines while "eliminating cumbersome requirements not based on scientific [!] evidence and doing more to attract highly qualified candidates from a variety of fields" (Paige 2002, viii). Included in "a variety of fields" are retired military personnel (i.e., "Troops to Teachers": see Paige 2002, 3), mostly men, a program which discloses both the authoritarianism of contemporary right-wing reform as well as its gender politics (see chapter 3).

In strengthening requirements in the academic disciplines, Paige's report echoes—without referencing—the Holmes movement, a reform of teacher education advanced *by* the field of education 15 years ago. In abbreviated form, the goals of Holmes Group—a consortium of research universities—included:

1. To make the education of teachers intellectually more solid.
2. To recognize differences in teachers' knowledge, skill, and commitment, in their education, certification, and work. If teachers are to become more effective professionals, we must distinguish between novices, competent members of the profession, and high-level professional leaders.
3. To create standards of entry to the profession—examinations and educational requirements—that are professionally relevant and intellectually defensible.

4. To connect our own institutions [research universities] to schools.
5. To make schools better places to work. (Holmes Group 1986, 4)

At least two of these goals—numbers 1 and 3—are prominent in the Paige report. In claiming of this initiative as it own and as "new," the dishonesty of the Bush Administration's demand for "quality teachers" is disclosed. Schools of education have not functioned to block the entry of qualified teachers to the profession; working conditions themselves—among them salaries but class size and professional autonomy as well—make the profession unappealing to many, except, perhaps, military personnel. For them, schools might represent a "step up."

It seems politicians will do anything but pay teachers more, an especially curious recalcitrance from right-wing politicians who forever pledge allegiance to the "wisdom" of the "free market." Make the public schools attractive places to work, such "wisdom" should suggest, and there will be an oversupply of teacher candidates. Reducing teachers to postal workers, carrying other people's mail (prepackaged, teacher-proof curriculum) and bullying those who prepare them (the education professorate) will only distort the "market" and thereby intensify the problem. But if the agenda is scapegoating and distracting the electorate, politicians can only look forward to the deterioration of the schools, a predictable "outcome" of these political tactics.

In "Demanding Highly Qualified Teachers" (Paige 2002, 4), the report focuses, as did the university-based Holmes Group, on "rigorous subject matter preparation" (5). "Again," Paige (6) reiterates, "the focus of the law is content knowledge." Unlike the Holmes proposals, Paige takes aim at the nation's schools of education. Without referencing it, he asserts that "scientific evidence raises questions about the value of attendance in schools of education" (8). What he means, apparently, is that the test scores of those taught by education-school graduates are not necessarily superior to those taught without education coursework.

"This new approach," Paige (2002, 20) suggests, evidently ignorant of the antecedent proposals such as those advanced by the Holmes Group, "would not necessarily mean the end of schools of education." "Rather," he continues, "it might signal a new beginning for these institutions, which could come to resemble graduate schools of business." Given that the right-wing has converted schools to skill factories and corporations, who can be surprised that Paige wants schools of education to become businesses as well? In support of his interest in detaching teacher certification from coursework in education (a "troubled marriage" to be sure: see chapter 7), Paige quotes James W. Fraser, dean of the school of education at Northeastern University in Boston:

The breaking up of our monopoly would force us to convince students, their tuition-paying parents and the school districts that do the hiring that our programs produce teaching candidates who are more qualified and skilled than candidates who obtained their training elsewhere or who come in with no training. (quoted in Paige 2002, 20–21)

Paige (21) comments: "Although schools of education would lose their 'exclusive franchise' over teacher preparation, they would likely emerge stronger in the long run."

Given the anti-intellectual political conditions in which we work—including the betrayal by our professional organizations—Paige might be right. If teacher certification were decoupled from coursework in education, if the "troubled marriage" between teachers and education schools was ended, then those who study education would do so out of intellectual interest. The field would suffer a cataclysmic contraction—education schools would become small, perhaps reorganized as small departments of education in Colleges of Arts and Sciences—but the field that survived (if one survived at all) would be an academic, intellectual field, one worthy of the name.

The academic strength of schools of education is, however, not Paige's concern. Paige's—the Bush Administration's—proposals are similar to those already advanced by the Holmes Group and by curriculum theorists (see Pinar 1989). But the Paige report is not about the facts; it is about constructing a scapegoat and a self-serving fantasy of a future that can never arrive. As Paul Shaker and Elizabeth Heilman (2002, 1) have pointed out, government and its "advocacy academicians" (like Diane Ravitch; see Wraga 2001) are committed to silencing the education professoriate in order to control the curriculum America's schoolchildren are taught.

By alleging that problem of teacher quality is a function of "high barriers" and "low standards" (Paige 2002, 12), and that hordes of "talented individuals" are being "thwarted" (15) from entering the profession by "mandated education courses, unpaid student teaching, and the hoops and hurdles of the state certification bureaucracy" (40), Paige is attributing the problem of teacher quality to schools of education, not to teacher pay and unsatisfactory working conditions. "If only" we raise standards for "verbal ability and content knowledge" (23), teachers will demonstrate "quality" and student test-scores will soar. This is a safe move politically (scapegoating a relatively defenseless field), but it is a falsification of the facts, and, I suspect, Paige and his appointees—such as Sclafani—know it.

This political manipulation of teacher education is not unique to the United States. In the United Kingdom, the right-wing assault on academic freedom and progressive education seems to have started a decade later than in it did in the United States. In the late 1960s in Britain the "Black Papers" were published, a series of well-publicized critiques of progressive education made mostly by arts and sciences professors. It was not, John Furlong (2002) reports, until 1979 and the election of right-wing prime minister Margaret

Thatcher that those behind the Black Papers enjoyed influence. At that time attention became focused on teacher education, the bastion of what was characterized as the "liberal education elite" (quoted in Furlong 2002, 23).

The assault on academic freedom that the British government's control of teacher education enacts seems more aggressive, more totalitarian than in the United States. In the United Kingdom, education professors' influence over teacher education has been sharply restricted and monitored; schools' responsibilities in training programs (the official discourse is now teacher "training" rather than teacher "education") have been substantially increased, a curious development given that politicians' long-standing criticism of the schools would seem to classify them as the last place prospective teachers should look for innovation (Furlong 2002).

In the United Kingdom two agencies enforce governmental control of teacher education. The Teacher Training Agency (TTA) funds and manages all teacher education courses while Ofsted enforces this management, collecting "objective evidence about schools (and teacher education courses) and reporting on their failings" (Lawlor 1993, 7; quoted in Furlong 2002, 23). As Bush officials (such as Sclafani and Paige) advocate and as NCATE standards specify, Ofsted inspectors judge the quality of individual university courses by assessing the impact of trainee's teaching on children's learning (Furlong 2002). This political assault on academic freedom has been effective; Furlong (2002, 24) reports that the voices of "those in higher education had been successfully silenced." In the preparation of public school teachers, academic freedom has, in England, been erased.

As in the United States, not only the right wing exploits public education for political purposes. When the Labour Party came to power in 1997, officials continued inspection protocols and schedules. At the same time, Labour government officials took direct control of course content by detailing "standards of competence" and specifying a "national curriculum" for teacher education dictating curriculum content, pedagogy, and assessment in the fields of literacy, numeracy, science and information technology. Recently, officials have also introduced numeracy and literacy tests for student teachers in addition to more formal entrance qualifications (Furlong 2002).

Unlike the situation in the United States, governmental intervention in teacher education in England has been enforced through two central agencies (TTA and Ofsted). These bureaucracies, Furlong reports, have specified the curriculum content of teacher training programs; they have "policed implementation through rigorous inspection regimes" (Furlong 2002, 24). Without meaningful public debate (the case in the United States as well), the government's anti-intellectual agenda has been, simply, imposed. As in the United States, teacher educators in England have opposed both the fact of governmental intervention in the academic process and the specific curriculum content that the government imposed (Furlong 2002). More effectively than has the U.S. government (to date), the British government has de-profession-alized teaching by destroying teacher autonomy and erasing academic free-dom. The totalitarian future English novelists (such as Aldous Huxley and George Orwell) famously feared in the 20th century has, in the sphere of British teacher education at least, arrived.

IV
KEEPING HOPE ALIVE

[C]urriculum is an important topic for public debate.
It shapes the society we are and hope to become.
—Frank H. T. Rhodes (2001, B10)

My final prayer: O my body, make of me
always a man who questions!
—Frantz Fanon (1967, 232)

Eternal vigilance is the price of liberty.
—Ida B. Wells (1970, 415)

It should be needless to say that the preparation of thoughtful and informed teachers cannot occur in such totalitarian circumstances. Nor will it occur if stipulated as a form of social engineering, figuring out how to get students to score higher on standardized tests, although higher test scores could be an in-cidental consequence of understanding curriculum as complicated conversa-tion. The professional preparation of teachers *is* the project of academic un-derstanding, but not narrowly conceived as professional training in the school subjects as they exist (i.e., academic vocationalism) and in bureau-cratic regimen of the school-as-business.

The professional preparation of teachers requires understanding curricu-lum as interdisciplinary, grounded in self-formation and historical moment. When the curriculum is severed into school subjects, educational experience becomes fragmented. As Linda McNeil (2000, 13) points out: "This *fragmen-tation* of course content tended to disembody the curriculum, divorcing it from the cultures and interests and prior knowledge of the students, from the teachers' knowledge of the subject, and from the epistemologies, the ways of knowing, within the subject itself."

Teachers' loyalties must be broader than to the school subject(s) they are hired to teach; they must be intellectually expansive, interdisciplinary in range. Teacher loyalties must include the educational institution itself, ex-pressed as an intellectual concern for the overall school program and those enrolled in it. As many university faculty appreciate, our work as teachers and scholars requires that we understand the context—not only intellectual but also institutional—in which that work proceeds. What appears to be (or is presented disingenuously as) merely "administrative" matters can threaten academic freedom and, thereby, the educational enterprise itself.

In many institutions—perhaps most of all in overadministered private universities—faculty control over important academic matters, such as academic emphases, has already been usurped by bureaucrats. Certainly this is the case at the University of Rochester, where Daniel Noah Moses had enrolled to study for the Ph.D. in History with Christopher Lasch. After Lasch's death in 1994, as part of a general administrative restructuring of the University (the so-called "Renaissance Plan"), the famous (slave historian Eugene Genovese had also taught at Rochester) University of Rochester Department of History was "refocused," which is to say, "down-sized." Moses (1999) reports that the central administration had determined that the Department could not sustain its "ratings" without Lasch's presence. "Instead of supporting the department under these circumstances," Moses (1999, 87) reports, "the administration chose to downsize it." No doubt Christopher Lasch (1995, 192–193) had (not only) the University of Rochester in mind when he wrote:

It is corporate control, not academic radicalism, that has "corrupted higher education." It is corporate control that has diverted social resources from the humanities into military and technological research, fostered as obsession with quantification that has destroyed the social sciences, replaced English language with bureaucratic jargon, and created a top-heavy administrative apparatus whose educational vision begins and ends with the bottom line.

In the professional preparation of teachers converge multiple projects of intellectual understanding, including understanding the essential antagonism between "business thinking" and the process of education. Professional teacher education cannot guarantee success as measured by student performance on standardized examinations. A well-prepared teacher may not perform well in certain settings, with certain students, at certain schools, and even when they do, they may not, despite their best efforts, enable their students to obtain higher scores on standardized tests. After all, student learning, while influenced in important and essential ways by teaching, is primarily a function of study (see Doll 1998; McClintock 1971). Teaching represents an (educational) opportunity offered, not a (business) service rendered. "Accountability" is an empty and pernicious political slogan, a gendered and racialized subjugation that disables teachers from the thoughtful performance of their profession.

Try as we may, teachers will not "reach" all students, especially students who do not study (or who cannot study, due, for instance, to conditions at home), who decline to listen and participate (or, due to their psychological or physiological states, cannot listen and participate) in class. Intelligence plays no small part, of course, although the ratio of "nature" to "nurture" remains unresolved. Of course we cannot change genetics, but we teachers can and must conduct ourselves as if "nurture" is the primary determinant in educational accomplishment. Teachers are responsible for being well-informed and self-aware, for being pedagogically spirited and adaptable and ethically committed, for making every effort to engage students intellectually and psychosocially. But it is sheer (political) nonsense to assert that teachers are accountable for students' learning. Students (and, secondarily, their parents and caregivers) are accountable for their educational accomplishment. *Teachers provide opportunities; students are responsible for taking advantage of them.*

Curriculum theorists appreciate these facts; we reject the political nonsense about "accountability" even when, due to legislation, we are required to report the rhetoric in our teacher education classes. We understand that the point of academic work is understanding, to self-reflexively engage our students in understanding the curriculum and those political, psycho-social, and gendered *milieux* in which it is taught and studied. We are clear that the project of understanding is no retreat from the everyday world of "practice" into some ivory-tower panopticon. Scholarly understanding *is* a form of *praxis*.

Traditionally, when curriculum had been conceived as a conversation, the concept connoted "conversing" with those great usually white male minds of western civilization whose ideas presumably transcended the temporal and cultural locales of their origin. That patriarchal and Eurocentric concept is no longer in fashion, for good reason. European high culture is no longer the center of American or Western civilization, especially as that is codified and theorized in academic scholarship and inquiry (McCarthy 1998). But the political decentering of European knowledges and knowing hardly means that curriculum is no longer students' and teachers' conversations with ideas, including European ones, as these are recorded in primary source material, textbooks, and other curricular artifacts and technologies.

Curriculum remains pre-eminently that conversation, but it is also a conversation among the participants, one which supports and explores the possibilities of unpredicted and novel events, unplanned destinations, conversation which incorporates life history and politics and popular culture as well as official, institutional, bureaucratized knowledge. While hardly turning away from the problems of the everyday classroom and the practical pedagogue, to understand curriculum today requires acknowledging the limits of teaching technique and bureaucratic procedure. Curriculum conceived as a "complicated conversation" cannot be framed as another technique that will somehow get the American educational engine humming smoothly again. Education is, of course, no mechanical affair, and yet, astonishingly, much of the field and the public still seems to proceed on the assumption that if we only make the appropriate adjustments—in the curriculum, teaching, learning, administration, counseling, perhaps the establishment of "standards"—then those test scores will soar. It is a mad, mostly male, fantasy.

The school curriculum (especially the secondary school curriculum) is a somewhat arbitrary political settlement of what Herbert Kliebard (1986) has characterized as the struggle for the American curriculum. As we saw in chapter 3, we educators lost that struggle; right-wing politicians and businessmen (often intersecting categories), allied with our vocationally minded colleagues in the natural sciences, social sciences, and humanities, won. The children lost. With its emphasis on the bottom line, the school increasingly becomes a business, no longer a factory perhaps, but certainly a corporation (Fiske 1991). Factory or corporation, schools become (knowledge and skill) businesses, not institutions of education.

What we have today—still, unbelievably—is 19th-century faculty psychology, contemporary versions of that presumably long-ago discredited idea that the mind is a muscle which must be exercised by all the basic weights (academic disciplines) if it is to bulge. Once bulging, clearly visible by high test scores, America will be rich, powerful, ready for the new millennium. Poverty and crime will disappear and the G.N.P. will seek the sky. In addition to this masculinized fantasy which conflates "mind" with "muscles" and test scores with national supremacy and economic productivity, present-day general curriculum requirements also represent a negotiated settlement among competing constituencies, most powerful of which are the sciences and mathematics. With extensive secondary-school curricular prerequisites for college admission closely linked with two years of "general education" at the university-level, each of the politically powerful academic disciplines gets a piece of the student enrollment (i.e., budget) pie.

While many are, of course, sincere in believing that "general education" makes for a "well-rounded" individual, forcing students to study the "major" fields also props up enrollment and employment in those fields. The curricular arrangement that stabilized after Sputnik is not, as we educators know (and despite the pious rhetoric), only about the education of students or the preparation of citizens and workers (see Penn State 2002). Animating the present vocationalism—academic and that of the workplace—is the masculinist, militaristic, and economic fantasy that academic achievement (as measured by standardized tests; "excellence" in mathematics and science is crucial) creates the conditions for national supremacy, understood today primarily as economic prosperity, but cultural hegemony and continued military dominance as well.

Serious students of curriculum theory already know this unhappy story. The progressive dream (Pilder 1974) may have been over long ago, but then it always was a dream, was it not? Dewey (1916) must have known his was a losing gamble, even if it was a gamble he was compelled, for his own as well as for the nation's sake, to wage. And even while the public sphere has almost always been dominated to varying degrees by conservative, sometimes reactionary, political and economic interests, individual teachers have continued—partly due to the influence of much maligned education professors—to work to realize that American dream of democratization and self-realization.

Individual teachers have always helped to keep hope alive, our faith— "our" denoting those of us in the academic field of education and in teacher preparation specifically—that individual educators can somehow find ways to work with children outside official directives and bureaucratic inertia, outside that patriarchal public sphere dominated by right-wing politics and capitalistic economics. Surely our situation is no worse than that faced by those Americans whose testimonies of suffering and struggle we glimpsed in chapters 2 and 4.

Despite the stacked deck, the overwhelming odds, the great gamble—the progressive dream of democratization and self-realization, inextricably intertwined as each depends upon and extends the other—must again be waged by those of us committed to the project of public education. Those children in our classrooms compel us to continue to converse, privately and in public, inspired by those who have gone before us, those who faced odds much worse than we face today.

V

RECAPTURING THE CURRICULUM

A new idea is an unsettling of received beliefs;
otherwise, it would not be a new idea.
—John Dewey (1991 [1927], 59)

The training of the schools we need today more than ever, - the
training of deft hands, quick eyes and ears, and above all the
broader, deeper, higher culture of gifted minds and pure hearts.
—W. E. B. Du Bois (1995/1996 [1903], 40)

Simply stated, faculty members must recapture the curriculum.
—Frank H. T. Rhodes (2001, B8)

If curriculum theorists could be heard, if we could teach the American public that education is not a business, in other words, if political conditions shifted so that curriculum theorists were able to influence the school curriculum, what would it look like? First of all, there would be no "it," no monolithic school curriculum. As a former president of Cornell University noted, no ideal curriculum exists for every institution (Rhodes 2001). While he is speaking of higher education, the point holds for public school curriculum as well.

If curriculum theorists were in charge, there would be multiple sites of (ongoing) curricular experimentation.

The curricular stranglehold universities have held over the curriculum of high schools will have to be loosened if there is to be more individualized curricular options, including opportunities for specialization. There is no *educational* reason why *everyone* must take advanced algebra or chemistry or study Shakespeare. Nor is there any educational reason these subjects must be kept compartmentalized within aggressively patrolled disciplines. Discussing the curriculum of the natural sciences, Frank H. T. Rhodes (2001, B9) appreciates that the *educational* point of such study is to situate the natural sciences in human society, not to study each in "isolation."

Led by those, like Rhodes, who understand that educational significance of interdisciplinary study, universities might participate supportively in the creation of smaller, less anonymous, possibly even theme-based high schools (such as schools for the arts or the natural sciences). Even "vocational" schools might be academic (see Kincheloe 1999). There might be many different organizations of public-funded, independent schools, requiring, perhaps, a breakup of the monolithic public system as we have known it, possibly through the redistribution of funding, such as vouchers or other forms of public support distributed directly to parents and others responsible for the care of children.

Many scholars remain loyal to the comprehensive public high school partly out of tradition, partly out of faith, mostly out of opposition to the right-wing's stipulation of school reform as "marketization" and the introduction of "business-like" competition among schools. I am not opposed to continuance of the comprehensive high school, but its curriculum must be reconfigured radically. With curricular and pedagogical revolution at the secondary level, middle and elementary school curriculum could change as well.

Curricular experimentation does not come easily to the comprehensive public high school. A voucher system might, if bureaucratic regulation of educational programs were decentralized and academic vocationalism weakened, make such curricular experimentation more likely. With carefully monitored, rigidly enforced funding equalization formulae, funding inequities could be no greater than now, and perhaps less. What would be greater than now are, for instance, opportunities for marginalized groups to intensify their study of their histories and cultures, build on their strengths, and construct curriculum linked specifically to their existential projects, grounded in the processes of their self-formation in a society is not yet born (see, for instance, Lomotey and Rivers 1998).

While there might be many schools emphasizing specific and changing issues of specific individuals and groups, no doubt there would still be some number of comprehensive high schools, probably some number of which not very unlike those in existence today. After all, not all parents and students are dissatisfied, especially those in well-funded suburban districts in the Northeast, Midwest, and West. Moreover, there are those parents who will choose a multicultural and ideologically diverse educational experience for their children (although these are not common consequences of the comprehensive high school today). Other parents will choose a school whose curriculum more specifically addresses their aspirations for their children, including aspirations for study of school subjects closely allied with the existing academic disciplines. As exist today, there would be schools which emphasize the sciences, others the arts, others mathematics, others foreign languages, social sciences (including community projects and social work), literature (creative writing as well), music, others technology, others vocational preparation.

The traditional wisdom of the curriculum field—and of some outside it (see, for instance, Schlesinger 1991)—held that the break-up of the public school would mean the break-up of American common culture. Given the cultural and political power of capitalism and the attendant commodification of social life in America, a "common culture" will persist. The shopping mall, not the civic square, is the symbol of "common culture" in the United States today. While democracy and education are irrevocably linked, the comprehensive public high school has long ceased to be a site for democratic development, if it ever was (Spring 1972, 1986, 1989). The construction of a democratic public sphere cannot get underway if politically vulnerable groups— including political groups on the Left—continue to be worn down by the corrosive effects of day-to-day racism, heterosexism, classism, and sexism, while kept ignorant of their heritage.

Of course, the proliferation of schools more closely identified with the religious, gendered, and political interests of various sectors of the population will hardly resolve the vexed relations among education, culture, and politics. It will still be necessary to debate curriculum issues as public issues, to study teaching and learning autobiographically and psychoanalytically, to connect the school subjects with self-formation, society, history, and the workplace. But specialized and smaller schools might reduce the massive alienation of the public school from the public, end its political isolation, dissolve its bureaucratic self-enclosure. Smaller and specialized schools could allow for the negotiation of more extensive and more intense parental involvement, when desired and possible.

Most importantly, the proliferation of specialized schools should allow for greater curriculum experimentation, a possibility of special interest to those of us who appreciate that the curriculum is the intellectual and organizational center of educational experience. There are compelling educational reasons why, for instance, student alienation (including bullying), school violence generally, and human sexuality should be studied by interested students and faculty in interdisciplinary courses, conferences, and projects. The curriculum need not mirror higher education's bureaucratic compartmentalization of knowledge according to established and self-interested academic disciplines. (There is every educational reason why colleges and universities also need to engage in fundamental curricular experimentation, and not only for students and faculty associated with in-house Honors Colleges.) Finally, this proliferation of specialized schools might also shake current private and parochial schools out of their complacency and sense of superiority, in some cases, bigotry and classism. No longer could they compete against (what is, at least, perceived to be) a weary and decaying public school system.

To staff such schools, I endorse a variety of entries to the teaching profession, including so-called "fast-track" options for mature and experienced individuals, provided these persons are mentored closely and commence immediately the academic (i.e., professional) study of education. Of course, those who cannot conceive of public education but only of vocational training in the academic disciplines tend to be suspicious, even dismissive, of such study. For these, teacher education amounts to a series of "hurdles" to teaching. In our time, academic vocationalism substitutes for the education of the American public.

Whether "fast" or "slow," teacher education (if it remains at all) must be reconceived from a skills-identified induction into the school bureaucracy to the interdisciplinary, theoretical, and autobiographical study of educational experience in which curriculum and teaching are understood as complicated conversations toward the construction of a democratic public sphere. Informed by curriculum theory, teacher preparation becomes the education of self-reflexive, private-and-public intellectuals, intellectuals whose primarily loyalty is multiple, shared among their academic discipline(s), the social reconstruction of the institution and society in which they teach, and the intellectual and psycho-social development of the students they teach. Multiple loyalties require multiple curriculum designs, not the simple-minded alignment of the school subject with the academic disciplines (although, of course, there will be educators who choose this design). Opportunities for curricular experimentation are educational expressions of academic freedom.

Whether the present organization of public education remains or is radically reorganized, public schoolteachers must be granted greater academic freedom, must be granted some control over the curriculum and the means by which it is taught and tested. As well, teachers must exercise what limited academic freedom they enjoy, and press against it limits, becoming private-and-public intellectuals, "amateurs" in Edward Said's (1996) sense (see chapter 7). This is made extraordinarily and unnecessarily difficult when curriculum is tied to assessment.

Linking the curriculum to standardized exams means curricular and intellectual standardization. Such standardization does not only make a nightmare of education in the present; as Linda McNeil (2000, 3) appreciates, "the long-term effects of standardization are even more damaging: *over the long term, standardization creates inequities, widening the gap between the quality of education for poor and minority youth and that of more privileged students."* Moreover, *"[s]tandardization undermines academic standards"* (McNeil 2000, 6). It means the erasure of academic freedom, and, consequently, lost opportunities for originality, creativity, dissent, and discovery, the very *raisons d'être* for educational institutions.

Many teachers seem ill-prepared to exercise even the limited academic freedom they enjoy, let alone press against its limits. Too many teachers—prospective and practicing—remain trapped within vocational conceptions of their profession. The mathematics teacher (for example) who asks, in a teacher education class, how curriculum theory will help him be a better algebra teacher illustrates this ignorance. There is in the question no professional sense of the school as educational community, of faculty concerned about an overall school program engaging individual students who have specific and evolving interests, of raising questions beyond the boundaries of the school subjects, of exercising academic freedom to trouble taken-for-granted conceptions of those subjects, as well as studying how those subjects inform the public and private issues students and their parents face as citizens, as individuals, as humanity (see Kumashiro in press). The enemies of public education are not all in government; some are enrolled in the classes we teach.

The student's question is narrowly vocational, expressing too many prospective teachers' sense of having an instructional responsibility only for delivering one's subject. His is a technician's sense of "craft." Teaching is (mis)understood as a behavioral "skill" (itself a term of [in]convenience crafted by academic psychology). His loyalty is "vertical" toward what he imagines (or is told) constitutes higher education or toward the workplace, not "horizontal" toward the students and society, not as a participant in a school curriculum as a public conversation, as intellectually engaging the school community. His question illustrates the anti-intellectualism of teachers who fail to appreciate that their vocation *is* theory, that it requires intellectual interdisciplinary understanding. Teachers' vocation also requires knowledge—historical and theoretical—of the institution in which they teach. Finally, teachers might more fully appreciate and be allowed to demonstrate how the subjects they teach illumine the issues of the day. That is how theory makes the teacher "better," by enlarging and complicating teachers' intellectual sense of their professional calling, by animating teachers' intellectual engagement with their students' interests and situation, by compelling teachers to appreciate their professional practice as an ongoing theoretical preoccupation.

While "practice" is a theoretical question and "theory" is a form of intellectual practice, the two ought not to disappear into each other. Given the situation in the schools, we professors might play the two off each other, as Madeleine Grumet suggested more than 20 years ago. By emphasizing theory as practice and practice as theoretical activity, we might complicate the experience of both domains, while challenging the difference in status between the two. For Grumet, the distinctiveness of each domain provides opportunities to intensify the focus of both:

> Too often, curriculum theory has been tainted with the self-conscious complexity of academic work, disdaining practical activity in order to maintain the class privilege that clings to the abstract in order to aggrandize its status. Although the field situation provides a context where curriculum theory and practice confront one another, our objective ought not to be to resolve their differences, reducing one to the dimensions of the other. No longer must contemplation be reserved for the privileged; rather, it becomes a mode of analysis which challenges unjust privilege. Theory must not reinforce class differences but help dissolve them. Theory must not hang alienated from practice in some timeless realm of unchanging, arrogant truth. Rather, let us play theory and practice against each other so as to disclose their limitations, and in so doing enlarge the capacity and intensify the focus of each. (Pinar and Grumet 1988 [1981], 99; quoted in Pinar et al. 1995, 41)

This view resonates with Ted Aoki's (in press), who regarded theory and practice as "twin moments of the same reality. Rather than seeing theory as leading into practice, we need now more than ever to see it as a reflective moment in *praxis*." The two spheres are distinct but inevitably interrelated in, as Aoki might put it, generative tension.

Despite the theory's reduction to specialization and practice's institutionalization as bureaucratic protocols, many working in higher education still remember that control of the curriculum is a prerequisite to exercising their profession. Many still remember that when curriculum is tied to standardized examinations, intellectual life is standardized. Academic freedom is compromised, if not erased, when educators must focus upon what others—testmakers—have identified as key knowledge and "skills." In so doing, the educational point of the University—and the public school—disappears.

When Texas state legislators proposed standardized exams for students enrolled in the University of Texas system, Betty Travis, chairwoman of the University of Texas System Faculty Advisory Council (which represents the faculty associations at each of the system's nine regular campuses and six medical centers) replied: "While we certainly support accountability, we have serious concerns and strong opposition to [the testing proposal]." Faculty members at the University of Texas pointed out that "standardized texts will eventually result in standardized curriculum, which in turn disallows flexibility and innovation and undermines the fundamental principles of academic freedom" (quoted in Schmidt 2000, A35). How one yearns to hear the American Association of Colleges for Teacher Education (AACTE) or the National Council for Accreditation of Teacher Education (NCATE) or the National

Education Association (NEA) or the American Federation of Teachers (AFT) make such a declaration.

Nor is the intrusion of government into university academic affairs limited to the state of Texas, although it is the presidential administration of a former Texas governor—George W. Bush—which has suggested that colleges and universities be held accountable for retaining students and graduating them in a "timely fashion" (Burd 2002, A23). In contrast to public school administrators, "many" college officials objected to the Bush administration proposal to hold them accountable for the performance of their students. In a letter to U.S. Secretary of Education Rod Paige, Nils Hasselmo, president of the Association of American Universities, warned that if the administration delves too deeply into issues of institutional quality, it will "assure an adversarial relationship with the higher-education community from the onset of the reauthorization process" (quoted in Burd 2002, A23). He might have added that this apparently administrative matter is in fact academic, as it provides governmental support for grade inflation.

Because the public schools have long ago capitulated to government intrusion, including control of the curriculum, we curriculum theorists exercise little influence over the public school curriculum. But we do still enjoy some (albeit, diminishing) control over the curriculum—the education courses—we teach at colleges and universities, at least in terms of the books we ask students to read, the discussions we lead, the questions on which we examine these prospective and practicing teachers. In these classes, undergraduate and graduate, we can demonstrate what it means to teach not as technicians, but as progressive private-and-public intellectuals committed to democratization and self-realization, to the creation of a new public sphere. We can exercise the academic freedom still institutionalized in colleges and universities to trouble unexamined assumptions regarding the miseducation of the American public.

Drawing upon research in the various disciplines in the humanities and social sciences, we curriculum theorists can create curricular *montages*—this book is, I hope, an example—of academic knowledge, interdisciplinary in scope, hybrid in nature that prospective and practicing teachers might study in order to understand the nature of the public project to which they claim allegiance: education. In the juxtaposition of such scholarship is the possibility of teaching something "new," something "critical," something that is more than simply the sum of its parts, an effort to persuade prospective and practicing teachers that we must teach beyond contractual obligations, for self-realization and democratization, for self-mobilization and social reconstruction. We must pedagogically witness to the educational ideal of interdisciplinarity, situated in self-formation, relationally linked to society, grounded in the historical moment. Public education means the education of the public.

10

The Education of the
American Public

"THE GREAT WHITE SWITCH":
THE NATION GOES SOUTH

So where is the passion that was once invested in the Left?
—Kobena Mercer (1994, 280)

The South has been crucial, if not indispensable, to the renewed
success of the Republicans in presidential politics.
—Earl Black and Merle Black (1992, 11)

That's the South's trouble. Ignorant. Doesn't know anything.
—Lillian Smith (1972 [1944], 365)

That last sentence may seem an outrageous generalization; it is. Or it may
seem, simply, a fiction; it is. It is a sentence from Lillian Smith's (herself a
southerner and civil rights activist) novel *Strange Fruit*, a thought (to himself)
by an intellectually progressive but politically ineffectual character named
Prentiss Reid, editor of the newspaper in a small southern town where a
lynching has occurred. I quote it because, as the South continues to elect U.S.
presidents, Americans—especially outside this region—must become clear
about the political and cultural character of the South. Lillian Smith was
clear: Southern progressives all too often keep their views to themselves.

Preferring amiability to racial justice, too many progressive white southerners have kept their complaints to themselves. Of course, without a public
sphere such complaints have seemed only "personal," and many of those who

233

expressed them, at least in the 19th century, had to flee for their lives, as the famous cases of George Washington Cable and Andrew Sledd illustrate (see Pinar 2001). As Earl and Merle Black (1992) know, the South is no monolith politically, but its regional and racial reactionary politics has too often made it act as if it were.

Let us be clear: the political Left in this nation, including the progressive movement in public education, was defeated not only by its own excesses and miscalculations. American political progressivism was defeated by the (white) South. The defeat of the Left in the United States was a consequence of the South's political ascendancy in presidential politics after 1964. In allegiance with "conservatives" nationwide, the reactionary (and racialized and gendered) politics of the white South defused the revolutionary potential of the 1960s while blocking future political gains by women (the defeat of the Equal Rights Amendment), and are now rolling back even the modest political gains made by African Americans, such as "affirmative action."

Born in West Virginia, raised in Pennsylvania and (mostly) Ohio, I taught high-school English outside New York City (on Long Island). After finishing the Ph.D. at Ohio State, I taught for 13 years in upstate New York (at the University of Rochester). As of this writing, I am in my 18th year in the Deep South. That makes me no expert, of course, but it does render silence no option. It seems to me that southern, especially white southern, instincts are often, indeed, usually, mistaken. Not southern instincts for pleasure and the private life, mind you; these are consciously cultivated and enthusiastically practiced (except, of course, for the sizeable minority captured by "evangelical Christianity"). For me, the personalism and sensuality of the South were (and remain) a welcomed contrast to the austere Midwest of my childhood.

But southern pleasure in the sensual and the private is animated, in part, by southern abjection of the civic. As we saw in chapter 4, the civic sphere was never developed in the South as a self-disinterested collective space in which private sacrifice was willingly made for public gain. Undeveloped in the antebellum South, the public sphere was repudiated as it became occupied by Yankee soldiers during the War and by the Freedmen's Bureau afterward. After the collapse of Reconstruction in 1877, white southerners reclaimed the public sphere as theirs, not as a self-disinterested collectivity for the advancement of all, but as a projective screen on which to act out their often violent racial, sexual, and religious fantasies (which were, not uncommonly, conflated). The desegregation of the public schools in the mid-20th century restimulated white southerners' disidentification with—contempt for—the public sphere. Progressives in the South—a prominent exception is Morris Dees and his colleagues at the Southern Poverty Law Center in Montgomery, Alabama—have tended, like Lillian Smith's character, to keep their thoughts to themselves.

Not so southern reactionaries. These (especially white male) southerners continue to feel quite entitled to express their intense (sometimes violent) opposition to progressive causes, from Emancipation in the 19th century, to women's suffrage and reproductive rights, anti-lynching legislation, and the Equal Rights Amendment in the 20th century, and, now, civil rights for lesbians and gay men. Trent Lott is no exception; many white southerners (and "conservatives" nationwide) share his nostalgia for the racial and gender hierarchies of the past, for the "Lost Cause."

Is it not curious that the great-great-great-grandchildren of Confederates, (especially white) southerners are among the most rabidly "patriotic" in the nation? Descendants of those who championed an agrarian society to which capitalism came late and was then contested, (especially white male) southerners are among the most enthusiastic today about "free enterprise," even requiring the study of it by public-school students in Louisiana. Southerners—in alliance with pro-business conservatives and the religious right (intersecting but not identical categories, of course)—have, since 1968, shifted the American nation sharply to the right. The South lost the War but has won the peace. The American nation lost; the nation has "gone South." Public education is but one casualty.

The present historical moment in the United States continues to be defined politically by the Right. Without voting fraud in a southern state, George W. Bush would not be President. (Another southerner would have, alas, been elected President.) Despite the corruption of the corporate sector—the Enron and WorldCom scandals may well represent the tip of an iceberg rather than exceptions to the rule—the largely uncritical adoration of "business" (not only as a model for schooling but, for many, a model for life) continues, certainly on the Right. As I hope you are clear by now, academic—intellectual—freedom is imperiled by those who only understand schools and universities as businesses. A school that is a skill or knowledge factory is a business, not a school.

While "conservatives" in the United States are no monolith—there are important differences, for instance, between many "cultural" and "economic" conservatives—they continue their assault on the public sphere, including education as a public project. Not only do many conservatives embrace the "privatization" of the public sphere, more than a few embrace its incorporation into (fundamentalist) Christianity, ending the constitutionally mandated separation of church and state. For many of these right-wing radicals, progressive public education is an unintelligible conception. These ongoing right-wing threats to the American nation cannot be understood without appreciating the reactionary role of the (white) South in presidential politics and in the establishment of right-wing hegemony in the United States.

The entire nation has moved to the Right since 1968. It could not have done so—nor do I think it would have done so—without the reactionary rejection of progressive causes by the majority of European-Americans living in the American South. The historic if unholy alliance between northern and southern Democrats came apart, predictably, over the issue of race, especially as the struggle over civil rights for African Americans played out in American presidential politics. When the national Democratic party shifted decisively to a pro-civil rights position during the early 1960s, Earl and Merle Black (1992) observe, southern Democratic politicians correctly predicted the loss of support among white "conservatives" in the South.

Shortly after he signed the Civil Rights Act of 1964, President Lyndon B. Johnson told an aide, "I think we just delivered the South to the Republican party for a long time to come" (quoted in Black and Black 1992, 6). Black and Black (1992, 345) call this shift of political allegiance "the Great White Switch." They quote Thomas B. Edsall, who observed that "direct appeals to racial prejudice may no longer be acceptable in American politics, [but] in an indirect and sometimes subliminal way, [race] remains a driving force in the battle today between Republicans and Democrats" (quoted in Black and Black 1992, 7).

What this means is that so-called "conservative" values—Black and Black (1992, 9) list "traditional family values, the importance of religion, support for capital punishment, and opposition to gun control" and I would add opposition to abortion and opposition to civil rights for lesbians and gay men— preserve traces of earlier racist recalcitrance. They are "deferred and displaced." The reactionary energy that animates white southerners' sometime fanatical (on occasion, even homicidal) engagement with these issues suggests the presence of the past (as we saw in chapter 4). While southern "conservatism" cannot be reduced to residues of racial hatred—it is broader and more complex than that—it cannot be understood apart from it either. What Lillian Smith understood to be true in the South more than 50 years ago remains, to a shocking extent, present today:

> Southern tradition, segregation, states' rights have soaked up the fears of our people; little private fantasies of childhood have crept there for hiding, unacknowledged arsenals of hate have been stored there, and a loyalty covering up a lack of self-criticism has glazed the words over with sanctity. No wonder the saying of them aloud can stir anxieties until there are times when it seems we have lost our grasp on reality. (Smith 1963 [1949], 135)

What is needed in the South is, still, Reconstruction.

The South has not only cast its spell on much of the nation, it has, apparently, cast its spell on one of America's great historians. After leaving upstate New York (where he taught for many years at the University of Rochester) for Georgia, Marxist (and co-editor, with Elizabeth Fox-Genovese, of the short-lived scholarly periodical *Marxist Perspectives*) slave historian Eugene Genovese became "the Old South's least likely defender" (Applebome 1998). In introducing his commentary on "the southern tradition," Genovese (1994, ix) tells us: "There are a great many reasons for my southern partisanship, the most important of which arose from my early recognition that the people of the South, across lines of race, class and sex, are as generous, gracious, courteous, decent—in a word, civilized—as any people it has ever been my privilege to get to know."

Given the history of racism and violence in the South (more extensive and intense than in any other region [see Ayers 1984]), to characterize southerners as "gracious" seems strange indeed. Given his brilliance as a historian, gullibility seems an unlikely explanation. But then many accomplished northerners have been fooled by white southern "sincerity," not least among them 19th-century social reformer Frances Willard, as Ida B. Wells discovered (see Pinar 2001, chapter 8, section IV).

Nineteenth-century black feminist and schoolteacher Anna Julia Cooper knew that the surface of southern (white) "civilization" was that only, a surface covering-up systemic violence and collective hatred. Cooper also knew that northern whites were too often susceptible to believing what they saw (i.e., the southern social surface, expressed as southern "hospitality" and "charm"). More than 100 years ago Cooper (1998/1892, 97) wrote:

> One of the most singular facts about the unwritten history of this country is the consummate ability with which southern influence, southern ideas and southern ideals, have from the very beginning even up to the present day, dictated to and domineered over the brain and sinew of this nation. Without wealth, without education, without inventions, arts, sciences, or industries, without wellnigh every one of the progressive ideas and impulses which have made this country great, prosperous and happy, personally indolent and practically stupid, poor in everything but bluster and self-esteem, the southerner has nevertheless with Italian finesse and exquisite skill, uniformly and invariably, so manipulated Northern sentiment as to succeed sooner or later in carrying his point and shaping the policy of this government to suit his purposes.

Southern political ascendancy and its rerouting of racial hatred into other issues (such as opposition to civil rights for Americans who are lesbian and gay) seem lost on Genovese who, while acknowledging that southern conservatism now resonates well beyond the South, now imagines that "despite continued temptations and bad moments, their movement shows signs of exorcising the racism that has marred much of its history" (1994, 6). Now that "the curse of Ham" (see Pinar 2003c) has been dispelled (at least in Genovese's imagination), there is, evidently, no need to remind readers of it at all: "Finally, I have not dwelt upon the racist legacy of the southern tradition because I assume that readers will join me in taking it as a given" (Genovese 1994, 9).

Genovese's southern sympathies become somewhat intelligible in light of his ideological past. Perhaps it is his (ex-?) Marxist loathing for capitalism and its commodification and fragmentation of social relations that animates his apparent embrace of reactionary southern conservatism: "Increasingly, they [southern conservatives] became critical of capitalism's cash-nexus, recognizing it as a revolutionary solvent of social relations, and especially grew fearful of the consequences of radical democracy and egalitarianism" (Genovese 1994, 23). He continues:

> Southern conservatism has always traced the evils of the modern world to the ascendancy of the profit motive and material acquisitiveness; to the conversation of small property on individual labor into accumulated capital manifested as financial assets; to the centralization and bureaucratization of management; to the extreme specialization of labor and the rise of consumerism; to an idolatrous cult of economic growth and scientific and technological progress; and to the destructive exploitation of nature. Thus, down to our own day, southern conservatives have opposed finance capitalism and have regarded socialism as the logical outcome of the capitalist centralization of economic and state power. (Genovese 1994, 34–35)

It would seem that it is the anti-capitalism of southern conservatism that provides the site of his capitulation to reactionary southern (white) culture. While his anti-capitalism and his own bitterness over the "Waterloo" of the left (35) make this capitulation plausible, they do not render it forgivable.

At one point it appears that Genovese has abandoned even his own anti-capitalism, asserting that those on the Left have been "blinded to those historic achievements of capitalism upon which any civilized society must build, not the least of which has been an economic performance that has expanded the possibility for individual freedom and political democracy for enormous numbers of people throughout the world" (Genovese 1994, 37). "For better and worse," Genovese (37–38) concludes, "capitalism, not socialism, has once again emerged as the world's greatest revolutionary and self-revolutionizing system."

Genovese is surely right on this point, namely that capitalism seems to guarantee—and for both better *and* worse—permanent, accelerating, pervasive revolution worldwide. (Bowers [2000] would have been more persuasive, and accurate, had he blamed capitalism, rather than computers specifically, for the destruction of traditional societies and the contemporary exploitation of the "biosphere.") Genovese (1994, 38) is also surely right when he asserts that "the great questions of our time require a simultaneous reassessment of socialist and bourgeois assumptions." But he is mistaken to look to the (white) South—at least in its past or present hegemonic forms—for any help in that reassessment.

In the politics of "school reform," white southern politicians exploit teachers' political vulnerability in order to shift responsibility for educational underachievement away from reactionary southern history and its racist culture, away from politicians' own "conservative" policies which fiscally starve public institutions, among them public schools, colleges, and universities. Southern politicians' rhetoric of "accountability" distracts public attention away from the larger problem of anti-intellectualism in American culture and in southern culture specifically, a problem politicians nationwide often exploit but rarely challenge.

Situated within these larger and intensifying crises of culture and politics, and within the right-wing ascendancy of the last 40 years, school reform generally and teacher education reform specifically become legible as political distractions from the failures of especially (but not only) presidential policies that have undermined (some would say dismantled) the public sphere in the United States, including its educational infrastructure. That region of the nation historically absent a highly developed public sphere, the American South, has provided key electoral support for those right-wing politicians who prefer to build prisons rather than adequately fund public schools. Welcome to "Oz."

Teachers study curriculum theory to understand what is happening to them, and to the children in their charge. Such study, and the complicated conversation that it supports, can provide the animation for self-mobilization and collective action to reconstruct the public sphere in education. Such action is speech itself, naming right-wing reform as the political enforcement of intellectual enslavement that it is. Taking inspiration from those who were physically enslaved in this country, in a region now dominating presidential elections, we educators must regain our dignity and in so doing, our attunement to what we know constitutes the process of education. Working from within, we will teach the children according to our own inner standards, and in so doing, reconstruct the public sphere in America.

II
CURRICULUM AS SOCIAL PSYCHOANALYSIS:
WAKING UP FROM THE NIGHTMARE
THAT IS THE PRESENT

Memory haunts and hovers like ghosts. Distance in time from these
memories does not bring psychological distance for many.
In fact, the reverse may be true.
—Marla Morris (2001a, 150)

To form itself, the public has to break existing political forms.
—John Dewey (1991 [1927], 31)

*We are gradually requiring of the educator that he shall free the
powers of each man and connect him with the rest of life.*
—Jane Addams (2002 [1902], 80)

Presentism (and its denial of the past) is hardly peculiar to the South. Christopher Lasch (1978) lamented its persistence as a central feature of contemporary American life; it is intensified in an imagistic culture associated with mass advertising and the culture industry, and in the presence of "radical evil." For Lasch (1984) this radical evil is Nazi Germany and the Holocaust, a historical fact, he argues, unassimilable by a rational mass consciousness (see also Morris 2001a). The unassimilability and unintelligibility of mass extermination coupled with an unstable public sphere partially created by the culture industry and threatened by nuclear war, resulted in a presentistic, solipsistic, narcissistic self (Lasch 1984).

As we have seen, there never was a stable public sphere in the South. Moreover, the denial of the past, fueled by an overdetermined emphasis upon the personal and the sensual, has meant little interest in the future, except in narrow economic terms. The cultural and political future of the South, in which African Americans, white southern progressives and relocated (liberal) northerners play more prominent roles, is denied as white southerners cling to the residues of racial and class privilege. The postmodern presentism of the privatized public sphere in the North intersects with the premodern presentism of the private (pretending to be public) sphere of the white South. The American culture of narcissism is not only national, it is regional.

Under such circumstances, the curricular task becomes the recovery of memory and history in ways that psychologically allow individuals to reenter politically the public sphere in privately meaningful and ethically committed ways. What we need is contemporary versions of "freedom schools" (see chapter 3, section IV). Presentism structures public school curricula in the South as it does nationwide. Part of the project of *currere* is to contradict presentism by self-consciously cultivating the temporality of subjectivity, insisting on the simultaneity of past, present, and future, a temporal complexity in which difference does not dissolve onto a flatted social surface. The education of the American public requires the cultivation of historicity as well as self-reflexivity, intellectuality, and erudition.

The education of the American public cannot be accomplished by playing "school." In too many (especially southern) schools, busy-work is mistaken for intellectual exploration, bureaucratic authority mistaken for intellectual and moral authority. But in the South, even more than in the North, curriculum too often becomes an anonymous Other whose linkages to everyday life are fragile and implicit. Apollonian and Dionysian impulses are profoundly alienated from each another in the South, a schizoid state of affairs evident in Louisiana, for instance, where Mardi Gras and radical Christian fundamentalism (such as that of evangelist Jimmy Swaggert, still based in Baton Rouge) coexist.

The curriculum tends to function in the South not unlike a secular version of biblical fundamentalism, in which the letter of text is mistaken for its spirit. In both versions, the South's distance from the centers of knowledge production recall its defeated and victimized status, its position of "recipient" of the (federal, juridical) Word. Patriarchal loyalty to the Other requires a strict, literal rendering of the text, stunting both intellectual and cultural development. Split off from rational articulation and integration with daily life, hedonism threatens to become all-consuming for those whose pleasure-seeking lacks rational restraint or sublimation. The pleasure of the text, to use Roland Barthes' (1978) felicitous phrase, is in principle difficult for many to experience in the South.

This cultural "splitting" is maintained by a presentism that assumes that a past forgotten is a past no longer present. As psychoanalysis has demonstrated and southern novelists like Faulkner have portrayed, the past remains, hovering like ghosts. Given the South's particular history, and given its sharp sense of "place," the past figures prominently in the southern present, despite protestations to the contrary. Even should southern schools adopt the most technically accurate and refined curriculum, until the South re-experiences its past in ways that allow it to recover memory and history, (especially white) southern students will not work through it. Culturally and psychosocially dysfunctional patterns will continue, deforming not only the South, but, given its pivotal role in presidential politics, the American nation as a whole.

I propose a curriculum of "place," an intellectually lived ground for the technical curricula (especially technology) being emphasized today. This is a curriculum of southern studies whose educational point is not a sentimentalization of the past, but a psychoanalytically-informed interdisciplinary study and re-experience of the past, so that white guilt can be experienced and acknowledged, and moral responsibility claimed. Perhaps African Americans will discover, to an extent all have not yet, their strengths, courage, and competence. Unless this process occurs collectively and individually, socially and subjectively, the South will probably continue to live out—in denial—its history of relative poverty, defeat, racism, and class privilege.

As Lewis Simpson observes in his classic *The Dispossessed Garden*, the South lost both history and memory in defending its agrarian way of life, in its denial of its status as, in Simpson's phrase, the "garden of chattel." The southern literary Renaissance of the early 20th century, most prominently associated with the names of William Faulkner, Robert Penn Warren, Eudora Welty, and Thomas Wolfe, involved the recovery of both history and memory. The presence of the past in the present is portrayed, for instance, in this remarkable passage from William Faulkner's *Intruder in the Dust*. It suggests the meaning of the Battle of Gettysburg for white southern consciousness.

> It's all now see. Yesterday wont be over until tomorrow and tomorrow began ten thousand years ago. For every Southern [white] boy fourteen years old, not once but whenever he wants it, there is the instant when it's still not yet two o'clock on that July afternoon in 1863, the brigades are in position behind the rail fence, the guns are laid and ready in the woods, and the furled flags are already loosened to break out, and Pickett himself with his long oiled ringlets and his hat in one hand probably and his sword in the other looking up the hill waiting for Longstreet to give the word and it's all in the balance, it hasn't happened yet, it hasn't even begun yet, it not only hasn't begun yet but there is still time for it not to begin against that position and those circumstances which made more men that Garnett and Kemper and Armstead [*sic*] and Wilcox look grave yet it's going to begin, we all know that, we have come too far with too much at stake and that moment doesn't need even a fourteen-year-old boy to think this time. Maybe this time with all this much to lose and all this much to gain; Pennsylvania, Maryland, the world, the golden dome of Washington itself to crown with desperate and unbelievable victory the gamble, the case made two years ago; or to anyone who ever sailed even a skiff under a quilt sail, the moment in 1492 when somebody thought This is it; the absolute edge of no return, to turn back now and make home or sail irrevocably on and either find land or plunge over the world's roaring rim. (Faulkner 1948, 194–195)

What has been achieved in the southern literary imagination remains only partially achieved in white southern mass culture. Recent economic gains, reversing slowly the century-old economic underdevelopment of the region, coupled with a cultural "imperialism" of the mass media (southern "accents" continue to disappear from television and radio for example), support (especially white male) southerners in their repression of history, a history that differs painfully from that of the North. This pain is comprised by, in addition to its contrasting economic history, its absence of that moral self-righteousness associated with New England Puritanism, accompanied as that is by a sense of invincibility, optimism, and guilt. It is painful for many (white) southerners to remember that the South lost the only war (as a region) it waged. The pain repressed produces pessimism, which in its turn supports nostalgia, which in turn supports provincialism, conservatism, and the racial class system. The democratic legacy and potential of the New England town meeting is missing in the plantation South with its acute, if denied, system of racial caste (Williamson 1984; Woodward 1968).

The repression of memory and history is accompanied by distortions of various kinds, including political, social, racial, and psychological distortions. These distortions function to undermine the South's efforts to develop the intelligence and economic competitiveness of its citizens. Thus, the greatest incentive for the South today to unearth its past is not the intrinsic worth of the project, although it is, of course, intrinsically worthwhile. The incentive today would be to create that individual and social awareness that is a fundamental concomitant to the development of intelligence in its various modes, including technical, psychosocial, and aesthetic intelligence (Gardner 1983). Without self-understanding, there can be no social reconstruction.

Nor can the South compete economically with other regions of the country, particularly the Northeast and West Coast, until, in psychoanalytic fashion, it re-experiences its past in ways that will free the present from the past. To put the matter another way, the contemporary task of economic development requires a simultaneous cultural reconstruction, a curricular provocation of which might be progressive southern studies. These programs must not function as pretexts for (white) nostalgia. The curriculum would be comprised of politically critical and informed analyses of the "world the slaveholders made." Genovese's early studies of slavery and of African-American history generally represent one such perspective, a perspective that would be supplemented by not only conservative historians, but by African-American historians and writers, including but hardly limited to Maya Angelou, James Baldwin, Anna Julia Cooper, W. E. B. Du Bois, Alice Walker, Ida B. Wells, Richard Wright (see Doll 2000).

A central theme of these southern studies would be the multiracial character of the South, the profound ways in which African Americans and European Americans have become two sides of the same cultural coin. Only when southern whites comprehend that their experience is inseparable from that of southern African Americans (and vice versa) can the history of southern culture be re-experienced, psychologically accepted, and its genocidal aspects perhaps forgiven and surpassed. Only when there is no more defensive rhetoric regarding a "New South" will we know that the region has (finally) undergone Reconstruction.

Obviously, this is an enormous curricular and cultural undertaking. However, the scope and complexity of the task cannot function as rationalizations not to attempt the educational reconstruction of the South. The educational development of the South, in a postindustrial period (just dawning in the Deep South) when economic and cultural development are intertwined, depends on it. The future of public education depends on it. The fate of the nation depends on the educational reconstruction of the South.

The history of class, race, and gender within European-American and African-American sectors, must be made explicit, understood and lived through. As noted in chapter 4, the presence of slaves blurred class distinctions between the small aristocracy and the larger working and poor white classes, with the effect of blinding the white working class and poor whites generally to their victimization by the planter class post-bellum power elites, undermining their efforts to economically and culturally further themselves.

Indeed, poor and lower middle-class southern whites continue to misunderstand their status vis-à-vis the white upper class, and too often displace their frustration onto each other and onto African-Americans. Racism remains the key issue here, and so I list it first in this interdisciplinary curriculum for southern studies. Due to its intimacy with race, class is second. The aforementioned class issues can be delineated and taught in an integrated study of the literature, history, economics, and sociology of the South. A history and analysis of class relations within the African-American sector are essential. Third, a history of gender is required to comprehend the particular ways that women, both European- and African-American, were conceptualized and socially placed (Fox-Genovese 1988).

The often heroic history of African-American women, as they supported slave families in which African-American men were marginalized by white slaveowners, needs to be taught and psychologically incorporated (Gray 1999 [1985]). The leadership of the anti-lynching campaign by Ida B. Wells is a story all Americans might learn (Schechter 1997; Ware 1992; Wells 1970). The pervasive homoeroticism between the white slaveholders and their black male slaves, transfigured after Reconstruction into a collective fantasy of African-American desire for white women is, I argue in *The Gender of Racial Politics and Violence in America*, key to understanding white racism. The passive aggression of slaveholders toward their wives and daughters as they mystified them into objects of hyper-femininity and social uselessness needs to be theorized and taught. Also to be taught would be the sophisticated responses of these women, including their strategies of self-affirmation and empowerment, as well as their displacement of frustration onto each other and upon their racial captives (Faust 1996).

The struggle, courage, and triumph of African-American men, as they often appeared to comply with their masters but retained and sometimes strengthened an autonomous and undefeated psychological and cultural core—which led 100 years later to the 1960s Civil Rights movement, to African-American nationalism and separatism—needs to be detailed. As nightmarish, as wantonly destructive as white men's sexual, political, and economic exploitation of black women has been, the oppression of black men contained—contains—one additional element. There was a specific if unnamed psycho-sexual exploitation as the white man obsessed over the black man's sexuality, his body, his phallus, "his" alleged desire for the white "lady." As James Baldwin (1985, 192) has observed: "[t]he entire nation, has spent a hundred years avoiding the question of the place of the black man in it." Each of these thematizations needs to be studied and re-experienced and integrated in the present (Genovese 1968; Wiegman 1995; Williamson 1984).

Finally, the configuration of elements involved in the South/North relationship needs to be examined and experienced, including what Clement terms "northernizing the south" (Clement 1983). Those of us who have been born and/or have lived in the North but who live now in the South must participate in this examination, as our memory of and history with the South, while perhaps not repressed, is deformed. What is deformed includes our insistence upon the exclusively moral character of the Civil War, contributing to our self-righteousness at our perceived moral superiority, our pretensions regarding the absence of racism in the North, and our assumed cultural (including linguistic) sophistication and superiority. All of this gets mixed up with a regional version of racism, of course, and this, too, must be confronted directly.

While history and literature would constitute the two major disciplines comprising this conception of southern studies, the other disciplines comprising the humanities, the arts, and the social sciences obviously have curricular roles to play. Given the racial and gender tendencies of these fields, departments of African American and Women's Studies need to be involved in central ways. The social psychoanalytic potential of critically informed southern studies programs represents a historical opportunity for the social reconstruction of the South. Further, there are specific elements of the southern experience as well as of this curricular process, that can provide exemplars, both curricular and cultural, for the rest of the nation. These are suggested briefly by the following items:

- Progressive southern studies could provide a provocative study in confronting educationally the cultural dilemma specified by Christopher Lasch, namely, presentism, solipsism, political passivity, and ethical relativism. An interdisciplinary program in southern studies would be taught with the aim of re-experiencing denied elements of the past, which, when critically reintegrated, might help provide the psychology of social commitment, as well as remove "blocks"—internalized and institutionalized—to the development of intelligence.
- Given the southern penchant for narrative and for place, political and cultural histories of the South can usefully and congruently be situated in life histories of individual students. The literature of (especially African American) autobiography provides an instructional method and agenda for this social psychoanalytic and educational process. Such pedagogical juxtaposition of the concrete and the abstract would provide an important opportunity to study further the autobiographical experience of education.

- Individual autobiographical work needs to be complemented by group process. Groups led by specialists, and comprised by African-American and European-American men and women of varying class locations and sexual orientations would work to renegotiate in the interpersonal lived sphere, currently vertical and alienated, more horizontal and inclusive terms of social organization.
- The relations among the past, the imagination, life history, collective experience, and the development of intelligence in its several modes can be specified and studied with select populations. Longitudinal studies reminiscent of the Eight-Year Study (see Pinar et al. 1995, 133–139) can provide important information regarding the extent to which these studies further, educationally and economically, those participating.

Students of curriculum theory will recognize here the employment of several strands of contemporary curriculum research: the political, the autobiographical, the phenomenological and the gender-focused (see Pinar et al. 1995). Interdisciplinary courses that draw upon students' prior knowledge as well as introducing "new" knowledge in the various disciplines represent sound practice of curriculum theory, particularly when these abstract traditions are then situated in the concrete lives of individuals and groups.

Curriculum in this sense becomes a place of origin as well as destination, a "ground" from which intelligence can develop, and a "figure" for presenting new perceptions and reviewing old ones. With a point made in a different context, Kaja Silverman's (2000, 62) sense of the significance of the past underlines the educational potential of this curriculum of social psychoanalysis:

> [T]he subject . . . does not seek to bury, forget, or transcend the past. Rather, this subject holds himself always open to new possibilities for the deployment of that signifying constellation which most profoundly individualize him. He is receptive to the resurfacing in the present and future of what has been—not as an exercise in narcissistic solipsism, but rather as the extension in ever new directions of his capacity to care.

In this temporal and ethical sense, curriculum as a social psychoanalysis represents an educational incorporation of the culturally excluded ("race"), the denied (class), and the bifurcated (gender).

Obviously, the obstacles are many and jagged; they are, for many southern whites, intensely psychological and cultural. Progressive southern studies are, by definition, uncomfortable for those who take "white privilege" for granted. "A pedagogy of discomfort," Megan Boler (1999, 176–177) has astutely observed, "begins by inviting educators and students to engage in critical inquiry regarding values and cherished beliefs, and to examine con-

structed self-images in relation to how one has learned to perceive others."
Despite the discomfort, some southern white students will commit themselves
to work through, as individuals and as "southern whites," the residues of 300
years of southern history.

The obstacles blocking the institutionalization of progressive southern
studies are not only psychological and cultural; they are political as well.
Against the odds, progressives in the South—a future coalition of white and
black southerners in allegiance with some of us who have migrated here from
the North, organized, perhaps, by the Southern Poverty Law Center in
Montgomery—may someday succeed in institutionalizing the project. In the
South, it is a project "deferred and displaced" for 140 years. We engage in the
Reconstruction of the South not only for the South's sake, but for the na-
tion's sake. The hour is late and the sense of emergency acute.

III
"NEW MODES OF LIFE, EROTICISM, AND SOCIAL RELATIONS"

We have not yet reached our ideal in American civilization.
—Anna Julia Cooper (1998/1892, 54)

We are thus brought to a conception of Democracy not merely
as a sentiment which desires the well-being of all men,
nor yet as a creed which believes in the essential dignity
and equality of all men, but as that which afford
a rule of living as well as a test of faith.
—Jane Addams (2002 [1902], 7)

Politics is not a branch of morals; it is submerged in morals.
—John Dewey (1991 [1927], 41–42)

Our task as the new century begins is nothing less than the intellectual formation of a public sphere in education, a resuscitation of the progressive project,
in which we understand that self-realization and democratization are inextricably intertwined. That is, in addition to providing competent individuals for
the workplace and for higher education, we must renew our commitment to
the democratization of American society, a sociopolitical and economic process that requires the psycho-social and intellectual education of the self-
reflexive individual.

That means that academic knowledge as well as popular culture must be
made available in novel and changing curricular forms so that individual students and groups might collaboratively explore in academic terms their felt as

well as intellectual interests. These felt interests must be supported, if deepened and widened, guided by self-reflexive educators—private-and-public intellectuals—whose own interests remain alive and present in the tutelage of their students. The curriculum—individualized, constantly in flux—provides the intellectual and social forms by means of which the individual comes to form, as Stefan Jonsson appreciates. Speaking of Robert Musil (with my insertion bracketed), Jonsson (2000, 140–141) points out:

> The social order provides the forms that enable an individual to *be*, in the most elementary sense of the word. These forms determine the nature and meaning of all human expressions. Only by using and thus realizing these forms [including curricular forms, intellectual subjects which shape the human subject] can the human being emerge as a subject for itself and in itself.

But such realization cannot be forced.

The curriculum driven by standardized tests and structured by academic vocationalism tends to be split off from students' subjective attachments. The psychoanalytic notion of "transitional objects," while ordinarily applied to toys and other objects by means of which very young children move from the maternal body to engagement with the world, can help us understand how the curriculum might function as a bridge between the social and subjective. Lasch points out that children outgrow the need for transitional objects, but only because—Lasch (in 1984, 194) quotes Winnicott to make the point—the "transitional phenomena have become diffused, have become spread out over the whole intermediate territory between 'inner psychic reality' and the 'external world as perceived by two persons in common,' that is to say, over the whole cultural field."

It is not, of course, over the "whole cultural field" that the individual becomes engaged, but only those elements of it which "speak" (however obliquely) to the self in its "biographical situation." That is why student and faculty interests must animate academic study. Without subjective interest influencing the curriculum, students become split off, learning either to "do school" for "good grades" or performing their lack of "motivation" in a variety of, including, violent ways, requiring, perhaps, "special education." The educational point of the curriculum is to draw students out of themselves into unknown (to them) terrains of the "cultural field," enabling them to engage the world with passion and competence while never breaking the bridges of psychic attachment that makes the process of education subjectively meaningful. It is "the symbolism of transitional objects," Lasch (1984, 194) observes, that "occupies the borderland between subjectivity and objectivity."

For too long the institutionalized practices of the education have relied on punishment, not pleasure. As Kaja Silverman (2000, 46) points out (after

Lacan), "it is through the practice of desire rather than through its renuncia-
tion that humans approach what has traditionally been called virtue. Indeed,
it is the relinquishing of desire that, for Lacan, represents 'sin'." To emphasize the point Silverman quotes from Lacan's Seminar VII: "The only thing
of which one can [finally] be guilty is of having given ground relative to one's
desire" (quoted in Silverman 2000, 47).

The point of public education is not self-abandonment nor that suspen-
sion, until adulthood, of satisfaction too many—including "successful"—
schools require (see Pope 2001). The point of public education is not to become "accountable," forced through "modes of address" to positions of
"gracious submission" to the political and business status quo. The point of
public education is to become an individual, a citizen, a human subject engaged with intelligence and passion in the problems and pleasures of his or
her life, problems and pleasures bound up with the problems and pleasures of
everyone else in the nation, on this planet. "Through education," Megan
Boler (1999, 200) reminds, "we invite one another to risk 'living at the edge of
our skin,' where we find the greatest hope of revisioning ourselves."

If curriculum theory endeavors to understand the educational significance
(i.e., its meaning for self and society) of the curriculum across the academic
disciplines, we must revision our research to exhibit such interdisciplinary
range and interest. In contrast to subject matter specializations which now
dominate Departments of Curriculum and Instruction, specializations that
focus, for instance, upon the teaching of English or science or mathematics
(only teaching them more effectively), curriculum theory aspires to understand the overall educational significance not only of the school curriculum,
but of the "curriculum" writ large, including popular culture, historical moment, life history, all intersecting and embodied in the specific students sitting
in our classrooms.

To focus on the educational significance of schooling for the culture at
large means returning academic knowledge to the individual him- or herself,
teaching not only what is, for instance, historical knowledge, but also suggesting its possible consequences for the individual's self-formation, allowing
that knowledge to shape the individual coming to social form. It means assuming the position of the private-and-public intellectual, especially now that
this tradition is so attenuated (Jacoby 1987) and defamed (Posner 2001). It is
to suggest the significance of academic knowledge for the society at large. We
might aspire to become, in Edward Said's (1996, 82) sense, intellectuals as
"amateurs," not only "professionals" as academic vocationalism requires.

Discussing the shift in Philip Rieff's pedagogical position from public intellectual to "teacher" (here a self-enclosed concept recoiling from a "dying
culture"), Lasch (1995, 226–227) observes that "now that the public arena
seems to have been irreversibly corrupted by the aggressive marketing of

ideas, the decision to think of oneself as a teacher rather than a public intellectual is one that many others besides Rieff have reluctantly made." In the concept of "private-and-public intellectual," it is possible, even necessary, to combine the two conceptions of our pedagogical work.

By hyphenating "public-and-private," I am suggesting just such a connection between the subjective and the social, the private and the public, evident, for instance, in those African-American autobiographical practices surveyed in chapter 2. To speak from subjectivities of black suffering required attunement to the public sphere as it was experienced in the private. Such autobiographical testimony required a "double consciousness" to remind oneself and others that this world was not *the* world, that everything could change, that someday everything will change.

Slave narratives and fiction as well as those African-American autobiographies and literature written after "Emancipation" were means of self-protection as well as public expression, means of subjective excavation as well as social solidarity and political intervention. Recall that, in speaking of Linda Brent (Harriet Jacobs), Joanne Braxton (1989, 16) observed that "language is her first line of defense." She is speaking of physical defense (her use of "sass"), but she is also alluding to speech as a mode of psychological self-defense, a means of self-affirmation, self-understanding, and social resistance. In her movement toward literacy and heightened self-respect, Braxton reports, Charlotte Forten employed books as means of knowing, avenues of entering worlds from which she had been excluded. Books become passages out of her isolation.

There is, as I have emphasized, no parallel between the suffering of slaves (and freed people) and the political subjugation of contemporary public-school teachers in America today. While racism and misogyny have been "deferred and displaced" into the sphere of public education, wherein the intellectual freedom of teachers and students have been restricted by right-wing politicians using commonsense appeals to "accountability," racism and misogyny remain pervasive across American culture. Teachers have not absorbed the misogyny and racism intended for women and African Americans, leaving these groups free of hatred and prejudice. But teachers cannot comprehend their situation today unless they appreciate that they, *too*, are victims of these prejudices, disguised through the language of "business."

While we are not entitled to make the same order of moral claim, teachers who are subjugated in positions of "gracious submission" might well study the lives and work of Linda Brent, Charlotte Forten, Sojourner Truth, Harriet Tubman, and Ida B. Wells. Despite what for us must seem impossible conditions, these black women still found the inner courage and social solidarity to carry on, to "keep hope alive," to remember that *this* world is not *the* world. For the sake of the children in our classrooms, we teachers might take heart from their political courage and inner strength. In our repudiation of the status quo, we might act, not as wounded or defeated victims in "mortal educational combat" but, rather, as fierce midwives to (improbable) worlds not yet born. It is long past time for us to "talk back," to use "sass." Our pedagogical labor is crucial if "new modes of life, eroticism, and social relations" are to be created, cultivated, and institutionalized.

This ethical imperative structures the project of intellectual understanding today, a project that requires knowledge not only of the school subject one is employed to teach, but knowledge of the processes of education and the institution of the school, the organizational and intellectual center of which is the curriculum. By definition, teachers are students of education. After 30 years of autobiographical research, I suggest they are students of their own education as well. The individualized as well as bureaucratized ways teachers conceive of themselves, their subjects, and their students reflect modes of self-formation and the structures of public expression. Teacher's life histories provide the thematic precedents and structures of their self-reflexive relationships with themselves. Louis Althusser (1993, 169–170) was clear about the self-reflexive nature of his philosophical work: "I was greatly struck and still am by something Marx said to the effect that the philosopher expressed in his concepts (in his conception of philosophy, that is) his 'theoretical relationship with himself'." That "theoretical relationship" with oneself can be explored and recast through autobiographical reflection, through conversation with oneself.

Conversation occurs both intersubjectively *and* intrasubjectively, in rooms of our own. There we turn away from the maelstrom of everyday life, and in solitude and silence we can hear ourselves, including the otherness, the alterity, within. "Conversation and silence," Mary Elizabeth Moore (2002, 225) observes, "naturally lead to culmination and new beginnings." Passage is what William E. Doll, Jr. (2002, 49) has in mind when he points out that "conversation" derives from the Latin *conversare*, meaning "to turn oneself about."

Conversation, Doll points out, derives from the same Proto-Indo-European root as does the word *converge*, meaning "to approach the same point from different directions . . . to tend toward a common conclusion" (*American Heritage Dictionary*; quoted in Doll 2002, 49). "Thus," Doll (49) concludes, "there is a historical binding between conversation and convergence— through personal conversation we turn ourselves about and converge or come together. In conversation lie our hopes for both convergence and transformation." "Conversation is," he notes (quoting Gadamer), "a process of coming to an understanding" (Gadamer 1993 [1960], 385; quoted in Doll 2002, 49).

In studying ourselves, in elaborating and, perhaps, recasting our theoretical relationships with ourselves, we cannot forget the inextricability of the social and the subjective (Goodson 1998). Nor will we forget that the "self" we attempt to understand is, finally, illusory (Hwu 1998). But for teachers dispersed along a jagged, crumbling, social surface, the embrace of the private, the cultivation of subjectivity, is a political, not narcissistic, act. From the privacy of inner space, one can conduct serious (and playful) conversation with oneself, affirming the reality of one's lived experience in the face of brutal bureaucratic and political Orwellianism, wherein the scapegoating of teachers is camouflaged as concern for children: "leave no child behind."

The ethical imperative that informs our professional labor as educators and scholars is no simple "application" of an abstract ideal. There is here no application of theory into practice. Ewa Plonowska Ziarek's (2001, 1) neologism "dissensus" underscores that understanding occurs through conversation, conflict, and uncertainty. Such an ethics refers to what she deems an "irreducible dilemma of freedom and obligation," what she terms an "ethos of becoming" and an "ethos of alterity," one that structures a "non-appropriative relation to the Other" (Ziarek 2001, 2). So conceived, the educational project is nothing less than the composition of "new modes of life" (2). If NCATE would conceive of the "conceptual framework" standard as "dissensus," then, perhaps, one could become interested. Even then, however, all faculty need not necessary "share" the same "vision" of conflict, disagreement, and uncertainty.

Academic—intellectual—freedom must be our primary professional standard. Such freedom is the prerequisite for the "complicated conversation" that can connect self to society, making the classroom a civic square as well as a room of one's own. To claim this freedom we educators must, despite the distractions of the present, face the anti-intellectualism embedded in our profession. Too often we have mistaken busywork for academic work, authoritarianism for authority, indifference for professional dignity. To reaffirm our positions as teachers means remaining students. To become private-and-public intellectuals, we must be always studying across the disciplines, as well as reading in depth in at least one.

Teachers should probably be enrolled in universities each term, and not only in education departments or in the subject they teach, although study in these fields are obviously important. Teachers must also study fields outside their immediate expertise and interest; they will benefit from the study of interdisciplinary fields, especially, given the history of our present situation, African-American studies, and Women's and Gender Studies. When teachers come to us education professors, we must not (only) commiserate with them, we must provide provocative intellectual challenges.

Our primary commitment is to the academic—intellectual—understanding of self and society in the historical moment, the democratization of American culture. Such a commitment means we value academic knowledge and knowing, the "life of the mind," as these enliven and enrich the concrete lives of our students, their lives as individuals and as citizens. Of course, we teach "basic skills" and "core knowledge," but always in lived relation to those whom we teach. We must abandon infantilized positions from which we demand to know "what works." We must focus upon enlivening the educational opportunities we offer, working in every way ethically possible to encourage our students to take advantage of these opportunities. But we are not responsible for their learning. Students are responsible for their own learning. They deserve praise when they succeed, and they—and, secondarily, their parents—must take responsibility when they decline (or are unable) to learn.

When we curriculum theorists explicate the relations among curriculum, culture, the individual, and society, we are not engaged in some socially disinterested analytic exercise. We are employing academic knowledge, as did Jane Addams, to address the problems of society and culture. As Ziarek (2001, 16) notes in a different context, "far from offering a privatized ethics . . . [we seek] terms of praxis aiming to invent new modes of life, eroticism, and social relations."

In the short term, such invention requires that we work to reduce the political influence of business and religion in the United States, those twin and intersecting forces of anti-intellectualism in American culture Richard Hofstadter identified. This is not to endorse either socialism or secularism. But it is to insist that rhetoric of business be restricted to business organizations, not forced onto the profession of education where it has no business. It is to insist that spirituality remain a private matter, not politicized and recoded as educational policy, where it too often has meant the imposition of intellectual constraints if not outright censorship (see Zimmerman 2002).

Nor do I imagine the invention of "new modes of life" as obsessively futuristic, unmindful of the past (nor does Ziarek, no doubt). "A denial of the past," Lasch (1978, xviii) points out, "superficially progressive and optimistic, proves on closer analysis to embody the despair of a society that cannot face the future." As the method of *currere* aspires to support temporality in the character structure of the individual, curriculum theory insists that the education of the public is necessarily and profoundly historical. While not segregated in courses so labeled (characteristic of the system of academic vocationalism), historicity infuses all subjects, however interdisciplinary and interest-driven.

Such a project breathes life in a progressive commitment currently on display only in the museum. It is to reformulate the Deweyan commitment to democracy and education in light of our situation, our time, our lives, and the lives of our and others' children, all children. The first time round, "to many Americans," William L. Van Deburg (1984, 86) reminds, "progressivism was for whites only." Today, as this book illustrates, African-American history and culture comprise the conceptual center of contemporary curriculum theory in America.

At its most simple and basic, progressivism (*not* its anti-intellectual misrepresentation by otherwise distinguished historians such as Richard Hofstadter) is the historical throughline between the field of education 100 years ago and the contemporary field, specifically curriculum theory. I want to claim the progressive tradition while disavowing its excesses, including its past racialization and its tendencies to reduce education to social reform or child-centeredness, as well as its naive confidence in the casual relations among the three (i.e., social engineering).

Despite these weaknesses and its more current defamation by right-wing ideologues and distinguished historians, progressivism is the intellectual and political tradition that insists on the potential of academic knowledge for subjective and social reconstruction. Such a complex—William Doll might say "chaotic" (Doll 1993)—view of knowledge is quite congruent with the understanding of curriculum as a "complicated conversation" (Pinar et al. 1995, 848), disclosing as it does the relational character of ideas, in relation not only one to the other, but pointing as well to their embodiment and personification in individual lives, their origin and expression in social movements and trends, their rootedness in the historical past, their foreshadowing of our individual and national futures, and our future as a species as well.

Our planetary future is difficult to imagine outside those economic, political, and cultural transformations labeled loosely as "globalization." As David Held and his colleagues advise: "We need to refire our political imagination so that we do not remain politically passive in the face of these regional and global shifts" (Held et al. 1999, 450). Such "refiring" must include working toward what Held and his colleagues term "double-democratization." In allegiance with private-and-public intellectuals worldwide—in forums such as the International Association for the Advancement of Curriculum Studies (www.iaacs.org)—let us employ academic knowledge in the service of democratization, not only within nation-states, but within regions and across the globe:

> [D]emocracy needs to be rethought as a "double-sided process." By a double-sided process—or process of double democratization—is meant not just the deepening of democracy within a national community . . . but also the extension of democratic forms and processes across territorial borders. . . . The core of this project involves reconceiving legitimate political authority. (Held et al. 1999, 450)

Certainly we teachers must reconceive our notions of legitimate political authority in the United States. To do so, we must engage in serious autobiographical labor to break those internalized "modes of address" that keep us smashed on the social surface, unable to remember the past and too distracted by bureaucratic busywork to focus on the future. In this sense, "double-democratization" means not only local and global democratization, it means subjective and social democratization, the curricular construction of private-and-public spheres in curriculum and teaching.

Despite our public and private subjugation, despite the anti-intellectualism around us and within us, let us recommit ourselves to the study of our history, to work toward our future, committed to intellectual understanding, an interdisciplinary form of *praxis* requiring regression, progression, analysis, and synthesis. Self-understanding, self-mobilization, and social reconstruction characterize the *educational* experience of academic knowledge in schools that serve the species, not only the "economy." Such a fundamental reconceptualization of the American public education is not, however, utopian. "Schooling," Christopher Lasch (1995, 160) reminds, is not "a cure-all for everything that ails us."

As did the founder of American public education, Horace Mann, too many Americas today still believe that good schools can eradicate crime, eliminate poverty, construct committed citizens out of "abandoned and outcast children," and serve as the "great equalizer" between rich and poor (quoted phrases are Mann's, quoted in Lasch 1995, 160). We might have done better, Lasch suggests, had we started out less ambitiously. "If there is one lesson we might have been expected to learn in the 150 years since Horace Mann took charge of the schools of Massachusetts," Lasch (1995, 160) writes, "it is that the schools can't save society." He notes crime and poverty have not disappeared and the gap between rich and poor only widens. "Maybe," he suggests, "the time has come—if it hasn't already passed—to start all over again" (160).

Lasch is right. While scapegoating teachers, the last three decades of school "reform" are aimed at making the present system "work." Politicians understand that the authoritarianism is the only way to force children to excel at tasks in which they have little interest. Test-driven curriculum and instruction are the means of such authoritarianism, deflecting attention away from its intensely political motives and anti-educational effects. As Lasch (1995, 162) himself acknowledges, "[p]eople readily acquire such knowledge as they can put to good use." Especially after Sputnik, schools are not permitted to provide opportunities for students to put academic knowledge "to good use." Like a pyramid scheme, academic vocationalism justifies the acquisition of academic knowledge because it leads to more knowledge, someday resulting in a credential enabling, presumably, upward mobility. Academic vocationalism fails to insist on connecting academic knowledge to self-formation and historical moment, what Lasch himself—as a public intellectual—so powerfully did.

"What democracy requires," Lasch (1995, 162) points out, "is vigorous public debate not information." The notion of "complicated conversation" includes "vigorous public debate" but it is broader, supporting solitary study and discovery in rooms of one's own as well as in classrooms as civic squares. Complaining about the surfeit of information, Lasch (1996, 162–163) acknowledges that democracy "needs information too, but the kind of information it needs can be generated only by debate." While in agreement with him, I insist on expanding Lasch's conception as a curriculum theory, including, even emphasizing debate, but supporting a broad range of intellectual pursuits, some of which will be conducted in solitude and might not always result in public expression. Acknowledging that subjective interest is the prerequisite for erudition (but thinking still only of public debate), Lasch (1995, 163) points out:

> We do not know what we need to know until we ask the right questions, and we can identify the right questions only by subjecting our own ideas about the world to the test of public controversy. Information, usually seen as the precondition of debate, is better understood as its byproduct. When we get into arguments that focus and fully engage our attention, we become avid seekers of relevant information. Otherwise we take in information passively—if we take it in at all.

This is a strong critique of academic vocationalism. Except for his exclusive focus on the concept of "debate," it is a succinct statement of curriculum as "complicated conversation."

Lasch is thinking not of the public school but of journalism, reporting that political debate began to decline at the beginning of the 20th century, at about the same time when the press was becoming more "responsible," more "professional," after behavioral and social science (then its formative moment), more "objective." In the early 19th century, Lasch (1995, 163) reports, the press had been "fiercely partisan." It was Walter Lippmann, he continues, who articulated most forcefully the view that the role of the press was to "circulate information, not to encourage argument" (Lasch 1995, 170).

"Lippmann had forgotten," Lasch (170) surmises, "that our search for reliable information it itself guided by the questions that arise during arguments about a given course of action. It is only by subjecting our preference and projects to the test of debate that we come to understand what we know and what we still need to learn." I would supplement the word "debate" with "public scrutiny and judgment," but the educational point is well taken: curriculum as complicated conversation must be linked to subjective investment and public expression. "In short," Lasch (170) summarizes, expressing what every teacher knows, "we come to know our own minds only by explaining ourselves to others." While it includes debate and argument, this is a broader concept than either.

"If we insist on argument [especially understood as "teaching," as in explaining ourselves to others, which he suggests above] as the essence of education," Lasch (1995, 171) writes, sounding for the moment like a curriculum theorist,

> we will defend democracy not as the most efficient but as the most educational form of government, one that extends the circle of debate as widely as possible and thus forces all citizens to articulate their views [in the civic square that is the classroom], to put their views at risk, and to cultivate the virtues of eloquence, clarity of thought and expression, and sound judgement.

Directing confronting the structuring of education for the production of specialized elites (Conant's aristocracy of talent), Lasch (1995, 171) insists that "direct democracy" must be "re-create[d] . . . on a large scale." While he is thinking of the press, not the school, the concept upon which he fastens— the town meeting—expresses well the concept of the classroom as civic square. While reductive as a model for all educational activity, it expresses succinctly what it means to reconstruct the public sphere in curriculum and teaching. If we supplement it by including opportunities for individual exploration and discovery, sometimes in solitude, we have the rudiments of what it means to reconstruct the subjective and social spheres in curriculum and teaching.

None of this is exactly new, as it is, Lasch notes, what Dewey argued in *The Public and Its Problems* (1927), a book written in reply to Lippmann (and from which I have quoted several times in this study). Anticipating the contemporary "auditory turn" in which the hegemony of visuality is contested (see, for instance, Levin 1993), and in curriculum theory specifically (see Aoki in press), Lasch, relying on James Carey's work (1989), points out that Dewey's concept of communication emphasized the ear rather than the eye (see 1995, 172). Lasch quotes Dewey (in 1995, 172):

> Conversation has a vital import lacking in the fixed and frozen words of written speech. . . . The connections of the ear with vital and outgoing thought and emotion are immensely closer and more varied than those of the eye. Vision is a spectator; hearing is a participator.

The hegemony of visuality accompanies the ahistorical presentism and political passivity of the American culture of narcissism. Without the lived sense of temporality the method of *currere* encourages, we are consigned to the social surface, and what we see is what we get. When we listen to the past we become attuned to the future. Then we can understand the present, which we *can* reconstruct. Subjective and social reconstruction is our professional obligation as educators in this nightmarish moment of anti-intellectualism and political subjugation. Alone and together, let us participate in complicated conversation with ourselves and with colleagues worldwide. Let us construct an increasingly sophisticated and auditory field of education, one worthy of those schoolteachers and students who, each day, nearly everywhere on the globe, labor to understand themselves and the world they inhabit. May our "complicated conversation" complicate theirs—and yours.

Appendix:
Curriculum Studies Journals,
Organizations, and Conferences

Journals

1. *Journal of Critical Inquiry into Curriculum and Instruction*
2. *Journal of Curriculum Studies*
3. *Curriculum Inquiry*
4. *JCT: The Journal of Curriculum Theorizing*
5. *Journal of the American Association for the Advancement of Curriculum Studies*
6. *Journal of the International Association for the Advancement of Curriculum Studies*

Organizations

1. American Association for the Advancement of Curriculum Studies (AAACS) website: http://aaacs.info
2. American Educational Research Association (AERA): Division B: Curriculum Studies http://aera.net
3. Association for Supervision and Curriculum Development (ASCD)
4. Association for Teaching and Curriculum (ATC)
5. International Association for the Advancement of Curriculum Studies (IAACS) Website: www.iaacs.org

Conferences

Annual Conference of the American Association for the Advancement of Curriculum Studies

Bergamo Conference on Curriculum Theory and Classroom Practice (organized by the Editors of *JCT*) Website: http://orgs.bloomu.edu/jct/

Curriculum and Pedagogy Conference: http://www.ed.asu.edu/candp/main.html

Triennial Conference of the International Association for the Advancement of Curriculum Studies: www.iaacs.org

AMERICAN ASSOCIATION FOR THE
ADVANCEMENT OF CURRICULUM STUDIES

Professional Ethics and Standards for Scholars in Curriculum Studies

1. Commitment to teach all major sectors of scholarship in the field, even those critical of one's own point of view.
2. Commitment to interdisciplinarity, including arts-based research, as source and method of curriculum inquiry.
3. Commitment to curriculum history and theory, as "memory" and "future" of the field.
4. Commitment to a wide spectrum of research and inquiry, from the theoretical to practical, school-based and community based research, as well pedagogical intervention and, of course, curricular experimentation.
5. Commitment to internationalization, multiculturalism, and social justice.
6. Commitment to the overall school program, including extra-curricular activities and their relationship to traditionally academic studies, aware always that curriculum must be connected to life history, self-formation, society, and historical moment.
7. Commitment to the advancement of the field, through teaching, research, and service, including service to professional organizations, scholarly journals, and the promotion of graduate education in curriculum studies.

Accreditation Standards

8. Curriculum studies courses must be taught by faculty with terminal degrees in curriculum studies or who have demonstrated, through scholarship and conference participation, a sustained and sophisticated understanding of curriculum studies.

9. Undergraduate teacher education programs should contain at least one curriculum studies course, or significant curriculum-studies content within a more general course.

10. Graduate programs in all specializations within the broad field of education should contain at least one curriculum studies course.

11. Graduate programs in curriculum studies should contain at least one course in a) curriculum history, b) curriculum theory, and c) internationalization.

Approved April 19, 2003

References

Addams, Jane (2002 [1902]). *Democracy and social ethics.* [Introduction by Charlene Haddock Seigfried.] Urbana: University of Illinois Press.

Allen, Beverly (Ed.). (1982). *Pier Paolo Pasolini: The poetics of heresy.* Saratoga, CA: Anma Libri and Co.

Althusser, Louis (1993). *The future lasts a long time and the facts.* [Edited by Olivier Corpet and Yann Moulier Boutang. Translated by Richard Veasey.] London: Chatto & Windus.

Ames, Jessie Daniel (1942). *The changing character of lynching.* Atlanta: Commission on Interracial Cooperation. [Reprinted in 1972 by AMS Press, New York.]

Anderson, Benedict (1991 [1983]). *Imagined communities: Reflections on the origin and spread of nationalism.* London: Verso.

Andrews, William L. (Ed.). (1993). *African American autobiography: A collection of critical essays.* Englewood Cliffs, NJ: Prentice Hall.

Aoki, Douglas Sadao (2002, Spring). The price of teaching: Love, evasion, and the subordination of knowledge. *JCT* (18) 1, 21–39.

Aoki, Ted T. (1983). Experiencing ethnicity as a Japanese Canadian teacher: Reflections on a personal curriculum. *Curriculum Inquiry,* (13), 3.

Aoki, Ted T. (in press). *Curriculum in a new key: The collected works of Ted T. Aoki.* [With a preface by Rita L. Irwin and an introduction by William F. Pinar.] Mahwah, NJ: Lawrence Erlbaum Associates.

Appel, Stephen (Ed.). (1999). *Psychoanalysis and pedagogy.* Westport, CT: Bergin & Garvey.

Applebee, Arthur N. (1996). *Curriculum as conversation: Transforming traditions of teaching and learning.* Chicago: University of Chicago Press.

Applebome, Peter (1998, March 7). Could the Old South be resurrected? Cherished ideas of the Confederacy (not slavery) find new backers. New York: *New York Times* (on line).

Asher, Nina (2001, October). *In contemplation: A curriculum for healing.* Paper presented at the Bergamo Conference on Curriculum Theory and Classroom Practice, Dayton, Ohio.

Atwell-Vasey, Wendy (1998a). *Nourishing words: Bridging private reading and public teaching*. Albany: State University of New York Press.

Atwell-Vasey, Wendy (1998b). Psychoanalytic feminism and the powerful teacher. In William F. Pinar (Ed.), *Curriculum: Toward new identities* (143–156). New York: Garland.

Ayers, Edward L. (1984). *Vengeance and justice: Crime and punishment in the nineteenth century American South*. New York: Oxford University Press.

Ayers, Edward L. (1992). *The promise of the new south: Life after Reconstruction*. New York: Oxford University Press.

Ayers, William (1993). *To teach: The journey of a teacher*. [Foreword by H. Kohl.] New York: Teachers College Press.

Baker, Bernadette M. (2001). *In perpetual motion: Theories of power, educational history, and the child*. New York: Peter Lang.

Baldwin, James (1985). *The price of the ticket*. New York: St. Martin's Press.

Baldwin, James (1998). Going to meet the man. In David R. Roediger (Ed.), *Black on white: Black writers on what it means to be white* (255–273). New York: Schocken Books. [First published in 1965 by Dial Press.]

Barthes, Roland (1974). *S/Z*. [Trans. Richard Miller.] New York: Hill and Wang. [Paris: Editions du Seul, 1970.]

Barthes, Roland (1978). *The pleasure of the text*. [Trans. Richard Miller.] New York: Hill and Wang.

Barthes, Roland (1981). *Camera lucida: Reflections on photography*. [Trans. Richard Howard.] New York: Hill and Wang.

Barone, Tom (2000). *Aesthetics, politics, and educational inquiry*. New York: Peter Lang.

Barrow, R. (1984). *Giving teaching back to teachers: A critical introduction to curriculum theory*. Totowa, NJ: Barnes & Noble.

Bataille, Georges (1991). *The accursed share, vols. II and III: The history of eroticism and sovereignty*. [Trans. Robert Hurley.] New York: Zone.

Bederman, Gail (1995). *Manliness and civilization: A cultural history of gender and race in the United States, 1880–1917*. Chicago: University of Chicago Press.

Benstock, Shari (1988). Authorizing the autobiographical. In Shari Benstock (Ed.), *The private self: Theory and practice of women's autobiographical writings* (10–33). Chapel Hill and London: University of North Carolina Press.

Berlant, Lauren (1991). *The anatomy of national fantasy: Hawthorne, utopia and everyday life*. Chicago: University of Chicago Press.

Bersani, Leo (1995). *Homos*. Cambridge, MA: Harvard University Press.

Bestor, Arthur (1953). *Educational wastelands: The retreat from learning in our public schools*. Urbana: University of Illinois Press.

Beyer, Landon, Feinberg, Walter, Pagano, JoAnne and Whitson, Anthony J. (1989). *Preparing teachers as professionals: The role of educational studies and other liberal disciplines*. New York: Teachers College Press.

Black, Earl and Black, Merle (1992). *The vital South: How presidents are elected*. Cambridge, MA: Harvard University Press.

Blee, Katherine M. (1991). *Women of the Klan: Racism and gender in the 1920s*. Berkeley: University of California Press.

Block, Alan A. (1997). *I'm only bleeding: Education as the practice of social violence against the child*. New York: Peter Lang.

Block, Alan A. (1998). Curriculum as affichiste: Popular culture and identity. In William F. Pinar (Ed.), *Curriculum: Toward new identities* (325–341). New York: Garland.

Boa, Elizabeth (1996). *Kafka: Gender, class, and race in the letters and fictions.* Oxford: Clarendon Press.

Boler, Megan (1999). *Feeling power: Emotions and education.* New York: Routledge.

Bollas, C. (1995). *Cracking up: The work of unconscious experience.* New York: Hill and Wang.

Bonacich, Edna (1972). A theory of ethnic antagonism: The split labor market. *American Sociological Review* 37, 547–559.

Bonacich, Edna (1975). Abolition, the extension of slavery, and the position of free blacks: A study of split labor markets in the United States, 1830–1863. *American Journal of Sociology* 83, 601–128.

Bordo, Susan (1993). *Unbearable weight: Feminism, western culture, and the body.* Berkeley and Los Angeles: University of California Press.

Bowers, C. A. (1995). *Educating for an ecologically sustainable culture.* Albany: State University of New York Press.

Bowers, C. A. (2000). *Let them eat data: How computers affect education, cultural diversity and the prospects of ecological sustainability.* Athens: University of Georgia.

Braxton, Joanne M. (1989). *Black women writing autobiography: A tradition within a tradition.* Philadelphia, PA: Temple University Press.

Brennan, Teresa and Jay, Martin (Eds.). (1996). *Vision in context: Historical and contemporary perspectives on sight.* New York: Routledge.

Britzman, Deborah P. (1998). *Lost subjects, contested objects: Toward a psychoanalytic inquiry of learning.* Albany, NY: State University of New York Press.

Britzman, Deborah (2000). If the story cannot end: Deferred action, ambivalence, and difficult knowledge. In Roger I. Simon, Sharon Rosenberg and Claudia Eppert (Eds.), *Between hope and despair: Pedagogy and the remembrance of historical trauma* (27–57). Lanham, MD: Rowman & Littlefield.

Brombert, Victor (1978). *The romantic prison: The French tradition.* Princeton, NJ: Princeton University Press.

Brown, Norman O. (1959). *Life against death: The psychoanalytical meaning of history.* Middletown, CT: Wesleyan University Press.

Brown, Richard Maxwell (1975). *Strain of violence: Historical studies of American violence and vigilantism.* New York: Oxford University Press.

Brown, Roger (1965). *Social psychology.* New York: The Free Press.

Brownmiller, Susan (1993 [1975]). *Against our will: Men, women, and rape.* New York: Fawcett Columbine.

Brundage, W. Fitzhugh (1993). *Lynching in the new South: Georgia and Virginia, 1880–1930.* Urbana: University of Illinois Press.

Bruner, Jerome S. (1977). Preface to reissued *The process of education.* Cambridge, MA: Harvard University Press.

Bruner, Jerome S. (1977 [1960]). *The process of education.* Cambridge, MA: Harvard University Press.

Bruner, Jerome S. (1996). *The culture of education.* Cambridge, MA: Harvard University Press.

Buckley, Sandra (1991). "Penguin in bondage": A graphic tale of Japanese comic books. In C. Penley and A. Ross (Eds.), *Technoculture* (135–161). Minneapolis: University of Minnesota Press.

Bulhan, Hussein Abdilahi (1985). *Frantz Fanon and the psychology of oppression.* New York & London: Plenum Press.

Burbules, Nicholas (1993). *Dialogue in teaching.* New York: Teachers College Press.

Burbules, Nicholas C. (2000). The limits of dialogue as a critical pedagogy. In Peter Trifonas (Ed.), *Revolutionary pedagogies: Cultural politics, instituting education, and the discourse of theory* (251–273). New York: Routledge/Falmer.

Burd, Stephen (2002, September 20). Accountability or meddling? *The Chronicle of Higher Education*, A-23–25.

Burke, S. (1992). *The death and return of the author: Criticism and subjectivity in Barthes, Foucault, and Derrida*. Edinburgh, Scotland: Edinburgh University Press.

Butler, Judith (1990). *Gender trouble*. New York: Routledge.

Butler, Judith (1993). *Bodies that matter: On the discursive limits of "sex."* New York and London: Routledge.

Butterfield, Stephen (1974). *Black autobiography in America*. Amherst, MA: University of Massachusetts Press.

Bystrom, Dianne G. (1996). Beyond the hearings: The continuing effects of Hill vs. Thomas on women and men, the workplace, and politics. In Sandra L. Ragan, Dianne G. Bystrom, Lynda Lee Kaid and Christina S. Beck (Eds.), *The lynching of language: Gender, politics, and power in the Hill-Thomas hearings* (260–282). Urbana & Chicago: University of Illinois Press.

Cannella, Gaile S. (1998). Early childhood education: A call for the construction of revolutionary images. In William F. Pinar (Ed.), *Curriculum: Toward new identities* (157–184). New York: Garland.

Cantril, H. (1941). *The psychology of social movements*. New York: John Wiley.

Carby, Hazel V. (1987). *Reconstructing womanhood: The emergence of the Afro-American novelist*. New York: Oxford University Press.

Carby, Hazel V. (1993). "Hear my voice, ye careless daughters." In William L. Andrews (Ed.), *African American autobiography: A collection of critical essays* (59–76). Englewood Cliffs, NJ: Prentice Hall.

Carby, Hazel V. (1998). *Race men*. Cambridge, MA: Harvard University Press.

Carey, James W. (1989). *Communication as culture*. Boston: Unwin Hyman.

Carlson, Dennis (2002). *Leaving safe harbors: Toward a new progressivism in American education and public life*. New York: Routledge.

Carnes, Mark C. and Griffen, Clyde (Eds.). (1990). *Meanings for manhood: Constructions of masculinity in Victorian America*. Chicago: University of Chicago Press.

Carson, Clayborne (1981). *In struggle: SNCC and the black awakening of the 1960s*. Cambridge, MA: Harvard University Press.

Cash, W. J. (1941). *The mind of the South*. New York: Alfred Knopf.

Castenell, Jr., Louis A. and Pinar, William F. (1993). Introduction. In Louis A. Castenell, Jr. and William F. Pinar (Eds.), *Understanding curriculum as racial text: Representations of identity and difference in education* (1–30). Albany: State University of New York Press.

Cavell, Stanley (1994). *A pitch of philosophy*. Cambridge, MA: Harvard University Press.

Chang, B. G. (1996). *Deconstructing communication: Representation, subject, and economic exchange*. Minneapolis: University of Minnesota Press.

Chodorow, Nancy J. (1978). *The reproduction of mothering*. Berkeley: University of California Press.

Christian, Barbara (1985). *Black feminist criticism: Perspectives on black women writers*. New York: Pergamon Press.

Chronicle of Higher Education (2002, August 2). Peer review. Vol. XLVIII (47), A9.

Churchill, Ward and Wall, Jim Vander (1988). *Agents of repression: The FBI's secret wars against the Black Panther Party and the American Indian Movement*. Boston, MA: South End Press.

Cixous, Hélene (1992). We who are free, are we free? In Barbara Johnson (Ed.), *Freedom and interpretation: The Oxford Amnesty lectures* (17–44). New York: Basic Books.

Cleaver, Eldridge (1968). *Soul on ice.* New York: Dell.

Clement, Richard (1983). *Northernizing the South.* Athens: University of Georgia Press.

Clifford, Geraldine Joncich and Guthrie, James W. (1988). *Ed school: A brief for professional education.* Chicago: University of Chicago Press.

Cluster, Dick (Ed.). (1979). *They should have served that cup of coffee: 7 radicals remember the 60s.* Boston: South End Press.

Collins, Patricia H. (1991). *Black feminist thought: Knowledge, consciousness, ands the politics of empowerment.* New York: Routledge.

Comer, James P. (2003, January 24). Making schools of education bridges to better learning. *Chronicle of Higher Education* B20.

Conant, James B. (1963). *The education of American teachers.* New York: McGraw-Hill.

Cooper, Anna Julia (1998 [1892]). A voice from the South. In Charles Lemert and Esme Bhan (Eds.), *The voice of Anna Julia Cooper* (51–196). Lanham, MD: Rowan & Littlefield.

Cooper, William J., Jr. (1978). *The South and the politics of slavery.* Baton Rouge: Louisiana State University Press.

Crary, Jonathan (2002). *Suspensions of perception: Attention, spectacle, and modern culture.* Cambridge, MA: MIT Press/an October Book.

Cremin, Lawrence A. (1961). *The transformation of the school: Progressivism in American education, 1876–1957.* New York: Alfred A. Knopf.

Cuban, Larry and Shipps, Dorothy (2000). *Reconstructing the common good in education.* Stanford, CA: Stanford University Press.

Cudjoe, Selwyn R. (1984). Maya Angelou and the autobiographical statement. In Mari Evans (Ed.), *Black women writers* (6–24). Garden City, NY: Anchor Books.

Cummins, Eric (1994). *The rise and fall of California's radical prison movement.* Stanford, CA: Stanford University Press.

Cutler, James Elbert (1905). *Lynch law: An investigation into the history of lynching in the United States.* New York: Longmans, Green.

Dabbs, James McBride (1964). *Who speaks for the South?* New York: Funk & Wagnalls.

Daignault, Jacques (1992). Traces at work from different places. In William F. Pinar and William M. Reynolds (Eds.), *Understanding curriculum as phenomenological and deconstructed text* (195–215). New York: Teachers College Press.

Daspit, Toby A. and Weaver, John A. (Eds.). (2000). *Popular culture and critical pedagogy.* New York: Garland.

Davies, Bronwyn (2000). *A body of writing 1990–1999.* Walnut Creek, CA: AltaMira.

De Castell, Suzanne (1999). On finding one's lace in the text: Literary as a technology of self-formation. In William F. Pinar (Ed.), *Contemporary curriculum discourses: Twenty years of JCT* (398–411). New York: Peter Lang.

Decosta-Willis, Miriam (Ed.). (1995). *The Memphis diary of Ida B. Wells.* [Foreword by Mary Helen Washington. Afterward by Dorothy Sterling.] Boston, MA: Beacon Press.

Deleuze, Gilles (1986). *Foucault.* [Foreword by Paul A. Bové. Translated and edited by Sean Hand.] Minneapolis: University of Minnesota Press.

Deleuze, Gilles (1993). *The fold: Leibniz and the Baroque.* [Forward and translation by T. Conley.] Minneapolis and London: University of Minnesota Press.

Deleuze, Gilles and Guattari, Félix (1987). *A thousand plateaus: Capitalism and schizophrenia.* [Trans. and foreword by Brian Massumi.] Minneapolis: University of Minnesota Press.

Derrida, Jacques (1976 [1967]). *Of grammatology*. [Trans. by G. Spivak.] Baltimore, MD: Johns Hopkins University Press. [Originally published in French, 1967.]

Dewey, John (1916). *Democracy and education*. New York: Macmillan.

Dewey, John (1938). *Experience and education*. New York: Macmillan.

Dewey, John (1962 [1934]). *A common faith*. New Haven, CT: Yale University Press.

Dewey, John (1991 [1927]). *The public and its problems*. Athens: Ohio University Press.

Dimitriadis, Greg and McCarthy, Cameron (2001). *Reading & teaching the postcolonial: From Baldwin to Basquiat and beyond*. New York: Teachers College Press.

Disch, Lisa and Kane, Mary Jo (1996). When a looker is really a bitch: Lisa Olson, sport, and the heterosexual matrix. In Ruth-Ellen B. Joeres and Barbara Laslett (Eds.), *The second signs reader: Feminist scholarship* (326–356). Chicago: University of Chicago Press.

Doll, Mary Aswell (2000). *Like letters in running water: A mythopoetics of curriculum*. Mahwah, NJ: Lawrence Erlbaum Associates.

Doll, Jr., William E. (1993). *A post-modern perspective on curriculum*. New York: Teachers College Press.

Doll, Jr., William E. (1998). Curriculum and concepts of control. [Assisted by Al Alcazar.] In William F. Pinar (Ed.), *Curriculum: Toward new identities* (295–323). New York: Garland.

Doll, Jr., William E. (2002). Ghosts and the curriculum. In William E. Doll, Jr. and Noel Gough (Eds.), *Curriculum visions* (23–70). New York: Peter Lang.

Du Bois, W. E. B. (1975 [1935]). *Black reconstruction in America*. New York: Atheneum.

Du Bois, W. E. B. (1982 [1903]). *The souls of black folk*. New York: New American Library.

Du Bois, W. E. B. (1995/1996 [1903]). The souls of black folk. In Herb Boyd and Robert L. Allen (Eds.), *Brotherman: The odyssey of black men in America* (36–40). New York: Ballantine/One World.

Duncan, Martha G. (1996). *Romantic outlaws, beloved prisons: The unconscious meanings of crime and punishment*. New York: New York University Press.

Dunlop, Rishma (1999). *Boundary bay: A novel*. Vancouver, British Columbia, Canada: University of British Columbia, Faculty of Education, unpublished Ph.D. dissertation.

Earle, William (1972). *The autobiographical consciousness: A philosophical inquiry into existence*. Chicago: Quandrangle Books.

Edelman, Lee (1994). Seeing things: Representation, the scene of surveillance and the spectacle of gay male sex. In Jonathan Goldberg (Ed.), *Reclaiming Sodom* (265–287). New York: Routledge.

Edgerton, Susan Huddleston (1996). *Translating the curriculum: Multiculturalism into cultural studies*. New York: Routledge.

Egan, Kieran (1992). *Imagination in teaching and learning*. Chicago: University of Chicago Press. [Published in Canada by the Althouse Press, London, Ontario. The reference is to this edition.]

Egéa-Kuehne, Denise (2001). Derrida's ethics of affirmation: The challenge of educational rights and responsibility. In Gert J. J. Biesta and Denise Egéa-Kuehne (Eds.), *Derrida & Education* (186–208). London: Routledge.

Eisenstein, Elizabeth L. (1979). *The printing press as an agent of change: Communications and cultural transformations in early modern Europe*. New York: Cambridge University Press.

Eisner, Elliot W. (1979). *The educational imagination: On the design and evaluation of school programs*. New York: Macmillan.

Elkins, Stanley M. (1959). *Slavery: A problem in American institutional and intellectual life.* Chicago: University of Chicago Press.

Ellison, Ralph (1972/1952). *Invisible man.* New York: Vintage.

Ellison, Ralph (1995). *Shadow and act.* New York: Vantage Books. [1995 edition published by Vintage.]

Ellsworth, Elizabeth (1997). *Teaching positions: Difference, pedagogy, and the power of address.* New York: Teachers College Press.

Elmore, Richard (1993). School decentralization: Who gains? who loses? In J. Hannaway and M. Carnoy (Eds.), *Decentralization and school improvement: Can we fulfill the promise?* (33–55). San Francisco, CA: Jossey-Bass.

Elshtain, Jean Bethke (2002). *Jane Addams and the dream of American democracy.* New York: Basic Books.

Eppert, Claudia (2000). Relearning questions: Responding to the ethical address of past and present others. In Roger I. Simon, Sharon Rosenberg and Claudia Eppert (Eds.), *Between hope and despair: Pedagogy and the remembrance of historical trauma* (213–230). Lanham, MD: Rowman & Littlefield.

Evans, Sara (1979). *Personal politics.* New York: Vintage.

Fabbri, Paolo (1994). Free/indirect/discourse. In Patrick Rumble and Bart Testa (Eds.), *Pier Paolo Pasolini: Contemporary perspectives* (78–87). Toronto: University of Toronto Press.

Fairclough, Adam (1995/1999). *Race and democracy: The civil rights struggle in Louisiana, 1915–1972.* [Paperback edition: 1999.] Athens: University of Georgia Press.

Fanon, Frantz (1967). *Black skin, white masks.* [Trans. by Charles Lam Markmann.] New York: Grove Weidenfeld. [Originally published in French under the title *Peau Noire, Masques Blancs,* copyright 1952 by Editions du Seuil, Paris.]

Faulkner, William (1946). *The sound and the fury.* New York: Vintage.

Faulkner, William (1948). *Intruder in the dust.* New York: Random House.

Faust, Drew Gilpin (1996). *Mothers of invention. Women of the slaveholding south in the American civil war.* Chapel Hill: University of North Carolina Press.

Fehlman, S. (1987). *Jacques Lacan and the adventure of insight.* Cambridge, MA: Harvard University Press.

Fiedler, Leslie (1948). "Come back to the raft ag'in, Huck Honey!" *Partisan Review* 15, 664–711.

Fiedler, Leslie A. (1966). *Love and death in the American novel.* [Revised edition.] New York: Stein and Day.

Filene, Peter G. (1998). *Him/her/self.* [3rd edition; 1st edition published in 1974 by Harcourt, Brace, Jovanovich.] Baltimore, MD: Johns Hopkins University Press.

Fiske, E. (1991). *Smart schools, smart kids.* New York: Simon & Schuster.

Flax, Jane (1987). Re-membering the selves: The repressed gendered. *Michigan Quarterly Review, 26*(1), 92–110.

Foner, Eric (1988). *Reconstruction: America's unfinished revolution, 1863–1877.* New York: Harper & Row.

Forten, Charlotte L. (1961). *The journal of Charlotte L. Forten: A free negro in the slave era.* New York: Macmillan.

Foucault, Michel (1973). *The birth of the clinic: An archaeology of medical perception.* [Trans. A. M. Sheridan.] New York: Pantheon.

Foucault, Michel (1988). *Madness and civilization.* [Trans. Richard Howard.] New York: Vintage.

Foucault, Michel (1995 [1979]). *Discipline and punish: The birth of the prison*. [Trans. by Alan Sheridan.] New York: Vintage.

Foucault, Michel (1990, 1988). *Politics, philosophy, culture: Interviews and other writings 1977–1984*. [Edited with an introduction by Lawrence D. Kritzman.] New York and London: Routledge.

Fox-Genovese, Elizabeth (1988). *Within the plantation household: Black and white women of the old South*. Chapel Hill: University of North Carolina Press.

Franklin, John Hope (1970). Foreword to Ida B. Wells' *Crusade for justice* (ix–xi). Chicago: University of Chicago Press.

Freire, Paulo (1968). *Pedagogy of the oppressed*. New York: Seabury.

Freud, Sigmund (1955). *The standard edition of the complete works of Sigmund Freud*. Volume 17. [Ed. James Strachey.] London: Hogarth Press.

Freyre, Gilberto (1963). *New world in the tropics*. New York: Vintage.

Friedenberg, Edgar (1962). *The vanishing adolescent*. New York: Dell.

Friedman, Susan Stanford (1988). Women's autobiographical selves: Theory and practice. In Shari Benstock (Ed.), *The private self: Theory and practice of women's autobiographical writings* (34–62). Chapel Hill and London: University of North Carolina Press.

Friedrich, Pia (1982). *Pier Paolo Pasolini*. Boston: Twayne Publishers.

Furlong, John (2002, August–September). Ideology and reform in teacher education in England. *Educational Researcher* 31 (6), 23–25.

Gadamer, H.-G. (1993). *Truth and method*. In C. J. Weinsheimer and D. G. Marshall (Trans.). New York: Continuam.

Gardner, Howard (1983). *Frames of mind: The theory of multiple intelligences*. New York: Basic Books.

Gates, Jr., Henry Louis (1988). *The signifying monkey: A theory of Afro-American literary criticism*. New York: Oxford University Press.

Gates, Jr., Henry Louis (1992). *Loose canons: Notes on the culture wars*. New York: Oxford University Press.

Gates, Jr., Henry Louis (1996). *Colored people: A memoir*. New York: Alfred A. Knopf.

Gaztambide-Fernández, Rubén and Sears, James (2004). *Curriculum work as public moral enterprise*. Lanham, MD: Rowman & Littlefield.

Genovese, Eugene D. (1964). *The political economy of slavery*. New York: Pantheon.

Genovese, Eugene D. (1968). *In red and black*. New York: Pantheon.

Genovese, Eugene D. (1994). *The southern tradition: The achievements and limitations of American conservatism*. Cambridge, MA: Harvard University Press.

Gerassi, John (1966). *The boys of Boise; Furor, vice, and folly in an American city*. New York: Macmillan.

Gilmore, David D. (1990). *Manhood in the making*. New Haven: Yale University Press.

Gilmore, David D. (2001). *Misogyny: The male malady*. Philadelphia: University of Pennsylvania Press.

Gilmore, Leigh (1994). *Autobiographics: A feminist theory of women's self-representation*. Ithaca, NY: Cornell University Press.

Giroux, Henry A. (1999). *The mouse that roared: Disney and the end of innocence*. Lanham, MD: Rowman & Littlefield.

Glissant, Edouard (2002, April 19). The poetics of the world: Global thinking and unforeseeable events. Baton Rouge, Louisiana: Chancellor's Distinguished Lecture.

Gollnick, Donna (2002, September 5). *The Power of Title II Report Card Data: Unraveling the USDOE Recommendations to NCATE*. Address to the NCATE 2000 Clinic for Louisiana Institutions: A Partnership Approach to Enhancing Teacher Quality and Accountability. Baton Rouge: Claiborne Conference Center.

Goodson, Ivor (1998). Storying the self: Life politics and the study of the teacher's life and work. In William F. Pinar (Ed.), *Curriculum: Toward new identities* (3–20). New York: Garland.

Gordon, Lewis R. (1995). *Bad faith and antiblack racism*. Atlantic Highlands, NJ: Humanities Press.

Gough, Annette (1998). Beyond Eurocentrism in science education: Promises and problematics from a feminist poststructuralist perspective. In William F. Pinar (Ed.), *Curriculum: Toward new identities* (185–209). New York: Garland.

Gough, Noel (1994). Narration, reflection, diffraction: Aspects of fiction in educational inquiry. *Australian Educational Researcher* 21 (3), 47–76.

Gough, Noel (1998). Reflections and diffractions: Functions of fiction in curriculum inquiry. In William F. Pinar (Ed.), *Curriculum: Toward new identities* (93–127). New York: Garland.

Gough, Noel (2002). Voicing curriculum visions. In William E. Doll, Jr. and Noel Gough (Eds.), *Curriculum visions* (1–22). New York: Peter Lang.

Graff, Gerald (1992). *Beyond the culture wars: How teaching the conflicts can revitalize American education*. New York: Norton.

Graham, Robert (1989). Autobiography and education. *Journal of Educational Thought* 23 (2), 92–105.

Graham, Robert (1991). *Reading and writing the self: Autobiography in education and the curriculum*. New York: Teachers College Press.

Gray, Deborah (1999 [1985]). *Ar'n't I a woman? Female slaves in the plantation South*. New York: Norton.

Greene, Maxine (1995). *Releasing the imagination*. San Francisco: Jossey-Bass.

Greene, Naomi (1990). *Pier Paolo Pasolini: Cinema as heresy*. Princeton, NJ: Princeton University Press.

Gregorian, Vartan (2001, August 17). Teacher education must become colleges' central preoccupation. *The Chronicle of Higher Education*, B7–8.

Grice, H. (1975). Logic and conversation. In P. Cole and J. L. Morgan (Eds.), *Syntax and semantics* (41–58). [Vol. 3.] New York: Seminar Press.

Griffen, Larry J., Clark, Paula, and Sandberg, Joanne, C. (1997). Narrative and event: Lynching and historical sociology. In W. Fitzhugh Brundage (Ed.), *Under sentence of death: Lynching in the south* (24–47). Chapel Hill: University of North Carolina Press.

Griswold, Robert L. (1998). The "flabby American," the body, and the cold war. In Laura McCall and Donald Yacovone (Eds.), *A shared experience: Men, women, and the history of gender* (323–348). New York: New York University Press.

Grumet, Madeleine R. (1976). Psychoanalytic foundations. In William F. Pinar and Madeleine R. Grumet, *Toward a poor curriculum* (111–146). Dubuque, IA: Kendall/Hunt.

Grumet, Madeleine R. (1988). *Bitter milk: Women and teaching*. Amherst: University of Massachusetts Press.

Gunn, Janet (1982). *Autobiography: Toward a politics of experience*. Philadelphia: University of Pennsylvania Press.

Gunning, Sandra (1996). *Race, rape, and lynching: The red record of American literature, 1890–1912*. New York: Oxford University Press

Gusdorf, Georges (1980). Conditions and limits of autobiography. In James Olney (Ed.), *Autobiography: Essays theoretical and critical* (28–48). Princeton, NJ: Princeton University Press.

Habermas, Jurgen (1970). *Knowledge and human interests.* Boston, MA: Beacon.

Habermas, Jurgen (1979). *Communication and the evolution of society.* [T. McCarthy, trans.] Boston, MA: Beacon Press.

Hall, Jacquelyn Dowd (1979). *Revolt against chivalry: Jessie Daniel Ames and the women's campaign against lynching.* New York: Columbia University Press.

Halperin, David M. (1990). *One hundred years of homosexuality.* New York: Routledge.

Hannaford, Ivan (1996). *Race: The history of an idea in the west.* [Foreword by Bernard Crick.] Baltimore, MD: Johns Hopkins University Press.

Haraway, Donna (1991). *Simians, cyborgs, and women: The reinvention of nature.* New York: Routledge.

Hardt, Michael and Negri, Antonio (2000). *Empire.* Cambridge, MA: Harvard University Press.

Harris, Trudier (1984). *Exorcising blackness: Historical and literary lynching and burning rituals.* Bloomington: Indiana University Press.

Hartman, Saidiya V. (1997). *Scenes of subjection: Terror, slavery, and self-making in nineteenth century America.* New York: Oxford University Press.

Hasebe-Ludt, Erika and Hurren, Wanda (Eds.). (2003). *Curriculum intertext: Place, language, pedagogy.* New York: Peter Lang.

Hatem, Mervat (1986). The politics of sexuality and gender in segregated patriarchal system: The case of eighteenth- and nineteenth-century Egypt. *Feminist Studies* 12, 281–288.

Haycock, Kati (2002, September 6). Good teaching matters . . . a lot. *Address to the NCATE 2000 Clinic for Louisiana Institutions: A Partnership Approach to Enhancing Teacher Quality and Accountability.* Baton Rouge: Claiborne Conference Center.

Haynes, Carolyn A. (1998). *Divine destiny: Gender and race in nineteenth-century Protestantism.* Jackson: University Press of Mississippi.

Held, David, McGrew, Athony, Goldblatt, David, Perraton, Jonathan (1999). *Global transformations: Politics, economics and culture.* Stanford, CA: Stanford University Press.

Henderson, James and Kesson, Kathleen (2001). Curriculum work as public intellectual leadership. In Kris Sloan and James T. Sears (Eds.), *Democratic curriculum theory & practice: Retrieving public spaces* (1–24). Troy, NY: Educator's International Press.

Hernton, Calvin C. (1988 [1965]). *Sex and racism in America.* New York: Doubleday (Anchor).

Hlebowitsh, Peter (1993). *Radical curriculum theory reconsidered: A historical approach.* New York: Teachers College Press.

Hodes, Martha (1993, January). The sexualization of reconstruction politics: White women and black men in the South after the Civil War. *Journal of the History of Sexuality* 3 (3), 402–417.

Hodge, Charles (2002, September 5). Overview of NCATE's Expectations for the Unit's Conceptual Framework. *Address to the NCATE 2000 Clinic for Louisiana Institutions: A Partnership Approach to Enhancing Teacher Quality and Accountability.* Baton Rouge: Claiborne Conference Center.

Hofstadter, Richard (1962). *Anti-intellectualism in American life.* New York: Vintage.

Holmes Group (1986). *Tomorrow's teachers.* East Lansing, MI: The Holmes Group, Inc.

Hooks, bell (1981). *Ain't I a woman.* Boston: South End Press.

Hooks, bell (1994). Feminism inside: Toward a black body politic. In Thelma Golden (Ed.), *Black male: Representations of masculinity in contemporary American art* (127–140). New York: Whitney Museum of American Art (Harry N. Abrams, Inc.).

Hope, Trevor (1994). The "returns" of cartography: Mapping identity-in (-) difference. *Differences* 6 (2+3), 208–211.

Howell, Linda (1995). The cyborg manifesto revisited: Issues and methods for technocultural feminism. In Richard Dellamora (Ed.), *Postmodern apocalypse: Theory and cultural practice at the end* (199–218). Philadelphia: University of Pennsylvania Press.

Huebner, Dwayne E. (1999). *The lure of the transcendent.* Mahwah, NJ: Lawrence Erlbaum Associates.

Hughes, John Starrett (1990). The madness of separate spheres: Insanity and masculinity in Victorian Alabama. In Mark C. Carnes and Clyde Griffen (Eds.), *Meanings for manhood: Constructions of masculinity in Victorian America* (53–66). Chicago: University of Chicago Press.

Hull, Gloria T. (1987). *Color, sex, and poetry: Three women writers of the Harlem Renaissance.* Bloomington: Indiana University Press.

Hwu, Wen-Song (1998). Curriculum, transcendence, and Zen/Taoism: Critical ontology of the self. In William F. Pinar (Ed.), *Curriculum: Toward new identities* (21–40). New York: Garland.

Imig, David G. and Earley, Penelope M. (2002, January 18). *Speech to LSU College of Education Faculty.* Baton Rouge: Louisiana State University.

Izenberg, Gerald N. (2000). *Modernism and masculinity: Mann, Wedekind, Kandinsky through World War I.* Chicago: University of Chicago Press.

Jackson, Philip W. (1999). *John Dewey and the lessons of art.* New Haven, CT: Yale University Press.

Jacobs, Harriet A. (1987/1861). *Incidents in the life of a slave girl, written by herself.* [Edited by Jean Fagan Yellin.] Cambridge, MA: Harvard University Press.

Jacoby, Russell (1987). *The last intellectuals.* New York: Basic Books.

jagodzinski, jan (Ed.). (2002). *Pedagogical desire: Authority, seduction, transference, and the question of ethics.* Westport, CT: Bergin & Garvey.

James, William (1970). *Pragmatism; and four essays from "the meaning of truth."* Cleveland: World Publishing.

Jay, Martin (1993). *Downcast eyes: The denigration of vision in twentieth-century French thought.* Berkeley: University of California Press.

Johnson, Jr., James Weldon (1933). *Along this way.* New York: Viking.

Jonsson, Stefan (2000). *Subject without nation: Robert Musil and the history of modern identity.* Durham, NC: Duke University Press.

Jordan, Winthrop D. (1968). *White over black.* Chapel Hill: University of North Carolina Press.

Kimball, Roger (1990). *Tenured radicals: How politics has corrupted our higher education.* New York: Harper & Row.

Kimmel, Michael S. (1990). Baseball and the reconstitution of American masculinity, 1880–1920. In Michael A. Messner and Don Sabo (Eds.), *Sport, men, and the gender order* (55–65). Champaign, IL: Human Kinetics.

Kimmel, Michael S. (1994). Consuming manhood: The feminization of American culture and the recreation of the male body, 1832–1920. In Laurence Goldstein (Ed.), *The male body* (12–41). Ann Arbor: University of Michigan Press.

Kimmel, Michael S. (1996). *Manhood in America: A cultural history.* New York: Free Press.

Kincheloe, Joe L. (1999). Schools where Ronnie and Brandon would have excelled. In William F. Pinar (Ed.), *Contemporary curriculum discourses* (346–363). New York: Peter Lang.

Kincheloe, Joe L. (2002). *The sign of the burger: McDonald's and the culture of power.* Philadelphia: Temple University Press.

Kincheloe, Joe L. and Steinberg, Shirley (1993). A tentative description of post-formal thinking: The critical confrontation with cognitive theory. *Harvard Educational Review* 63 (3), 296–320.

King, M. C. (1973). The politics of sexual stereotypes. *Black Scholar* 4 (6–7), 12–23.

Kliebard, Herbert M. (1970). Persistent issues in historical perspective. *Educational Comment*, 31–41. [Also in William F. Pinar (Ed.) (1975a), *Curriculum theorizing: The reconceptualists* (39–50). Berkeley: McCutchan. Reissued in 2000 as *Curriculum theorizing: The reconceptualization.* Troy, NY: Educator's International Press.]

Kliebard, Herbert M. (1975). Bureaucracy and curriculum theory. In William F. Pinar (Ed.), *Curriculum theorizing: The reconceptualists* (51–69). Berkeley, CA: McCutchan. [Reissued in 2000 as *Curriculum theorizing: The reconceptualization.* Troy, NY: Educator's International Press.]

Kliebard, Herbert M. (1986). *The struggle for the American curriculum 1893–1958.* Boston: Routledge & Kegan Paul.

Koerner, James D. (1963). *The miseducation of American teachers.* Baltimore, MD: Penguin.

Kohli, Wendy (1995). Educating for emancipatory rationality. In Wendy Kohli (Ed.), *Critical conversations in philosophy of education* (103–115). New York: Routledge.

Kridel, Craig and Newman, Vicky (2003). A random harvest: A multiplicity of studies in American curriculum history research. In William F. Pinar (Ed.), *International handbook of curriculum research* (637–650). Mahwah, NJ: Lawrence Erlbaum Associates.

Kuhn, Thomas (1962). *The structure of scientific revolutions.* Chicago: University of Chicago Press.

Kumashiro, Kevin (in press). *Crisis, uncertainty, and hope: Learning to teach against oppression.* New York: Routledge Falmer.

Laing, R. D. (1970). *Knots.* London: Tavistock Publications.

Landow, George P. (1992). *Hypertext: The convergence of contemporary critical theory and technology.* Baltimore: Johns Hopkins University Press.

Langness, L. L. and Frank, Gelya (1981). *Lives: An anthropological approach to biography.* Novato, CA: Chandler & Sharp Publishers.

Laplanche, J. and Pontalis, J. B. (1973). *The language of psychoanalysis.* [Trans. by Donald Nicholson-Smith.] New York: Norton.

Lasch, Christopher (1978). *The culture of narcissism: American life in an age of diminishing expectations.* New York: Norton.

Lasch, Christopher (1984). *The minimal self: Psychic survival in troubled times.* New York: Norton.

Lasch, Christopher (1995). *The revolt of the elites and the betrayal of democracy.* New York: Norton.

Lather, Patti (1994). The absent presence: Patriarchy, capitalism, and the nature of teacher work. In L. Stone (Ed.), *The education feminist reader* (242–251). New York: Routledge.

Lawlor, S. (1993). *Inspecting the school inspectors.* London: Centre for Policy Studies.

Le Clair, Thomas (1981, March 21). "The language must now sweat": A conversation with Toni Morrison. *New Republic*, 75–78.

Ledbetter, Mark (1996). *Victims and the postmodern narrative or doing violence to the body: An ethic of reading and writing.* New York: St. Martin's Press.

Leiner, Marvin (1994). *Sexual politics in Cuba: Machismo, homosexuality, and AIDS.* Boulder, CO: Westview Press.

Lemelle, Jr., Anthony J. (1995). *Black male deviance*. Westport, CT: Praeger.

Lemert, Charles and Bhan, Esure (Eds.). (1998). *The voice of Anna Julia Cooper*. Lanham, MD: Rowman and Littlefield.

Lesko, Nancy (2000). Preparing to teach (teach marked out) coach: Tracking the gendered relations of dominance on and off the football field. In Nancy Lesko (Ed.), *Masculinities at School* (187–212). Thousand Oaks, CA: Sage.

Lesko, Nancy (2001). *Act your age! A cultural construction of adolescence*. New York: Routledge/Falmer.

Levin, David Michael (Ed.). (1993). *Modernity and the hegemony of vision* (1–29). Berkeley: University of California Press.

Lévy, Pierre (2001). *Cyberculture*. [Trans. by Robert Bononno.] Minneapolis: University of Minnesota Press.

Lewes, Kenneth (1988). *The psychoanalytic theory of male homosexuality*. New York: New American Library.

Lewis, David Levering (1997 [1979]). *When Harlem was in vogue*. New York: Penguin.

Lomotey, Kofi and Rivers, Shariba (1998). Models of excellence: Independent African-centered schools. In William F. Pinar (Ed.), *Curriculum: Toward new identities* (343–353). New York: Garland.

Lorde, Audre (1982). *Afterimages*. In *Chosen poems old and new*. New York: Norton & Co.

Lukacher, Ned (1986). *Primal scenes: Literature, philosophy, psychoanalysis*. Ithaca, NY: Cornell University Press.

Lyotard, Jean-Francois (1993). *The postmodern explained*. [Afterward by Wlad Godzich.] Minneapolis: University of Minnesota Press.

Macdonald, James B. (1995). *Theory as a prayerful act: Collected essays*. [Edited by Bradley Macdonald; introduced by William F. Pinar.] New York: Peter Lang.

Mailer, Norman (1957). *The white negro*. San Francisco: City Lights.

McCarthy, Cameron (1998). The uses of culture: Canon formation, postcolonial literature, and the multicultural project. In William F. Pinar (Ed.), *Curriculum: Toward new identities* (253–262). New York: Garland.

McClintock, R. (1971). Toward a place for study in a world of instruction. *Teachers College Record* 73 (20), 161–205.

McDowell, Deborah (1993). In the first place: Making Frederick Douglass and the Afro-American narrative tradition. In William L. Andrews (Ed.), *African American autobiography: A collection of critical essays* (36–58). Englewood Cliffs, NJ: Prentice Hall.

McKnight, E. Douglas (2003). *Schooling, the Puritan imperative, and the molding of an American national identity: Education's "errand into the wilderness."* Mahwah, NJ: Lawrence Erlbaum Associates.

McLaren, Peter (1994). *Life in schools: An introduction to critical pedagogy in the foundations of education*. [2nd edition.] New York: Longman.

McLaren, Peter (1998). Revolution and reality. [An interview with Carmel Borg, Peter Mayo, Ronald Sultana.] In William F. Pinar (Ed.), *Curriculum: Toward new identities* (354–376). New York: Garland.

McLuhan, Marshall (1962). *Gutenberg galaxy: The making of typographic man*. Toronto: University of Toronto Press.

McNeil, Linda M. (2000). *Contradictions of school reform: Educational costs of standardized testing*. New York: Routledge.

Mehlman, Jeffrey (1971/1974). *A structural study of autobiography: Proust, Leiris, Sartre, Lévi-Strauss*. Ithaca, NY: Cornell University Press.

Mercer, Kobena (1994). *Welcome to the jungle: New positions in black cultural studies.* New York: Routledge.

Merleau-Ponty, Maurcie (1966). *Phenomenology of perception.* London: Routledge and Kegan Paul.

Merrill, James (1993). *A different person: A memoir.* New York: Alfred A. Knopf.

Miller, James E. (1993). *The passion of Michel Foucault.* New York: Simon & Schuster.

Miller, Janet L. (1990). *Creating spaces and finding voices: Teachers collaborating for empowerment.* Albany, NY: State University of New York Press.

Miller, Janet L. (in press). *The sound of silence breaking and other essays: Working the tension in curriculum theory.* New York: Peter Lang.

Mitchell, Margaret (1954). *Gone with the wind.* New York: Permabooks.

Mitchell, Ted (2000). Turning points: Reconstruction and the growth of national influence in education. In Larry Cuban and Dorothy Shipps (Eds.), *Reconstructing the common good in education: Coping with intractable dilemmas* (13–31). Stanford, CA: Stanford University Press.

Mitchell, W. J. T. (1994). *Picture theory: Essays on verbal and visual representation.* Chicago: University of Chicago Press.

Molnar, Alex (2002). The commercialization of America's schools. In William E. Doll, Jr. and Noel Gough (Eds.), *Curriculum visions* (203–212). New York: Peter Lang.

Monette, Paul (1992). *Becoming a man: Half a life story.* San Francisco, CA: Harper.

Moore, Mary Elizabeth Mullino (2002). Curriculum: A journey through complexity, community, conversation, culmination. In William E. Doll, Jr. and Noel Gough (Eds.), *Curriculum visions* (219–227). New York: Peter Lang.

Moriarty, Michael (1991). *Roland Barthes.* Stanford, CA: Stanford University Press.

Morris, Marla (2001a). *Holocaust and curriculum.* Mahwah, NJ: Lawrence Erlbaum Associates.

Morris, Marla (2001b). *Academic work as threat.* Paper presented at the Bergamo Conference on Curriculum Theory and Classroom Practice, Dayton, Ohio, October 25–28.

Morrison, Toni (1971, August 22). What the black woman thinks about women's lib. *New York Times Magazine.*

Morrison, Toni (1989, Winter). Unspeakable things unspoken: The Afro-American presence in American literature. *Michigan Quarterly,* 1–34.

Morrison, Toni (1992). *Playing in the dark: Whiteness and the literary imagination.* Cambridge, MA: Harvard University Press.

Moses, Daniel Noah (1999, Spring). Distinguishing a university from a shopping mall. *The NEA Higher Education Journal* 15 (1), 85–96.

Moynihan, Daniel P. (1965). *The Negro family: The case for national action.* Office of Policy, Planning and Research, Department of Labor. Washington, DC: Government Printing Office.

Munoz, José Esteban (1996). Famous and dandy like B. 'n' Andy: Race, Pop, and Basquiat. In Jennifer Doyle, Jonathan Flatley, and José Esteban Munoz (Eds.), *Pop out: Queer Warhol* (144–179). Durham and London: Duke University Press.

Munro, Petra (1998). Engendering curriculum history. In William F. Pinar (Ed.), *Curriculum: Toward new identities* (263–294). New York: Garland.

Munro, Petra (2002, September 5–6). *Personal communications during the NCATE 2000 Clinic for Louisiana Institutions: A Partnership Approach to Enhancing Teacher Quality and Accountability.* Baton Rouge: Claiborne Conference Center.

Murtadha-Watts, Khaula (2000). Theorizing urban black masculinity construction in an African-centered school. In Nancy Lesko (Ed.), *Masculinities at school* (49–71). Thousand Oaks, CA: Sage.

Musil, Robert (1955 [1905]). *Young Torless*. [Preface by Alan Pryce-Jones.] New York: Pantheon Books.

Musil, Robert (1990). *Precision and soul: Essays and addresses*. [Edited and translated by Burton Pike and David S. Luft.] Chicago and London: University of Chicago Press.

Musil, Robert (1995 [1979]). *The man without qualities*. [Trans. by Sophie Perkins and Burton Pike.] New York: Knopf. The 1979 edition quoted in the introduction was published in London by Secker and Warburg. Foreword by Elithne Wilkins. Trans. Ernst Kaiser.

Myrdal, Gunnar (1962 [1944]). *An American dilemma: The negro problem and modern democracy*. New York: Harper & Row.

National Commission on Excellence in Education (1983). *A nation at risk: The imperative for educational reform*. Washington, DC: United States Department of Education.

Nietzsche, Friedrich (1983a). On the uses and disadvantages of history for life (Essay 2, foreword). In *Untimely meditations* (trans. R. J. Hollingdale). New York and London: Cambridge University Press.

Nietzsche, Friedrich (1983b). Schopenhauer as education (Essay 3, sections 7 and 8). In *Untimely meditations* (trans. R. J. Hollingdale). New York and London: Cambridge University Press.

Oakeshott, Michael (1959). *The voice of poetry in the conversation of mankind*. London: Bowes & Bowes.

Olney, James (Ed.). (1980). *Autobiography: Essays theoretical and critical*. Princeton, NJ: Princeton University Press.

Ong, Walter J. (1982). *Orality and literacy: The technologizing of the word*. London: Methuen.

O'Shea, A. (1993). Review of *Sentimental education: Schooling, popular culture and the regulation of liberty*. In *Media, Culture and Society* 15, 503–510.

Page, Reba N. (2001, June/July). Reshaping graduate preparation in educational research methods: One school's experience. *Educational Researcher* 30 (5), 19–25.

Pagano, Jo Anne (1999 [1981]). The curriculum field: Emergence of a discipline. In William F. Pinar (Ed.), *Contemporary curriculum discourses: Twenty years of JCT* (82–105). New York: Peter Lang.

Paige, Rod (2002). *Meeting the highly qualified teachers challenge: The Secretary's annual report on teacher quality*. Washington, DC: U.S. Department of Education, Office of Post-secondary Education.

Pask, Kevin (1995). Cyborg economies: Desire and labor in the *Terminator* films. In Richard Dellamora (Ed.), *Postmodern apocalypse: Theory and cultural practice at the end* (182–198). Philadelphia: University of Pennsylvania Press.

Patton, Paul (2000). *Deleuze and the political*. London: Routledge.

Penley, Constance (1991). Brownian motion: Women, tactics, and technology. In C. Penley and A. Ross (Eds.), *Technoculture* (135–161). Minneapolis: University of Minnesota Press.

Penn State (2002). *Students in the balance: General education in the research university*. University Park: The Penn State Symposium on General Education.

Pfeil, Fred (1995). *White guys*. London: Verso.

Phillips, Ulrich Bonnell (1963). *Life and labor in the old South*. New York: Grosset and Dunlap.

Pilder, William (1974). In the stillness is the dancing. In William F. Pinar (Ed.), *Heightened consciousness, cultural revolution, and curriculum theory: The proceedings of the Rochester conference* (117–129). Berkeley, CA: McCutchan.

Pinar, William F. (1989, January/February). A reconceptualization of teacher education. *Journal of Teacher Education*, 9–12.

Pinar, William F. (1994). *Autobiography, politics, and sexuality: Essays in curriculum theory 1972–1992*. New York: Peter Lang.

Pinar, William F. (1999a). *Contemporary curriculum discourses: Twenty years of* JCT. New York: Peter Lang.

Pinar, William F. (1999b). Gracious submission. *Educational Researcher* 28 (1), 14–15.

Pinar, William F. (2001). *The gender of racial politics and violence in America: Lynching, prison rape, and the crisis of masculinity*. New York: Peter Lang.

Pinar, William, F. (2002). The medicated body: Drugs and Daslin. In Sherry Shapiro and Svi Shapiro (Eds.), *Body movements: Pedagogy, politics, and social change* (283–315). Cresskill, NJ: Hampton Press.

Pinar, William F. (Ed.). (2003a). *International handbook of curriculum research*. Mahwah, NJ: Lawrence Erlbaum Associates.

Pinar, William F. (2003b). The internationalization of curriculum studies. In Donna Trueit, Hongyu Wang, William E. Doll, Jr., and William F. Pinar (Eds.), *The internationalization of curriculum studies*. New York: Peter Lang.

Pinar, William F. (2003c). Inside Noah's tent: The sodomitical genesis of "race" in the Christian imagination. In Peter Pericles Trifonas (Ed.), *Pedagogies of difference* (155–187). New York: RoutledgeFalmer.

Pinar, William F. and Grumet, Madeleine R. (1976). *Toward a poor curriculum*. Dubuque, IA: Kendall/Hunt.

Pinar, William F. and Grumet, Madeleine R. (1988). Socratic *caesura* and the theory-practice relationship. In William F. Pinar (Ed.), *Contemporary curriculum discourses* (92–100). Scottsdale, AZ: Gorsuch Scarisbrick. [First published In M. Lawn and L. Barton (Eds.), *Rethinking Curriculum Studies* (20–42). London: Croom Helm.]

Pinar, William F., Reynolds, William M., Slattery, Patrick, and Taubman, Peter M. (1995). *Understanding curriculum: An introduction to historical and contemporary curriculum discourses*. New York: Peter Lang.

Pine, Richard (1995). *The thief of reason: Oscar Wilde and modern Ireland*. New York: St. Martin's Press.

Polanyi, Michael (1958). *Personal knowledge*. London: Routledge and Kegan Paul.

Pope, Denise Clark (2001). *Doing school: How we are creating a generation of stressed out, materialistic, and miseducated students*. New Haven, CT: Yale University Press.

Posner, Richard (2001). *Public intellectuals: A study of decline*. Cambridge, MA: Harvard University Press.

Potter, David (1968). *The South and the sectional conflict*. Baton Rouge: Louisiana State University Press.

Pronger, Brian (1990). *The arena of masculinity: Sports, homosexuality and the meaning of sex*. New York: St. Martin's Press.

Quinn, Molly (2001). *Going out, not knowing whither: Education, the upward journey, and the faith of reason*. New York: Peter Lang.

Rabinowitz, Paula (1987, Winter). Eccentric memories: A conversation with Maxine Hong Kingston. *Michigan Quarterly Review* 26 (1), 177–187.

Ragan, Sandra L., Bystrom, Dianne G., Kaid, Lynda Lee and Beck, Christina S. (Eds.). (1996). *The lynching of language: Gender, politics, and power in the Hill-Thomas hearings*. [Foreword by Julia T. Wood.] Urbana & Chicago: University of Illinois Press.

Ransby, B. (1992). The gang rape of Anita Hill and the assault upon all women of African descent. In R. Chrisman and R. L. Allen (Eds.), *Court of Appeal* (169–175). New York: Ballantine Books.

Raper, Arthur F. (1969 [1933]). *The tragedy of lynching*. Montclair, NJ: Patterson Smith. [First printing 1933, University of North Carolina Press.]

Rhodes, Frank H. T. (2001, September 14). A battle plan for professors to recapture the curriculum. *Chronicle of Higher Education*, B7–B10.

Rickover, H. (1959). *Education and freedom*. New York: E. Dutton.

Rickover, H. (1963). *American education—A national failure: The problem of our schools and what we can learn from England*. New York: E. Dutton.

Riley-Taylor, Elaine (2002). *Ecology, spirituality & education: Curriculum for relational knowing*. New York: Peter Lang.

Ronell, Avital (1992a). *Crack wars*. Lincoln: University of Nebraska Press.

Ronell, Avital (1992b). Video/television/Rodney King: Twelve steps beyond the pleasure principle. *Differences* 4 (2), 1–15.

Rooney, E. (1989). *Seductive reasoning: Pluralism as the problematic of contemporary literary theory*. Ithaca, NY: Cornell University Press.

Root, E. Merrill (1958). *Brainwashing in the high schools: An examination of American history textbooks*. New York: Devin-Adair.

Roper, Cynthia S., Chanslor, Mike, and Bystrom, Dianne G. (1996). Sex, race, and politics: An intercultural communication approach to the Hill-Thomas hearings. In Sandra L. Ragan, Dianne G. Bystrom, Lynda Lee Kaid, and Christina S. Beck (Eds.), *The lynching of language: Gender, politics, and power in the Hill-Thomas Hearings* (44–60). Urbana & Chicago: University of Illinois Press.

Rorty, Richard (1991). *Essays on Heidegger and others. Philosophical papers. Volume 2*. Cambridge and New York: Cambridge University Press.

Ross, Andrew (1991). Hacking away at the counterculture. In C. Penley and A. Ross (Eds.), *Technoculture* (107–134). Minneapolis and Oxford: University of Minnesota Press.

Rugg, Harold (1963). *Imagination*. New York: Harper & Row.

Said, Edward W. (1975). *Beginnings: Intention and method*. New York: Basic Books.

Said, Edward W. (1996). *Representations of the intellectual: The 1993 Reith lectures*. New York: Vintage.

Sartre, Jean-Paul (1981). *The family idiot: Gustave Flaubert 1821–1857*. [Trans. by Carol Cosman.] Chicago and London: University of Chicago Press.

Sarup, Madan (1992). *Jacques Lacan*. Toronto: University of Toronto Press.

Savran, David (1998). *Taking it a like a man: White masculinity, masochism, and contemporary American culture*. Princeton, NJ: Princeton University Press.

Schechter, Patricia A. (1997). Unsettled business: Ida B. Wells against lynching, or, how antilynching got its gender. In W. Fitzhugh Brundage (Ed.), *Under sentence of death: Lynching in the south* (292–317). Chapel Hill: University of North Carolina Press.

Schlesinger, Jr., Arthur (1991). *The disuniting of America*. New York: Whittle Direct Books.

Schmidt, Peter (2000, October 6). Faculty outcry greets proposal for competency texts at U. of Texas. *Chronicle of Higher Education*, A 35, 38.

Schubert, William H., Schubert, Ann Lynn Lopez, Thomas, Thomas P., Carroll, Wayne M. (2002). *Curriculum books: The First hundred years*. [Second Edition.] New York: Peter Lang.

Schwab, Joseph (1978). *Science, curriculum and liberal education: Selected essays, Joseph J. Schwab*. [Edited I. Westbury and N. Wilkof.] Chicago, IL: University of Chicago Press.

Sclafani, Susan K. (2002, September 5). *Teacher quality as a national priority*. Address to the NCATE 2000 Clinic for Louisiana Institutions: A Partnership Approach to Enhancing Teacher Quality and Accountability. Baton Rouge: Claiborne Conference Center.

Seale, Bobby (1978). *A lonely rage.* [Foreword by James Baldwin.] New York: Times Books.

Sears, James T. (2001, October 13). *Writing literally, speaking publicly: Curriculum work.* Workshop led at the 2nd annual Curriculum & Pedagogy Conference, Victoria, British Columbia, Canada.

Shaker, Paul and Heilman, Elizabeth E. (2002, January). Advocacy versus authority—Silencing the education professoriate. *AAACS Policy Perspectives* 3 (1), 1–6.

Shapiro, Herbert (1988). *White violence and black response: From reconstruction to Montgomery.* Amherst: University of Massachusetts Press.

Silberman, Charles (1970). *Crisis in the classroom: The remaking of American education.* New York: Random House.

Silverman, Kaja (1992). *Male subjectivity at the margins.* New York & London: Routledge.

Silverman, Kaja (2000). *World spectators.* Stanford, CA: Stanford University Press.

Simon, Roger I., Rosenberg, Sharon and Eppert, Claudia (Eds.). (2000). *Between hope and despair: Pedagogy and the remembrance of historical trauma.* Lanham, MD: Rowman & Littlefield.

Simpson, David (2002). *Situatedness, or, why we keep saying where we're coming from.* Durham, NC: Duke University Press.

Simpson, Lewis (1983). *The dispossessed garden.* Baton Rouge: Louisiana State University Press.

Simpson, Mark (1994). *Male impersonators: Men performing masculinity.* [Foreword by Alan Sinfield.] New York: Routledge.

Sizer, Ted (1984). *Horace's compromise: The dilemma of the American high school.* Boston, MA: Houghton Mifflin.

Slattery, Patrick and Rapp, Dana (2002). *Ethics and the foundations of education: Teaching convictions in a postmodern world.* Boston: Allyn & Bacon.

Sloan, Kris and Sears, James T. (Eds.). (2001). *Democratic curriculum theory & practice: Retrieving public spaces.* Troy, NY: Educator's International Press.

Smith, Lillian (1963 [1949]). *Killers of the dream.* [Revised and enlarged edition. First published in 1949 by Norton & Co.] Garden City, NY: Anchor Books.

Smith, Lillian (1972 [1944]). *Strange fruit.* San Diego, CA: Harvest.

Smith, Valerie (1987). *Self-discovery and authority in Afro-American narrative.* Cambridge, MA: Harvard University Press.

Spring, Joel (1972). *Education and the rise of the corporate state.* Boston, MA: Beacon Press.

Spring, Joel (1976). *The sorting machine.* New York: David McKay.

Spring, Joel (1986). *The American high school 1642–1985: Varieties of historical interpretation and development of American education.* New York: Longman.

Spring, Joel (1989). *The sorting machine revisited: National educational policy since 1945.* New York: Longman.

Steinberg, Shirley R. (1997). The bitch who has everything. In Shirley R. Steinberg and Joe L. Kincheloe (Eds.), *Kinderculture: The corporate construction of childhood* (207–218). Boulder, CO: Westview.

Steinberg, Shirley R. (1999). Early childhood as a gendered construction. In William F. Pinar (Ed.), *Contemporary curriculum discourses* (474–480). New York: Peter Lang.

Stokes, Mason (2001). *The color of sex: Whiteness, heterosexuality, & the fictions of white supremacy.* Durham, NC: Duke University Press.

Stoler, Ann Laura (1995). *Race and the education of desire: Foucault's history of sexuality and the colonial order of things.* Durham, NC: Duke University Press.

Stoller, Peter (1997). *Sensuous scholarship.* Philadelphia: University of Pennsylvania Press.

Stowe, Steven M. (1987). *Intimacy and power in the Old South: Ritual in the lives of the planters.* Baltimore, MD: Johns Hopkins University Press.

Sullivan, Harry Stack (1965). *Collected works.* New York: Norton.

Sumara, Dennis J. and Davis, Brent (1998). Unskinning curriculum. In William F. Pinar (Ed.), *Curriculum: Toward new identities* (75–92). New York: Garland.

Summers, Lawrence H. (2001). *President Lawrence H. Summers' Address at the 2001 President's Weekend at HGSE.* http://www.gse.harvard.edu/pw2001/

Sundquist, Eric J. (1993). *To wake the nations: Race in the making of American literature.* Cambridge, MA: Harvard University Press.

Taubman, Peter Maas (1990 [1992]). Achieving the right distance. *Educational Theory* 40 (1), 121–133. [Reprinted in W. Pinar and W. Reynolds (Eds.), *Understanding curriculum as phenomenological and deconstructed text* (216–233). New York: Teachers College Press.]

Taylor, Mark C. (1980). *Journeys to selfhood: Hegel and Kierkegaard.* Berkeley: University of California Press.

Tolnay, Stewart E. and Beck, E. M. (1995). *A festival of violence: An analysis of southern lynchings, 1882–1930.* Urbana: University of Illinois Press.

Torres, Sasha (1996). The caped crusader of camp: Pop, camp, and the *Batman* television series. In Jennifer Doyle, Jonathan Flatley, and José Esteban Munoz (Eds.), *Pop out: Queer Warhol* (238–255). Durham and London: Duke University Press.

Trifonas, Peter Pericles (Ed.). (2000). *Revolutionary pedagogies.* New York: Routledge.

Trifonas, Peter Pericles (Ed.). (2003). *Pedagogies of difference.* New York: Routledge-Falmer.

Trueit, Donna (2002). Speaking of ghosts. . . . In William E. Doll, Jr. and Noel Gough (Eds.), *Curriculum visions* (267–280). New York: Peter Lang.

Truth, Sojourner (1968 [1878]). *Narrative of Sojourner Truth, a bondwoman of olden time.* [Olive Gilbert, comp.] New York: Arno.

Tyack, David (1993). School governance in the United States: Historical puzzles and anomalies. In J. Hannaway and M. Carnoy (Eds.), *Decentralization and school improvement: Can we fulfill the promise?* (1–32). San Francisco, CA: Jossey-Bass Publishers.

Tyack, David and Hansot, Elizabeth (1990). *Learning together: A history of coeducation in American schools.* New Haven, CT: Yale University Press.

Tyler, Ralph (1949). *Basic principles of curriculum and instruction.* Chicago, IL: University of Chicago Press.

Van Deburg, William L. (1984). *Slavery & race in American popular culture.* Madison: University of Wisconsin Press.

Walker, Alice (1985). *The color purple.* New York: Pocket Books.

Wallace, Michele (1990). *Invisibility blues: From pop to theory.* London: Verso.

Wang, Hongyu (2002a). The call from the stranger. In William E. Doll, Jr. and Noel Gough (Eds.), *Curriculum visions* (287–299). New York: Peter Lang.

Ware, Vron (1992). *Beyond the pale: White women, racism and history.* London: Verso.

Warner, Coleman (2002, April 4). Union chief chides education scholars. New Orleans: *The Times-Picayune,* B-1, B-2.

Warnke, Georgia (1993). Ocularcentrism and social criticism. In David Michael Levin (Ed.), *Modernity and the hegemony of vision* (287–308). Berkeley: University of California Press.

Washington, Mary Helen (Ed.). (1987). *Invented lives: Narratives of black women 1860–1960.* Garden City, NY: Doubleday/Anchor.

Weaver, John A. (2001). *The limits of usefulness or six steps to anti-intellectualism in the excellent corporate university.* Paper presented at the Bergamo Conference on Curriculum Theory and Classroom Practice, Dayton, Ohio, October 25–28.

Weaver, John A., Appelbaum, Peter M., and Morris, Marla (Eds.). (2001). *(Post) modern science (education): Propositions and alternative paths.* New York: Peter Lang.

Webber, Julie A. (2003). *Failure to hold: Politics, proto-citizenship and school violence.* Landham, MD: Rowman & Littlefield.

Weintraub, Karl Joachim (1978). *The value of the individual: Self and circumstance in autobiography.* Chicago: University of Chicago Press.

Wells, Ida B. (1970). *Crusade for justice: The autobiography of Ida B. Wells.* [Edited by Alfreda Duster.] Chicago: University of Chicago Press.

Wells-Barnett, Ida B. (1977 [1901]). Lynching and the excuse for it. Addams, Jane (1977/1901). Respect for law. In Jane Addams and Ida B. Wells, *Lynching and rape: An exchange of views* (28–34). [Edited, and with an introduction, by Bettina Aptheker.] Chicago: University of Illinois, Occasional Paper No. 25.

Wertham, Fredric (1953/1954). *Seduction of the innocent.* New York: Rinehart and Co.

Westbrook, Robert (1991). *John Dewey and American philosophy.* Ithaca, NY: Cornell University Press.

White, Deborah Gray (1985). *Ar'n't I a woman? Female slaves in the plantation South.* New York: Norton.

White, Walter (1929). *Rope and faggot: A biography of judge lynch.* New York: Alfred A. Knopf.

Whites, LeeAnn (1992, Summer). Rebecca Latimer Felton and the wife's farm: The class and racial politics of gender reform. *Georgia Historical Quarterly* 75, 368–372.

Wiegman, Robyn (1993, January). The anatomy of lynching. *Journal of the History of Sexuality* 3 (3), 445–467.

Wiegman, Robyn (1995). *American anatomies: Theorizing race and gender.* Durham, NC: Duke University Press.

Williamson, Joel (1984). *The crucible of race: Black-white relations in the American South since emancipation.* New York: Oxford University Press.

Willinsky, John (1998). *Learning to divide the world: Education at empire's end.* Minneapolis: University of Minnesota Press.

Willinsky, John (1999). *Technologies of knowing: A proposal for the human sciences.* Boston: Beacon Press.

Willinsky, John (2001, January–February). The strategic education research program and the public value of research. *Educational Researcher* 30 (1), 5–14.

Willis, Ellen (1984). Radical feminism and feminist radicalism. In Sohnya Sayres et al. (Eds.), *The 60s without apology.* Minneapolis: University of Minnesota Press.

Wilmore, Gayraud S. (1983). *Black religion and black radicalism: An interpretation of the religious history of Afro-American people.* [Second edition.] Maryknoll, NY: Orbis Books.

Wood, Julia T. (1996). Foreword: Continuing the conversation about Hill and Thomas. In Sandra L. Ragan, Dianne G. Bystrom, Lynda Lee Kaid, and Christina S. Beck (Eds.), *The lynching of language: Gender, politics, and power in the Hill-Thomas hearings* (ix–xiii). Urbana & Chicago: University of Illinois Press.

Woodward, C. Vann (1968). *The burden of southern history.* Baton Rouge: Louisiana State University Press.

Worth, Robert F. (1998, spring). A legacy of a lynching. *American Scholar* 67 (2), 65–77.

Wraga, William G. (1999, January–February). Extracting sun-beams out of cucumbers": The retreat from practice in reconceptualized curriculum studies. *Educational Researcher* (28) 1, 4–13.

Wraga, William G. (2001, October). Left out: The villainization of progressive education in the United States. *Educational Researcher* 30 (7), 34–39.

Wraga, William (2002, August–September). Recovering curriculum practice: Continuing the conversation. *Educational Researcher* (31) 6, 17–19.

Wright, Elizabeth (1996, Spring). Review of Renata Salecl's *The spoils of freedom: Psychoanalysis and feminism after the fall of socialism.* [London & New York: Routledge, 1994]. *Journal for the Psychoanalysis of Culture and Society* 1 (1), 146–148.

Wright, George C. (1990). *Racial violence in Kentucky, 1865–1940: Lynchings, mob rule, and "legal lynchings."* Baton Rouge: Louisiana State University Press.

Wright, Richard (1945). *Black boy.* New York: Harper & Brothers.

Young-Bruehl, Elisabeth (1996). *The anatomy of prejudices.* Cambridge, MA: Harvard University Press.

Zangrando, Robert L. (1980). *The N.A.A.C.P. Crusade against lynching, 1909–1950.* Philadelphia: Temple University Press.

Ziarek, Ewa Plonowska (2001). *An ethics of dissensus: Postmodernity, feminism, and the politics of radical democracy.* Stanford, CA: Stanford University Press.

Zimmerman, Jonathan (2002). *Whose America? Culture wars in the public schools.* Cambridge, MA: Harvard University Press.

Zinn, Howard (1965, November 23). Schools in context: The Mississippi idea. *The Nation*, 10.

Zizek, Slavoj (1998). Love thy neighbor? No, thanks! ? In Christopher Lane (Ed.), *The psychoanalysis of race* (154–175). New York: Columbia University Press.

Author Index

Subject Index